VideoHound's
MOVIE
LaughLines

Quips, Quotes, and
Clever Comebacks

VideoHound's MOVIE LaughLines

Quips, Quotes, and Clever Comebacks

VISIBLE INK PRESS

DETROIT • WASHINGTON, D.C. • TORONTO

VideoHound's
M VIE
LaughLines

Quips, Quotes, and
Clever Comebacks

Most Visible Ink Press™ books are available at special quantity discounts when purchased in bulk by corporations, organizations, or groups. Customized printings, special imprints, messages, and excerpts can be produced to meet your needs. For more information, contact Special Markets Manager, Gale Research Inc., 835 Penobscot Bldg., Detroit, MI 48226.

ISBN 0-7876-0699-5

Credits

Chief Quote Gatherer
Carl Forget

Editor
Hilary Weber

Contributing Editors
Julia Furtaw
Terri Schell
Christine Tomassini
Beth A. Fhaner
Kelly M. Cross
Devra M. Sladics
Michelle Banks
James Craddock
Carol Schwartz

Managing Editor
Martin Connors

Technical Support
Roger Valade

Typesetter
Marco Di Vita,
Graphix Group

Design Supervisor
Cynthia Baldwin

Cover and Page Design
Michelle S. DiMercurio

Copywriter
Susan Stefani

Photo Coordinator
Barbara Yarrow
Pamela Hayes

VideoHound's Personal Illustrator
Terry Colon

Production
Mary Beth Trimper
Dorothy Maki
Evi Seoud
Shanna Heilveil
Wendy Blurton

Publicity
Jennifer Sweetland

Marketing Manager
Lauri Taylor

Photos courtesy of The Kobal Collection

A Cunning Canine™ Production

Contents

Introduction

by VideoHound

- What a sad business, being funny.

- Very sad, if they don't laugh.

The ballerina, Terry (Claire Trevor) and the clown,
Calvero (Charlie Chaplin) in *Limelight* (1952).

Dying is easy. Comedy is hard.

Alan Swan (Peter O'Toole) quoting Edmund King in *My
Favorite Year* (1982).

I have a very pessimistic view of life... I feel that life is
divided into the horrible and the miserable. These are the
two categories, you know. The horrible would be, like terminal cases, blind people, cripples. I don't know how they get
through life. It's amazing to me. And the miserable is everyone else. So when you go through life, you should be thankful
you're miserable because you're very lucky to be miserable.

Alvy Singer (Woody Allen) to Annie (Diane Keaton) in
Annie Hall (1977).

Making people laugh, whether they be miserable or horrible, is
hard work. Tickling the cinematic funny bone is an art frequently fouled
by writers, directors, and performers who *think* they're funny, usually at
the viewer's expense. But when film comedy works, the payoff is pure
bliss. *VideoHound's Movie LaughLines* collects more than two thousand

---

of these priceless screen moments, ranging from the beginning of cinema to today's comedy hits, so that you, the lucky reader, can browse and chuckle (or groan) to your heart's content. Humor of all kinds is represented: slapstick; screwball; romantic; sarcastic; raunchy; black; controversial; stand-up, sit down, and heel, boy! Knowing the importance of being a well-rounded canine, VideoHound has not limited himself to mere comedies from which to extract funny lines. No, indeed. Witty lines from otherwise straight dramas or action adventures are served for the discriminating comic palate. Famous tragic-couple Bogart and Bacall, certainly not known as comedians, even manage a line or two for comedic posterity.

Arranged by movie release year within 100 broad categories ranging from "Sex n' Celibacy" to "No Pun Intended," the quotes proceed in ascending order by date. Thus, first you'll find the classic standards, ("Today I shot an elephant in my pajamas...") because, well, what would comedy be without them? But you'll also discover (or rediscover) surprisingly modern-sounding quotes from more obscure movies of the golden age of cinema. Fueled by a unsurpassed collection of writers and directors like Francis Goodrich, Anita Loos, and Preston Sturges, the films of the 1930s and '40s produced a bevy of amusing remarks and wry repartee. Mae West, W.C. Fields, The Marx Brothers, and The Three Stooges are all representative of this age and have some of the best laugh lines in movie history.

VideoHound's Movie LaughLines even tracks how classic dialogue has evolved over movie history, with great lines morphing their way into different films with slightly different words or meanings. For example, VideoHound traces this variation on a Dirty Harry "Do you feel lucky, punk?" rant as spoken by Sgt. Jack Colt (Emilio Estevez) in *National Lampoon's Loaded Weapon:* "I know what you're thinking, punk. You're thinking, did he fire 173 times, or 174? Well, do you feel lucky, punk?"

Unlike most movie quote books, each quote identifies the characters speaking and the actors portraying them, the name of the movie, year released, and occasionally, other information to set the scene. Two dozen, er, seven indexes provide quick answers to nagging questions. Search for a quote by movie title, cast member, character name, writer, director, quotation keyword, or, our favorite, decade (if someone said it in the 50s, you can look it up).

You'll enjoy pestering what's left of your friends with some of these great lines, and hey, here's more ammo for annoying phone answering machine greetings. You'll love doing impressions while outfitted with some of the great lines in movie history, here rendered in all of their accurate glory, complete with the occasional word or idea sure to offend someone in the family. With *VideoHound's Movie LaughLines* as your guide to the inane and insane, you may find yourself the hit of the next business meeting, blind date, or encounter with a movie scriptwriter (but be careful of those quote duels). These small bits of cinematic chatter as uttered by the immortals of filmdom will entertain you for moments on end, and help you relive the movie-going experience without having to actually invest hours watching the flicks.

'Nuff said?

You can't spend the rest of your life crying. It annoys people in the movies.

Felix Ungar (Walter Matthau) to Oscar Madison
(Jack Lemmon) in *The Odd Couple* (1968).

Category List

Sex 'n' Celibacy

Lust

Vixens and Vamps

Hunka, Hunka, Burnin' Love

Hey, Baby! What's Your Sign?

Lip Service

Datin' & Relatin'

Lovestruck

I Do, I Do

The Ol' Ball and Chain

Cheatin' Hearts

Breakin' Up Is Hard? To Do

I Vant to Be Alone

She Said...

He Said...

Women

Men

Cat Fights

Tough Guys

Pals

All in the Family

Ohh, Baby!

Growing Pains

It's All Geek to Me

Yellow Bellies

It Sucks to Be Me....

Faces Only a Mother Could Love

You Loook Mahvelous!

Spare Tires

If I Only Had a Brain

Brains Waves

Doctors Orders or Take Two Aspirin and Call Me in the Morning

Lawyers or That's a Mouthpiece

Stop the Presses!

Just the Facts, Ma'am

Check, Please...

Working Stiffs

On the Grift

Take the Money and Run

Brother, Can Ya Spare a Dime?

Bargain Basement

Pearls of Wisdom

Bad Advice

Life Sucks, Then You Die

Philosophy 101

Artsy Fartsy

Roll Over Beethoven

Shall We Dance?

Green Eggs and Hamlet

You Oughta Be in Pictures

Name Dropping

The Name Game

What's Your Number?

Talk Talk

No Pun Intended

Cracking Wise

In Other Words...YES!

Riddle Me This...

Look It Up!

Mangled Metaphors

Tongue Twisters

Tall Tales

Express Yourself

Well, Excuuuuuse Me!

See Ya, Wouldn't Wanna Be Ya!

Duh!

Say, What?

Greetings & Salutations

Threats or Why, I Oughta...

"Punch" Lines

Big City, Bright Lines

The Grass Is Always Greener

Away Down South

Foreign Correspondence

Francophiles & Francophobes

It's About Time

Doin' Time

Sin & Vice

Make That a Double!

What Are the Odds?

Holy Quotes!

Miss(ed) Manners

Hygiene Hijinks

Auto-Rama

He Shoots, He Scores!

Purely Political

War...What Is It Good For?

They're Coming to Take Me Away, Ha

Cosmic Quips

Fashion Faux Pas

Idol Worship

Upper Crusty

Food, Glorious Food

Animal Crackers

Non-PC

No Absence of Malice

Things that Go Bump in the Night

Psycho-Killers, Qu'est-ce que c'est?

Parts Is Parts

Over My Dead Body

Quotes Section

It takes two to get one in trouble.

> Lady Lou (Mae West) to Sally Glynn (Rochelle Hudson) in
> *She Done Him Wrong* (1933).

- Let me hold your hand.

  - No, no! You start by holding my hand and pretty soon you'll be shuffling the whole deck.

> Empress Agrippa (Verree Teasdale) and Eddie/Oedipus
> (Eddie Cantor) in *Roman Scandals* (1933).

Not 'Anytime Annie'?! (...) She only said 'no' once and then she couldn't hear the question.

> Andy Lee (George E. Stone) speaking of Ann Lowell
> (Ginger Rogers) in *42nd Street* (1933).

What other hobbies have you got?

> Wolf J. Flywheel (Groucho Marx) to Giuseppe, the father
> of twelve kids in *The Big Store* (1941).

- Why is it that whenever he's around I'm all wet?

  - In more ways than one.

> Phyllis (Dorothy Lamour) having her hair washed when
> Sebastian (Cornel Wilde) walks by in *The Greatest Show
> on Earth* (1952).

Meet me in the bedroom in five minutes, and bring a cattle prod.

> Detective Phil Moscowitz (Tatsuya Mihashi) to Suki Yaki
> (Akike Wakabayashi). Chinese actors in
> a story narrated in English by Woody Allen, in
> *What's Up, Tiger Lily?* (1966).

You Swedish tease!

> Max Bialystock (Zero Mostel) to his secretary Ulla (Lee
> Meredith) in *The Producers* (1967).

- I'll take a pill and go to sleep.

  - Why take a pill when you can take a girl.

> Felix Madison (Jack Lemmon) and Oscar Ungar (Walter
> Matthau) in *The Odd Couple* (1968).

Henry's bed is Henry's province. He can people it with sheep for all I care—which on occasion he's done.

> Eleanor of Aquitaine (Katharine Hepburn) in
> *The Lion in Winter* (1968).

In prison, I remember this psychiatrist asked if I had a girl and I said no. And he said: Do you think sex is dirty? And I said it is if you do it right.

> Virgil Starkwell (Woody Allen) in *Take the Money and
> Run* (1969).

I once stole a pornographic book that was printed in braille. I used to rub the dirty parts.

Felding Mellish (Woody Allen) in *Bananas* (1971).

- You went to a university? It's hard to believe. For what?

    - Cosmetic, sexual technique and poetry.

    - No kidding!? They teach you sexual technique in school?

    - You have to know it in case something goes wrong with the machine.

    - What do you do? Switch to manual?

    - Where did you learn about sex?

    - Me? From my mother. When I was a little kid I asked her where babies came from and she thought I said rabies. She said from a dog bite and a week later a lady on our block gave birth to triplets. I thought she was bitten by a Great Dane.

Miles Monroe (Woody Allen) defrosted in the year 2173 after 200 years of cryogenetic sleep meets Luna Schlosser (Diane Keaton) in *Sleeper* (1973). The machine is an orgasmatron.

Sleeper

- What were you thinking about while we were doing it?

    - Willie Mays.

    - Do you always think about baseball players when you're making love?

    - Keeps me going.

- Yeah! I couldn't figure out why you kept saying 'slide.'

Linda (Diane Keaton) and Allan (Woody Allen) in
Play It Again, Sam (1972).

With most grievous dispatch I will open the latch and get to her snatch.

The Fool (Woody Allen) trying to open the Queen's (Lynn
Redgrave) chastity belt in *Everything You Always Wanted
to Know About Sex *But Were Afraid to Ask* (1972).

- Do you want to perform sex with me?
- Perform sex? I don't think I'm up to a performance but I'll rehearse with you if you like?
- Okay. I just thought you might want to. They have a machine here.
- Machine!? I'm not getting into that thing. I'm strictly a hand operator. I don't like anything with moving parts that are not my own.

Luna Schlosser (Diane Keaton) inviting Miles Monroe
(Woody Allen) into the orgasmatron in *Sleeper* (1973).

I went to a brothel once in my life. I got hiccups. It was over like that. (*Snaps his fingers.*)

Boris (Woody Allen) in *Love and Death* (1975).

- Jeez, you're old-fashioned, aren't you?
- From the waist up.

Philip Marlowe (Robert Mitchum) and Velma Grayle
(Charlotte Rampling) in *Farewell, My Lovely* (1975).

- Sex without love is an empty experience.
- Yes, but as empty experiences go, it's one of the best.

Sonja (Diane Keaton) and Boris (Woody Allen) in
Love and Death (1975).

That was the most fun I ever had without laughing.

> Alvy Singer (Woody Allen) after making love with Annie
> (Diane Keaton) in *Annie Hall* (1977).

I think there's too much burden placed on the orgasm to make up for the empty areas in life.

> Alvy Singer (Woody Allen) to Pam (Shelley Duvall) in
> *Annie Hall* (1977).

As Balzac said: There goes another novel.

> Alvy Singer (Woody Allen) after making love with Annie
> (Diane Keaton) in *Annie Hall* (1977).

He said how he thought Moby Dick was a venereal disease.

> Crazy Marlin Borunki (Dom DeLuise) remembering how
> his Polish father ruined his date in *The End* (1978).

Goddammit, I knew it! You can always tell a virgin on account the white of the eyes ain't clear.

> Henry Moon (Jack Nicholson) to his new wife Julia Tate
> (Mary Steenburgen) in *Goin' South* (1978).

Greg, honey, is it supposed to be this soft?

> Babs Jensen (Martha Smith) fiddling with her boyfriend in
> his car in *National Lampoon's Animal House* (1978).

Nothing worth knowing can be understood with the mind. Everything really valuable has to enter you through a different opening.

> Isaac Davis (Woody Allen) to Mary Wilke (Diane Keaton)
> in *Manhattan* (1979).

Don't knock masturbation, it's sex with someone I love.

Alvy Singer (Woody Allen) in *Annie Hall* (1977). Off-screen Woody Allen also said: "I believe that sex is a beautiful thing between two people. Between five, it's fantastic."

Have you ever seen a grown man naked, Tommy?

Captain Oveur (Peter Graves) in *Airplane!* (1980).

- Sexuality was born in wetness.

- It's easier that way.

Jack Burroughs (Alan Alda) and Claudia Zimmer (Rita Moreno) in *The Four Seasons* (1981).

Oh Bob? Do I have any openings that this man could fit? (or fill?)

Empress Nympho (Madeline Kahn) asking her manservant if a new muscle-bound slave could be put to good use in *History of the World: Part I* (1981).

No, we're not homosexuals, but we're willing to learn.

Russell's (Harold Ramis) answer to the recruiting sergeant at the army recruiting center in *Stripes* (1981).

Sex alleviates tension and love causes it.

Andrew (Woody Allen) in *A Midsummer Night's Sex Comedy* (1982).

You've cleared my sinuses for the summer.

Andrew (Woody Allen) after making love to his wife Adrian (Mary Steenburgen) in *A Midsummer Night's Sex Comedy* (1982).

- Some people think suicide is the ultimate act of self-absorption.

- I thought masturbation was the ultimate act of self-absorption.

Sam (Tom Berenger) and Harold (Kevin Kline) in *The Big Chill* (1983).

- I have got a headache.

   - I don't want to touch your head.

Allison (Jennifer Jason Leigh) on her wedding night with
Julio (Taylor Negron) in *Easy Money* (1983).

I've been in prison for three years. My dick gets hard after the wind blows.

Reggie Hammond (Eddie Murphy) in *48 HRS.* (1983).

- Something is missing when you're not in love.

   - Yeah, fear and desperation.

Emily (Susan Sarandon) and Joe (Richard Dreyfuss) after
making love, both being in love with someone else in *The
Buddy System* (1984).

- What's so important about sex?

   - That's like saying: what's so important about laughing or Duke Ellington or the World Series? It's one of those things that makes you feel like you're really living, like you're glad to be alive.

   - I am already glad to be alive. I don't need to play tonsil hockey with some English tart to feel good.

Edwina Cutwater (Lily Tomlin) and Roger Cobb (Steve
Martin) sharing the same body in *All of Me* (1984).

- Susan, where have you been?

   - All over.

   - Anybody I know?

Susan (Madonna) and her girlfriend in
Desperately Seeking Susan (1985).

Dave lost interest in me and I lost interest in sex. I went shopping for gratification. That's like sex without a climax.

> Barbara Whiteman (Bette Midler) to Jerry Baskin (Nick Nolte) in *Down and Out in Beverly Hills* (1986).

Want to sneak a peak at stiffy?

> Harvey Fairchild (Jack Lemmon) to his wife Gillian (Julie Andrews) in *That's Life!* (1986).

- Could you have ruined yourself somehow?

  - How could I ruin myself?

  - I don't know. Excessive masturbation?

  - Hey! Are you gonna start knocking my hobbies?

> Hannah (Mia Farrow) and Mickey (Woody Allen) after being told that Mickey's sperm count is too low for babies in *Hannah and Her Sisters* (1986).

- I've never tried a *ménage à trois*. Have you?

- With Steve!? Oh, God! It was hard enough to get him alone and even then it wasn't hard enough.

> Trish (Glenne Headly) and Frankie (Ann Magnuson) in *Making Mr. Right* (1987).

You're in more dire need of a blow job than any white man in history.

> Adrian Cronauer (Robin Williams) to Sgt. Maj. Dickerson (J.T. Walsh) in *Good Morning, Vietnam* (1987).

Does the phrase needle-dick, the bug f**ker, mean anything to you?

> Sandy (Bette Midler) to a cop in *Outrageous Fortune* (1987).

I would appreciate that you not act like a walking hard-on when we work together.

> Bill (Emilio Estevez) to Chris (Richard Dreyfuss) in
> *Stakeout* (1987).

Casual sex! What are you talking about? This is, like, my best suit.

> David (Martin Short) on his third date with cautious
> Kathy (Annette O'Toole) in *Cross My Heart* (1987).

Making love is like hitting a baseball. You've just got to relax and concentrate.

> Annie Savoy's (Susan Sarandon) opening monologue in
> *Bull Durham* (1988).

They say that sex is the theater of the poor. You're not going to stage the Beggar's Opera, are you?

> Oscar Wilde (Nickolas Grace) to Alfred Taylor (Stratford
> Johns) in *Salome's Last Dance* (1988).

- That's right, Miranda, I'm going to Greece for the sex. Sex for breakfast, sex for dinner, sex for tea, and sex for supper.

  - Sounds like a marvelous diet, love.

  - It is.

  - Have you ever heard of it? It's called the F-plan.

> Shirley (Pauline Collins) shouting at her outraged daughter when
> a delivery man walks by to offer his comment in *Shirley Valentine*
> (1989)

- You know, if I told Joe I was going to Greece for a week he'd think I was going for the sex.

  - Well, let him.

  - I'm not particularly fond of it, sex. I think sex is like a supermarket, you know, overrated. Just a lot of pushing and shoving and you still come out of it with very little at the end.

Shirley (Pauline Collins) planning her trip to Greece with Jane (Alison Steadman) in *Shirley Valentine* (1989).

A dirty mind is a terrible thing to waste.

Ouiser Boudreaux (Shirley MacLaine) in *Steel Magnolias* (1989).

He'd bend over for a pack of cigarettes.

Jerry Beck (Don Johnson) in *Dead Bang* (1989).

- He's very deep! He's not like that.

- Yes, very deep is exactly where he want's to put it.

Alice Tate (Mia Farrow) and her Muse (Bernadette Peters) about Alice's college teacher in *Alice* (1990).

Man! I had a boner with a capital 'O'.

Sailor Ripley (Nicolas Cage) in *Wild at Heart* (1990).

Stand by for a fascist invasion!

Vicky (Elizabeth McGovern) about to have intercourse with Jerry (Beau Bridges) in *Women & Men. Stories of Seduction* (1990).

I sure hate sex sometimes. His sex in particular.

Vicky (Elizabeth McGovern) thinking of Jerry (Beau Bridges) in *Women & Men. Stories of Seduction* (1990).

Nicolas Cage and Laura Dern are *Wild at Heart*

- Lieutenant Ravine, how do you like sleeping with a murderess?

- It's better than to be sleeping with a Ninja Turtle.

Ned Ravine (Armand Assante) to a reporter at the courthouse in *Fatal Instinct* (1993).

You know I'm a sucker for a soft dick, Sherman.

Maria Ruskin (Melanie Griffith) to Sherman McCoy (Tom Hanks) in *The Bonfires of the Vanities* (1990).

Women need a reason to have sex. Men just need a place.

Mitch Robbins (Billy Crystal) in *City Slickers* (1991).

- How you doin', Patty?

- I can still get it wet. How about you, Gino?

- Me!? I can't believe you can still eat with that mouth.

Gino Felino (Steven Seagal) and Patty (Gina Gershon) in *Out for Justice* (1991).

I love being single. I never had so much sex since I was a Boy Scout leader.

Frank Drebin (Leslie Nielsen) to Jane Spencer (Priscilla Presley) in *The Naked Gun 2 1/2: The Smell of Fear* (1991).

Just remember, this is a mercy f**k.

Ellen Stone (Dyan Cannon) consenting to have sex with her ex-husband Harry (Danny Aiello) to keep him from jumping out the window and as an alternative to re-marriage in *The Pickle* (1993).

Colonel, these men have taken a supreme vow of celibacy, like their fathers and their fathers before them. They haven't seen a woman in decades.

Topper Harley (Charlie Sheen) speaking of Buddhist monks in *Hot Shots! Part Deux* (1993).

- You're a virgin!

  - No!... I'm a gentleman.

Kevin Walker (David Alan Grier) and his younger
brother Darryl (Daman Wayans) in *Blankman* (1994).

- You can't get enough of me.

  - Typically male point of view.

  - How do you figure?

  - Show some bedroom proficiency you think you're
Gods. What about what we do for you?

  - Women? Women as lovers are basically the same. They
just have to be there.

  - Be there!?

  - Making a male climax isn't at all challenging. Insert
somewhere close, preferably moist, thrust, repeat.

  - How flattering.

  - Now, making a woman come therein lies a challenge.

  - Oh, you think so?

  - A woman makes a guy come, it's standard. A guy makes
a woman come, it's talent.

  - And I actually dig you.

  - Something wrong?

  - I'm insulted. Believe me, Don Juan, it takes more than
that to get a guy off. Just being there, as you put it, is not
enough.

  - Hmm. I've touched a nerve.

  - I'm astonished to hear you trivialize my role in our sex
life.

  - It wasn't directed at you. I was making a generalization.

  - You're making a generalization about broads.

Why don't you just light your tampon and blow your box apart because it's the only bang you're ever going to get, sweetheart.

Bernadette (Terence Stamp) to a temperamental (and ugly) woman in *The Adventures of Priscilla, Queen of the Desert* (1994).

- Those are my opinions based on the few women who were goodly enough to sleep with me.

- How many?

- How many what?

- How many different girls have you slept with?

- How many different girls... Didn't we have this discussion before?

- We might have. I don't really remember. How many?

- Including you?

- It better be up to and including me.

- Twelve.

Dante (Brian O'Halloran) and Veronica (Marilyn Ghigliotti) in *Clerks* (1994).

After sex, you smoke. That's a rule.

The three boys confusing voyeurism with sex after paying $103.00 (in loose change) to see V's (Melanie Griffith) breasts in *Milk Money* (1994).

Lust

Eyeing three beautiful smiling girls:

Larry-I'll take the blond.

Moe-I'll take the brunette.

Curly-I'll take the black and tan.

Larry-Hey, there's four of 'em.

Moe-We'll throw the other to the dogs.

Curly-Woof, woof, woof.

In *Restless Knights* (1935).

- My, what a fiery nature!

  - Let's throw another log on it.

> Sal (Dorothy Lamour) kissing Chester Hooton (Bob Hope)
> in *The Road to Utopia* (1945).

Have you been marooned on a desert island or do you find it difficult to concentrate?

> Adrienne Fromsett (Audrey Totter) to Philip Marlowe
> (Robert Montgomery) whose eyes keep following the
> pretty secretary around the room in *Lady in the Lake*
> (1946).

- Why are you always chasing women?

  - I'll tell you as soon as I catch one.

> Carmen Navarro (Carmen Miranda) and her fiance
> Lionel Deveraux (Groucho Marx) in *Copacabana* (1947).

- What a gown!

  - How did you put that on? With a spray gun?

> Scat Sweeney (Bing Crosby) and 'Hot Lips' Barton (Bob
> Hope) to Lucia de Andrade (Dorothy Lamour) in *The
> Road to Rio* (1947).

Ah, what a candy counter!

> Stanley Snodgrass (Bob Hope) admiring Irene Bailey
> (Arlene Dahl) in *Here Come the Girls* (1953).

If you ever decide to swim the channel, I'd like to handle the grease job.

> Tony (Robert Wagner) ogling Holly's (Debbie Reynolds)
> legs in *Say One For Me* (1959).

The Naked Gun: From the Files of Police Squad!

Ah, Cassandra. What a babe. Schwing! She'd give a dog a bone.

Wayne Campbell (Mike Myers) speaking of his girlfriend Cassandra (Tia Carrere) in *Wayne's World 2* (1993).

That body was put together by somebody very close to God.

Leo Schneider (Joseph Bologna) commenting on a woman's beauty in *Chapter Two* (1979).

- Who are you?

- Just your average, horny little devil.

Alexandra 'Alex' Medford (Cher) and Daryl Van Horne (Jack Nicholson) in *The Witches of Eastwick* (1987).

- You like?

- Parts of me are already applauding.

Nick Deezy (Jeff Goldblum) to a woman wearing lace panties and garters in *Vibes* (1988).

Her hair was the color of gold in old paintings. She had a full set of curves and the kind of legs you'd kinda love to suck on for a day. She was giving me a look I could feel in my hip pocket.

Lt. Frank Drebin (Leslie Nielsen) about Jane Spencer (Priscilla Presley) in *The Naked Gun: From the Files of Police Squad!* (1988).

I have a hard-on for you the size of Florida.

Parry (Robin Williams) to Lydia Sinclair (Amanda Plummer) in *The Fisher King* (1991).

There she was. Just like I remembered her. A delicately beautiful face and a body that could melt a cheese sandwich from across the room.

> Lt. Frank Drebin (Leslie Nielsen) describing Jane Spencer (Priscilla Presley), his old flame, in *The Naked Gun 2 1/2: The Smell of Fear* (1991).

Vixens and Vamps

Ah, Joe, come here. Crawl to me, baby, crawl to me.

> Maudie Triplet (Mae West) kissing Joe Anton (George Raft) in *Night After Night* (1932).

- The horoscope. Keep this where you can consult it frequently.

  - All right, I'll take it to bed with me.

> Rajah (Nigel de Brulier) and Tira (Mae West) in *I'm No Angel* (1933).

Am I making myself clear, boys?

> Tira's (Mae West) exit line from the stage in *I'm No Angel* (1933).

It's my fortune. When I was born with this face, it was the same as striking oil.

> Tira (Mae West) in *I'm No Angel* (1933).

- I'll never forget you.

  - Nobody ever does.

> Kirk Lawrence (Kent Taylor) and Tira (Mae West) in *I'm No Angel* (1933).

One figure can sometimes add up to a lot.

> Tira (Mae West) in *I'm No Angel* (1933).

- I was under the impression you were a one-man woman.

  - I am. One man at a time.

> Tira's (Mae West) answer to her maid in *I'm No Angel*
> (1933).

When I'm good, I'm very good. When I'm bad, I'm even better.

> Tira (Mae West) in *I'm No Angel* (1933). Ann Jillian
> repeated the line in *Mae West* (1986).

- Why did you admit knowing so many men in your life?

  - It's not the men in your life that count, it's the life in your men.

> Tira (Mae West) in *I'm No Angel* (1933). Off-screen and
> as Marlo in *Sextette* (1978) she repeated the line slightly
> differently: "It's not the men in my life that counts, it's the
> life in my men."

Come up and see me sometime.

> Tira (Mae West) on the phone to one of the jury men in
> *I'm No Angel* (1933).

- Are those absolutely necessary? You know, I wasn't born with them.

  - No, but a lot of men would have been safer if you had.

  - I don't know. Hands ain't everything.

> Lady Lou (Mae West) after killing her rival, Russian Rita
> (Rafaela Ottiano), when Captain Cummings (Cary Grant)
> comes to put the cuffs on her in *She Done Him Wrong*
> (1933).

- You-bad-girl.

- You'll find out.

> Captain Cummings (Cary Grant) who treathens Lady Lou (Mae West) with marriage in *She Done Him Wrong* (1933).

- Haven't you ever met a man who could make you happy?

- Sure, lots of times.

> Captain Cummings (Cary Grant) and Lady Lou (Mae West) in *She Done Him Wrong* (1933).

When women go wrong, men go right after them.

> Lady Lou (Mae West) answering Sally Glynn's (Rochelle Hudson) question: Who'd want me after what I've done?, in *She Done Him Wrong* (1933).

Come up again, any time.

> Lady Lou (Mae West), first to Serge Stanieff (Gilbert Roland), and later, to Captain Cummings (Cary Grant) in *She Done Him Wrong* (1933).

- So, you met a man who wouldn't fall for you, hey?

- Who wants him to fall? Why, he'd be the kind a woman would have to marry to get rid of.

> Gus Jordan (Noah Beery, Sr.) and Lady Lou (Mae West) speaking of Captain Cummings (Cary Grant) in *She Done Him Wrong* (1933).

- May we ask what types of men you prefer?

- Just two: domestic and foreign.

> Ruby Carter's (Mae West) answer to a group of admirers in *Belle of the Nineties* (1934).

Why don't you come up sometime, see me? I'm home every evening.

Lady Lou (Mae West) to Captain Cummings/The Hawk (Cary Grant) in *She Done Him Wrong* (1933). One of her best known one-liners better remembered simply as: "Come up and see me sometime." Variations include: (1) "Come up Wednesday, that's amateur night." (2) "Come up, I'll tell your future." (3) "Don't be afraid, I won't tell." (4) After marrying the Earl of Stratton, she sings it in the last scene of *Goin' to Town* (1935): "Now that I'm a lady, come up and see me sometime." Ann Jillian repeated the line in *Mae West* (1986): "Why don't you come up sometime?"

It's better to be looked over than overlooked.

> Ruby Carter (Mae West) in *Belle of the Nineties* (1934).

- What's the rush, where's the fire?
  - In your eyes, big boy, in your eyes.

> Cleo Borden (Mae West) in *Goin' to Town* (1935).

I'm a woman of very few words, but lots of action.

> Cleo Borden (Mae West) in *Goin' to Town* (1935).

- You ain't scared of me because they say I'm a bad man?
  - I'm a good woman for a bad man.

> Buck Gonzales (Fred Kohler) and Cleo Borden (Mae West) in *Goin' to Town* (1935).

She's got those eyes that run up and down men like a searchlight.

> Olga (Dennie Moore), the manicurist, characterizing Chrystal Allen (Joan Crawford) in *The Women* (1939).

I will smolder, I'll siren, I'll vamp him to a crisp.

> Karin/Kathryn Borg (Greta Garbo) about being a 'smoldering siren' or 'vamp' to her husband Lawrence Blake (Melvyn Douglas) in *Two-Faced Woman* (1941).

- I could make you forget.
  - But not for long and not enough. For that you'd have to have a heart.

> Senora Camargo (Nina Vale) and Laurence Gerard (Dick Powell) in *Cornered* (1945).

- She couldn't be all bad, no one is.

   - She comes the closest.

Jeff Bailey (Robert Mitchum) speaking about Kathie
Moffet (Jane Greer) in *Out of the Past* (1947).

- I believe you know Lois?

   - If I didn't I certainly do now.

Frank Benson (Bob Hope) introducing his date, who is
showing a lot of cleavage, to his ex-wife Elaine (Jane
Wyman) in *How to Commit Marriage* (1969).

Behaving like some ludicrous little underage *femme fatale*.
You're about as fatale as an after dinner mint.

Brian Roberts (Michael York) to Sally Bowles (Liza
Minnelli) in *Cabaret* (1972).

- I guess you could say I'm half saint, half whore.

   - I'm just hoping I get the half that eats.

Sonja (Diane Keaton) and Boris (Woody Allen) in *Love
and Death* (1975).

I'm not bad, I'm just drawn that way.

Jessica Rabbit (voice of Kathleen Turner) in *Who Framed
Roger Rabbit?* (1988).

I've been a very bad girl, but you have to admit I was very,
very good at it.

Miss Sharon Stone (Halle Berry) to Fred (John Goodman)
in *The Flintstones* (1994).

Hunka, Hunka, Burnin' Love

- You belong at Vassar.

- If there's a double meaning in that, I got it.

Football players Jojo Jordan (Eddie Bracken) and girl-crazy Manuelito (Desi Arnaz) in *Too Many Girls* (1940).

- That Bitsy is strickly a one woman man.

- So am I. One tonight and one tomorrow night.

Private Johnny Grey (Victor Mature) in *Seven Days' Leave* (1942).

- He's pretty fresh, isn't he?

- Well, he's in the fresh air all the time.

Molly (Jean Arthur) and Waco (Charles Winninger) about Duke (John Wayne) in *A Lady Takes a Chance* (1943).

- Why did you say I run after everything in skirts?

- I didn't.

- You did.

- I said anything.

French captain Henri Rochard (Cary Grant) and the American lieutenant Catherine Gates (Ann Sheridan) in *I Was a Male War Bride* (1949).

It is widely held that too much wine will dull a man's desire. Indeed, it will, in a dull man.

The narrator (Michael MacLiammoir) in *Tom Jones* (1963).

He's too beautiful. He's too much twisted steel and sex appeal. I can't be with a guy who looks like I won him in a raffle.

> Dorinda Durston (Holly Hunter) speaking about Ted Baker (Brad Johnson) in *Always* (1989).

Hey, Baby! What's Your Sign?

Don't go away and leave me alone.... You stay and I'll go away.

> Mr. Hammer (Groucho Marx) whom has a unique way of flirting with Mrs. Potter (Margaret Dumont) in *The Cocoanuts* (1929).

Look at her! A-wiggling and a-pouting and a-butting up with that rubber mouth of hers just like a snake putting a spell on a bird.

> Jim Bridger (Tully Marshall), a wagon train scout, about Felice (Lily Damita) making eyes at Clint Belmet (Gary Cooper) in *Fighting Caravans* (1931).

Oh, Professor, you're so full of whimsy.

> Cora (Thelma Todd) to Professor Quincy Adams Wagstaff (Groucho Marx) in *Horse Feathers* (1932).

- Do your eyes bother you?

  - No. Why?

  - They bother me.

> Jerry 'Babe' Stewart (Clark Gable) flirting with librarian Connie Randall (Carole Lombard) in *No Man of Her Own* (1932).

- That twinkle in your eye, wrap it up for me, will you? (...)

  - You write the words and the music, don't you?

> Jerry 'Babe' Stewart (Clark Gable) flirting with Connie Randall (Carole Lombard) in *No Man of Her Own* (1932).

Where do we park it, sweets?

> Professor Quail (W.C. Fields) flirting with the lovely Peggy Hopkins Joyce in *International House* (1933).

Cigarette-me, Cossack.

> Cleo Borden (Mae West) flirting with a Russian in *Goin' to Town* (1935).

- Oh! Hold me closer! Closer! Closer!

  - If I hold you any closer, I'll be in back of you.

> Flo (Esther Muir) and Dr. Hugo Z. Hackenbush (Groucho Marx) in *A Day at the Races* (1937).

If you loved me like I love you, I'd love you better than Irish stew. Boo-boop-a-doo.

> Oliver Hardy serenading Anna (Della Lind) in *Swiss Miss* (1938).

I know. You've forgotten those few nights on the Riviera when we sat beneath the Mediterranean skies, moonlight bathing in the Mediterranean Sea. We were young, gay, reckless. The night I drank champagne from your slipper, two quarts. It would have held more but you were wearing innersoles. Oh! Hildegard.

> J. Cheever Loophole (Groucho Marx) flirting with Mrs.
> Susannah Dukesbury (Margaret Dumont) in *At the Circus*
> (1939).

You get a canoe later and I'll paddle you.

> S. Quentin Quale (Groucho Marx) flirting with an Indian
> girl in *Go West* (1940).

Is that your own hair or did you scalp an angel?

> Larry Haines (Bob Hope) flirting with Karen Bentley
> (Madeleine Carroll) in *My Favorite Blonde* (1942).

Lady-My! What a beautiful head of bone you have.
Curly-I bet you tell that to all the guys.

> In *Booby Dupes* (1945).

Groucho Marx and
Margaret Dumont

I'm just a coward with water in my blood, but when I'm near you it starts to boil and bubbling and every little bubble starts to bubble, and every little bubble's bubble bubbles. Honest, Mimi, I'm fizzing all over for you.

Beaucaire (Bob Hope) courting
Mimi (Joan Caulfield) in
Monsieur Beaucaire (1946).

- You're the most beautiful girl I've ever seen.

  - Am I really?

- No, but I don't mind lying if it's going to get me somewhere.

> Ronald Kornblow (Groucho Marx) and Beatrice Reiner (Lisette Verea) in *A Night in Casablanca* (1946).

- Say, dream girl, how would you like to get into the movies?

- Why, have you got any passes?

- No, but I could make a few.

> Lionel Deveraux (Groucho Marx) flirting with a chorus girl in *Copacabana* (1947).

Toots, I'd love to cover you with furs and automobiles.

> Moe flirting with Miss Lulu in *Half-Wit's Holiday* (1947).

Are you doing anything you couldn't be doing better with somebody else?

> Jed Towers (Richard Widmark) calling Nell (Marilyn Monroe) in the hotel room across the court in *Don't Bother to Knock* (1952).

I sure like the way you draw the Bat Lady. Lovely lines. I like the way your bone structure is... structured. Dandy tabeleus stat coxnemius.

> Rick Todd (Dean Martin) flirting with fellow artist Abigail Parker (Dorothy Malone) in *Artists and Models* (1955).

- I like the way you look.

- Since when?

- Does it have to be retroactive?

> Actress Deborah Vaughn (Janis Paige) flirting with critic Larry Mackay (David Niven) in *Please Don't Eat the Daisies* (1960).

- Do you have any idea of the kind of woman that I really am?

- No, but I have high hopes.

- I'll tell you what I'm like. I know what I want when I see what I want, and when I see what I want, I want it.

- Do you see it?

- I see it.

- Do you want it?

- I want it.

- You got it.

> Diane (Joan Collins) and Chester Babcock (Bob Hope) in
> *The Road to Hong Kong* (1962).

- You know, Chester, you're the sort of man that I could love.

- Could you?

- Oh yes, I could, Chester. I could love you body and soul.

- They're available, in that order.

> Diane (Joan Collins) and Chester Babcock (Bob Hope) in
> *The Road to Hong Kong* (1962).

- What are you doing Saturday night?

- Committing suicide.

- What about Friday night?

> Allan (Woody Allen) flirting with a woman in a museum
> in *Play It Again, Sam* (1972).

I love the way your eyes curl up when you look at me.

> Nick Gardenia (Chevy Chase) flirting with his ex-wife
> Glenda Park (Goldie Hawn) in *Seems Like Old Times*
> (1980).

- I'll tell you. If I want to call you I will. If I don't, I won't.

- Well, if I'm around I'll be there and if I'm not, I won't.

Flirting between Chico (Perry King) and Frannie (Maria Smith) in *The Lords of Flatbush* (1974).

A man sees a beautiful chicken, he cannot help being inquisitive.

Inspector Jacques Clouseau (Peter Sellers), disguised as a playboy and flirting with Lady Lytton (Catherine Schell) in *The Return of the Pink Panther* (1982).

- I'm not wearing a bra, Johnny.

  - That makes two of us.

Johnny Kelly (Michael Keaton) and a chorus girl in *Johnny Dangerously* (1984).

- You know, I saw you sitting in the bus. I was gonna come back but...

  - But you're too bashful.

  - That's right, but now that we've met I'm growing some self-confidence.

  - Oh, good. Then it will be easier for you to deal with rejection.

Jack Harrison (Jeff Goldblum) flirting with Elizabeth (Teresa Ganzel) in *Transylvania 6-5000* (1985).

That was flirting? (...) That was, I like your ass, can I wear it as a hat?

Ed Furillo (Bruno Kirby) to Mitch Robbins (Billy Crystal) in *City Slickers* (1991).

- Mrs. Oglethorpe, you look wonderful. I could make love to you right here and now.

  - Roland, please! Let's keep this on a professional level.

  - Very well then. I'll charge you fifty bucks a pop.

Shyster lawyer Roland T. Flakfizer (John Turturro) flirting with the wealthy and old Mrs. Lilian Oglethorpe (Nancy Marchand) in *Brain Donors* (1992).

You are like wet sand in my underwear.

> Cindy (Rosie Perez) to her flirting boss in *Untamed Heart*
> (1993).

- How would you like to curl up with a good book?

  - In your dreams!

> Adventure (voice of Patrick Stewart) flirting with Fantasy
> (voice of Whoopi Goldberg) in *The Pagemaster* (1994).

- Hey, you like breakfast burritos? I know a great place across the border. I takes thirty-five minutes.

  - We just had pie.

  - They're really good burritos.

  - My mother told me never to go with strangers.

  - Well, we'll swing by and pick her up. Where does she live?

  - Rhode Island.

  - All right. Forty-five minutes. We'll put her in the back.

> Kevin (Michael Keaton) inviting Julia (Geena Davis) to
> ride across the border in his sports car in *Speechless*
> (1994).

Lip Service

■ □ □ □ □ □ □ □ □ ■

I'd love to kiss you, but I just washed my hair.

> Madge (Bette Davis), with a thick accent ("Ah'd love t' kiss
> you but ah jes washed mah hayah"), in *Cabin in the
> Cotton* (1932).

- For one kiss of your lips I'd give half my life.

  - See me tomorrow and I'll kiss you twice.

> Ivan Valadov (Ivan Lebedeff) and Cleo Borden (Mae
> West) in *Goin' to Town* (1935).

Bette Davis

Ah! My beautiful one. (...) I love you madly. (...) Kiss me! I can feel the hot blood pumping through your varicosed veins.

> Banjo (Jimmy Durante) to the nurse in *The Man Who Came to Dinner* (1942).

Am I the first girl you never kissed?

> Maria Acuna (Rita Hayworth) to Robert Davis (Fred Astaire) in *You Were Never Lovelier* (1942).

He kissed me... right on the north and south.

> Dot/Dorothy Bryant (Laraine Day) in *Mr. Lucky* (1943).

Your lipstick is on crooked.

> Philip Marlowe (Robert Montgomery) to Adrienne Fromsett (Audrey Totter) in *Lady in the Lake* (1946).

Anybody who'd kiss me would kiss anybody.

> Wilber 'Squeezebox' McCoy (Lou Costello) in *Comin' Round the Mountain* (1951).

I like to kiss this girl because she has just the type of lips I like, one on top and one on the bottom.

> Junior (Bob Hope) in *Son of Paleface* (1952).

- Give me a kiss to get me in the mood. Just one.

- Very well. Just one.

- I'll give you a sample just in case we're cast away on a desert island. (They kiss.) Well?

- Better bring a deck of cards.

> Pipo Papolino (Bob Hope), soliciting a kiss from Francesca Bruni (Audrey Dalton) before going out to impersonate Casanova in *Casanova's Big Night* (1954).

Come on, give your mommy a big sloppy kiss.

Martha (Elizabeth Taylor) to George (Richard Burton) in *Who's Afraid of Virginia Woolf?* (1966).

- Your lips are fire.

- I know. Saves a fortune in matches.

> Francesca Bruni (Audrey Dalton) and Pipo Papolino (Bob Hope) in *Casanova's Big Night* (1954).

I'm glad we tried it a second time. It's better when two people do it.

> Feathers (Angie Dickinson) kissing John T. Chance (John Wayne) in *Rio Bravo* (1959).

If you want more call for refills.

> Buddy Love (Jerry Lewis) after kissing Stella Purdy (Stella Stevens) in *The Nutty Professor* (1963).

Just marking my place.

> Simon Dermott (Peter O'Toole) pressing his fingers to Nicole Bonnet's (Audrey Hepburn) lips in *How to Steal a Million* (1966).

Kiss my eyes, kiss my neck, kiss my Ankh.

> Jewish lawyer Harold Fine (Peter Sellers) turned into a fetishist hippie after eating brownies asking Nancy (Leigh Taylor-Young) to kiss his Ankh pendant in *I Love You, Alice B. Toklas!* (1968).

Now, give me a kiss and say goodnight. (*Leans forward.*) No tongues!

Elizabeth (Madeline Kahn) to her fiancé Freddy
Frankenstein (Gene Wilder) in Young Frankenstein
(1974).

What is it, Nick? You need some chopsticks or some lip gloss or something, because your lips keep getting stuck on your teeth. Or is that your idea of a smile?

Jo-Ann Vallenari (Michelle Pfeiffer) to Lt. Nick Frescia
(Kurt Russell) in Tequila Sunrise (1988).

I'm back! I've got lips again and I'm going to use them, baby. It's me! I'm your elephant of joy.

King of the Moon (Robin Williams), whose head, re-
united with his body, is rushing to his queen in The
Adventures of Baron Munchausen (1989).

- Kiss me, beautiful.

   - Do you mind if I throw up first?

Vicky (Elizabeth McGovern) and Jerry (Beau Bridges) in
Women & Men. Stories of Seduction (1990).

Datin' & Relatin'

- I'm as gentle as a plowhorse and powerful interested in education.

   - Then I hope you come to some of my classes. I have several little boys just your age.

The Virginian (Gary Cooper) courting the new school
marm Molly Wood (Mary Brian) in The Virginian (1929).

- I hope I pick up something good this time. I'm always getting school teachers.

   - Why not? You've got a lot to learn yet.

Sailors Bilge Smith (Randolph Scott) and 'Bake' Baker (Fred Astaire) on shore leave in *Follow the Fleet* (1936).

- If you were only a man!

   - If you weren't a woman!

Margit Agnew (Myrna Loy) and Charlie Lodge (William Powell) in *Double Wedding* (1937).

When I dress for a date with you, it will be a suit of armor and brass knuckles.

Dixie Daisy (Barbara Stanwyck) in *Lady of Burlesque* (1943).

This may come as a shock to you, but there are some men who don't end every sentence with a proposition.

Jan Morrow (Doris Day) to Brad Allen (Rock Hudson) in *Pillow Talk* (1959).

A relationship, I think, is like a shark. You know, it has to constantly move forward or it dies. And I think what we have on our hands is a dead shark.

Alvy Singer (Woody Allen) to Annie (Diane Keaton) in *Annie Hall* (1977).

I ran out of gas.

   I had a flat tire.

   I didn't have enough money for cab fare.

   My tux didn't come back from the cleaners.

   An old friend came in from out of town.

- Naturally something happens. You put the vibes to thirty million chicks something is gonna happen.

- That's the idea, Rat. That's the attitude.

- The attitude?

- Yeah. The attitude dictates that you don't care whether she comes, stays, lays or prays. I mean whatever happens your toes are still tapping. Now, when you've got that, then you have got the attitude.

Mark 'Rat' Ratner (Brian Backer) taking points on how to pick up girls from cool Mike Damone (Robert Romanus) in Fast Times at Ridgemont High *(1982).*

Someone stole my car.

There was an earthquake, a terrible flood.

... It wasn't my fault, I swear to God.

Joliet Jake Blues' (John Belushi) list of excuses for leaving his fiancée, the Mystery Woman (Carrie Fisher), at the altar in The Blues Brothers *(1980).*

Juliet left me. I feel like I've been hit with a wet frying pan.

Rigby Reardon (Steve Martin) in Dead Men Don't Wear Plaid *(1982).*

You're either a romantic fool or you're an idiot. I don't know which is worse.

Denise (Elizabeth McGovern) to Terry (Steve Guttenberg) in The Bedroom Window *(1986).*

I must like him, I'm shaving above the knees.

Kathy (Annette O'Toole) preparing for her third date with David in Cross My Heart *(1987).*

- You and me... It's time we got something going. I'm free tonight.

- Oh, I'd like that, Joey, but I think I'd rather eat worms and die.

- Hey! You know my worm doesn't have a hook.

Joey O'Brien (Robin Williams) flirting with a co-worker in Cadillac Man *(1990).*

- You're late!

- You're stunning.

- You're forgiven.

Vivian Ward (Julia Roberts) and her date Edward Lewis (Richard Gere) in Pretty Woman *(1990).*

- I thought you liked Nadine?

- I do. I did, until she got me that stupid plant. Believe me, when a lady gives you a plant it's her little way of testing you; like if you can take care of it it's a sign to her that she can move the relationship to the next level. Trust me. When a woman gives you something that you have to water, feed, or take for a walk, it's time to dump.

> Carl (Gailard Sartain) and Ray (Ted Danson) in *Getting Even with Dad* (1994).

- Do you like movies?

- Yes. Yes, I do. I love movies. Do you know what I especially love are good movies.

- Ohhh, you're kidding. I love good movies too.

- Really, oh. Do you know what I hate are bad movies.

- Me too! We're so alike.

- I think that dinner is probably one of my favorite meals of the day.

- Mine too! This is downright eerie.

It's Pat—The Movie

- Oh, do you know another thing I hate? Senseless evil.

- I'm not even going to tell you because you won't believe it.

> Pat (Julia Sweeney) and Chris (David Foley) finding common grounds to fall in love in *It's Pat—The Movie* (1994).

- When it comes to relationships everybody is a used car salesman.

- Is that your philosophy: Don't trust anyone?

- No, you gotta trust people. You just can't trust the warranty.

Simon B. Wilder (Joe Pesci) and Monty/Montgomery
Quesler (Brendan Fraser) in *With Honors* (1994).

Lovestruck

Love flies out the door when money comes innuendo.

Groucho (Groucho Marx) in *Monkey Business* (1931).

- You'll get a divorce!

- But I love him! How can I get a divorce?

- I'll tan your behind!

- It won't do any good. Love is greater that a tanned behind.

Peachum (Fritz Rasp), the king of beggars, to his
daughter Polly (Carola Neher) who secretly married
Mack the Knife (Rudolph Forster) in *The Threepenny
Opera* (1931).

- Maudie, do you believe in love at first sight?

- I don't know but it saves an awful lot of time.

Mabel Jellyman (Alison Skipworth) and Maudie Triplet
(Mae West) in *Night After Night* (1932).

It's the old story: boy meets girl, Romeo and Juliet, Minneapolis and St. Paul.

Dr. Hugo Hackenbush (Groucho Marx) in *A Day at the
Races* (1937).

- You mean to say you just stood there and let me beat up a defenseless woman?

- I did, Mr. Cook.

- Where's your sense of chivalry?

- MY chivalry? Aren't you just a trifle confused, Mr. Cook? You hit her.

- That's entirely different. I love her.

> Wally Cook (Fredric March) and Oliver Stone (Walter Connolly) in *Nothing Sacred* (1937).

Don't leave me Susannah. Can't you see I love you? There, you dragged it out of me. I love you, all of you. I love you feverishly. Have you got a thermometer on you?

> J. Cheever Loophole (Groucho Marx) flirting with Mrs. Dukesbury (Margaret Dumont) in *At the Circus* (1939).

Love is a romantic designation for a most ordinary, biological, or shall we say chemical, process. A lot of nonsense is talked and written about it.

> Lena 'Ninotchka' Yakushova (Greta Garbo), a Russian Bolshevik, to Count Leon Bressart (Melvyn Douglas) in *Ninotchka* (1939).

- Gee, you're really smitten, aren't you, Charlie?

- Yeah! The trouble with me is when I'm smitten I stay smut.

> Charlie McCarthy (voice of Edgar Bergen) and the soda jerk in *Look Who's Laughing* (1941).

Don't give me that honey again. Love is something that gives you one room, two chins, and three kids.

> Gloria Lyons (Lucille Ball) to Ruby, her dresser in *The Big Street* (1942).

Love is like champagne, marriage is the headache, and divorce is the aspirin tablet.

Charlie McCarthy (voice of Edgar Bergen) in *Look Who's Laughing* (1941).

- I'm in love.

  - Nonsense! This is only delayed adolescence.

Maggie Cutler (Bette Davis) and Sheridan 'Sheri' Whiteside (Monty Woolley) in *The Man Who Came to Dinner* (1942).

- But Mortimer, you're going to love me for my mind too.

  - One thing at a time.

Elaine Harper (Priscilla Lane) just married to Mortimer Brewster (Cary Grant) in *Arsenic and Old Lace* (1944).

- I think he's stuck on you. What's the matter with him?

  - It's only natural that you wouldn't understand, Henri.

  - It certainly is.

  - You see, you chase after anything in skirts, anything. They're all the same to you. But lots of men can tell them apart. Believe me, sometimes they find one they like better than the others. That's called love. You probably haven't experienced it but you must have read about it somewhere.

Capt. Henri Rochard (Cary Grant) and Lt. Catherine Gates (Ann Sheridan) speaking of her admirer in *I Was a Male War Bride* (1949).

Miss Singleton, don't you worry about love because a girl built like you is going to collide right on with it one of these days.

Steve Williams (John Wayne) to Miss Singleton (Donna Reed) in *Trouble Along the Way* (1953).

When a man and a woman see each other and like each other they oughta come together—wham!—like a couple of taxis on Broadway.

Stella (Thelma Ritter) to Jeff/L.B. Jeffries (James Stewart) in *Rear Window* (1954).

You don't know what love is. To you, it's just another four-letter word.

Brick Pollit (Paul Newman) to his father Big Daddy (Burl Ives) in *Cat on a Hot Tin Roof* (1958).

- Jonathan, I just don't happen to love you.

- How do you know? Love isn't an opinion, it's a chemical reaction.

Jan Morrow (Doris Day) and Jonathan Forbes (Tony Randall) in *Pillow Talk* (1959).

- You know, Chester, you're the sort of man that I could love.

- Could you?

- Oh yes, I could, Chester. I could love you body and soul.

- They're available, in that order.

Diane (Joan Collins) and Chester Babcock (Bob Hope) in *The Road to Hong Kong* (1962).

I always say that to love yourself is the beginning of a life-long romance and after watching you, I know that you and you will be very happy together.

Stella Purdy (Stella Stevens) to Julius Kelp/Buddy Love (Jerry Lewis) in *The Nutty Professor* (1963).

All I know is my heart was really pounding and I felt a funny tingling all over. I don't know. I was either in love or I had smallpox.

Virgil Starkwell (Woody Allen) walking in the park with Louise (Janet Margolin) in *Take the Money and Run* (1969).

-I love you! I love you!

- Oh say it in French. Please say it in French.

- I don't know French.

- Oh please, please.

- What about Hebrew?

-Oohhhhh!

Felding Mellish (Woody Allen) making love with Nancy (Louise Lasser) in *Bananas* (1971).

Is this love or only infatuation of the body?

Natalie Landauer (Marisa Berenson) to Sally Bowles (Liza Minnelli) about having been 'pounced' upon by Fritz in *Cabaret* (1972).

Don't touch me unless you love me.

Joe Frady (Warren Beatty) to a redneck bar brawler hinting at his girlish long hair in *The Parallax View* (1974).

- Natasha, to love is to suffer. To avoid suffering one must not love. But then one suffers from not loving. Therefore to love is to suffer, not to love is to suffer. To suffer is to suffer. To be happy is to love. To be happy then is to suffer. But suffering makes one unhappy. Therefore, to be unhappy one must love, or love to suffer, or suffer from too much happiness. I hope you're getting this down.

- I never want to marry. I just want to get divorced.

Sonja's (Diane Keaton) advice to young Natasha (Jessica Harper) about love and marriage in *Love and Death* (1975).

- Do you love me?

- Love is too weak a word... I luuurv you. I LOOve you. I luff you, two f's.

Annie (Diane Keaton) and Alvy Singer (Woody Allen) in *Annie Hall* (1977).

I've always loved you.

Gruppenfuhrer (Eugene J. Anthony) to the Neo-Nazi leader (Henry Gibson) falling from the sky in a red car in *The Blues Brothers* (1980).

- Haven't you heard of the sexual revolution?

- Who won? Hum? It used to be sex was the only free thing. No longer. Alimony! Palimony! It's all financial. Love is an illusion.

- It's the only illusion that counts, my friend.

- Says who?

- Anyone who's ever been in love.

- Love sucks!

- So's your attitude.

> Kirbo (Emilio Estevez) and Kevin (Andrew McCarthy) in *St. Elmo's Fire* (1985).

- I love you so much it hurts.

- That's because you're leaning on my fork.

> Arthur Bach (Dudley Moore) and his wife Linda (Liza Minnelli) in *Arthur 2: On the Rocks* (1988).

- You said you loved me.

- I meant it at the time.

- Well, what is it? A viral love, kind of a twenty-four hour thing?

> Suzanne Vale (Meryl Streep) and Jack Falkner (Dennis Quaid) in *Postcards from the Edge* (1990).

Mike Myers and Dana Carvey in *Wayne's World*

Yes! Yes! I am guilty. Guilty of love in the first degree.

> Celeste Talbert (Sally Field) in a soap opera within *Soapdish* (1991).

- Tell me. When that first show is over, will you still love me when I'm an incredibly humongoid giant star?

- Yeah.

- Will you still love me when I'm in my hanging-out-with-Ravi-Shankar phase?

- Yeah.

- Will you still love me when I'm in my carbohydrate-sequined-jump-suit-young-girls-in-cotton-panties-waking-up-in-a-pool-of-your-own-vomit-bloated-purple-dead-on-the-toilet phase?

- Yeah.

- OK! Party!

Wayne Campbell (Mike Myers) and Cassandra (Tia Carrere) in *Wayne's World* (1992).

Through all the ups and... downs, I've come to realize that what we call love is really the exchange of energy over time. It's simple quantum mechanics. You take water for example. Sometimes it's water, sometimes it's ice. Sometimes steam or vapor. It's always the same H-two-O. It only changes it's properties. Your mother is like that. She's like water. I made the decision a long time ago just to love her basic properties.

Maj. Hank Marshall (Tommy Lee Jones) explaining to his daughters his love for his star-struck eccentric wife Carly (Jessica Lange) in *Blue Sky* (1994).

I Do, I Do

- Well, what do you say, girls? Are we all going to get married?

- All of us?

- All of us!

- Yes, but that's bigamy!

- Yes, and it's big-of-me too. It's big of all of us. Let's be big for a change. I'm sick of these conventional marriages.

One woman and one man was good enough for your grand-mother, but who wants to marry your grandmother?

> Captain Jeffrey Spaulding (Groucho Marx) proposing marriage to both Mrs. Rittenhouse (Margaret Dumont) and Mrs. Whitehead (Margaret Irving) in *Animal Crackers* (1930).

I wouldn't marry you to keep warm on an iceberg!

> Jimmy Wade (Roland Young) to Trixie (Lillian Roth) in *Madam Satan* (1930).

So, you're leaving me for marriage.

> Newspaper editor Walter Burns (Adolphe Menjou) to his star reporter Hildy Johnson (Pat O'Brien) in *The Front Page* (1931).

Married! I can see you now, in the kitchen, bending over a hot stove, but I can't see the stove.

> Rufus T. Firefly (Groucho Marx) flirting with Gloria Teasdale (Margaret Dumont) in *Duck Soup* (1933).

I wouldn't marry you if you were young, which you can't be, if you were honest, but you never were, or if you were about to die tomorrow, which is too much to hope for.

> Bo Peep (Charlotte Henry) to Silas Barnaby (Henry Kleinach) in *March of the Wooden Soldiers* (Original title: *Babes in Toyland*) (1934).

- This poor little thing is married, unhappily married. Now isn't that criminal?

- It's no crime to be married. It just shows a weakness on the part of men that women take advantage of.

Hortense (Alice Brady), speaking for her niece Mimi (Ginger Rogers), to lawyer Egbert Fitzgerald (Edward Everett Horton) in *The Gay Divorcee* (1934).

You must understand that a man, to be married, must be broad-minded.

Oliver Hardy to Stan Laurel when he sees his wife kissing another man in *The Bohemian Girl* (1936).

She may be his wife, but she's engaged to me.

Warren Haggerty (Spencer Tracy) whose fiancée Gladys Benton (Jean Harlow) is temporarily married to Bill Chandler (William Powell) in *Libeled Lady* (1936).

Moe-We're not going to build nothing. We're on our honeymoon.

Curly-Soitanly. I got married so I could retire.

The boys, newly married, are refusing to build a house in *The Sitter-Downers* (1937).

Emily, I have a little confession to make. I really am a horse doctor, but marry me and I'll never look at another horse.

Dr. Hugo Hackenbush (Groucho Marx) and Emily Upjohn (Margaret Dumont) in *A Day at the Races* (1937).

- You know, you only go on a honeymoon once. Wouldn't you like to go to Paris for a few days, then Venice, then home to your own little love nest?

- George! I didn't know you cared?

- Wait a minute, wait a minute! You can't leave Reggie like this.

- Oh, don't be silly. We can't take him with us on our honeymoon.

> George's (George Burns) suggestion to Gracie (Gracie Allen) about her honeymoon with Reggie (Ray Noble) backfires on him in *A Damsel in Distress* (1937).

You know, getting married is like buying a new horse or going into a strange saloon....

> Larson E. Whipsnade (W.C. Fields) to his daughter Vicky (Constance Moore) in *You Can't Cheat an Honest Man* (1939).

I can see it all now. I come home from a hard day's work. I whistle for the dog, and my wife comes out.

> Curly in *Yes, We Have No Bonanza* (1939).

- Married men live longer.

  - Nonsense. It only seems longer.

> Fabian, the Great Ventriloquist (Richard Cortez) and Alf, his puppet, in *Mr. Moto's Last Warning* (1939).

But Mrs. Callahan, you know that he'd rather be cheated by me than married to you.

> Frenchy (Marlene Dietrich) who won the pants off Boris (Mischa Auer), Mrs. Callahan's (Una Merkel) husband in *Destry Rides Again* (1939).

Are you married or happy?

> Moe as a census taker in *No Census, No Feeling* (1940). Curly to a block of ice he's about to shave in *An Ache in Every Stake* (1941).

- Marriage is a strong institution, Charlie.

- So is Alcatraz, but I wouldn't want to live in it.

Julie Patterson (Lucille Ball) and Charlie McCarthy (voice of Edgar Bergen) in *Look Who's Laughing* (1941).

My heart is a bargain today. Will you have me?

Cuthbert J. Twillie (W.C. Fields) proposing marriage to Flower Belle Lee (Mae West) in *My Little Chickadee* (1940).

D.H.-You got the right angle, honey. You marry for love. I did.

Dresser-All five times.

Sandra-And you've still got another arm.

D.H.-Yeah and I wish I was an octopus.

Dresser-You are.

D.H.-Slip me that handcuff, will you, honey.

Diamond Hand (Eve Arden) with one wrist full of diamond bracelets, a dresser and Sandra (Hedy Lamarr) in *Ziegfeld Girl* (1941).

- You'll be marrying yourself someday.
- Marrying myself! I wouldn't be legal.

Charlie McCarthy (voice of Edgar Bergen) in *Look Who's Laughing* (1941).

Nobody ever sends me flowers anymore. After a woman gets married, her husband decides she can't smell anymore.

Delphina Acuna (Barbara Brown) to her husband Eduardo (Adolphe Menjou) in *You Were Never Lovelier* (1942).

Are you married or happy, Miss Kelly?

Ralph Edwards to a woman in the audience of the radio show Truth or Consequences in *Seven Days' Leave* (1942).

Responsibility for recording a marriage has always been up to the woman. If it wasn't for her, marriage would have disappeared long since. No man is going to jeopardize his present or poison his future with a lot of little brats hollering around the house, unless he's forced to. It's up to the woman to knock him down, hard time, and drag him in front of two witnesses immediately, if not sooner. Any time after that, it's too late.

Attorney Johnson (Alan Bridge) to Trudy Kockenlocker (Betty Hutton) in *The Miracle of Morgan's Creek* (1944).

Please, Marabelle, if you'll marry me this once I'll never ask you-allllll again.

Moe, a Southern gentleman, proposes marriage to Marabelle in *Uncivil War Birds* (1946).

Mrs. Hawkins, marriage is nothing but a three-ring circus: first the engagement ring, and then the wedding ring, and then the suffering.

Chester Wooley (Lou Costello) refusing to marry the Widow Hawkins (Marjorie Main) in *The Wistful Widow of Wagon Gap* (1947).

- Marriage is very healthy, sir. Married men live much longer than bachelors.

- If that's true, they're only trying to outlive their wives so they can be bachelors again.

The dresser and Tom Bowen (Fred Astaire) in *Royal Wedding* (1951).

- Looks like we're in the cold.
- Perhaps we should keep each other warm.

- Listen, buster, the only way you can keep me warm is to wrap me up in a marriage license.

> Angel (Gloria Grahame) and Sebastian (Cornel Wilde), old lovers abandoned by their new ones in *The Greatest Show on Earth* (1952).

She can love who she pleases, but she must marry the man I choose.

> Squire Western (Hugh Griffith) speaking of his daughter Sophie (Susannah York) in *Tom Jones* (1963).

Most men are the marrying sort, poor devils.

> Professor Henry Higgins (Rex Harrison) to Eliza Doolittle (Audrey Hepburn) in *My Fair Lady* (1964).

I've been married thirty-eight years and I don't regret one day of it... The one day of it I don't regret was August 2nd, 1936. She was off visiting her ailing mother at the time.

> Judge Blackstone (Sidney Blackmer) to Stanley Ford (Jack Lemmon) in *How to Murder Your Wife* (1965).

Marriage is not a basic fact of nature, it's an invention. It's like the infield fly rule. It exists only because women say so, and like idiots we just go following along.

> Stanley Ford (Jack Lemmon) on trial for allegedly murdering his wife in *How to Murder Your Wife* (1965).

- What kind of people just sit like that with nothing to say to each other?

- Married people?

> Mark (Albert Finney) and Joanna (Audrey Hepburn) early in *Two for the Road* (1967), a question which is

asked again twice by Audrey Hepburn at other moments
during the movie with an explanation too simple to see.

Love! What love? Love is ten minutes. Love is before, marriage is after. You meet a girl one night, you don't know if
you're going to make it, that's love. When you wake up in
the morning, that's marriage.

Murray (Herb Edelman) to Harold Fine (Peter Sellers) in *I
Love You, Alice B. Toklas!* (1968).

I'm old-fashioned. I don't believe in extramarital relationships. I think people should mate for life, like pigeons or
Catholics.

Isaac Davis (Woody Allen) to Tracy (Mariel Hemingway)
in *Manhattan* (1979).

- They are now going to recite their vows. Martha.

- You-ness, me-ness, us-ness, we-ness, your-ness, my-
ness, our-ness, happiness.

A Cosmos wedding ceremony presided by Reverend
Spike (Tom Smothers) with Martha (Sally Kellerman)
pronouncing her marital vows in *Serial* (1980).

- Why don't we smarten up and marry each other?

- Because you're an alcoholic and I'm gay. We'd have
trouble getting our kids into a good school.

Georgia Hines (Marsha Mason) and Jimmy (James Coco)
in *Only When I Laugh* (1981).

- Were you ever married, Mr. Trabucco?

- Once; but I got rid of her. Now I just lease.

Victor Clooney (Jack Lemmon) and Trabucco (Walter
Matthau) in *Buddy Buddy* (1981).

You can't bring logic into this. We're talking about marriage. Marriage is like the Middle East. There's no solution.

Shirley (Pauline Collins) in Shirley Valentine (1989).

I can't believe I've been married five years. Seems like yesterday. And you know how lousy a day yesterday was.

Thornton Melon (Rodney Dangerfield) to Lou (Burt Young) about his second marriage in Back to School (1986).

Life after death is as improbable as sex after marriage.

Mrs. White (Madeline Kahn) in Clue (1986).

The Monchine 40 says: Marriage is this. He goes off to fight the Turks and you put on a lock. (*2nd definition.*) Marriage is this. You cook and clean and bring him martinis. (*3rd definition.*) The modern marriage. There are no rules or responsibilities, but if he does something wrong you can set him on fire while he sleeps and go on a talk show where everybody will forgive you and love you.

The Council Chief (Tony Jay), consulting a large dictionary, to Celeste (Kim Basinger) in My Stepmother is an Alien (1988).

- Marriages don't break up on account of infidelity. It's just a symbol that something else is wrong.

  - Really?! Well, that symbol is f**king my wife.

Jess (Bruno Kirby) and Harry (Billy Crystal) in When Harry Met Sally (1989).

You can't bring logic into this. We're talking about marriage. Marriage is like the Middle East. There's no solution.

Shirley (Pauline Collins) in Shirley Valentine (1989).

You know, I used to think you were crazy for marrying that man. Then, for a few years, I thought you were butting for punishment. Now I realize you must be on a mission from God.

> Ouiser Boudreaux (Shirley MacLaine) in *Steel Magnolias* (1989).

- Are you going to marry her?

- Garth, marriage is punishment for shoplifting in some countries.

> Garth Algar (Dana Carvey) and Wayne Campbell (Mike Myers) in *Wayne's World* (1992).

The Ol' Ball and Chain

I think you're above all women, but below zero.

> Bob Brooks (Reginald Denny) to his wife Angela (Kay Johnson) in *Madam Satan* (1930). At the end of the movie, once her disguise as Madam Satan is uncovered, she tells him: You told me I was below zero so I raised the temperature.

Mrs. Briggs, I've known and respected your husband for many years... and what's good enough for him is good enough for me.

> Groucho (Groucho Marx) to Lucille Briggs (Thelma Todd), grabbing her hand and pulling her down in *Monkey Business* (1931).

My slogan: Your wife is safe with Tonetti—he prefers spaghetti.

> Rodolfo Tonetti (Erik Rhodes), a professional at posing as the third party in divorce cases in *The Gay Divorcee* (1934).

Captain-Pardon me, Sir. Is your wife a blond or a brunette?

Moe-Well, Sir, I really can't say. When she first married me everybody accused her of being lightheaded.

> Moe is Major Hide in *Uncivil Warriors* (1935).

I wouldn't go on living with you if you were dipped in platinum.

> Lucy Warrimer (Irene Dunne) to her soon-to-be ex-husband Jerry (Cary Grant) in *The Awful Truth* (1937).

My wife is so mean she barks at the dog.

> Fiesta (Akim Tamiroff) in *Union Pacific* (1939).

A husband is what's left of a sweetheart after the nerve has been killed.

> Lou (Lou Costello) in *One Night in the Tropics* (1940).

After all, what a husband doesn't know won't hurt his wife.

> Anna (Maude Eburne) to Maria Tura (Carole Lombard) about her rendezvous with a young flyer in *To Be or Not to Be* (1942).

Jose-How dare you hug my wife in front of my eyes?

Curly-Turn around and I'll hug her behind your back.

> In Mexico in *What's the Matador?* (1942).

- Sir! This lady is my wife. You should be ashamed!

- If this lady is your wife, *you* should be ashamed.

> Ronald Kornblow (Groucho Marx) in *A Night in Casablanca* (1946).

- George, do you know my wife's an angel?

   - You're lucky. Mine's living.

> Tom Watson (Bud Abbott) and George Bell (Lou Costello)
> in *Lost in Alaska* (1952).

- I didn't mean any harm.

   - That's when you do the most damage.

   - We all make mistakes.

   - You specialize in them.

   - Only little ones.

> Ann Shankland (Rita Hayworth) visiting her ex-husband
> John Malcolm (Burt Lancaster) in England in *Separate
> Tables* (1958).

- Bob.

   - Frank.

   - I'm miserable. I might as well admit it. What do you call it when you hate the woman you love?

   - A wife.

> Frank Broderick (Henry Fonda) and Bob Weston (Tony
> Curtis) in *Sex and the Single Girl* (1964).

- Mrs. Benson, your husband is a very attractive man, but first, for the record, I am not in the habit of meeting a gentleman at one o'clock and crawling in his bed at three-thirty.

   - I never accused you of crawling into bed with a gentleman.

> Lois Gray (Maureen Arthur) and Frank Benson's (Bob
> Hope) ex-wife Elaine (Jane Wyman) in *How to Commit
> Marriage* (1969).

- You know, Glenda, there was a time when you had a pretty good sense of humor.

- I remember it. It was the day I married you.

Nick Gardenia (Chevy Chase) and his ex-wife Glenda Park (Goldie Hawn) in *Seems Like Old Times* (1980).

- Shouldn't we kiss or shake hands or something?

- Let's save it for when you leave.

Bill Waren (Alan Alda) and his ex-wife Hannah Warren (Jane Fonda) in *California Suite* (1978).

Forgive I should mention it, but you know, when your wife was my wife, your wife was some wife. I only hope my wife is your wife like your wife was my wife... You know what I mean?

Movie director Lazlo Karansky (Ringo Starr) about his ex-wife to Sir Michael Barrington (Timothy Dalton) about his new bride Marlo Manners (Mae West) in *Sextette* (1978).

He called me a baboon! He thinks I'm his wife.

Al Czervik (Rodney Dangerfield) to Judge Smelis (Ted Knight) in *Caddyshack* (1980).

- Yes, master.

- I am not your master, you are my wife.

- Right, I am your wife, master.

- Go away, Lupi. I cannot stand subordination.

- Neither can I. I'll stay away.

Lupi (Carol Kane) and Radu (John Byner) in *Transylvania 6-5000* (1985).

Husbands should be like Kleenex: soft, strong, and disposable.

Mrs. White (Madeline Kahn), who had five husbands in *Clue* (1986).

You used to have a wild side. Sometimes I feel like I married Jimi Hendrix and he turned into Oliver North.

> Pam Marshetta (Bonnie Bedelia) to her Vietnam veteran coal mining husband Gary (Fred Ward) in *The Prince of Pennsylvania* (1988).

His wife is poison, but he thinks she's Betty Crocker.

> R.K. Maroon (Alan Tilvern) to Eddie Valiant (Bob Hoskins) speaking about Roger's wife, Jessica Rabbit in *Who Framed Roger Rabbit?* (1988).

I wouldn't live with you if the world was flooded with piss and you lived in a tree.

> Julie (Martha Plimpton) to Tod (Keanu Reeves) in *Parenthood* (1989).

The Addams Family

Don't torture yourself, Gomez. That's my job.

> Morticia (Anjelica Huston) to Gomez (Raul Julia) in *The Addams Family* (1991).

Is it up yet?

> Ernest Menville (Bruce Willis) asking the maid if his wife, Madeline Ashton (Meryl Streep), is awake in *Death Becomes Her* (1992).

- You oughta get a husband, Coonie. You wouldn't be so mean.

  - I had a husband. That's how I got this way.

> Frank/Francis (Richard Harris) and Coonie (Shirley MacLaine) in *Wrestling Ernest Hemingway* (1993).

- Mother, Fred is a loving husband and a good provider.

- Oh, really?! What has he ever provided you besides shade? Oh, Wilma, you could have married Elliot Firestone, the man who invented the wheel. Instead you married Fred Flintstone, the man who invented the excuse.

> Wilma (Elizabeth Perkins) and her mother Pearl
> (Elizabeth Taylor) in *The Flintstones* (1994).

Cheatin' Hearts

- All those opera pretenders, acrobats, that Italian bicycle rider I told you about, they're all lies. The only man in my life is that cavalier in there. Oscar Jaffe.

- What are you trying to tell me?

- I was completely loyal to him.

- Loyal?!

- Of course... he watched me like a hawk.

> Lily Garland (Carole Lombard) to her fiancé George
> Smith (Ralph Forbes) about Oscar Jaffe/O.J. (John
> Barrymore) in *Twentieth Century* (1934).

Why the hell did you ever say 'I do' to me when you're still saying 'I did' to him?

Ira Park (Charles Grodin) to his wife Glenda (Goldie Hawn) about her ex-husband Nick Gardenia (Chevy Chase) in *Seems Like Old Times* (1980).

- It's unbelievable. I come home to find a man in the same boat with me and my wife says: "What does it matter?"

- You certainly don't want me to waste a lot of time giving you a long explanation?

- No, but I think a husband is entitled to an inkling.

> Joseph Tura (Jack Benny) finding Lt. Sobinski in his bed
> and slippers, and his wife Maria (Carole Lombard) in a
> hurry to find and kill the spy Professor Siletsky in *To Be or
> Not to Be* (1942).

If I don't come back, I forgive you for what happened between you and Sobinski. But if I do, it's another matter.

> Jospeh Tura (Jack Benny) to his wife Maria (Carole Lombard) in *To Be or Not to Be* (1942).

I won't let myself fall in love with a man who won't trust me no matter what I might do.

> Lorelei Lee (Marilyn Monroe) to Mr. Esmond in *Gentlemen Prefer Blondes* (1953).

Shirley Valentine

Millie, would you sit down a minute. (...) It's the kind of thing you should hear sitting up.

> Marvin Michaels (Walter Matthau) about to explain the other woman in his bed to his wife Millie (Elaine May) in *California Suite* (1978).

Any man who does less is less than a man.

> Giuseppe (Richard Libertini) explaining to Claude Eastman (Dudley Moore), while chopping lettuce, what should be done to an unfaithful wife in *Unfaithfully Yours* (1983).

Jane divorced her husband. I never knew him. It was before I met her. Apparently she came home from work unexpectedly one morning and found him in bed with the milkman. Honest to God! The milkman. Well, from that day forward I noticed (*whispers*) she never takes milk in her tea.

> Shirley (Pauline Collins) having tea with her friend Jane (Alison Steadman) while talking to the camera in *Shirley Valentine* (1989).

Breakin' Up Is Hard? To Do

You can't have a divorce on an empty stomach.

Aunt Hortense (Alice Brady) to Mimi (Ginger Rogers) in *The Gay Divorcee* (1934).

I swear, if you existed, I'd divorce you.

Martha (Elizabeth Taylor) to her husband George (Richard Burton) in *Who's Afraid of Virginia Woolf?* (1966).

- Divorce is a terrible thing.

- Oh! It can be if you haven't the right solicitor.

Felix Madison (Jack Lemmon) and the English sisters in *The Odd Couple* (1968).

- You gave her more than half?

- We're having a friendly divorce. She and her lawyer are friends.

The Gay Divorcee

Lois Gray (Maureen Arthur) surprised that Frank Benson's (Bob Hope) ex-wife gets 60% of their house in *How to Commit Marriage* (1969).

- Were you ever married, Mr. Trabucco?

- Once but I got rid of her. Now I just lease.

Victor Clooney (Jack Lemmon) and Trabucco (Walter Matthau) in *Buddy Buddy* (1981).

Consider that a divorce.

> Doug Quaid (Arnold Schwarzenegger) shooting his wife
> Lori (Sharon Stone) in *Total Recall* (1990).

Divorce? In California? That's exactly what she wants you to do. You have no talent for poverty.

> Helen Sharp (Goldie Hawn) to Ernest Menville (Bruce
> Willis) in *Death Becomes Her* (1992).

I thought it was for life but the nice judge gave me a full pardon.

Tracy Lord (Katharine Hepburn) to C.K. Dexter Haven (Cary Grant) about her divorce in *The Philadelphia Story* (1940).

I Vant to Be Alone

I want to be alone.

> Grusinskaya (Greta Garbo) as the reclusive artist in
> *Grand Hotel* (1932). She also says: I just want to be
> alone.

- I want to be mysterious, I want to be alone.

 - Don't try that. You're not Swedish.

 - I don't have to be. It took her five years to smile. I sang in my third picture.

> Cherry Chester/Sarah Brown (Margaret Sullavan) and
> Boyce 'Boycy' Medford (Beulah Bondi) in *The Moon's
> Our Home* (1936).

When I finish my work, I want my solitude and my privitation.

> Fidelia (Hattie McDaniel) to Anne Hilton (Claudette
> Colbert) in *Since You Went Away* (1944).

Greta Garbo

- How do you like your coffee?
- Alone!

Dummond Hall (Jeff Chandler) and Lynn Markham (Joan
Crawford) in *Female on the Beach* (1955).

Never let one man worry your mind. Find 'em, fool 'em and
forget 'em.

Tira's (Mae West) leitmotif in *I'm No Angel* (1933).

It's difficult to explain a man like him to a man like you.

Klara Novak (Margaret Sullavan) to Alfred Kralik (James
Stewart) who, in fact, is both her secret correspondent
and her boss in *The Shop Around the Corner* (1940).

Let's all be manly!

Amanda Bonner (Katharine Hepburn) in *Adam's Rib* (1949).

He's like an animal. He has an animal's habits. There's even
something subhuman about him. Thousands of years have
passed him right by and there he is, Stanley Kowalski, sur-
vivor of the stone age, bearing the raw meat home after the
killing, the jungle and you. You! You're waiting for him.
Maybe he'll strike you or maybe he'll grunt and kiss you.

Blanche Du Bois (Vivien Leigh) to her sister Stella
Kowalski (Kim Hunter) about her husband Stanley
(Marlon Brando) in *A Streetcar Named Desire* (1951).

It takes more than big, broad shoulders to make a man,
Harvey.

Helen Ramirez (Katy Jurado) to Harvey Pell (Lloyd
Bridges) in *High Noon* (1952).

Men! Can't live with 'em, can't shoot 'em.

Wendy (Mare Winningham) and Julie (Ally Sheedy) in *St. Elmo's Fire* (1985). This line has known many variations simply by changing the first word or rephrasing it slightly. Examples: (1) "Boys! Can't live with 'em, can't shoot 'em." Corky (Winona Ryder) in *Night on Earth* (1991). (2) "Kids! Can't live with 'em, can't shoot 'em." Grandpa Gustafson (Burgess Meredith) in *Grumpy Old Men* (1993). (3) "Women! Can't live with 'em, can't kill 'em." Gibs (Tom Arnold) in *True Lies* (1994). (4) "People! Can't live with 'em, can't live without 'em." Pat (Julia Sweeney) in *It's Pat—The Movie* (1994).

- Do you smoke?

  - Yes, I do.

  - Good, a man should have an occupation of some sort.

> Lady Bracknell (Edith Evans), not terribly fond of Jack Worthing (Michael Redgrave), in *The Importance of Being Earnest* (1952).

You gentlemen date back one hundred thousand years. You oughta be wearing leopard skins and carrying clubs. Politics! Business! What is so masculine about a conversation that a woman can't enter into?

> Lesley Benedict (Elizabeth Taylor) in *Giant* (1956).

We wouldn't be caught dead with men. Rough, hairy beasts. Eight hands. And they all want just one thing from a girl.

> Jerry (Jack Lemmon) disguised as a woman in *Some Like It Hot* (1959). An opinion shared by Jayne Mansfield who said, off screen: Men are those creatures with two legs and eight hands.

- I don't quite understand. Am I being stupid?

  - No, you're being a man, which is sometimes the same thing.

> Frank Beardsley (Henry Fonda) and Helen North (Lucille Ball) in *Yours, Mine and Ours* (1968).

They're either married or gay. And if they're not gay, they've just broken up with the most wonderful woman in the world or they've just broken up with a bitch who looks just like me. They're in transition from a monogamous relationship and they need more space or they're tired of space but they just can't commit or they want to commit but they're afraid to get close. They want to get close, you don't want to get near them.

Meg (Mary Kay Place) to
Sarah (Glenn Close) on the
subject of dating in *The Big
Chill* (1983).

I will try to be as
direct and honest with
you as I possibly can. I
think, no, I am posi-
tive, that you are the
most unattractive man
I have ever met in my
entire life. You know,
in the short time that
we have been together
you have demon-

The Witches of Eastwick

strated every loathsome characteristics of the male personality and even discovered a few new ones. You are physically
repulsive, intellectually retarded, you're morally reprehensible,
vulgar, insensitive, selfish, stupid. You have no taste, a lousy
sense of humour and you smell. You're not even interesting
enough to make me sick.

Alexandra 'Alex' Medford (Cher) to Daryl Van Horne
(Jack Nicholson) in *The Witches of Eastwick* (1987).

I always thought men you like vanished with the dinosaur and
the wooley mammoth, but here you are, big as life. Amazing.

Dr. Theodora Cushing (Frances Fisher) to Harry Archer
(Daniel Baldwin) in *Attack of the 50 Ft. Woman* (1993).

- All men are pigs!

- Ah, pigs: an omnivorous, domesticated, cloven hoof
vertibrate that defecates the same place it consumes.

- Exactly.

Prymaat Conehead (Jane Curtin) having a chit-chat about men!! with her
neighbor in *Coneheads* (1993).

You two-timing bastard! I hope your prostate falls out!

> Peaches Jordan (Jada Pinkett) watching a soap opera in
> *A Low Down Dirty Shame* (1994).

He Said...

∎▫▫▫▫▫▫▫▫▫∎

Women are like elephants to me. I like to look at them but I wouldn't want to own one.

> Commodore Orlando Jackson (W.C. Fields) in *Mississippi* (1935).

There's a Miss Cooper waiting outside for me. She's another one of those dizzy, silly, maladjusted females who can't make up her mind. I'll probably find out she hasn't got one.

> Doctor Tony Flag (Fred Astaire) before his first meeting with
> Amanda Cooper (Ginger Rogers), who overhears the comment
> and sets out to contradict him in *Carefree* (1938).

Great ladies and gallant street girls have a lot in common.

> Preston Dillard (Henry Fonda) in *Jezebel* (1938).

She's so deliciously low, so horribly dirty (...) I shall make a duchess of this draggle-tailed guttersnipe.

> Professor Henry Higgins (Leslie Howard) speaking of Eliza
> Doolittle (Wendy Hiller) in *Pygmalion* (1938). Rex Harrison has
> the same line in the musical version *My Fair Lady* (1964).

There's only two ways to handle women... and nobody knows what they are.

> Bill Yard (George Cleveland) in *Valley of the Sun* (1942).

Ever know a woman who wasn't a doll or a dame?

> Waldo Lydecker (Clifton Webb) to Det. Mark McPherson
> (Dana Andrews) in *Laura* (1944).

Statistics show that there are more women in the world than anything else—except insects.

> Johnny Farrell (Glenn Ford) who seems to think that it
> wouldn't be a tragedy if Ballin Mundson (George
> Macready) lost Gilda (Rita Hayworth) in *Gilda* (1946).

- I suppose, being a woman, you can't help it.
  - Can't help what?
  - Making a fool of yourself.

> The Ghost/Captain Daniel Gregg (Rex Harrison), having
> claimed that "jealousy is a disease of the flesh," is
> somewhat disturbed at seeing Lucy Muir (Gene Tierney)
> with Miles Fairley (George Sanders) in *The Ghost and
> Mrs. Muir* (1947).

It's my experience that women will do anything for money.

> The Ghost/Captain Daniel Gregg (Rex Harrison) to Lucy
> Muir (Gene Tierney) in *The Ghost and Mrs. Muir* (1947).

Ah! Ah! Danger ahead! Two of 'em!
  - Be happy! You only find the right woman once.
  - That many times?

> Henri Baurel (Georges Guétary) and Adam Cook (Oscar
> Levant) in *An American in Paris* (1951).

A woman can smell mink through six inches of lead.

> Emil J. Keck (Groucho Marx) in *Double Dynamite* (1951).

Women are like oranges. When you've squeezed one, you've squeezed them all.

> Pipo Papolino (Bob Hope) posing as Casanova in
> *Casanova's Big Night* (1954).

Let me tell you a little secret about women. Now, the reason they're called the opposite sex is because when they start to holler 'I hate ya' you can bet money, marbles or chalk that they mean exactly the opposite.

> Pa Larkin (Paul Douglas) to Lorenzo Charlton/Charly
> (Tony Randall) in *The Mating Game* (1959).

I tell you, it's a whole different sex.

> Jerry/Daphne (Jack Lemmon) in women's clothes in *Some
> Like It Hot* (1959).

Do women think it's feminine to be so illogical or can't they help it?

> Joshua (Cary Grant) to Eugena (Audrey Hepburn) in
> *Charade* (1963).

I'd prefer a new version of the Spanish Inquisition than to ever let a woman into my life.

> Professor Henry Higgins (Rex Harrison) in *My Fair Lady*
> (1964).

I'm very grateful she's a woman and so easy to forget.

> Professor Henry Higgins (Rex Harrison) in *My Fair Lady*
> (1964).

I like a girl in a bikini. No concealed weapons.

> Scaramanga (Christopher Lee) in *The Man with the
> Golden Gun* (1974).

I warn you, Tanya the Lotus Eater, I am opposed to the Women's Libs. Man is the master and women's place is in the home.

> Inspector Jacques Clouseau (Peter Sellers) to Tanya the Lotus Eater, a S & M prostitute in *Revenge of the Pink Panther* (1978).

All dames are alike. They reach down your throat so they can grab your heart, they pull it out, they throw it on the floor and they step on it with their high heels. They spit on it. They shove it in the oven and the cook the shit out of it. Then they slice it into little pieces, slam on a hunk of toast and serve it to you. And they expect you to say: thanks honey, it's delicious!

> Rigby Reardon (Steve Martin) in *Dead Men Don't Wear Plaid* (1982).

A woman is a hole! Isn't that what they say? All the futility of the world pouring into her.

> Daryl Van Horne (Jack Nicholson) in *The Witches of Eastwick* (1987).

Let me ask you something. You're all church-going folks.(...) Do you think God knew what He was doing when He created woman? No shit! I really want to know. Or do you think it was another one of His minor mistakes like tidal waves, earthquakes, floods? (...) What's the matter? You don't think God makes mistakes? Of course He does. We all make mistakes. But when we make mistakes, they call it evil. When God makes mistakes, they call it nature. So what do you think? Women! A mistake? Or did He do it to us on purpose? Because I really want to know. Because if it's a mistake, maybe we can do something about it. Find a cure, invent a vaccine, build up our immune system... a little exercise. You know, twenty push-ups a day and you never have to be afflicted with women again.

Daryl Van Horne (Jack Nicholson) in The Witches of Eastwick (1987).

- There are two kinds of women: high maintenance and low maintenance.

  - And Ingrid Bergman is low maintenance?

  - An LM definitely.

Harry Burns (Billy Crystal) and Sally Albright (Meg Ryan) in When Harry Met Sally (1989).

- Harry, we are just going to be friends.

  - You realize, of course, that we can never be friends.

  - Why not?

  - What I'm saying is, and this is not a come-on in any way, shape or form, is that men and women can't be friends because the sex part always gets in the way. (...) Because no man can be friends with a woman he finds attractive. He always wants to have sex with her.

  - So, you're saying that a man can be friends with a woman he finds unattractive.

  - No, you pretty much want to nail them too.

Sally Albright (Meg Ryan) and Harry Burns (Billy Crystal) in When Harry Met Sally (1989).

- I don't like dames!

  - Good! Me neither.

The Kid (Charlie Corsmo) and Tess Trueheart (Glenne Headly) in Dick Tracy (1990).

- Oh dear Lord, what's the matter with women anyway?

- Please don't call me women.

Hodie (Peter Weller) and Kit (Molly Ringwald) in *Women & Men. Stories of Seduction* (1990).

Women are like a beautiful bed of flowers.... Of course there's a weed here and there.

Chester Lee (Rodney Dangerfield) revises his statement when a punk with purplish-pink spikes and bangs walks by in *Ladybugs* (1992).

Billy Crystal and Meg Ryan in *When Harry Met Sally*

- Women are one of life's great mysteries. To some guys women are like a big jigsaw puzzle with pieces that just don't fit. I think the soul of a woman is darker than a back alley, and more tangled than a telephone cord, and colder than an Eskimo pie in Anchorage, but those guys don't even have a clue. When you know women the way I do, you know exactly what makes them tick, what makes them hum, what makes them jiggle up and down when they walk. There are two kinds of women in the world and I've known them both: one will take you for a fast ride on a bumpy road with no seat belt, the other kind...

- Gee, knock off the chatter, will you, Ned?

Ned Ravine's (Armand Assante) voiceover monologue and Arch's (John Witherspoon) comment at the beginning of *Fatal Instinct* (1993) establish the mood for a parody of *film noirs* of the 1940s and early 1950s.

A woman is like a slingshot: the greater the resistance, the further you can get with 'em.

Reverend Jonas Nightengale (Steve Martin) in *Leap of Faith* (1993).

Babes are like a bad song. Once you get 'em stuck in your head you can't get 'em out again.

Spanky (Travis Tedford), president of the He-man Womun-Haters Club in *The Little Rascals* (1994).

- All raise your right hand... your other right hand:

I. (*Repeated in chorus by the club members.*)

- Stymie. (*Obviously they repeat his name instead of their own.*)

- Member of the He-Man Womun-Haters Club. (*Chorus.*)

- Do solemnly swear to be a he-man and hate women, and not play with them, and not touch them unless I have to, and especially never to fall in love, and if I do, may I die slowly and painfully and suffer for hours or until I scream bloody murder. (Chorus).

Stymie (Kevin Jamal Woods) and the Little Rascals swearing allegiance to the He-Man Womun-Haters Club in *The Little Rascals* (1994).

Spanky-And now... the choosing of the driver.

Froggy-Our driver should be a man who's all He-man.

Porky-A He-man so manly that if he fell off a building he'd go out of his way to land on a girl.

Spanky (Travis Tedford), Froggy (Jordan Warkol) and Porky (Zachary Mabry) choosing a driver for The Blur, their prized go-cart, in *The Little Rascals* (1994).

Babes are like a bad song. Once you get 'em stuck in your head you can't get 'em out again.

Spanky (Travis Tedford) president of the He-man Womun Haters Club in *The Little Rascals* (1994).

Women

There are no girls gone wrong, there are bad girls found out.

Ruby Carter (Mae West) in *Belle of the Nineties* (1934).

I was just wondering what makes dames like you so dizzy.

> Peter Warne's (Clark Gable) answer to Ellie's (Claudette Colbert) question "What are you thinking about?" in *It Happened One Night* (1934).

- He said I'm cheap. (...) He meant I was dishonest.

- Darling, all women are dishonest. If they weren't, the world would be divided into two classes of people: old maids and bachelors. Look. That's dishonest (*holds up lipstick*), plucking your eyebrows is dishonest, the rouge on your cheeks is dishonest, and a fat woman in a girdle, wooo!, that's highway robbery. If marrying a nice boy like Bill is the wrong idea don't tell me that starving and waiting for Prince Charming to ride up on a white horse is the right one.

> Nicole De Cortillon (Danielle Darrieux) and Gloria Patterson (Helen Broderick) about conning millionnaire Bill into marriage in *The Rage of Paris* (1938)

Don't make an issue of my womanhood.

> Lena 'Ninotchka' Yakushova (Greta Garbo) to the Russian trade delegates Buljanoff, Iranoff and Kopalski greating her at the Paris train station in *Ninotchka* (1939).

There's only two ways to handle women... and nobody knows what they are.

> Bill Yard (George Cleveland) in *Valley of the Sun* (1942).

The way to a woman's heart is to get her out of the kitchen.

> Warrick (Sir Cedric Hardwicke) in *Valley of the Sun* (1942).

I don't know what the Good Lord was about when he made a female out of a perfectly good rib.

> John Fraser (Ward Bond) to Captain Chris Holden (Gary Cooper) in *Unconquered* (1947).

I'd say she's doing a woman's hardest job: juggling wolves.

> Lisa Carol Fremont (Grace Kelly) to Jeff/L.B. Jeffries (James Stewart) about Miss Torso, an attractive ballet dancer surrounded by men in the apartment across the yard in *Rear Window* (1954).

- Can you look like yes and act like no? Can you entice them, lure them, then pospone, evade, delay? It needs a special kind of experience and skill. This a nice girl has not learned.

- No. This is what a nice girl has learned best.

> Dr. Prokosch (Oscar Homolka) trying to dissuade his student, Cathy (Kim Novak), from posing as the in-house girlfriend of three married men and one divorcé for her thesis in sociology in *Boys' Night Out* (1962).

A woman without a man is like a trailer without a car; it ain't going nowhere.

> Polly the Pistol (Kim Novak) to Zelda Spooner (Felicia Farr) in *Kiss Me, Stupid* (1964).

Women have to emancipate themselves in order to emancipate men so that they can emancipate each other where it counts the most.

> Maggie Dubois (Natalie Wood) to newspaper editor Henry Goodbody (Arthur O'Connell), because he wouldn't or couldn't tell the color of her stockings in *The Great Race* (1965).

Actually, I don't dislike women, I merely distrust them. The twinkle in the eye and the arsenic in the soup.

> Sherlock Holmes (Robert Stephens) in *The Private Life of Sherlock Holmes* (1970).

You're an emancipated woman, learn to lose.

> Lawrence 'Larry the Liquidator' Garfield (Danny DeVito) to Kate Sullivan (Penelope Ann Miller) in *Other People's Money* (1991).

I'm not one of these guys who's going to look upon you as an object (...) because I look upon a woman as a whole.

> Harry Bliss (Jack Nicholson) to Joan Spruance (Ellen Barkin) in *Man Trouble* (1992).

Funny thing about women. They'll do anything to keep up appearances. Take Lola Cain. She'd rather look like a hard-case with bloody knuckles than a soft touch with a soiled reputation. Still, I had to admit, there was something about her that made me sweat bullets.

> Ned Ravine's (Armand Assante) thoughts about Lola Cain (Sean Young) in *Fatal Instinct* (1993) are reminescent of voiceover monologues in film noirs the 1940s and early 1950s.

- Women! Ain't they perfect?

  - Not always.

  - Yes they are. They're perfect. Don't matter if they're skinny, fat, blonde or blue. If a woman is willing to give you her love, Harvard, it's the greatest gift in the world. Makes you taller, makes you smart, makes your teeth shine.... Boy, oh boy, women are perfect.

  - Keep your voice low.

Behind every great man is a woman and thank heaven I have Lilian Oglethorpe because, quite frankly, I enjoy the shade.

Roland T. Flakfizer (John Turturro) introducing, in a Groucho-like manner, Mrs. Lilian Oglethorpe (Nancy Marchand) at a press conference in *Brain Donors* (1992).

- Perfect love and perfect ache. Joy when you first see 'em and get to know 'em, ache when you leave 'em. Joy, ache. Joy, ache. Joy, ache.

> Simon B. Wilder (Joe Pesci) to Harvard student Jeff (Josh Hamilton) in *With Honors* (1994).

Men

As for me, I'm going back in the closet where men are empty overcoats.

> Groucho (Groucho Marx) to Lucille (Thelma Todd) in *Monkey Business* (1931).

- I'm wild about you.

- Some of the wildest men make the best pets.

> Ace Lamont (John Miljan) and Ruby Carter (Mae West) in *Belle of the Nineties* (1934).

- All my life I've been looking for a man that's big, handsome, and got plenty of money.

- Hmmm, what you've been looking for is three men.

> The maid, Jasmsine (Libby Taylor), and Ruby Carter (Mae West) in *Belle of the Nineties* (1934).

Don't ever let a man put anything over on you outside of an umbrella.

> Ruby Carter (Mae West) to her maid Jasmine (Libby Taylor) in *Belle of the Nineties* (1934).

- Women do have it worse than men, don't they?

- I don't know. I'm not a man.

> Hans Pinneberg (Douglass Montgomery) and the gynecologist's nurse (Hedda Hopper) in *Little Man, What Now?* (1934).

The man who gets you is going to have a lifetime of misery.

> David Huxley (Cary Grant) to Susan Vance (Katharine
> Hepburn) in *Bringing Up Baby* (1938).

- Somebody strap me down!

   - Oh! So that's the kind of man you are.

   - You mean there's another kind?

> Jim Taylor (Bob Hope) and Marina Von Minden (Vera
> Zorina) in *Louisiana Purchase* (1941).

- For eight hours of every day Mr. Curtis is up to his hips in beautiful girls and we all look alike to him.

   - Really?

   - Yes. To a hungry man a lamb chop is a tasty dish but to the butcher it's just another hunk of meat.

> Marge (Sunnie O'Dea) to co-dancer Sheila Winthrop
> (Rita Hayworth), who never misses as opportunity to
> dance with Robert Curtis (Fred Astaire) in *You'll Never
> Get Rich* (1941).

A fellah like that reminds me of a side of pork: streak of fat, streak of lean, streak of good, streak of mean.

> Mrs. Reverend Varner (Marjorie Main) to Elizabeth
> Cotton (Lana Turner) about gambler Candy Johnson
> (Clark Gable) in *Honky Tonk* (1941).

- That Bitsy is strictly a one woman man.

   - So am I. One tonight and one tomorrow night.

> Private Johnny Grey (Victor Mature) in *Seven Days'
> Leave* (1942).

- You don't understand. Every night, when the moon is full, I turn into a wolf.

- You and fifty million other guys.

> Lawrence Talbon/Wolfman (Lon Chaney, Jr.) and Wilbur Grey (Lou Costello) in *Abbott and Costello Meet Frankenstein* (1948).

Getting better acquainted with him is like making a pet out of a polecat.

> Calamity Jane (Doris Day) speaking of Wild Bill Hickok (Howard Keel) in *Calamity Jane* (1953).

- Maybe one day she'll find her happiness.

  - Yeah, and some man will lose his.

> Stella (Thelma Ritter) and Jeff/L.B. Jeffries (James Stewart) talking about Miss Loneliheart in the apartment across the yard in *Rear Window* (1954).

- You're an arrogant, self-centered, male chauvinist pig.

  - You're just being sweet to me because I'm a man.

> Ruth Loomis (Jill Clayburgh) and Dan Snow (Walter Matthau) in *First Monday in October* (1981).

We're VIPs: Very Immense Penises.

> Booger (Curtis Armstrong) in *Revenge of the Nerds II: Nerds in Paradise* (1987).

- Phillip is completely true to Susan.

- Men aren't true to anything. They will have sex with a tree.

Catherine (Rita Wilson) and Blanche Munchnick (Madeline Kahn) in *Mixed Nuts* (1994).

- All men are pigs!

  - Ah, pigs: an omnivorous, domesticated, cloven hoof vertibrate that defecates the same place it consumes.

  - Exactly.

> Prymaat Conehead (Jane Curtin) having a chit-chat about Men!! with her neighbor in *Coneheads* (1993).

Spanky-And now... the choosing of the driver.

Froggy-Our driver should be a man who's all He-man.

Porky-A He-man so manly that if he fell off a building he'd go out of his way to land on a girl.

> Spanky (Travis Tedford), Froggy (Jordan Warkol) and
> Porky (Zachary Mabry) choosing a driver for The Blur,
> their prized go-cart, in *The Little Rascals* (1994).

Cat Fights

- I was reading a book the other day. (...) It's all about civilization or something, a nutty kind of book. Do you know that the guy said that machinery is going to take the place of every profession?

- Oh, dear, that's something you need never worry about.

> Kitty Packard (Jean Harlow) and Carlotta Vance (Marie
> Dressler) in *Dinner at Eight* (1933). Off-screen Harlow
> once asked a producer: "What kind of whore am I now?"

As long as they have sidewalks, you've got a job.

> Nan Prescott (Joan Blondell) to Vivian Rich (Claire Dodd)
> in *Footlight Parade* (1933).

Must have been tough on your mother not having any children.

> Ann Lowell (Ginger Rogers) to a bitchy co-dancer in
> *42nd Street* (1933).

Do you know that she makes forty-five dollars a week and sends her mother a hundred of it.

> Ann Lowell/Anytime Annie (Ginger Rogers) maligning a
> co-dancer in *42nd Street* (1933).

In my days, women with hair like that didn't come out at night.

> Aunt Kate (Elizabeth Patterson) about Mavis Arden (Mae West) in *Go West, Young Man* (1936).

When I go back to my room, you're the only thing I want to find missing.

> Jean Maitland (Ginger Rogers) to her roommate Linda Shaw (Gail Patrick) in *Stage Door* (1937).

- It would be a terrific innovation if you could get your mind to stretch a little further than the next wisecrack.

  - You know, I tried that once and it didn't snap back into place.

> Terry Randall (Katharine Hepburn) and Eve (Eve Arden) in *Stage Door* (1937).

I'll bet you could boil a terrific pan of water.

> Jean Maitland (Ginger Rogers) to Terry Randall (Katharine Hepburn) in *Stage Door* (1937).

I see that in addition to your other charms you have that insolence generated by an inferior upbringing.

> Terry Randall (Katharine Hepburn) to Jean Maitland (Ginger Rogers) in *Stage Door* (1937).

You may as well go to perdition in ermine. You're sure to come back in rags.

> Terry Randall (Katharine Hepburn) lending her roommate Jean Maitland (Ginger Rogers) a fur coat for her date with producer Anthony Powell (Adolphe Menjou) in *Stage Door* (1937).

- I bet Miss Swallow knows poison ivy when she sees it.

  - I bet poison ivy runs when it sees her.

> David Huxley (Cary Grant) and Susan Vance (Katharine Hepburn) speaking of David's fiancée in *Bringing Up Baby* (1938).

I'd like to make a dress for her: half tar and half feathers.

> Lily Belle Callahan (Una Merkel) speaking of Frenchy (Marlene Dietrich) in *Destry Rides Again* (1939).

There's a name for you ladies, but it isn't used in high society... outside of a kennel.

> Crystal Allen's (Joan Crawford) exit line in *The Women* (1939).

This is the kind of woman that makes whole civilizations topple.

> Miss Bragg (Kathleen Howard) speaking of Sugarpuss O'Shea (Barbara Stanwyck) in *Ball of Fire* (1941).

That dame is a lump of mud.

> Gloria Lyons (Lucille Ball) about a co-performer in *The Big Street* (1942)

Don't take that patronizing tone with me, you flea-bitten Cleopatra.

> Sheri(dan) Whiteside (Monty Wolley) to Maggie Cutler (Bette Davis) in *The Man Who Came to Dinner* (1942).

Clara Tate is a copyrighted nuisance.

> Mrs. Mott (Ethel Barrymore) about her busybody neighbor in *None But the Lonely Heart* (1944).

Lucille Ball

You peroxide kissing bug... I'll pull that blond hair by its black roots. Put 'em up!

> Edwina Fulton (Ginger Rogers) to Lois Laurel (Marilyn Monroe) in *Monkey Business* (1952).

I must say, Mrs. Burnside, you're everything I ever expected... and quite a bit more.

> Mame Dennis (Rosalind Russell) meeting her future mother-in-law in *Auntie Mame* (1958).

But, you can't play Scrabble... not with grown-up people!

> Hilary Rhyall (Deborah Kerr) to Hattie Durant (Jean Simmons) in *The Grass Is Greener* (1960).

- It's been a pleasure meeting you, Miss London. (...) I never miss any of your performances. It's heart-warming to see that your vivacity is not merely stagecraft, your beauty is more than make-up and amber lights.

  - She hates me.

> Charlotte Oar (Jessie Royce Landis), Parker's (Bob Hope) mother-in-law, to his ex-wife Ivy London (Marilyn Maxwell) in *Critic's Choice* (1963).

- What an enormous bed!

  - The German army was very large in those days.

> Mata Bond (Joanna Pettit) shown into the bedroom (closed since 1916) of her mother Mata Hari by Polo (Ronnie Corbett) in *Casino Royale* (1967).

- Did you ever see a girl carry a torch so high?

  - Yeah! Statue of Liberty.

> The dancers and Tallulah (Jodie Foster) speaking of Bleusy's (Florrie Dugger) infatuation for Bugsy in *Bugsy Malone* (1976).

- Lola, darling, you know there are only two things I dislike about you.

  - Really? What are they?

  - Your face.

Marina Rudd (Elizabeth Taylor) and Lola Brewster (Kim Novak) in *The Mirror Crack'd* (1980).

- Oh my! That kind of evening, hmm?

  - Not the kind you're used to. No money changed hands.

Sandy (Bette Midler) and Lauren (Shelley Long) in *Outrageous Fortune* (1987).

Come in, Mr. Butterworth.... Oh, you're not Mr. Butterworth. I can tell by the coat.

Linda Bach (Liza Minnelli) comparing beautiful Susan Johnson (Cynthia Sikes) to old Mr. Butterworth in *Arthur 2: On the Rocks* (1988).

- Really?! You're Roy's mother?

  - Hmm, hmm.

  - That's impossible!

  - Not quite, but I'm not sure who you are. Miss Langtry, was it?

  - I'm Roy's friend.

  - Yes, I imagine you're lots of people's friend.

  - Oh! Of course. Now that I see you in the light you're plenty old enough to be Roy's mother.

  - Aren't we all.

Myra Langtry (Annette Bening) and Lilly Dillon (Anjelica Huston) fighting for Roy's (John Cusack) affection in *The Grifters* (1990).

There are two things I don't like about you... your face. So how about shutting both of 'em.

Mitzi (Hugo Weaving) to Felicia (Guy Pearce) in *The Adventures of Priscilla, Queen of the Desert* (1994).

What's on her mind—if I may so flatter her?

> Kit (Molly Ringwald) jealous of another woman in
> *Women & Men: Stories of Seduction* (1990).

Gosh! I'm glad you came. I didn't know if you would. I spoke to my P.R. woman and she said "Madeline Ashton goes to the opening of an envelope."

> Helen Sharp (Goldie Hawn) to Madeline Ashton (Meryl
> Streep) in *Death Becomes Her* (1992).

Tough Guys

Them's five-finger words!

> James (Jimmy Durante) in *Speak Easily* (1932).

When you're slapped, you'll take it and like it.

> Sam Spade (Humphrey Bogart) to Joel Cairo (Peter Lorre)
> in *The Maltese Falcon* (1941).

All five of 'em hit me at once.

> Bill (W.C. Fields), who was knocked down by one man in
> *Never Give a Sucker an Even Break* (1941). Two of W.C.
> Fields catch-phrases were: (1) "I can lick my weight in
> wildflowers;" (2) "I'll fight anyone in pediatrics."

Drop that gun or I'll drill you. I've got a gun here that shoots bullets for twelve miles and throws rocks the rest of the way.

> Weejie (Lou Costello) in *Hit the Ice* (1943).

I'll take lemonade... in a dirty glass.

Clint Eastwood

Chester Hooton (Bob Hope) affecting to be mean, down and dirty in a Klondike Saloon in *The Road to Utopia* (1945). Still popular: "Give me a milk Steve... in a dirty glass." Devin Butler (Norman D. Golden II), the kid in *Cop and a Half* (1993).

He plum riled me.

'Painless' Peter Potter (Bob Hope), affecting a cowboy's accent, after ordering Bob to get out of town before sundown in *The Paleface* (1948).

I won't need it. He's a small lion.

Samson (Victor Mature) throwing away his spear before engaging in a hopelessly phony fight with a lion in *Samson and Delilah* (1949).

Well, it's a nice, soft night. So I think I'll go and join me comrades and talk a little treason.

Michaelen Flynn (Barry Fitzgerald) in *The Quiet Man* (1952).

I wanted to marry her when I saw the moonlight shining on the barrel of her father's shotgun.

Ali Hakim (Eddie Albert) in *Oklahoma!* (1955).

Go ahead! Make my day!

Dirty Harry Callahan (Clint Eastwood) urging an armed robber to make a play for is gun in *Sudden Impact.*

(1963). Also: (1) Marty McFly (Michael J. Fox) posing as Clint Eastwood in 1885 and facing some bad hombres in *Back to the Future—Part III* (1990). (2) Burt Simpson (Dabney Coleman) to a bad guy but in his case hoping to die in *Short Time* (1990). (3) Tom Burton (Rutger Hauer) in *Beyond Justice* (1992). (4) Fletch (Chevy Chase) in *Fletch* (1985). Variants: (1) "Go ahead, give me a reason. Make my year." Ralph (Danny DeVito) to Jack (Michael Douglas) in *The Jewel of the Nile* (1985). (2) "Go ahead! Make my billenium!" Betlegeuse (Michael Keaton) in *Beetlejuice* (1988). See also: *Last Action Hero* (1993).

I know what you're thinking, punk. You're thinking, did he fire six shots or only five? Well, to tell you the truth, in all this excitement, I've kinda lost track myself. But, being this is a .44 magnum, the most powerful handgun in the world, and would blow your head clean off, you've got to ask yourself one question: do I feel lucky? Well, do you, punk?

Dirty Harry/Harry Callahan (Clint Eastwood) to a bank robber in *Dirty Harry* (1963). Re-phrased for the age of automatic weapons in *National Lampoon's Loaded Weapon I* (1993). Sgt. Jack Colt (Emilio Estevez) asks the bad guy: "I know what you're thinking, punk. You're thinking, did he fire 173 times, or 174? Well, do you feel lucky, punk?"

- Remember! KAOS will do everything in it's power to try to stop you. You'll be in imminent danger and constant jeopardy facing death at every turn.

You talkin' to me?!

Travis Bickle (Robert De Niro), repeatedly, practicing his tough guy act in *Taxi Driver* (1976). (1) John Wayne, as John Bernard Brooks, has the same line at the beginning of *The Shootist* (1976) when a hold-up man asks for his wallet: "Are you talkin' to me?!" (2) Robberson (Chevy Chase), a suburbanite addicted to cop movies, practices that same stance and speech in front of a mirror in *Cops and Robbersons* (1994). (3) Cartoon characters are also belligerent but have better enunciation. In *The Lion King* (1994): "Are you talking to me?"

- Annddd loving it!

Commander Drury (Kenneth Mars) and Maxwell Smart (Don Adams) in *Get Smart, Again!* (1989). "Annddd loving it!" is Maxwell Smart's standard answer when told that a mission will put his life in danger in the *Get Smart* television series and Smart movies, including *The Nude Bomb* (1980).

You're so cool you piss ice cubes.

Donald Quinelle (Robin Williams) to Jack Locke (Jerry Reed) in *The Survivors* (1983).

I'm your worst nightmare! An eight year old with a badge.

Devon Butler (Norman D. Golden II), assisting detective Nick McKenna (Burt Reynols) for a day, gives a speeding ticket to the school principal in *Cop and a Half* (1993). Other variations: (1) Glen (Sam McMurray), in *Raising Arizona* (1987): "I'm your worst nightmare." (2) Father Jedediah Mayii (Leslie Nielsen), warning the devil within Nancy Aglet (Linda Blair), in *Repossessed* (1990): "I'm your worst nightmare." (3) Jigsaw (Tim Curry), in *National Lampoon's Loaded Weapon I* (1993): "I am your worst nightmare." (4) Jack Slater (Arnold Schwarzenegger), in *Last Action Hero* (1993): "You've seen these movies where they say, 'Make my day!' or 'I'm your worst nightmare!' Well, listen to this one: 'Rubber baby buggy bumpers.'" (5) Rock Reilly (Tom Berenger) engaging Eddie Devane (William McNamara) in a fist fight in *Chasers* (1994): "I'm gonna be your worst nightmare." (6) Herbert Cadbury (Jonathan Hyde) playing gin rummy with the prison lowlife (Rush Pearson) in *Richie Rich* (1994): "Welcome to your worst nightmare."

Let's show this prehistoric bitch how we do things down-town.

Dr. Peter Venkman (Bill Murray) to the ghostbusters,
speaking of Gozer in *Ghostbusters* (1984).

- Hey! You don't want to be in here!

  - When I want your opinion I'll beat it out of you.

Eddie Cusack's (Chuck Norris) answer to a bad guy in a
poolroom full of bad guys in *Code of Silence* (1985).

We're back, we're bad. You're black, I'm mad.

Sgt. Martin Riggs (Mel Gibson) to his partner Sgt. Roger
Murtaugh (Danny Glover) in *Lethal Weapon 2* (1989).

- Hey, Joe, want me to shoot this guy?

  - Shit, you shoot me in a dream you better wake up and apologize.

Mr. Blonde/Vic (Michael Madsen) and Mr. White/Larry
(Harvey Keitel), members of a five-men robbery team in
Reservoir Dogs (1992).

- Cigarette?

  - No, thanks. They're bad for you.

  - Yes, I know. I like things that are bad for me.

Lola Cain (Sean Young) and Ned Ravine (Armand
Assante) in *Fatal Instinct* (1993).

Pals

I thought we might run up a few curtains and make a batch of fudge while we decide what dress to wear to the country club dance.

Sarcastic prostitute (Jean Harlow) to Dennis Carson (Clark Gable) when he
tells her to be friendly with Barbara Willis (Mary Astor) in *Red Dust* (1932).

We may be friends, but every once in awhile we f**k each other.

> Olymic runner (Patrice Donnelly) speaking about competitor and lover (Mariel Hemingway) in *Personal Best* (1982).

- I thought you wanted to be my friend.

 - This is what I do with my friends.

> Beth Wexler (Rita Wilson) and Lawrence Bourne III (Tom Hanks), who is getting fresh with her in *Volunteers* (1985).

Betty Finn was a true friend, and I sold her out for a bunch of Swatch dogs and Diet Coke heads.

> Veronica (Winona Ryder) in *Heathers* (1989).

This could be the end of a beautiful friendship.

> Detective (Treat Williams) and partner (Joe Piscipo) as they become zombies in *Dead Heat* (1988).

All in the Family

- Your mother has her good points, Pat.

 - She sure has, and they stick out all over her!

> Pat Harrington (Del Henderson) and his daughter Pat(ricia) (Marion Davies) in the silent movie *The Patsy* (1928).

- So, you're Agnes.

 - Yes, ma'am.

 - My! What a striking resemblance between you and the butler.

- Yes, ma'am. You see, I'm twins.

> Lady Plumtree (Thelma Todd) and Agnes (Stan Laurel) in
> *Another Fine Mess* (1930).

Twins?! Are they both mine?

> Gussie (El Brendel), the comic relief, to his mother-in-law
> (Louise Carver) in *The Big Trail* (1931).

- Well, you suggested it, now you cut it.

- I don't know anything about cutting wood.

- Well, you ought to. You once told me your father was in the lumber business.

- Well, I know he was, but he was only in a small way.

- What do you mean, 'small way'?

- Well, he used to sell toothpicks.

- Well, go ahead and make some toothpicks. Be a chip off the old block.

> Ollie (Oliver Hardy) and Stan (Stan Laurel) cutting wood
> to pay for their meal in *One Good Turn* (1931).

Maybe I am a little headstrong, but I come by it honestly. My father was a little headstrong, my mother was a little armstrong. The headstrongs married the armstrongs and that's why darkies were born.

> Rufus T. Firefly (Groucho Marx) in *Duck Soup* (1933).

- You know, I had a wire from my sister today. She has a brand new little baby. She's married, you know.

- Is it a little girl or a boy?

- Well, I don't know yet. I'm dying to find out whether I'm an uncle or an aunt.

> Nurse Allen (Gracie Allen) and Doc Burns (George Burns) in
> *International House* (1933). Diana Lynn, as Emmy

Kockenlocker, has a similar line in *The Miracle of Morgan's Creek* (1944): "I was just wondering whether I'm an aunt or an uncle."

I was born at home because I wanted to be near mother.

Jim (William Powell) to Eleanor (Myrna Loy) in *Manhattan Melodrama* (1934). The Three Stooges had a similar routine in *Don't Throw That Knife* (1951). They are census takers practicing on each other. Shemp Howard dresses as a woman and Moe Howard knocks at his door: Where were you born Madam? In the hospital. I wanted to be near my mother.

- Speaking of relatives, Mrs. Colton, have your ancestors ever been traced?
- Yes, but they were too smart. They couldn't catch 'em.

Cleo Borden Colton (Mae West) to a society lady in *Goin' to Town* (1935).

I hope you will grow up to be as good a mother as your father.

Gracie Allen and George Burns

Stan Laurel to young Arline (Darle Hood) in *The Bohemian Girl* (1936).

- Where did you get such a nice father and mother?

- I took my time picking them.

Jim Lane (Clark Gable) and Ann Barton (Myrna Loy) in *Test Pilot* (1938).

Moe-What was your family decomposed of?

Curly-Well, I'll tell you. It was a litter of three and I was the one they kept.

Census takers in No Census, No Feeling (1940).

Larry-Who darned our socks and pressed our shirts when we were helpless little squirts?

Curly-Mammy!

Moe-Who kept the buttons on our clothes? Who scrubbed our ears and blew our nose?

Curly-Mammy! Oh, Mammy! It's your little boy Sammy coming home from Alabamy. Put on those eggs and hammy. Don't flim-flam me, Mammy. Oh, Mammy!

The boys, disguised as refugee children (Moe is Johnny, Curly is Franky, Larry is Mable), have a little recitation for their new 'mammy' in All the World's a Stooge (1941).

If I could reach as high as my father's shoestrings, my whole life would be justified.

Woodrow Lafayette Pershing Truesmith (Eddie Bracken) beginning his speech for truth in Hail the Conquering Hero (1944).

Has your mother turned into an honest woman?

Adam Mercy (Randolph Scott) to the prison warden in Captain Kidd (1945).

The boys are census takers practicing on each other. Shemp pretends to be a woman:

Moe-Where were you born, madam?

Shemp-In the hospital.

Moe-Hospital?

Shemp-Yes, I wanted to be near my mother.

> In *Don't Throw that Knife* (1951).

Any son of yours would rise to great heights... aided by the hangman's noose.

> Captain Bonney (Hilary Brooke) to Captain Kidd (Charles Laughton) in *Abbott and Costello Meet Captain Kidd* (1952).

If he was the last man on earth and my sister the last woman, I'd still say no!

> Red Will Danaher (Victor McLaglen) refusing to let Sean Thornton (John Wayne) court his sister Mary Kate (Maureen O'Hara) in *The Quiet Man* (1952).

- That was one of my father's jokes.

 - What are you? One of your mother's?

> Chick Williams (Norman Wisdom) and Raymond Paine (Jason Robards) on the burlesque stage in *The Night They Raided Minsky's* (1968).

Don't ever hit your mother with a shovel. It leaves a dull impression on her mind.

> In *Butch Cassidy and the Sundance Kid* (1969).

- You're not our natural-born child...

 - You mean, I'm going to stay this color?

> The black, adoptive mother (Mabel King) of white Navin R. Johnson (Steve Martin) in *The Jerk* (1979).

- So I figured mom and dad didn't need me around any-more, not with fourteen mouths to feed.

- Your folks had fourteen kids?

- No, they ran a kennel.

> Johnny Kelly (Michael Keaton) and Lil Sheridan (Marilu
> Henner) in *Johnny Dangerously* (1984).

- You've gotten to be like a daughter to me and I want to share something with you.

- What's that, Mom Kelly?

- I go both ways.

> Ma Kelly (Maureen Stapleton) and Lil Sheridan (Marilu
> Henner) in *Johnny Dangerously* (1984).

That's it! I want out of this family.

> Jeanie Bueller (Jennifer Grey) in *Ferris Bueller's Day Off*
> (1986).

- You're Arthur, aren't you? Stanford Bach's boy?

- That's right.

- The shame of the family, the wastrel, the public drunk.

- Oh, you say that as if it were a bad thing.

> Kendal Winchester (David O'Brien) and Arthur Bach
> (Dudley Moore) in *Arthur 2: On the Rocks* (1988).

They're family and I love them but they do look like they've all been carved out of cream cheese.

> Clairee Belcher (Olympia Dukakis) in *Steel Magnolias*
> (1989).

If I had to live with my mother I would stab myself six times.

> Ann Napolitano (Mercedes Ruehl) in *The Fisher King*
> (1991).

- Wait a second. I think you should know. It's likely that Steve will look at you as a father figure.

- You know what, it's already starting to happen. I'm trying to fill those shoes. I'm doing the best I can.

- I understand, but you should realize this is a father that Steve might want to put a bullet through.

- How does he feel about his uncle?

Dr. Aaron (Diane Wiest) and Al Percolo (Albert Brooks) speaking about baseball star Steve Nebraska (Lane Smith) in *The Scout* (1994).

You need a mother very, very badly.

Peter Banning's daughter Moira (Caroline Goodall) to Captain James Hook (Dustin Hoffman) in *Hook* (1991).

If I wanted a big brother I wouldn't have killed mine.

Harlan 'Flat Top' Myerson (Tom Whitenight) to Paul Blake (Scott Bakula) in *Necessary Roughness* (1991).

- She's my sister...

- Sister! Our blood isn't even at the same temperature.

Joseph Donelly (Tom Cruise) and Shannon Christie (Nicole Kidman), who resents being associated to Joseph in this way in *Far and Away* (1992).

- I understand your boy Matthew has been seeing a lot of my daughter Kimberly.

- Yes, Dave. (Under his breath.) More than you know.

Dave Mullen (Tom Parks) and Chester Lee (Rodney Dangerfield) in *Ladybugs* (1992).

Ohh, Baby!

- I wonder what they got corraled in there anyhow?

- Babies! Aren't they? Never saw so many mavericks in my life.

- Shttt. Thems are kids and some of them are waiting to be christened. One, two, three... eleven beautiful sleeping angels. Hey, it be funny if they all got mixed up and christened wrong, wouldn't it? (...)

- Let's get busy before the parson gets to work.

The Virginian (Gary Cooper) and Steve (Richard Arlen) mixing the babies in *The Virginian* (1929). Later on Cooper hooks a baby bonnet to his friends belt and he gets a bunch of angry mothers wanting to skin him alive.)

- Chicolini, where were you born?

- I don't remember. I was too little.

The military prosecutor answered by Chicolini (Chico Marx), on trial for espionage in *Duck Soup* (1933).

His mother should have thrown him away and kept the stork.

Ruby Carter (Mae West) in *Belle of the Nineties* (1934). A similar joke was told on the *Abbott and Costello Program* by Elvia Allman, as Mrs. Niles, to Lou Costello: "The stork that brought you should have been arrested."

W.C. Fields

Go away, boy. You draw flies.

Larson E. Whipsnade (W.C. Fields) to a kid in *You Can't Cheat an Honest Man* (1939). Off-screen, Fields once said: (1) "I never met a kid I liked." (2) "Any man who hates small dogs and children can't be all bad." Fields once told a woman who complained that her son was "a tough little one": "Madam, there's no such thing as a tough child. If you parboil them first for seven hours, they always come out tender." When asked if he believed in the adage: Children should be seen and not heard, Fields. answered: "I believe children should neither be seen nor heard from ever again."

- Why he only got here and he's sleeping already.

- All babies sleep twenty hours a day, Jerry.

- I suppose that's the reason most of them never amount to anything.

> Jerry Cohan (Walter Huston) and his wife at the birth of
> their son in *Yankee Doodle Dandy* (1942).

Moe-Didn't you once tell me you were born in Oxford?

Curly-I don't remember. I was born awfully young.

> In *If a Body Meets a Body* (1945).

If I were your baby, I'd be swinging from a tree.

> Stella Purdy (Stella Stevens) to Julius Kelp/Buddy Love
> (Jerry Lewis) in *The Nutty Professor* (1963).

They're lovely kids. I've never seen a better argument for the pill.

> Dan Bartlett (Bob Hope) in *Cancel My Reservation*
> (1972).

The best thing about kids is making them.

> Thornton Melon (Rodney Dangerfield) in *Back to School*
> (1986).

You're short, your belly button sticks out too far, and you're a terrible burden to your mother.

> Dr. Peter Venkman (Bill Murray) speaking to Dana's
> (Sigourney Weaver) baby in *Ghostbusters II* (1989).

- Kids are happy when their mother is happy.

- No, they're not. Everyone says that but it's not true. Kids are happy if you're there. You give kids a choice, your mother in the next room on the verge of suicide versus your mother in Hawaii in ecstasy they choose suicide in the next room. Believe me.

> Arnold Moss (Dan Aykroyd) and Dotty Ingels (Julie Kavner) in *This Is My Life* (1992).

- I smell children.

- Sic 'em.

> The Sanderson witches, Mary (Kathy Najimy) and Winifred (Bette Midler), in *Hocus Pocus* (1993).

You know I always wanted a child and now I think I'll have one... on toast.

> Witch Winifred Sanderson (Bette Midler) in *Hocus Pocus* (1993).

Is it true that when you were born the doctor turned around and slapped your mother?

> Mitzi (Hugo Weaving) to Felicia (Guy Pearce) in *The Adventures of Priscilla, Queen of the Desert* (1994).

I was very artistic as a child. I started wearing make-up when I was six.

> Edie (Beverly D'Angelo) in *The Crazy Sitter* (1994).

- Spanky, me and Porky got an idea.

- Keep it. You might need it when you grow up.

- O.K.

> Buckwheat (Ross Elliot Bagley), Spanky (Travis Tedford), and Porky (Zachary Mabry) in *The Little Rascals* (1994).

- Is it a boy or a girl?

- No time. Look for yourself.

- It's Pat!

Mrs. Riley (Beverly Leech) and the obstetrician (Timothy Stack) in *It's Pat—The Movie* (1994).

Jane, having a baby is a big responsibility. It's like being in charge of sanitation at a Haitian jail.

> Frank Drebin (Leslie Nielsen) to wife Jane (Priscilla Presley) in *The Naked Gun 33 1/3—The Final Insult* (1994).

Kids! Ten seconds of joy, thirty years of misery.

> Gibs/Albert Gibson (Tom Arbold) in *True Lies* (1994).

Growing Pains

- How do you know it's exactly that old?

- Well, Professor Brown told me it was five hundred million years old when I first met him and that was three and a half years ago.

> The waiter (Eric Blore) to Guy Holden (Fred Astaire) and Mimi (Ginger Rogers) in *The Gay Divorcee* (1934).

- You make me think of my youth.

- Really? He must be a big boy by now.

> Martha Phelps (Margaret Dumont) and Wolf J. Flywheel (Groucho Marx) in *The Big Store* (1941).

- Will you stop calling me ma'am. It's Miss.

- Oh, I'm very sorry. I'm not very good at telling a woman's age by her face... ma'am.

> Lynn Hollister (John Wayne) to the information clerk in the train station in *Wheel of Fortune* (Former title: *A Man Betrayed*) (1941).

My great-aunt Elizabeth ate a box of chocolates every day of her life. She lived to be 102, and when she had been dead three days, she looked healthier than you.

> Sheridan 'Sheri' Whiteside (Monty Woolley) to his nurse in *The Man Who Came to Dinner* (1942).

- I haven't had food for two days and I still have the face of a ten-year-old boy.

- If I were you, I'd give it back to him because you're getting it all wrinkled.

> Doc (Bud Abbott) and Wishy (Lou Costello) in *Rio Rita* (1942).

You're only as old as your arteries.

> E.J. Waggleberry (Raymond Walburn) to Harold (Harold Lloyd) in *The Sin of Harold Diddlebock* (1947). And later: "A man is only as young as his ideas."

- Listen! I'm over twenty-one.

- Yeah, from the neck down you are.

> Gladys Glover (Judy Holliday) and Pete Sheppard (Jack Lemmon) in *It Should Happen to You* (1954).

- Yes, I've found a man. He's seven years old.

- In America, that's old enough.

> Cinzia Zaccardi (Sophia Loren) and her over-protective father Arturo (Eduardo Ciannelli) in *Houseboat* (1958).

Personally, I think it would be a bit tacky to wear diamonds before I'm forty.

> Holly Golightly (Audrey Hepburn) in *Breakfast at Tiffany's* (1961).

A man's not worth a cent until he's forty. We just pay him wages until then to make mistakes.

> Horace Vandergelder (Walter Matthau) to his long-time employee Cornelius (Michael Crawford) in *Hello, Dolly!* (1969).

Christine, I've reached that realistic age where I have to choose between having fun and a heart attack.

> Richard Morgan (Joseph Cotten) to Christine (Jacqueline Bisset) in *The Grasshopper* (1970).

How old is a woman like you?

> Willy Clark (Walter Matthau) to his nurse in *The Sunshine Boys* (1975).

Seventy-six to be exact, Mr. Diamond. How do I look so young? Quite simple. A complete vegetable diet, twelve hours of sleep and lots and lots of make-up.

> The multiple personality Lionel Twain (Truman Capote) in *Murder by Death* (1976).

I've aged, Sidney. I'm getting lines in my face. I look like a brand new steel-belted radial tire.

Diana Barrie (Maggie Smith) to Sydney Cochran (Michael Caine) in *California Suite* (1978).

Why do men have to get better looking when they get older? Remind me to bring it up at the Equal Rights Commission.

> Hannah Warren (Jane Fonda) to her ex-husband Bill (Alan Alda) in *California Suite* (1978).

- You're still a boy. When are you going to grow up?

- I am trying, Glenda. I grew a mustache but it fell off.

> Glenda Park (Goldie Hawn) and her ex-husband Nick Gardenia (Chevy Chase) in *Seems Like Old Times* (1980).

Is this your wife? A lovely lady. You're all right. You must've been something before electricity.

Al Czervik (Rodney Dangerfield) to Judge Smelis (Ted Knight) about his wife (Lois Kibbee) in *Caddyshack* (1980).

Happy 38! That's a contradiction in terms.

Roger Cobb (Steve Martin) in *All of Me* (1984).

The Big Chill

- It's not the same for men. Charlie Chaplin had babies when he was 73.

  - Yes, but he was too old to pick them up.

Sally (Meg Ryan) and Harry (Billy Crystal) in *When Harry Met Sally* (1989).

Here I sit on my ticking biological clock.

Meg (Mary Kay Place) in *The Big Chill* (1983).

Value this time in your life, kids, because this is the time in your life when you still have your choices. It goes by so fast. When you're a teenager, you think you can do anything and you do. Your twenties are a blur. Thirty, you raise your family, you make a little money and you think to yourself: What happened to my twenties? Forties, you grow a little pot belly, you grow another chin. The music starts to get too loud. One of your old girlfriends from high school becomes a grandmother. Fifties, you have a minor surgery. You'll call it 'a procedure' but it's a surgery. Sixties, you'll have a major surgery. The music is still loud but it doesn't matter because you can't hear it anyway. Seventies, you and the wife retire to Fort Lauderdale, start eating dinner at two o'clock in the afternoon. You have lunch around ten, breakfast the night before. Spend most of your time wandering around malls, looking for the ultimate soft yogurt and muttering: How come the kids don't call? The eighties, you have a major stroke. You end up blabbering to some Jamaican nurse that your wife can't stand and that you call mama. Any questions?

Mitch Robbins (Billy Crystal) addressing his son's class in
City Slickers (1991).

I'm an adult... technically.

Aging hippie Dennis Van Welker (Christopher Lloyd) in
Camp Nowhere (1994).

- I've been feeling this way since then. I was only sixteen and I knew it wouldn't work, but I'm twenty-two going on twenty-three. Can't you see how much I've grown since then?

- You mean you ain't wearing that trainer no more?

Peaches Jordan (Jada Pinkett) and Shame (Keenen Ivory
Wayans) in *A Low Down Dirty Shame* (1994). When she
walks away he says: "Peaches, I see something has
grown since you were sixteen."

It's All Geek to Me

- Do you have any hobbies?

- I collect spores, molds and fungus.

Janine Melnitz (Annie Potts) trying to flirt with Dr. Egon
Spengler (Harold Ramis) in *Ghostbusters* (1984).

Dork! You are a parent's wet dream.

> John Bender (Judd Nelson) to Brian Johnson (Anthony Michael Hall) in *The Breakfast Club* (1985).

Yellow Bellies

I don't want to walk around with my throat cut.

> Stanio (Stan Laurel) to Ollio (Oliver Hardy) after being threatened by the bandit Diavolo in *The Devil's Brother* (Former title: *Fra Diavolo*) (1933).

Listen, you all have to realize one thing, that I (*whispers so his wife won't hear*) am the master of this household.

> Harold Bissonette (W.C. Fields) to his daughter in *It's a Gift* (1934).

- Are you a man or a mouse?

  - You put a piece of cheese down there and you'll find out.

> Gil (Alan Jones) and Dr. Hugo Hackenbush (Groucho Marx) in *A Day at the Races* (1937).

Go up those stairs! Be brave! Do you want these people here to think I'm a coward?

> Algy Shaw (Bud Abbott) pressing Wellington Phlug (Lou Costello) to go up to the mysterious temple in *Pardon My Sarong* (1942).

- Are you scared? You have red blood, ain't you?

  - Yes, but I don't want to get it all over strangers.

> Jeffrey Peters (Bing Crosby) and Orville 'Turkey' Jackson (Bob Hope) in *The Road to Morocco* (1942).

I want my mama!

Lou (Lou Costello) in *One Night in the Tropics* (1940) and many other comedies, usually when he's scared.

I'll lead the way—go ahead.

> Policeman Moe pushing his partners Curly and Larry
> before him through every door in *Dizzy Detectives*
> (1943).

- Help him! You're a man, you've got blood in your veins.

- Yes, and I want to keep it there. It's the squirting kind.

> Count D'Armand (Cecil Kellaway) urging Beaucaire (Bob
> Hope) to help fight off their assailants in *Monsieur
> Beaucaire* (1946).

Brave men run in my family.

> 'Painless' Peter Potter (Bob Hope), a coward, in *The
> Paleface* (1948).

- I'm afraid!

- Wait a minute! Would you rather die a hero or live like
a rat?

- Get the cheese ready.

> Freddy Phillips (Lou Costello) and Casey Edwards (Bud
> Abbott) in *Abbott and Costello Meet the Killer, Boris
> Karloff* (1949).

Only a coward hits a coward.

> Humphrey (Bob Hope) to Cart Belknap (Bruce Cabot) in
> *Fancy Pants* (1950).

- Listen, just how big a coward are you?

- Well, I was captain of the Olympic Team.

> Roy (Roy Rogers) and Junior (Bob Hope) in *Son of
> Paleface* (1952).

Con man-You dirty crook!

  Shemp-Them's fighting words in my country.

  Con man-All right. Let's fight.

  Shemp-We're not in my country.

In Loose Loot (1953).

Don't be frightened, Francesca... I'm scared enough for all of us.

Pipo Papolino (Bob Hope) posing, briefly, as the great
swordsman Casanova in Casanova's Big Night (1954).

I'm too yellow to die!

The Great Wooley (Jerry Lewis) in The Geisha Boy
(1958).

- What are your religious views?

  - I'm a practicing coward.

Mrs. Barham (Joyce Grenfell) and Lt. Cmdr. Charles
Madison (James Garner), who discovered his 'new
religion' at Guadalcanal, in The Americanization of
Emily (1964).

You have the wrong guy. (...) I'm not the heroic type. Really! I was beaten up by Quakers.

Miles Monroe (Woody Allen) refusing to help the
revolution in the year 2173 in Sleeper (1973).

Wait, Master, it might be dangerous. You go first.

Igor (Marty Feldman) to Dr. Frederick Frankenstein (Gene
Wilder) in Young Frankenstein (1974).

- Aren't you going to see what's wrong with him?

Young Frankenstein

- I'd rather set my hair on fire and have it put out with a sledge hammer.

Ellis Fielding (Dan Aykroyd) asking the nurse (Nancy Parsons) to investigate the screams of Harry 'The Hippo' Gutterman (Dom DeLuise) in *Loose Cannons* (1990).

- Why don't we step outside and settle this like men?

- We are outside!

- Then why don't we step inside and settle it like women?

Shyster lawyer Roland T. Flakfizer (John Turturro) and sleazy lawyer Edmond Lazlo (John Lavident) in *Brain Donors* (1992).

Dad, eight percent of all household accidents involve ladders, another three percent involve trees. I'm looking at an eleven percent probability here.

Richard Tyler (Macaulay Culkin) refusing the climb to the tree house that his father is building for him in *The Pagemaster* (1994). Richard's fears are confirmed when his father falls out of the tree.

It Sucks to Be Me....

- What kind of girl are you?

- Just what you see. A tiny cog in the great wheel of evolution.

Count Leon Bressart (Melvyn Douglas) and the Russian Lena Yakushova 'Ninotchka' (Greta Garbo) in *Ninotchka* (1939).

I was a heel from the ground up.

> Francis Harrigan (John Payne) remembering his ill-treatment of Katie Blaine (Alice Faye) in *Tin Pan Alley* (1940).

Lady-He thinks I'm lying. Any half-wit can see I'm telling the truth.

Shemp-Yeah, I can see you're telling the truth.

> In *Crime on their Hands* (1948).

What's Casanova got that if I had I probably couldn't handle anyway?

> Pipo Papolino (Bob Hope) in *Casanova's Big Night* (1954).

I don't know how fast he moves but it takes an early bird to get the best of a worm like me.

> Jonathan Forbes (Tony Randall) bungling his metaphors in *Pillow Talk* (1959).

- Then she mentioned penis envy. Do you know about that?

- Me?! I'm one of the few males who suffer from that.

> Annie (Diane Keaton) relating her conversation with her analyst to Alvy Singer (Woody Allen) in *Annie Hall* (1977).

I'm a hopeless romantic in a male chauvinistic world.

> Robert(a) (John Lithgow), a transsexual in *The World According to Garp* (1982).

I've lost a woman—a whole woman.

> David (Albert Brooks) in *Lost in America* (1985).

—❝—

I'm a baaaaaaaad boy!

Herbie Brown (Lou Costello) in *Buck Private* (1941) and other comedies.

You want to know about bombing? Sweetheart, some nights the audience was so dead they were wearing toe tags.

> Dottie Ingels (Julie Kavner) about her debut as a stand-up comic in *This Is My Life* (1992).

I know why it's raining. I could have predicted it. It's raining because my goddamn wipers are all screwed up. If my wipers were O.K., the goddamn sun would be shining, at night.

> Bernie La Plante (Dustin Hoffman) in *Hero* (1992).

I'm not a Neanderthal! I'm a Co-magnum.

> Bouncer Ed Molloy (Andrew Dice Clay) telling the interrogation detectives that he's above that low evolutionary stage but not by much since he confuses Cro-magnon with Co-magnum in *Brain Smasher... A Love Story* (1993).

A woman wants someone like me, she goes to the pound and gets a three-legged dog.

> Phil Berquist (Daniel Stern) in *City Slickers II: The Legend of Curly's Gold* (1994).

Faces Only a Mother Could Love

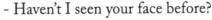

- Haven't I seen your face before?

  - Probably you've seen me at the Horse Show.

  - Jockey?

> Doc (W.C. Fields) and the very tall and toothy Miss Mason (Elise Cavanna) in *The Dentist* (1932).

I don't like his face or any part of him. He looks like a Bulgarian boll weevil mourning his first born.

> The impresario Thomas Barry (Ned Sparks) in *42nd Street* (1933).

You know, you wouldn't be a bad looking dame... if it wasn't for your face.

> Rudy Adams (Jean Harlow) to Gypsy (Dorothy Burgess) in *Hold Your Man* (1933).

That's the first forehead I ever saw that ran clear to the back of the neck.

> John Scott (John Wayne) about Kansas Charly's (Edward Chandler) baldness in *The Desert Trail* (1935).

How would you like to feel the way she looks?

> Otis B. Driftwood (Groucho Marx) looking at an ugly old hag in an operatic scene in *A Night at the Opera* (1935).

Thanks for the dance... cut yourself a slice of throat.

> Curly to his ugly date in *Hoi Polloi* (1935).

Is this the face that wrecked a thousand ships and burned the towerless tops of Eliam?

> Doc Boone (Thomas Mitchell) to his landlady throwing him out in *Stagecoach* (1939).

- The only dance I'll do with her is the elevator dance.

  - What's that?

  - No step.

> Wishy (Lou Costello) and Doc (Bud Abbott) in *Rio Rita* (1942).

- Wouldn't you marry a pretty girl like that?

- No, I'd rather marry a homely girl.

- Why?

- Well, if you marry a pretty girl like that, she's liable to run away.

- A homely girl is apt to run away too.

- Yeah, but who cares.

> Algy Shaw (Bud Abbott) and Wellington Phlug (Lou Costello) in *Pardon My Sarong* (1942). The same routine is repeated in *Buck Privates Come Home* (1947).

She ain't pretty. (...) I've seen better heads on malted milks.

> Mervin Milgrim (Lou Costello) in *Who Done It?* (1942).

- There's the girl you've got to make love to.

- No, Chic, I'm not going to make love to her.

- Why? She's only got a couple of buck teeth.

- What do I care how much she paid for 'em?

> Chic Larkin (Bud Abbott) and Mervin Milgrim (Lou Costello) in *Who Done It?* (1942).

I always said your face scares people. Why don't you throw it away?

> Moe in *Idle Roomers* (1944).

Sit down and take a load off my eyes.

> Sylvester the Great/Sylvester Crosby (Bob Hope) to Princess Margaret (Virginia Mayo) in *The Princess and the Pirate* (1944).

Where did you get that face? Hollywood?

> Mortimer Brewster (Cary Grant) to his brother Jonathan (Raymond Massey), whose face was redone in the image of Frankenstein by his plastic surgeon

friend and sidekick Dr.
Einstein (Peter Lorre) in
Arsenic and Old Lace
(1944).

Pity about the hair. I
suppose you've tried
everything?   Bear
grease...?

Shadwell (Gilbert
Roland) to Captain
Kidd (Charles
Laughton) in *Captain
Kidd* (1945).

I've seen happier faces
on canes.

Brad (Charlton Heston) to his board of directors in *The
Greatest Show on Earth* (1952).

Breakfast at Tiffany's

It's the kind of face you want to throw a brick at.

Gulley Jimson (Alec Guinness) about his sidekick Nosey
(Mike Morgan) in *The Horse's Mouth* (1958).

I've got to do something about the way I look. I mean, a girl
can't go to Sing Sing with a green face.

Holly Golightly (Audrey Hepburn) in
Breakfast at Tiffany's (1961).

You look like you put your face on backward this morning.

Bugsy (Scott Baio) to the bartender in
Bugsy Malone (1976).

I wouldn't take you to a dog fight if you were the defending
champ.

Henry Moon (Jack Nicholson) to a woman in *Goin' South* (1978).

In that wig you could play Lassie.

> Marina Rudd (Elizabeth Taylor) to Lola Brewster (Kim Novak) in *The Mirror Crack'd* (1980).

Look at that one. The last time I saw a mouth like that it had a hook in it.

> Al Czervik (Rodney Dangerfield) in *Caddyshack* (1980).

You look like an anemic turtle.

> Dr. Irving Finegarten (Robert Preston) to Polly Reed (Loretta Swit) in *S.O.B.* (1981).

Mary Jane Canary was a dear and selfless woman, but she looked like an unmade bed.

> Wyatt Earp (James Garner) about Calamity Jane in *Sunset* (1988).

I'll tell you one thing, she's not two-faced. If she were, she'd wear the other one.

> Chester Lee (Rodney Dangerfield) speaking about Coach Annie (Nancy Parsons) in *Ladybugs* (1992).

If she went to a dog show she'd win.

> Chester Lee (Rodney Dangerfield) speaking about Coach Annie (Nancy Parsons) in *Ladybugs* (1992).

Hey, let's beautify the neighborhood... stay indoors.

Chester Lee (Rodney Dangerfield) watching his neighbors in *Ladybugs* (1992).

I've had this mustache for thirteen years. How long have you had yours?

> Bill Reimers (Emilio Estevez) to Gina Garrett (Rosie O'Donnell) in *Another Stakeout* (1993).

You Loook Mahvelous!

Twenty years on the China seas and she never lost a spangle.

> Jamesy McArdle (Wallace Beery) watching China Doll Portland (Jean Harlow) walking down the steps in a spangled dress in *China Seas* (1935).

- Besides, Lucette is beautiful, too.

- Well, beauty is only skin deep.

- That's deep enough for me. I'm not a cannibal.

> Wishy (Lou Costello) and Doc (Bud Abbott) in *Rio Rita* (1942).

You're as beautiful as ever, my dear. It just takes longer now.

> Eduardo Acuna (Adolphe Menjou) to his wife Delphina (Barbara Brown) in *You Were Never Lovelier* (1942).

- Gee, you're pretty.

- I bet you say that to all the girls.

- Yes... it don't go over so good with the boys.

> Freddy Phillips (Lou Costello) and Angela Gordon (Lenore Aubert) in *Abbott and Costello Meet the Killer, Boris Karloff* (1949).

The prettier the bait, the better the catch. That's an old saying I just made up.

> Nick Charles (William Powell) in *Song of the Thin Man* (1947).

I understand how you feel. You don't have to worry. One of these days you're going to be just as pretty as Mademoiselle,

Look how she moves. Just like Jell-O on springs. She must have a built-in motor or something.

Jerry/Daphne (Jack Lemmon) to Joe/Josephine (Tony Curtis), watching Sugar Kane Kowa's (Marilyn Monroe) swinging hips on high heels in *Some Like It Hot* (1959). Off-screen M.M. once said: "People say I walk all wiggly and wobbly. I don't know what they mean. I just walk."

maybe prettier. You already got bone structure. When I was your age I didn't have no bone structure. Took me years to get bone structure. And don't think bone structure isn't important. Nobody started to call me Mademoiselle 'til I was seventeen and getting a little bone structure.

> Trixie Delight (Madeline Kahn) to Addie (Tatum O'Neal)
> in *Paper Moon* (1973).

I love the way you look. (...) You're my sweet-ass gal.

> Flap Horton (Jeff Daniels) to his wife Emma (Debra
> Winger) in *Terms of Endearment* (1983).

I never saw such beautiful landscaping. It looks like all the trees threw up.

> Chester Lee (Rodney Dangerfield) in *Ladybugs* (1992).

- What are you thinking about?

- Cassandra. She's a fox. In France she would be called La Renarde and she would be hunted with only her cunning to protect her.

- She's a babe.

- She's a robo-babe. In Latin she would be called baby-a-majora.

- If she were a president she'd be Babebraham Lincoln.

> Garth Algar (Dana Carvey) and Wayne Campbell (Mike
> Myers) speaking of Cassandra (Tia Carrere) in *Wayne's
> World* (1992).

Spare Tires

Tonight when the moon is sneaking around the clouds, I'll be sneaking around you. I'll meet you tonight under the moon. Oh! I can see you now; you and the moon. You wear a necktie so I'll know you.

Mr. Hammer (Groucho Marx) to Mrs. Potter (Margaret
Dumont) in *Cocoanuts* (1929).

Say! You cover a lot of ground yourself. You'd better beat it. I hear they're gonna tear you down and put up an office building where you're standing.

Rufus T. Firefly (Groucho Marx) to Gloria Teasdale
(Margaret Dumont) in *Duck Soup* (1933).

- My, you're gaining weight.

- Yes, I'll soon be your size.

Gwendolyn Hall (Geneva Mitchell) and Rita Vernon
(Mary Duncan) in *Morning Glory* (1933).

- All New York will be at your feet.

- Well! (*looking under the table*) There's plenty of room.

Herman Gottlieb (Siegfried Rumann) to Mrs. Claypool
(Margaret Dumont) and answered by Otis B. Driftwood
(Groucho Marx) in *A Night at the Opera* (1935).

- Never mind, dear, chin up.

- That's right, both of 'em.

Edith (Phyllis Povah) and Miriam (Paulette Goddard) in
The Women (1939).

I'm so hungry my spare tire's deflated.

Josh Mallon (Bing Crosby) in *The Road to Singapore* (1940).

Keep your chins up.

The Kid (Bob Hope) to Nellie Thursday (Jane Darwell) in
The Lemon Drop Kid (1951).

Being a fat narcissist isn't easy.

Maxwell Slaughter (Jackie Gleason) to the mirror in *Soldier in the Rain* (1963).

- I hate fat people!

  - You're fat.

  - Hate myself, too.

Capain Kidd (Charles Laughton) and Captain Bonney (Hilary Brooke) in *Abbott and Costello Meet Captain Kidd* (1952).

Back off, Moby Dick! How would you like flab parted in the front, too?

Frank Benson (Bob Hope) to fat Oliver Poe (Jackie Gleason) in *How to Commit Marriage* (1969).

Well, come see a fat old man sometime.

Rooster's (John Wayne) farewell words to Mattie (Kim Darby) in the last scene of *True Grit* (1969).

I'm so glad to see you. Not only have you kept your gorgeous figure but you added so much to it.

Lola Brewster (Kim Novak) to Marina Rudd (Elizabeth Taylor) in *The Mirror Crack'd* (1980).

Keep all your fat parts in one place.

Judge Alvin Valkenheiser (Dan Aykroyd) in *Nothing but Trouble* (1991).

Behind every great man is a woman and thank heaven I have Lilian Oglethorpe because, quite frankly, I enjoy the shade.

Roland T. Flakfizer (John Turturro) introducing, in a Groucho-like manner, Mrs. Lilian Oglethorpe (Nancy Marchand) at a press conference in *Brain Donors* (1992).

- I'm only one man.

- Not from the back.

> Fred (John Goodman) and Barney (Rick Moranis) in *The
> Flintstones* (1994).

- You two should be ashamed of yourselves.
  - I've got my hands full just being ashamed of him.
  - You've got your hands full when you scratch you neck.

> Wilma (Elizabeth Perkins), her mother Pearl (Elizabeth
> Taylor), and her husband Fred (John Goodman) in *The
> Flintstones* (1994).

If I Only Had a Brain

Doc-This kid is so dumb he doesn't know what time it is.

Golfer-By the way, what time is it?

Doc-I don't know.

> Doc (W.C. Fields) speaking of his caddy in *The Dentist*
> (1932).

Baravelli, you've got the brain of a four-year-old, and I bet
he was glad to get rid of it.

> Professor Quincy Adams Wagstaff (Groucho Marx) to
> student Baravelli (Chico Marx) in *Horse Feathers* (1932).

You know, I'm not as dumb as you look.

> Stan Laurel to Oliver Hardy in *Their First
> Mistake* (1932).

- It was that dumb brother of yours.

- Don't you call him dumb. Why, you've forgotten more than he'll never know, in his little finger.

> Oliver Hardy and his wife Fanny (Stan Laurel) in *Twice Two* (1932).

Well, baby, what's on your mind? If any.

> Nick Charles (William Powell) to Dorothy Wynant (Maureen O'Sullivan) in *The Thin Man* (1934).

I can gyp that gypsy anytime. You know, he's so dumb he's thicker than mud.

> Stan Laurel speaking of Oliver Hardy in *The Bohemian Girl* (1936).

What's on your stagnant mind?

> Barney Pells (Franchot Tone) to Mike Anthony (Clark Gable) in *Love on the Run* (1936).

Do you remember how dumb I used to be? Well, I'm better now.

> Stan Laurel to Oliver Hardy in *Block-Heads* (1938).

Larry-Is that the sun up there?

Curly-I don't know. I'm new around here.

> In *Nutty but Nice* (1940).

- Did you ever go to school, stupid?

- Yeah, and I came out the same way.

> Smoky Adams (Bud Abbott) and Pomery (Lou Costello) in *In the Navy* (1941). In *Rio Rita* (1942), as Wishy, and in *Little Giant* (1946), as Benny Miller, Lou answers: "Yes, Sir, but I came out...." As Joe Bascom/Harry Lambert he answers the same question sightly differently in *Mexican Hayride* (1948): "Of course I did, and I came out the same way."

Bud Abbott and Lou Costello

You're supposed to be a smart guy; if it was raining one hundred dollar bills, you'd be out looking for a dime you lost someplace.

Ann Mitchell (Barbara Stanwyck) to Henry Connel (James Gleason) in *Meet John Doe* (1941).

I am worried, terribly worried about you. Why don't you have your mind lifted?

Pat Jamieson (Spencer Tracy) to Edwina in *Without Love* (1945).

Colonel-Forward march! You fools... what's the matter with you?

Curly-I'm no fool.

Colonel-Forward march! You idiot.

In *Uncivil War Birds* (1946).

I wouldn't let that bother me, Sweetypie. You wouldn't know a clue if it bit you.

Photographer to journalist Patricia Hunter (Luana Walters) in *The Corpse Vanishes* (1947).

- What makes you so dumb?

- It just comes to me natural.

Ted (Bud Abbott) and Tommy (Lou Costello) in *The Noose Hangs High* (1948).

Moe-You know, he's the most intelligent imbecile I ever saw.

Shemp-Hey! What about me?

Moe-Oh, you're much smarter. You're just an imbecile.

Shemp insists on knowing where he stands compared to Larry in *Fuelin' Around* (1949).

Moe-We're in a tough spot, men.
Larry-Yeah, it's gonna take brains to get us outta here.
Moe-That's why I said we're in a tough spot.

> In *Who Done It?* (1949).

He's got nothing upstairs but brass knuckles.

> In *The Asphalt Jungle* (1950).

Remember, we're census takers, not ordinary idiots.

> Moe to Larry and Shemp in *Don't Throw That Knife* (1951).

I've got a photocell mind.

> Oliver 'Puddin Head' Johnson (Lou Costello) memorizing a map in *Abbott and Costello Meet Captain Kidd* (1952).

- How stupid can you get?
    - How stupid do you want me to be?

> Pete Patterson (Bud Abbott) and Freddie Franklin (Lou Costello) in *Abbott and Costello Meet the Mummy* (1955).

You know something? You read too many comic books!

> Jim Stark (James Dean) to a rocker in *Rebel Without a Cause* (1955).

You're so dumb you're adorable.

> Captain Cutshaw (Scott Wilson) to Doctor Hudson Kane (Stacy Keach) in *The Ninth Configuration* (1979).

- Are you stupid?

- No.

- A nincompoop? Moronic? Idiotic? Imbecilic? What are you laughing at?

- You went right by me and didn't know it.

Oliver 'Puddin Head' Johnson (Lou Costello) and the innkeeper in *Abbott and Costello Meet Captain Kidd* (1952).

Here, read this magazine. There are many pictures.

> Hobson (John Gielgud) to Arthur Bach (Dudley Moore) in
> *Arthur* (1981).

You're not too smart, are you? I like that in a man.

> Matty Walker (Kathleen Turner) to Ned Racine (William
> Hurt) in *Body Heat* (1981). This scene was parodied by
> Sean Young, as Lola Cain, and Armand Assante, as Ned
> Ravine, in *Fatal Instinct* (1993). "You really are incredibly
> stupid, aren't you? I like that in a man." "I'd be insulted,
> but I know you're serious."

You don't know crap from Christmas.

> Sissy (Cher) in *Come Back to the 5 & Dime Jimmy Dean,*
> *Jimmy Dean* (1982).

You're supposed to be stupid, son. Don't abuse the privilege.

> Braddock (Warren Oates) to Lymangood (Daniel Stern),
> a recruit who speaks out of turn in *Blue Thunder* (1983).

I want to be just like you. I figure all I need is a lobotomy and some tights.

> John Bender (Judd Nelson) to wrestler Andy Clark (Emilio
> Estevez) in *The Breakfast Club* (1985).

You couldn't find big time if you had a road map.

> Fast Eddy Felson (Paul Newman) to Vincent (Tom Cruise)
> in *The Color of Money* (1986).

I swear, you two are living testimony to the fact that it's better to be lucky than smart.

Buford Pope (Rip Torn) to Vernon (Jeff Bridges) and Nadine Hightower (Kim Basinger) in *Nadine* (1987).

Is English your second language?

Joanna Stayton (Goldie Hawn) (before her conversion into Annie Proffitt) to Dean (Kurt Russell) in *Overboard* (1987).

Body Heat

I'm speaking English. I'm terribly sorry if you find that confusing.

Angela Crispini (Debra Winger) to Tom O'Toole (Nick Nolte) in *Everybody Wins* (1990).

What what!? Is English your second language?

Carmen (Elizabeth Pena) to Cathy (Christina Applegate) in *Across the Moon* (1994).

Are we on the same page here?

Ned Trent (James Woods) pressing a point with a bomb disposal policeman in *The Specialist* (1994).

-I've been reading about the Emmaline Quincy....

-I didn't know you could read.

Johnny Angel (George Raft) to a gangster in *Johnny Angel* (1945).

I hope his dick is bigger than his I.Q.

> Alexandra 'Alex' Medford (Cher) in *The Witches of Eastwick* (1987).

Dumbest ass in captivity.

> Vera (Della Reese) to Bennie 'Snake Eyes' Wilson (Redd Foxx) in *Harlem Nights* (1989).

Act your age, not your shoe size!

> Kate Flax (Christina Ricci) to the her older sister Charlotte (Winona Ryder) in *Mermaids* (1990).

Jethro... your head is emptier than last year's bird nest. If your head was filled with dynamite, you wouldn't know how to blow your nose.

> Granny (Cloris Leachman) to Jethro (Diedrich Bader) in *The Beverly Hillbillies* (1993).

I don't look as dumb as I am.

> Ned Ravine (Armand Assante) to Lola Cain (Sean Young) in *Fatal Instinct* (1993). Reminescent of the 'dumb' jokes of the thirties such as these by Laurel and Hardy: (1) "You know, I'm not as dumb as you look." *Their First Mistake* (1932). (2) "Do you remember how dumb I used to be? Well, I'm better now." *Block-Heads* (1938).

Remember, Mud, just because you're smart it doesn't mean you can't be stupid. It's your constitutional right.

> Dennis Van Welker (Christopher Lloyd) to young Morris 'Mud' Himmel (Jonathan Jackson), who assimilates the lesson by the end of *Camp Nowhere* (1994).

- I'm worried, Cliff. He's smarter than we thought.

- He'd have to be to get himself dressed in the morning.

> Miss Sharon Stone (Halle Berry) and Cliff (Kyle
> MacLachlan) talking about their patsy Fred (John
> Goodman) in *The Flintstones* (1994).

- I've got half a mind...

- Don't flatter yourself.

- That's it! Where's my club, Wilma?

> Fred (John Goodman) and his mother-in-law Pearl
> (Elizabeth Taylor) in *The Flintstones* (1994).

The only difference between genius and stupidity, my boy, is that genius has its limits.

> Zeno (Turhan Bey) to Sammy Curtis (Trenton Knight) in
> *The Skateboard Kid II* (1994).

Brain Waves

That boy is so smart he'd dry snow and sell it for sugar.

> Honey Wiggin (Eugene Pallette) about *The Virginian*
> (1929) (Gary Cooper).

- Smart idea of yours.

- The only kind I have.

> Peggy Hopkins Joyce and Professor Quail (W.C. Fields),
> with typical Fieldsian humor, waiting in front of her room
> in a miniature car in *International House* (1933).

Moe-Sometimes you've got brain.

Larry-Thank you.

Moe-Don't let it go to your head.

> In *Horse Collars* (1935).

Boy! Have I got a brain.

Moe in *Mutts to You* (1938).

- I'm smart. I've got brains I haven't used yet.

- Well, don't let it go to your head.

Chester Wooley (Lou Costello) and Jake Frame (Gordon
Jones) in *The Wistful Widow of Wagon Gap* (1947).

For a guy without brains you're a genius.

Moe to Larry in *Crime on their Hands* (1948).

Doctors Orders or Take Two Aspirin and Call Me in the Morning

- We can't leave it outside!

- He might catch cold and die of ammonia.

- Not ammonia. He means pumonia.

Ollie (Oliver Hardy) and Stan (Stan Laurel) caught trying
to sneak a 'monkey' (gorilla) into a boarding house in
The Chimp (1932).

Doctor-What do you gentlemen know about medicine?

Larry-We graduated with the highest temperatures in our class.

In *Men in Black* (1934).

Moe-How about it, Doctor?

Curly-I don't like the sound of his bark.

> Moe and Curly are tree surgeons in *Some More of Samoa* (1941).

Moe-Needs a transfusion.

Curly-Certainly, a transfusion is less confusion.

> Moe and Curly are tree doctors in *Some More of Samoa* (1941).

Larry-I'll take some burnt toast and rotten eggs.

Moe/Curly-What?

Larry-I've got a tape worm and it's good enough for him.

> In *Beer Barrel Polecats* (1946). They did the same routine in *Three Sappy People* (1939) with Curly ordering the food. Lucille Ball, as Gloria Lyons, as the same joke in *The Big Street* (1942): "How's your tape worm, sister." Bing Crosby, as the secretary reading a letter in *Robin and the Seven Hoods* (1964): "Here's one where a lady has fourteen kids, they all have tape worms, they're gonna be evicted...."

Girl-The witch doctor is a bad man.

Larry-You can say that again.

Girl-The witch doctor is a bad man.

> The Native Girl (Jean Willes) and Larry (Larry Fine) in *Hula-La-La* (1951). This joke was used often in comedies including the *Police Squad* television series.

I should have listened to my psychiatrist. He told me not to trust anybody but him.

> Jonathan Forbes (Tony Randall) in *Pillow Talk* (1959).

Dr. Bradley is the greatest living argument for mercy killing.

Sheridan Whiteside (Monty Woolley) speaking of his doctor in *The Man Who Came to Dinner* (1942).

Well, maire, there's gratitude for you. You raise a patient, treat him like a son, slave all day over a hot endless couch and what do you get in return? They don't even invite you on their honeymoon.

Dr. Fritz Wolgang Sigismund Fassbender (Peter Sellers) to the mayor after the wedding ceremony uniting Michael James (Peter O'Toole) and Carole Werner (Romy Schneider) in *What's New Pussycat?* (1965).

- Is your work in the nature of a vocation?

- No, not quite. My grandfather wished it. He believes that if you can't join the ruling classes you must do your best to deplete them.

Michael Finsbury (Michael Caine), studying to be a surgeon, and Julia Finsbury (Nanette Newman) in *The Wrong Box* (1966).

This man treats crocodiles for acne.

Captain Cutshaw (Scott Wilson) speaking of Doctor Fell in *The Ninth Configuration* (1979).

Max-Doctor, how is he? Will he be all right?

Doc-I think so. His vital signs are encouraging, but he's very weak.

22-We have to ask him some questions.

Doc-He can't talk.

Max-Can he type?

Doc-I'm sorry. You can't go in there.

22-Doctor, it is absolutely vital that we speak to him. This is an international emergency. That man in there has information that could determine the fate of the entire world.

Max-22, do you mind? Let me handle this. I've dealt with doctors before. Now look, doctor, we want in!

Doc-No!

22-Please?

Doc-O.K.

Max-See.

Maxwell Smart (Don Adams), the doctor (David Adnopoz) and Agent 22 (Andrea Howard) in *The Nude Bomb* (1980).

- I want you to deal with your feelings, Suzanne, before they deal with you.

  - Do you always talk in bumper stickers?

Suzanne Vale's (Meryl Streep) answer to her doctor in *Postcards from the Edge* (1990).

I guess I'm doing what all shrinks do. To paraphrase Freud, I'm trying to turn her neurotic misery into general unhappiness so that she can be like the rest of us.

Isaac Barr (Richard Gere) speaking of Diana Baylor (Uma Thurman) in *Final Analysis* (1992).

Is it true that when you were born the doctor turned around and slapped your mother?

Mitzi (Hugo Weaving) to Felicia (Guy Pearce) in *The Adventures of Priscilla, Queen of the Desert* (1994).

- Now, don't forget to take your pills. Four every hour.

  - Dennis! That's one every four hours. (...)

  - Oh, it's not the first time that mistake's got me in trouble.

Aging hippie Dennis Van Welker (Christopher Lloyd) and young Morris 'Mud' Himmel (Jonathan Jackson) in *Camp Nowhere* (1994).

Lawyers or That's a Mouthpiece

-You're awfully shy for a lawyer

-You bet I am. I'm a shyster lawyer.

> Groucho (Groucho Marx) and Lucille (Thelma Todd) in
> *Monkey Business* (1931).

- Do you plead guilty or not guilty?

- Not guilty.

- On what grounds?

- We weren't on the ground, we were sleeping on a park bench.

> In court on a vagrancy charge, the first answer is by
> Oliver Hardy but the second, unfortunate one, is by Stan
> Laurel in *Scram* (1932).

Judge-Order! Order!

Curly-I'll have a ham sandwich.

> In a court of law in *Back to the Woods* (1937).

- Never mind what you think.

- Sorry, I can't talk without thinking, not being a lawyer.

> The prosecutor (Russell Hinks) insisting on immediate
> answers and Frank James (Henry Fonda) in *The Return of
> Frank James* (1940).

I thought he was a lawyer. Why isn't he out suing somebody?

> Jim Blandings (Cary Grant) in *Mr. Blandings Builds His
> Dream House* (1948).

Lawyers should never marry other lawyers. This is called inbreeding from which come idiot children and more lawyers.

Kip Lurie (David Wayne) to Amanda Bonner (Katharine Hepburn) who is married to a lawyer in *Adam's Rib* (1949).

I'm going to cut you into twelve pieces and feed you to the jury.

Lawyers Adam Bonner (Spencer Tracy) to his wife Amanda (Katharine Hepburn) in *Adam's Rib* (1949).

Katharine Hepburn and Spencer Tracy in *Adam's Rib*

These are my lawyers. All Harvard men.

Spats Columbo (George Raft) speaking of his thick-skulled musclebound bodyguards in *Some Like It Hot* (1959).

Of course he's upset, he's a lawyer. He's paid to be upset.

Stanley Ford (Jack Lemmon) in *How to Murder Your Wife* (1965).

Some men are heterosexual, and some men are homosexual, and some men don't think about sex at all. They become lawyers.

Boris Grushenko (Woody Allen) in *Love and Death* (1975).

- What about the law?

- The law!? Hey, this is the only country where the Constitution is written in pencil.

Philippa (Twiggy) and Jack Monicker (Robin Williams) in *Club Paradise* (1986).

You know Wally. He could find a loophole in the Ten Commandments.

Harry Hinkle (Jack Lemmon) about his shyster lawyer brother-in-law Wally (Walter Matthau) in *The Fortune Cookie* (1966).

I don't know who I am, but I'm sure I have a lawyer.

Joanna Stayton/Annie Proffitt (Goldie Hawn) coming out of her coma in *Overboard* (1987).

Of course I know what an attorney is. It's like a lawyer only the bills are bigger.

Harry Angel (Mickey Rourke) in *Angel Heart* (1987).

- What makes you think I'm a lawyer?

  - You've got that sharp useless look about you.

Edward Lewis (Richard Gere) and Vivian Ward (Julia Roberts) in *Pretty Woman* (1990).

- You know, it's too bad you want to be a lawyer.

  - Why is that?

  - Because we need more lawyers like we need more big white Moby Dicks.

Nick Styles (Denzel Washington) getting riled by a young girl in *Ricochet* (1991).

- Not so fast! (...) We need a contract.

  - A binding document with plenty of loopholes.

  - Sign that.

  - This paper is blank.

  - I'll fill it in later.

  - Fair enough. You're not going to cheat me or anything?

  - I give you my word as a gentleman.

  - Well, you had me until then.

  - All right, all right. A fifty-fifty split. (*He tears up the paper.*)

  - Ah, that's more like it.

- What about me?

- To show you there's no favoritism, Rocco and I will also split your salary fifty-fifty.

- Thanks.

- Which should keep you out of the high income bracket. Come to think of it, it should keep you out of any income bracket.

> Manager Rocco Meloncheck (Mel Smith), shyster lawyer
> Rolant T. Flakfizer (John Turturro) and Jacques (Bob
> Nelson) in a Marx Brothers-like contract signing routine
> in *Brain Donors* (1992).

- Mrs. Oglethorpe, as your trusted lawyer...

- You can use those two words together?

> Sleazy lawyer Edmond Lazlo (John Lavident) and shyster
> lawyer Roland T. Flakfizer (John Turturro) in *Brain Donors*
> (1992).

Lana Ravine is potential mother of my potential child and I challenge you, strike a blow for motherhood, strike a blow for the American justice system, put the can back in American, put the ju back in jurisprudence, put the con back in the constitution, and put the dom back in freedom.

> Defense attorney Ned Ravine (Armand Assante)
> addressing the jury in *Fatal Instinct* (1993).

You know nothing about the law. You're a used car salesman, Daniel. You're an ambulance chaser with a rank.

> JoAnne Galloway (Demi More) to Daniel Kaffee (Tom
> Cruise), a specialist of out-of-court plea-bargaining in *A
> Few Good Men* (1993).

Now, then. Let me remind you this is a trial; this is not a hearing. Even though both sides will be saying things and I will be hearing them, it is not a hearing. No doubt you will all be hearing the same things that I will be hearing. That's your privilege. However, once both sides have been heard then it will be my job to pass judgment. Obviously you can all pass judgment too, but it won't count. This is because I am the one who is the judge. Have I made myself clear to the plaintiff?

Judge Buckle (Alan Arkin) in *North* (1994).

Stop the Presses!

Moe-Press.
Larry-Press.
Curly-Pull.

The boys pretend to be reporters to get past the golf club attendant in *Three Little Beers* (1935) and to fool the racetrack guard in *Even as I.O.U.* (1942).

You're something that flies out of a jar when they take the lid off.

Sally Parker (Joan Crawford) to reporter Mike Anthony (Clark Gable) in *Love on the Run* (1936).

If I don't come back with the biggest story you ever handled, you can put me back in short pants and make me marble editor.

Wally Cook (Fredric March) to his editor Oliver Stone (Walter Connelly) in *Nothing Sacred* (1937).

You couldn't get a story in the papers if the Statue of Liberty came to life and bit the Big Apple.

Movie star Annabel Allison (Lucille Ball) to publicist Lenny Morgan (Jack Oakie) in *The Affairs of Annabel* (1938).

- I got rid of all those reporters.

- What did you tell them?

- I told them we were out of scotch.

> Nora Charles (Myrna Loy) and her husband Nick (William Powell) in *Another Thin Man* (1939).

His Girl Friday

- You can't quit, you're a newspaperman.

-That's why I'm getting out. I want to go someplace where I can be a woman.

> Walter Burns (Cary Grant) trying to persuade ex-wife Hildy Johnson (Rosalind Russell) from quitting her job at the paper for marriage in *His Girl Friday* (1940).

Reporter-I'm Brown. From the *Sun*.

Shemp-Oh, that's too bad. Are you peeling?

> In *Studio Stooges* (1950).

You never push a noun against a verb except to blow up something.

> Henry Drummond (Spencer Tracy) to journalist E.K. Hornbeck (Gene Kelly) in *Inherit the Wind* (1960).

You're talking to a guy with a bag on his head, cotton in his ears and a stick up his ass.

> Stanley White (Mickey Rourke) to a lady journalist questioning a mounted policeman in *Year of the Dragon* (1985).

She's pretending to be a person. She's really just a reporter.

News editor (Chevy Chase) speaking of Gale Gayley (Geena Davis) in *Hero* (1992).

You have reached the Los Angeles Times. If you would like to order a subscription, please press one. If your newspaper did not arrive this morning, press two. If you would like to place a classified add, press three. If you would like to speak to the editorial desk, city desk, national desk, international desk, sports desk, metro, view, or calendar sections, press the first three letters of the desk you desire followed by the star key in the case of the first three or the pound key in the case of the latter five.

Phillip (Steve Martin) phoning the Los Angeles Times in
Mixed Nuts (1994).

Just the Facts, Ma'am

- Just me and my memories. I'm practically a hermit.

- A hermit! I notice the table is set for four.

- That's nothing. My alarm clock is set for eight. That doesn't prove a thing.

Detective Henderson (Robert E. O'Connor) snooping in
Otis B. Driftwood's (Groucho Marx) room in *A Night at
the Opera* (1935).

Lou-You're a public servant, aren't you?

Cop-Yes!

Lou-Get me a glass of water.

Albert (Lou Costello) and a street cop in *In Society*
(1944).

This pen has been fired recently.

Inspector Clouseau (Peter Sellers) picking up the murder
weapon with his pen in *A Shot in the Dark* (1964).

I'm with the mattress police. There are no tags on these mattresses.

> Erwin Fletch (Chevy Chase) in *Fletch* (1986).

- I heard police work is dangerous.

  - It is. That's why I carry a big gun.

  - Aren't you afraid it might go off accidentally?

  - I used to have that problem.

  - What did you do about it?

  - I just think about baseball.

> Jane Spencer (Priscilla Presley) and Lt. Frank Drebin (Leslie Nielsen) in *The Naked Gun. From the Files of Police Squad!* (1988).

It's true what they say: cops and women don't mix. Like eating a spoonful of Drano. Sure, it'll clean you out but it'll leave you hollow inside.

> Lt. Frank Drebin (Leslie Nielsen) to Jane Spencer (Priscilla Presley) in *The Naked Gun: From the Files of Police Squad!* (1988).

- Do you mind if we frisk ourselves in a private place?
  - Siegfried!

> KAOS agent Siegfried (Bernie Kopell) and Maxwell Smart (Don Adams) frisking each other in a public park in *Get Smart, Again!* (1989).

Being a cop is like being a pitcher, Harry. To get the strikes you've got to risk your balls.

> Jack Moony (Bob Hoskins) in *Heart Condition* (1990).

I believe everything and I believe nothing. I suspect everyone and I suspect no one. I gather the facts, I examine the clues and before you know it the case is solved.

Inspector Clouseau (Peter Sellers) in *A Shot in the Dark* (1964).

Sylvester Stallone and
Sandra Bullock in
Demolition Man.

She cracked like a raw egg.

Detective Dominick Benti (M. Emmet
Walsh) about his interrogation of a
female suspect in *Narrow Margin*
(1990).

I fleshed you out as some blow-up-the-bad-guy-with-a-grin-He-man type but
now I realize that you're the moody-troubled-past-gunsligner-who-will-only-draw-when-he-must type.

Lanina Huxley's (Sandra Bullock)
impression of revived cop John
Spartan (Sylvester Stallone) in
Demolition Man (1993).

When you're a cop you see it all, and I
knew exactly how babies were made.

Ned Ravine (Armand Assante)
coming home early with the intention
of fulfilling his wife's dream for
children in *Fatal Instinct* (1993).

Look, lady, I am what I am and I do what I do. A few guys
make shoe laces, others lay sod, some make a good living
neutering animals. I'm a cop.

Frank Drebin (Leslie Nielsen) to Jane Spencer-Drebin
(Priscilla Presley) in *The Naked Gun 33 1/3—The Final
Insult* (1994).

Check, Please...

Ollie-Oh, *garçon*!

Waiter-Yes, sir?

Ollie-Bring me a *parfait*.

Waiter-Yes, sir.

Stan-Put one on my steak, too.

Ollie-You don't put *parfaits* on steaks. (*to the waiter*) Just cancel the *parfaits*. But bring me a small *demi tasse*.

Waiter-Yes, sir.

Stan-Oh, Gaston.

Waiter-Yes, sir?

Stan-Bring me one too, in a big cup.

Ollie-A big cup! Where were you brung up?

> Oliver Hardy attempts at sophistication in a restaurant are unwittingly sabotaged by Stan Laurel in *Below Zero* (1930).

- Your check, Sir.

- Nine dollars and forty cents! That's an outrage! If I were you, I wouldn't pay it.

> Otis B. Driftwood (Groucho Marx) who passes it on to his lady friend in *A Night at the Opera* (1935).

- The check, Sir!

- Is this check any good?

> Gordon Miller's (Groucho Marx) answer to the waiter in *Room Service* (1938).

Garçon! Another glass of milk and two fresh straws.

> Oliver Hardy ordering for himself and Stan Laurel in a French café in *The Flying Deuces* (1939).

- Oh, waiter!

  - That isn't a waiter, my dear. That's a butler.

  - Well, I can't yell 'Oh, butler!' can I? Maybe somebody's name is Butler.

> Miss Caswell (Marilyn Monroe) and Addison DeWitt
> (George Sanders) in *All About Eve* (1950).

Are you all together, or is it separate checks?

> Comicus (Mel Brooks), the waiter serving the Last Supper
> in *History of the World—Part 1* (1981).

If Roseanne had you for a waiter she'd be a size two.

> Doris Silverman (Olympia Dukakis) waiting for a menu in
> *The Cemetery Club* (1992).

Working Stiffs

- If it wasn't for your father you wouldn't be working for me for two weeks. You wouldn't even be working for me for two days. Not even for two minutes.
- Well, a girl can't ask for shorter hours than that.

> George (George Burns) and Gracie (Gracie Allen) in *A
> Damsel in Distress* (1937).

- Shouldn't you have been in two hours ago?

  - Why? What happened?

  - If you're not on time I'll have to get myself another stenographer.

  - Another stenographer? Do you think there's enough work for the two of us?

> George (George Burns) and Gracie (Gracie Allen) in *A
> Damsel in Distress* (1937).

- Did you type that letter I dictated last night?

- No. I didn't have time so I mailed them my notebook. I hope they can read my shorthand.

- You know, Gracie, I'm beginning to think that there's nothing up there. (*points to his own head.*)

- Oh, George, you're self-conscious.

> George (George Burns) and Gracie (Gracie Allen) in *A Damsel in Distress* (1937).

Our men can't even lay a hot iron in the eyes of a tax dodger without getting a black arrow in the throat. It's an outrage!

> Tax collector complaining to Sir Guy of Gisbourne (Basil Rathbone) in *The Adventures of Robin Hood* (1938).

- How do you ever make those funny things you say on the radio?

- Well, it's really very simple. I laugh first and then I think back until I come to a joke. (...) Of course, sometimes I can't think of a joke. (...) But then as long as I've laughed, no one can say that I haven't got laughs on my program.

> Fred Floogle (Fred Allen) and Jack Benny (as himself) in *It's in the Bag* (1945).

- Mac, you ever been in love?

- No, I've been a bartender all my life.

> Wyatt Earp (Henry Fonda) and Max (J. Farrell MacDonald) in *My Darling Clementine* (1946).

- I'll have your job for this!

- Aren't you a little too old for this type of work?

> Amos Strickland (Nicholas Joy) furious at bumbling bellboy Freddy (Lou Costello) in *Abbott and Costello Meet the Killer, Boris Karloff* (1949).

Find someone to type this.

Mr. Oliver Oxley (Charles Coburn) giving a letter to his secretary, Lois Laurel (Marilyn Monroe) (who is early at the office because her boss complains about her punctuation), in *Monkey Business* (1952).

Harrison Ford as
Indiana Jones

- I always heard you had talent.

- That was last year. This year I'm trying to earn a living.

> Betty Schaeffer (Nancy Olson) and Joe Gillis
> (William Holden) in *Sunset Boulevard*
> (1950).

- I thought archeologists were always funny little men searching for their mommies?

- Mummies!

> Willie Scott (Kate Capshaw) and
> Indy/Indiana Jones (Harrison Ford) in
> *Indiana Jones and the Temple of Doom*
> (1984).

- Arthur, honey, we're gonna have to become a two-income family.

- What!? You going to get a second job?

> Linda Bach (Liza Minnelli) and her husband
> Arthur (Dudley Moore) in *Arthur 2: On the
> Rocks* (1988).

On the Grift

- You told me about this yesterday.

- I know, but I left out a comma.

> Mrs. Potter (Margaret Dumont) and Mr. Hammer
> (Groucho Marx), who is trying to con her into buying
> Florida real estate in *Cocoanuts* (1929).

Here it is, Cocoanut Manor, forty-two hours from Times Square by railroad, sixteen hundred miles as the crow flies, eighteen hundred as the horse flies. There you are, Cocoanut Manor, glorifying the American sewer and the Florida sucker. Why, it's the most exclusive residential district in Florida. Nobody lives there.

> Mr. Hammer (Groucho Marx) trying to sell Florida real estate to Mrs. Potter (Margaret Dumont) in *Cocoanuts* (1929).

This is the age of chiselry! Everybody's got larceny in him.

> Bert Harris (James Cagney) to Ann Roberts (Joan Blondell) in *Blonde Crazy* (1931).

He's not that kind. Why if he was ever square with himself he'd take poison to get even.

> Kay Everly (Dorothy Mackail) to Connie Randall Stewart (Carole Lombard) about her gambler husband Jerry (Clark Gable) in *No Man of Her Own* (1932).

Oh Nicki! I love you because you know such lovely people.

> Nora Charles (Myrna Loy) to her husband Nick (William Powell) whose friends are usually cops, crooks or ex-cons in *The Thin Man* (1934).

Bartender-Hey! What about the money.

  Larry-It's a tin roof.

  Curly-A tin roof. It's on the house.

> The boys trying to con free drinks in *Horse Collars* (1935).

You wouldn't know them, darling. They're respectable.

> Nora Charles (Myrna Loy) to Nick Charles (William Powell) referring to his friends who are crooks, cops and ex-cons in *After the Thin Man* (1936).

Con man-It's $ 200.00 or nothing.
Curly-We'll take it for nothing.

> Con men selling the boys a treasure map in *Cash and Carry* (1937).

There must be some way of getting that money without getting in trouble with the Hays Office.

> J. Cheever Loophole (Groucho Marx) looking for a way to recuperate a wallet containing $10,000 that Peerless Pauline (Eve Arden) slipped into her bosom in *At the Circus* (1939).

- You must leave my room. We must have regard for certain conventions.

- One guy isn't enough, she's gotta have a convention. Oh, Susannah! Susannah! At last we're alone! (...) If only you knew how much I need you. Not because you have millions, I don't need millions. I'll tell you how much I need. Have you got a pencil? I left my typewriter in my other pants.

> Mrs. Dukesbury (Margaret Dumont) and J. Cheever Loophole (Groucho Marx) in *At the Circus* (1939).

They tell me he was so crooked that when he died they had to screw him into the ground.

> Wallie Campbell (Bob Hope) about his uncle in *The Cat and the Canary* (1939).

Salesman-You men ever sold anything?

Curly-Why certainly. Anything we could get our hands on.

Moe-The gentleman said sold, not stole.

> In *A Ducking They Did Go* (1939).

- You cheat!

  - The things worth having are worth cheating for.

> Cuthbert J. Twillie (W.C. Fields) disguised as the Masked Bandit to steal a kiss from his wife Flower Belle Lee (Mae West) in *My Little Chickadee* (1940).

- Have you got two tens for a five?

  - Yeah... Come on! Come on!

  - What's the matter with you? Something wrong?

  - Yeah. Fifteen dollars went south.

  - What do you mean?

  - You gave me a lot of fast talk. You said two tens for a five and I gave it to you.

  - Oh, you did. Wise guy. Okay. Here's your five, give me back my two tens.

  - That's better.

> Abbott (Bud Abbott) conning Lou (Lou Costello) out of $30.00 in *One Night in the Tropics* (1940).

- I've got a business proposition to make to you.

  - Yeah, you make the propositions and I get the business.

  - Do you remember that nice watch my father left me when he died?

  - Hmm, hmm.

  - I'm gonna let you have that for security.

  - Oh, well that's different. (...)

They're perfect gentlemen right down to their fingerprints.

Nora Charles (Myrna Loy) commenting to her husband Charles (William Powell) about his crooked friends in *Song of the Thin Man* (1947).

- You got the two dollars?

- Here it is, here's the two dollars.

- Fine, here's the pawn ticket.

Jeff Lambert (Bing Crosby) and Louey (Eddie 'Rochester' Anderson) in *Birth of the Blues* (1941).

- How dare you call Mr. Brooks a thief! Apologize at once. Tell him you're sorry.

- Mr. Brooks, I'm sorry you're a crook.

Melton (Alan Mowbray) and the bellboy Freddy (Lou Costello) in *Abbott and Costello Meet the Killer, Boris Karloff* (1949).

Anything to make a dishonest dollar.

Shemp in *He Cooked his Goose* (1952).

Thanks, Gisborne, but I'd rather keep you as an enemy because as long as I hate your guts I know I've got good taste.

Robbo (Frank Sinatra) refusing to join Guy Gisborne's (Peter Falk) mob in *Robin and the Seven Hoods* (1964).

- What's that?

- Iodine.

- Will it hurt?

- For a burglar you're not very brave, are you?

- I'm a society burglar. I don't expect people to rush about shooting me. Ouch!!! That hurt!

- Don't be such a baby. It's just a flesh wound.

- It happens to be my flesh.

- Well, you have to expect some occupational hazards. You broke in here to steal!

- Can we keep personalities out of this conversation?

Simon Dermott (Peter O'Toole) and Nicole Bonnet (Audrey Hepburn) in *How to Steal a Million* (1966).

Come on. Let's get out of here. The muggers will be here soon.

Oscar Ungar (Walter Matthau) to Felix Madison (Jack Lemmon) in *The Odd Couple* (1968).

Ruthless People

- I've got scruples too, you know. You know what that is, scruples?

- No, I don't know what it is, but if you got it, you can sure bet it belongs to somebody else.

Moses Pray (Ryan O'Neal) and Addie (Tatum O'Neal) in *Paper Moon* (1973).

You'd slit your own throat for two bits plus tax.

Danny Dan (Martin Lev) to Fat Sam (John Cassini) in *Bugsy Malone* (1976).

What is this? The bargain basement? I've been kidnapped by K-Mart?!

Kidnapped Barbara Stone (Bette Midler) whose ransom value is being "marked down" from $500,000 to $50,000 to $10,000 in *Ruthless People* (1986).

Inconceivable! You're trying to kidnap what I have rightfully stolen!

Vizzini (Wallace Shawn) to Westley/Robert the Pirate (Cary Elwes) in *The Princess Bride* (1987).

He was so crooked he could eat soup with a corkscrew.

> Myra Langtry (Annette Bening) about her old partner
> Cole Langley (J.T. Walsh) in *The Grifters* (1990).

- I'll give you a dime for every quarter you can lay on end.

- It's a bet.

- That's a dollar I owe you.

- Hey!

- That was the deal, a dime for every quarter.

> Roy Dillon (John Cusack) gives a dollar to the barfly and
> scoops up the quarters in *The Grifters* (1990).

- He died suddenly. He never even got the last rites for his last wrongs, Charlie.

- What did he die of?

- He wanted to work for somebody else.

- Ah, natural causes.

> Gang leader Case/Casey (Robert Patterson) making a
> point with Charlie McManus (Robbie Coltrane) who
> would also like to leave his employ in *Nuns on the Run*
> (1990).

Take the Money and Run

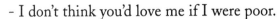

- I don't think you'd love me if I were poor.

- I might but I'd keep my mouth shut.

> Mr. Hammer (Groucho Marx) and Mrs. Potter (Margaret
> Dumont) in *Cocoanuts* (1929).

- Money don't mean a thing to me.

- No, I guess not, but with no heart and no brains it's all you've got. You'll need it.

> Tom Powers (James Cagney) and Mike Powers (Donald Cook) in *The Public Enemy* (1931).

Diamonds is my career.

> Lady Lou (Mae West) in *She Done Him Wrong* (1933).

The Thin Man

No gold digging for me. I take diamonds. We may be off the gold standard someday.

> Lady Lou (Mae West) in *She Done Him Wrong* (1933).

Don't make the same mistake twice, unless it pays.

> Ruby Carter (Mae West) in *Belle of the Nineties* (1934).

- I think it's a dirty trick to bring me all the way to New York just to make a widow out of me.

- You wouldn't be a widow long.

- You bet I wouldn't.

- Not with all your money.

> Nora Charles (Myrna Loy) and her husband Nick (William Powell) in *The Thin Man* (1934).

- How did you know I was here?

- I saw a group of men standing around a table. I knew there was only one woman in the world who could attract men like that—a woman with lots of money.

Nora Charles (Myrna Loy), the very rich and beautiful wife of Nick (William Powell) in *Another Thin Man* (1939).

- Martha, dear, there are many bonds that will hold us together through eternity.

- Really, Wolf? What are they?

- Your government bonds, your savings bonds, your liberty bonds, and maybe, in a year or two after we're married, who knows, maybe there'll be a little baby bond.

Wolf J. Flywheel (Groucho Marx) courting Martha Phelps (Margaret Dumont) in *The Big Store* (1941).

You sit around here and you spin your little web and you think the whole world revolves around you and your money. Well it doesn't, Mr. Potter. In the whole vast configuration of things I'd say you were nothing but a scurvy little spider.

George Bailey (James Stewart) to the rich and powerful Mr. Potter (Lionel Barrymore) in *It's a Wonderful Life* (1946).

- Is it the right size?

- Well, it can never be too big.

Lorelei Lee's (Marilyn Monroe) answer refers to the size of a diamond ring in *Gentlemen Prefer Blondes* (1953).

- You're here in Europe to buy a husband.

- The man I want doesn't have a price.

- That eliminates me.

John Robie (Cary Grant) and Frances Stevens (Grace Kelly) in *To Catch a Thief* (1955). Miss Kelly met her

future husband, Prince Rainier III of Monaco, during the
shooting of this film.

I want mine to wear glasses. (...) Men who wear glasses are
so much more gentle and sweet and helpless... They get
those weak eyes from reading... those long, tiny columns in
the *Wall Street Journal.*

> Sugar Kane Kowa (Marilyn Monroe) to Joe/Josephine
> (Tony Curtis) in *Some Like It Hot* (1959).

One thing I learned when I first started out: A man that
ain't got friends is poor, and he's going to stay poor until he
goes out and buys good ones. Me, I got the best.

> Big Jim (Edward G. Robinson) at his birthday party just
> before he's shot down by his friends in *Robin and the
> Seven Hoods* (1964).

I trust you will remember, Sir Arthur, when we come to the
matter of your fee, that you have been engaged to defend
me against extortion, not to subject me to it.

> Jessica Medicott (Katharine Hepburn) to Sir Arthur
> Granville-Jones (Laurence Olivier) in *Love Among the
> Ruins* (1975).

- Class isn't something you buy. Look at you. You've got a
five hundred dollar suit on and you're still a low-life.

 - Yeah! But I look good.

> Jack Cates (Nick Nolte) and Reggie Hammond (Eddie
> Murphy) in *48 HRS.* (1983).

- Did you have money or something? You were rich?

 - Oh, yeah. Very rich. Seven hundred and fifty million
dollars, and that was when seven hundred and fifty million
was considered a lot of money. I used to buy a new couch

I always say, a kiss on
the hand might feel
very good, but a
diamond tiara lasts
forever.

Lorelei Lee (Marilyn Monroe) to
Sir Francis Beekman (Charles
Coburn) in *Gentlemen Prefer
Blondes* (1953).

every week to match the *TV Guide*. I was rolling in it. I use to buy a new couch every week to match the *TV Guide...* What? You heard that one before?

Arthur Bach (Dudley Moore) to the bartender and
barflies in *Arthur 2: On the Rocks* (1988).

- You married for money?

  - I did no such thing. I married for a lot of money.

Neil (James Belushi) and Augie (John Candy) in *Once*
Upon a Crime (1991).

How did the market close? Hmmm. Well, roll over my amalgamated, split my utilities and double my capital venture overlaps. Now, call me in one hour and tell me what the hell I'm talking about.

Sleazy lawyer Roland T. Flakfizer (John Turturro) in a
Groucho-like role in *Brain Donors* (1992).

Brother, Can Ya Spare a Dime?

- We've got to do something to help that old lady.

  - I wish we could.

  - One good turn deserves another.

  - So do I neither.

  - What do you mean 'so do I neither'? Why don't you realize they're going to throw her into the streets.

  - But what can we do?

  - We've got to raise one hundred dollars.

  - One hundred dollars!

  - Yes.

- We couldn't even raise a thousand; we haven't got a dime.

> Ollie (Oliver Hardy) and Stan (Stan Laurel) in *One Good Turn* (1931).

I wasn't always rich. There was a time when I didn't know where my next husband was coming from.

> Lady Lou (Mae West) to her maid Pearl (Louise Beavers) in *She Done Him Wrong* (1933).

- We're seventy-four thousand dollars and a few pennies in the hole.

- What a magnificient failure. If I'm a genius, Oliver, it's because I'm a failure. Always remember that.

> Theater manager Oliver Webb (Walter Connelly) and producer-director Oscar Jaffe/O.J. (John Barrymore) in *Twentieth Century* (1934).

Oliver Hardy and Stan Laurel

Curly carrying a card asking for hand-outs:

Man- My good man, how long have you been starving?

*Curly-*Mister, I haven't tasted food for three days.

Man- Well, I wouldn't worry about it. It still tastes the same.

> In *Pop Goes the Easel* (1935).

Moe-Where's that dollar?

 Curly-Oh, no! Don't! That's my favorite dollar.

 Moe-What do you mean 'favorite dollar'?

 Curly-I raised it from a cent.

In *From Nurse to Worse* (1940).

Con man-If you find an honest man and he qualifies I'll give you a bonus of five thousand dollars.

 Moe-Can we have some money on account?

 Curly-Yeah, on account that we're broke.

In *So Long, Mr. Chumps* (1941).

- You don't want to end up with a loveless marriage, do you?

 - Me?! Loveless?!

 - That's right. Because if a girl spends all her time worrying about the money she doesn't have, how is she going to have any time for being in love? I want you to find happiness and stop having fun.

Lorelei Lee's (Marilyn Monroe) advice to Dorothy Shaw (Jane Russell) in *Gentlemen Prefer Blondes* (1953).

You're not more than one generation away from poor white trash, are you, Agent Starling?

Dr. Hannibal (the Cannibal) Lecter (Anthony Hopkins) to Clarice (Jodie Foster) in *Silence of the Lambs* (1991).

You're so cheap, you're wholesale.

Virginia Hill (Annette Bening) in a scene on a movie set in *Bugsy* (1991).

I was living in Queens with my two girls and we were all crammed into this unbelievably small house with my aunt Harriet. How small was it? It was so small that when you brushed your teeth you couldn't brush sideways.

Dottie Ingels's (Julie Kavner) voiceover monologue at the beginning of *This Is My Life* (1992).

- You know what the greatest nation in the world is, don't you?

- Well, I hope it's the U.S.A.

- Wrong. It's do-nation.

> Homeless Simon B. Wilder's (Joe Pesci) humorous way of
> soliciting in *With Honors* (1994).

Do you know why you hate me so much, Jeffrey? It's because I look the way you feel.

> Homeless bum Simon B. Wilder (Joe Pesci) to Harvard
> student Jeff (Josh Hamilton) in *With Honors* (1994).

Bargain Basement

You're just the man I wanted to see. If I show you how to save 20% would you be interested? Of course you would. In the first place, your overhead is too high and your brow is too low.

> Groucho (Groucho Marx) to mob boss Joe Helton
> (Rockliffe Fellowes) in *Monkey Business* (1931).

I...ain't much of a lover boy...there ain't much of a percentage in it.

> Clyde Barrow (Warren Beatty) in *Bonnie & Clyde* (1967).

For one dollar, I'll guess your weight, your height or your sex.

> Navin R. Johnson (Steve Martin) in the circus in *The Jerk*
> (1979).

How much for the women?

> Joliet Jake Blues (John Belushi) in *The Blues Brothers* (1980).

- She said it was a very good deal. And look, honey, it's a two-story house.

   - Two-story house! Before you buy it they give you one story, after you move in you get another story.

> Bess (Ilene Graff) and Chester Lee (Rodney Dangerfield) in *Ladybugs* (1992).

Pearls of Wisdom

A good motto is: Take all you can get and give as little as possible.

> Tira's (Mae West) advice to her friend Thelma in *I'm No Angel* (1933).

Be feminine and sweet... if you can blend the two.

> Aunt Hortense (Alice Brady) to Mimi (Ginger Rogers) on how to act with Guy Holden (Fred Astaire) in *The Gay Divorcee* (1934).

When in Bagdad, do as the bag-daddies do.

One of Patricia Harrington's (Marion Davies) catch-phrases in the silent movie *The Patsy* (1928).

Take it easy, honey. You'll last longer.

> Cleo Borden (Mae West) to her new husband Edward Carrington, Earl of Stratton (Paul Cavanaugh) in *Goin' to Town* (1935).

- Kitty, there's a sailor I want to meet. How do I go about it?

   - Are you kidding?

   - No. I mean are there any rules?

- Well, yes and no. Yes before you meet 'em and no after.

Shy Connie Martin (Harriet Hilliard (Nelson)) and Kitty
Collins (Lucille Ball) in Follow the Fleet (1936).

- Well, we're off. (...) You see, we're going to ride to the hounds in the morning. It's tally-ho at dawn.

- Yes, you have to get up very early in the morning to catch the fox.

- Yes, and stay up late at night to catch a minx.

Gloria Patterson (Helen Broderick) and Mr. Duncan
(Samuel S. Hinds) in The Rage of Paris (1938).

Take it from an expert, Ruby, a girl's best friend is a dollar.

Gloria Lyons (Lucille Ball) to her dresser Ruby in The Big
Street (1942).

Mother always said: If you're gonna catch a man, you may have to catch a cold too.

Christine Duncan (Esther Williams) explaining to her
roommate the necessity of a low neckline in Duchess of
Idaho (1950).

You can't spend the rest of your life crying. It annoys people in the movies.

Oscar Madison (Walter Matthau) to Felix Ungar (Jack
Lemmon) in The Odd Couple (1968).

It's a jungle out there. You've got to look out for number one... but don't step in number two.

Thornton Melon's (Rodney Dangerfield) graduation
speech in Back to School (1986).

You've got to have two things to win. You'ge got to have brains and you've got to have balls. You've got too much of

Beetlejuice

one and not enough of the other.

Fast Eddie Felson (Paul Newman) to Vince (Tom Cruise) in *The Color of Money* (1986).

Peggy, you know what a penis is? Stay away from it.

Mrs. Evelyn Kelcher (Barbara Harris) to Peggy Sue (Kathleen Turner) in *Peggy Sue Got Married* (1986).

Never trust the living!

Juno (Sylvia Sidney), the Coach, to her new ghosts Adam Maitland (Alec Baldwin) and his wife Barbara (Geena Davis) in *Beetlejuice* (1988).

Now, I want you to breathe through your eyelids.

Annie Savoy (Susan Sarandon) to Eddy Calvin 'Nuke' LaLoosh (Tim Robbins) to help him improve his pitching in *Bull Durham* (1988).

Never rub another man's rhubarb.

The Joker/Jack Napier's (Jack Nicholson) advice to Bruce Wayne (Michael Keaton) regarding Vicky Vale in *Batman* (1989).

My old man used to say, before he left this shitty world, never chase buses or women. You always get left behind.

Marlboro (Don Johnson) to Harley (Mickey Rourke) in *Harley Davidson and the Marlboro Man* (1991). Possibly a variation on a line by Dorothy Parker: "Never run after a bus or a man—there'll be another one along in a minute."

Bad Advice

-What's the secret?

- There's no secret, kid. Dames are simple. I never met one that didn't understand a slap on the mouth or a slug from a .45.

Allan (Woody Allen) and Bogey (Jerry Lacy) in Play It
Again, Sam (1972).

Don't play hard to get.

Jeff (Bill Murray) commenting on Michael
Dorsey/Dorothy Michaels' (Dustin Hoffman) female
disguise as Tootsie (1982).

- God hates me. That's what it is.

- Hate Him back. Works for me.

Roger Murtaugh (Danny Glover) and his new suicidal
partner Martin Riggs (Mel Gibson) in Lethal Weapon
(1987).

Give God a hard time, not me.

Charlie (Martin Sheen) to his father (Barnard Hughes) in
Da (1988).

Life Sucks, Then You Die

I don't read no papers and I don't listen to radios either. I know the world's been shaved by a drunken barber and I don't have to read about it.

Colonel (Walter Brennan) to Beanny (Irving Bacon) in
Meet John Doe (1941).

Blazing Saddles

Ilsa, I'm no good at being noble but it doesn't take much to see that the problems of three little people don't amount to a hill of beans in this crazy world.

Richard Blain/Rick's (Humphrey Bogart) farewell speech to Ilsa Lund (Ingrid Bergman) in *Casablanca* (1942). Rephrased by Peter Falk, as Lou Peckingpaugh, to Louise Fletcher, as Marlene Duchard, in *The Cheap Detective* (1978): You don't give a hill of beans about me, do you?

Story of my life. I always get the fuzzy end of the lollypop.

Sugar Kane (Marilyn Monroe) to Joe (Tony Curtis) in *Some Like It Hot* (1959).

What's happening in the clean world?

Sheriff Bart (Cleavon Little) to the Jim/Waco Kid (Gene Wilder) in *Blazing Saddles* (1974).

I have a very pessimistic view of life... I feel that life is divided into the horrible and the miserable. These are the two categories, you know. The horrible would be, like terminal cases, blind people, cripples. I don't know how they get through life. It's amazing to me. And the miserable is everyone else. So when you go through life, you should be thankful you're miserable because you're very lucky to be miserable.

Alvy Singer (Woody Allen) to Annie (Diane Keaton) in *Annie Hall* (1977).

- I thought I was gonna die.

- Oh! Sorry to disappoint you, but you're gonna live to enjoy all the glorious fruits of life: acne, shaving, premature ejaculation and your first divorce.

> Danny (Austin O'Brien) and Jack Slater (Arnold Schwarzenegger) in *Last Action Hero* (1993).

Hon, you know, it's not right to feel this shitty this time of the year, but this is life and when you go through it long enough you know what the flavor is... It sure ain't vanilla.

> Cindy (Rosie Perez) to her friend Caroline (Marisa Tomei) at Christmas time in *Untamed Heart* (1993).

Philosophy 101

Come easy, go easy.

> Stanio (Stan Laurel) after being robbed of their life's savings in *The Devil's Brother* (Former title: *Fra Diavolo*) (1933).

Life is but an empty bubble.

> Irene Bullock (Carole Lombard) playing a dramatic scene for the eyes and ears of Godfrey (William Powell) in *My Man Godfrey* (1936).

Ah, fill the cup. What boot is to repeat how time is slipping underneath our feet? Unborn tomorrow and dead yesterday. Why fret about them if today be sweet?

> Emil J. Keck (Groucho Marx) drinking champagne at Johnny Dalton's (Frank Sinatra) expense and urging him to 'live dangerously' in *Double Dynamite* (1951).

Life is just like a poker game. (...) First you hold a pretty hand, you make a pair, and then you get three of a kind and the first thing you know, you've got a full house.

> George Bell (Lou Costello) in *Lost in Alaska* (1952).

Let me tell you something, son. I've worked hard and I've become rich, friendless and mean. In America, that's about as far as you can go.

Horace Vandergelder (Walter Matthau) to his employee
Barnaby in *Hello, Dolly!* (1969).

I just wanna ride my machine without being hassled by the man!

Wyatt (Peter Fonda) in *Easy Rider* (1969).

Live! Otherwise you've got nothing to talk about in the locker room.

Maude (Ruth Gordon) to Harold (Bud Cort) in *Harold
and Maude* (1972).

- Miles, did you ever realize that God spelled backwards is dog?

- Yeah. So?

- Makes you think.

Luna Schlosser (Diane Keaton), a university graduate in
the year 2173, in which where Miles Monroe (Woody
Allen) has unfortunately been defrosted after a 200-year
sleep in *Sleeper* (1973).

- I see. You don't believe in science, and you don't believe that political systems work, and you don't believe in God.

- Right.

- So, then, what do you believe in?

- Sex and death. Two things that come once in my lifetime, but at least after death you're not noxious.

Luna Schlosser (Diane Keaton) and Miles Monroe
(Woody Allen) in *Sleeper* (1973).

To me nature is (...) spiders and bugs, and big fish eating little fish, and plants eating plants, and animals eating... It's like an enormous restaurant, that's the way I see it.

> Boris (Woody Allen) to Sonja (Diane Keaton) in *Love and Death* (1975).

A promise is like a thick blanket that leaves you shivering when the weather turns cold.

> Hyssops (James Coco) impersonating a prophet in *Holy Moses!* (1980).

Kevin, there are several quintessential moments in a man's life: losing his virginity, getting married, becoming a father and having the right girl smile at you.

> Kirbo (Emilio Estevez) to Kevin (Andrew McCarthy) in *St. Elmo's Fire* (1985).

Inside every so-called bad kid is a good kid waiting for someone to reach on down through the sleaze and the slime, pick him up and hose him off.

> Freddy Shoop (Mark Harmon) to Robin Bishop (Kirstie Alley) in *Summer School* (1987).

What if C-A-T really spelled dog?

> Ogre (Donald Gibb) having a brainstorm while smoking pot with the nerds in *Revenge of the Nerds II: Nerds in Paradise* (1987).

Don't be obsessed with your desires, Danny. The zen philosopher Basho once wrote: a flute with no holes is not a flute and a donut with no hole is a danish. He was a funny guy.

Ty Webb (Chevy Chase) to Danny Noonan (Michael O'Keefe) in *Caddyshack* (1980).

Susan Sarandon and
Kevin Costner in *Bull
Durham*

I believe in the Church of Baseball. I tried all the major religions and most of the minor ones. I've worshipped Buddha, Allah, Brahma, Vishnu, Siva, trees, mushrooms and Isodora Duncan. I know things. For instance: there are 108 beads in a Catholic rosary and there are 108 stitches in a baseball. When I learned that, I gave Jesus a chance. But it just didn't work out between us. The Lord laid out too much guilt on me. I prefer metaphysics to theology. You see, there's no guilt in baseball and it's never boring, which makes it like sex.

Annie Savoy's (Susan Sarandon) opening monologue in
Bull Durham (1988).

Opinions are like assholes—everybody has one.

Harry Callahan (Clint Eastwood) in *The Dead Pool* (1988).

You know, boys, there's three things in this world you need: respect for all kinds of life, a nice bowel movement on a regular basis, and a navy blazer.

Parry (Robin Williams) to the young torchers in *The
Fisher King* (1991).

Plato once said that the unexplained life is not worth living. Well, I agree. It wasn't until I took a long hard look at my own life that I realized what I really am. I'm me! It's not what you do that matters, it's who you are, and only then did I discover the truth: Chris is my other half and together we make a whole. I finally found a yin to go with my yang or is that yang to go with my yin. Well, in any case, I'm so lucky to be me!

> Pat's (Julia Sweeney) closing monologue tantalizing to the end our curiosity to know his or her true gender in *It's Pat—The Movie* (1994).

Artsy Fartsy

After all, we must remember that art is art. Still, on the other hand, water is water, isn't it? And east is east and west is west and if you take cranberries and stew them like apple sauce, it tastes much more like prunes than rhubarb does.

> Captain Jeffrey Spaulding (Groucho Marx) in *Animal Crackers* (1930).

Larry-Oh, an art school.

Moe-My old man used to draw.

Curly-Sure, he drew twenty years with one stroke of the pen.

> In *Pop Goes the Easel* (1935).

Painter-Gentlemen, I am an artiste.

Larry-I'm an artist too.

Curly-Oh, a pair of drawers.

> In *Pop Goes the Easel* (1935).

- Do you notice what that sign says, madam?

- Do not finger ART OBJECTS. Oh, I don't blame Art. If I were Art I'd object too. (*Laughs.*) I don't get it.

> Keggs (Reginald Gardiner), leading visitors through Tutney Castle, points a sign to Gracie (Gracie Allen) in *A Damsel in Distress* (1937).

- Look at that wall over there. Isn't that a beautiful wall?

- Beautiful.

- Do you know what that wall reminds me of?

- What?

- This one over here.

Tommy (Lou Costello) and Ted (Bud Abbott) in a chic restaurant in *The Noose Hangs High* (1948).

Moe Hailstone-Go burn the books.

Curly Pebble-Why burn the books?

Moe Hailstone-There are too many bookmakers. The bookies are overrunning the country. These are my orders.

In *You Nazty Spy!* (1940).

Miss Caswell is an actress, a graduate of the Copacabana School of Dramatic Arts.

Addison DeWitt (George Sanders) introducing his protégée (Marilyn Monroe) in *All About Eve* (1950).

A living, Mr. Temper, is made by selling something that everybody needs at least once a year and a million is made by producing something that everybody needs every single day. You artists, you painters produce nothing, that nobody needs, never.

Horace Vandergelder (Walter Matthau) to the young painter who wishes to marry his niece in *Hello, Dolly!* (1969).

Notice the whiskers. My God! You can almost reach out and touch them. That's the tip-off to a great work of art.

Vince Ricardo (Peter Falk) commenting on the 'Tiger on Black Velvet' painting in General Garcia's (Richard Libertini) art collection in *The In-Laws* (1979).

Millions of books written on every conceivable subject by all these great minds and in the end none of them knows anything more about the big questions of life than I do. Jesus! I read Socrates. You know, this guy used to knock off little Greek boys. What the hell does he have to teach me? And Nietzsche and his theory of eternal recurrence. He said that the life we live we're going to live over and over again the exact same way for eternity. Great! That means I'll have to sit through the Ice Capades again. It's not worth it.

Mickey (Woody Allen) on the
meaning of life in *Hannah and
Her Sisters* (1986)

I've got culture coming out of my ass.

Freddy (Steve Martin) in *Dirty
Rotten Scoundrels* (1988).

I make art till somebody dies. I am the world's first fully functioning homicidal artist.

The Joker/Jack Napier (Jack
Nicholson) to Vicky Vale (Kim
Basinger) in *Batman* (1989).

Jack Nicholson is The
Joker in *Batman*

Goose-stepping morons like yourself should try reading books instead of burning them.

Professor Jones (Sean Connery) to a Nazi colonel in
Indiana Jones and the Last Crusade (1989).

I do not see plays because I can nap at home for free, and I don't see movies because they're trash and they've got nothing but naked people in 'em, and I don't read books because if they're any good they're going to make them into a mini-series.

Ouiser Boudreaux (Shirley MacLaine) to Clairee Belcher
(Olympia Dukakis) in *Steel Magnolias* (1989).

She buys a new book every two days. She's into trash. What can you do?

Parry (Robin Williams) spying on the woman he loves in *The Fisher King* (1991).

You're like the Ernest Hemingway of bullshit.

Newton (Steve Martin) to Gwen (Goldie Hawn) in *Housesitter* (1992).

Roll Over Beethoven

Moe-I'm the best musician in the country.

Curly-Yeah, but how are you in the city?

Ted Healy and his Stooges appearing in the feature film *Dancing Lady* (1933).

I'm gonna sing Delilah. I've got a lot of respect for that dame. There's one lady barber that made good.

Cleo Borden (Mae West) staging an opera in *Goin' to Town* (1935).

What was that? High C or vitamin D?

Otis B. Driftwood (Groucho Marx) listening to an aria in *A Night at the Opera* (1935).

Oh, I had a much nicer voice—'til I ran a nail through it.

Stan Laurel with a soprano voice in *The Bohemian Girl* (1936).

- I didn't know you could play the piano. Do you play by ear?

- Oh, no. I use my hands like everybody else.

> Marsha Manning (Ginny Simms) and Weejie (Lou
> Costello) in *Hit the Ice* (1943).

Moe-How much money did you loan on this junk?

Larry-Cheap. Fifty dollars. That's a genuine stratosphere.

Moe-Stratosphere! Play some air.

> The boys are pawnbrokers in *Three Loan Wolves* (1946).

- How long you study music?

- Fifteen years.

- You know, two more years and you could have been a plumber.

> Faustino the Great (Chico Marx) and Mr. Lyons (Leon
> Belasco) in *Love Happy* (1949).

- Where's Goldfinger?

- Playing his golden harp.

> Pussy Galore (Honor Blackman) and James Bond (Sean
> Connery) in *Goldfinger* (1964).

Did you go to a rock concert? How was it? Was it heavy? Did it achieve total heavyocity?

> Alvy Singer (Woody Allen) to Annie (Diane Keaton) in
> *Annie Hall* (1977).

- What kind of music do you usually have here?

- Oh! We have both kind. We've got country and we've got western.

> Joliet Jake Blues (John Belushi) and Claire (Sheilah Wells)
> at Bob's Country Bunker in *The Blues Brothers* (1980).

Oh, my God! Where did that orchestra come from?!?!

> Shirley (Pauline Collins) making love on a boat in
> Greece, to the sound of orchestral music, in *Shirley
> Valentine* (1989).

Shall We Dance?

Moe's the name. Would you like to trip over the light fantasia?

> Moe inviting a lady to dance in *Three Smart Saps*
> (1942).

Lady-You're an unusual dancer.

Curly-I come from a family of dancers. My father died dancing... on the end of a rope.

> In *Three Smart Saps* (1942).

Go-go is an art form—it's interpretive dance with a rock 'n' roll background.

> Christina Whitaker in *Assault of the Killer Bimbos* (1987).

- You know the Great Volare?

- I knew him when he was the Pretty Good Volare.

> Mrs. Lilian Oglethorpe (Nancy Marchand) and Roland T.
> Flakfizer (John Turturro) speaking about the famous ballet
> dancer Roberto Volare in *Brain Donors* (1992).

- What are you doing here?

- To sign you for my ballet company.

- To sign ME for YOUR ballet company?

- I swear I just said that.

> Shyster lawyer Roland T. Flakfizer (John Turturro) and
> ballet dancer Roberto Volare (George De La Pena) in
> *Brain Donors* (1992).

- I don't dance for just anyone. I AM ballet. My dance shoes are in the Louvre in Paris.

- So what! Last year I left a raincoat in Cleveland.

- Do you realize what I was doing at the age of seven?

- I can imagine and you must be thankful you didn't go blind.

- I was dancing professionally.

- Whatever you want to call it: flogging the carrot, polishing the cue-stick, choking the chicken, clearing the snorkel.

> Ballet dancer Roberto Volare (George De La Pena) and
> Groucho-like shyster lawyer Roland T. Flakfizer (John
> Turturro) in *Brain Donors* (1992).

- Not a bad dip for a woman who's had four children.

- What are you talking about?! Two of them started with dips.

> Abe Silverman (Alan Manson) dancing with his wife
> Doris (Olympia Dukakis) in *The Cemetery Club* (1992).

Green Eggs and Hamlet

I'll walk in and make a scene that even Shakespeare couldn't top!

> Lil Andrews (Jean Harlow) in *Red-Headed Woman*
> (1932).

Shakespeare had his style and I have mine.

> Mae West to a producer who chided her for her misuse of Victor McLaglen in *Klondike Annie* (1936), pointing out that a movie could have two leading parts like Shakespeare's Romeo and Juliet.

What he did to Shakespeare we are doing now to Poland.

> Colonel Ehrhardt (Sig Ruman) speaking to and about Joseph Tura (Jack Benny) disguised as Professor Siletsky in *To Be or Not to Be* (1942).

I have a favorite quote about L.A. by William Shakespeare. He said: This other Eden, demi-paradise, this precious stone set in a silver sea, this earth, this realm, this... Los Angeles.

> Harris K. Telemacher (Steve Martin) in the opening monologue in *L. A. Story* (1991).

I want to write but I hate writing with my brother. Your whole relationship gets in the way. Can you imagine Hamlet written by William and Harvey Shakespeare?

> Eugene Morris Jerome (Corey Parker) in *Neil Simon's Broadway Bound* (1992).

- Hamlet's mama, she's the queen. (*Chorus by the new recruits.*)

- Marching in the final scene.

- Drinks a glass of funky wine.

- Now she's Satan's valentine.

> Sergeant Cass (Gregory Hines) drilling the new recruits at the end of *Renaissance Man* (1994).

You Oughta Be in Pictures

Curly-How are we going to get into pictures? We know nothing about movies.

Moe-There's a couple of thousand people in pictures now who know nothing about it. Three more won't make any difference.

In *Movie Maniacs* (1936).

Moe-Boy! This picture business is tougher to get into than I figured.

Larry-Don't worry. A bad beginning is a good ending.

Curly-Soitanly. If at first you don't succeed, keep on sucking till you do succeed.

Trying to get past the studio gates in *Movie Maniacs* (1936).

I didn't like the way he looked at me. (...) He makes you feel like you oughta run home and put on a tin overcoat.

Jean Maitland (Ginger Rogers) about producer Anthony Powell (Adolphe Menjou) in *Stage Door* (1937).

- You know, the chief's got a pip of a part for you in a new picture called *The Maid and the Man*. It's adapted from Hungaria. It's all about a little servant girl.

- You mean that piece of literary junk they've had around the studio for years? Why, they'd have to re-write that before the moths would eat it.

- Ah, you haven't read it lately. Listen, they've changed the middle, they tacked on a new end and built up a new beginning.

- Had its face lifted, eh?

> Publicist Lenny Morgan (Jack Oakie) and movie star
> Annabel Allison (Lucille Ball) in *The Affairs of Annabel*
> (1938).

- Don't these big empty houses scare you?

- Not me. I used to be in vaudeville.

> Cicily (Nydia Westman) and Wallie (Bob Hope) in *The
> Cat and the Canary* (1939).

As for you, baby, I've known dozens like you. Sappy kids with a heart like a curd dog that answers all the whistles and figures they're having a good time.

> Con artist Bill O'Brien (Douglas Fairbanks, Jr.) to out of
> work dancer Nina Barona (Rita Hayworth) in *Angels
> Over Broadway* (1940).

- Show business!

- Terrible, isn't it! What you have to go through to make a fortune.

> Don Bolton (Bob Hope) and Bert (Eddie Bracken) in
> *Caught in the Draft* (1941).

- It must be quite a struggle to achieve success in Hollywood?

- Oh, no. You just have to know which fork to use and which knife to stick in whose back.

> Tony Fairbanks (Dorothy Lamour) and Steve (Lynn
> Overman) in *Caught in the Draft* (1941).

- Are you nervous, Eugene?

- No, just my knees are nervous. They've never been on television before.

Abigail Parker (Dorothy Malone) and Eugene Fulstat
(Jerry Lewis) in *Artists and Models* (1955).

- What do you mean, kill the actors? Actors aren't animals, they're human beings.
- They are? Have you ever eaten with one?

Leo Bloom (Gene Wilder) and Max Bialystock (Zero
Mostel) in *The Producers* (1967).

He's a walking soap opera.

Oscar Madison (Walter Matthau) speaking of Felix
Ungar (Jack Lemmon) in *The Odd Couple* (1968).

What are you crying for? It's not a Lassie movie.

Jonathan (Jack Nicholson) to Jennifer (Carol Kane) after
the Ballbuster Parade, a slide show of Jonathan's ex-
girlfriends in *Carnal Knowledge* (1971).

As an actor, no one could touch him. As a human being, no one wanted to touch him.

Willy Clark (Walter Matthau) about his long-time partner
Al Lewis (George Burns) in *The Sunshine Boys* (1975).

I won't do this until the dancing dildos know their steps. I'm an actress.

Mary La Rue (Alexandra Morgan) in *The First Nudie
Musical* (1975).

Did you know that King Kong the First was just three feet six inches tall? He only came up to Fay Wray's belly button.

- You know the old saying: Once an actress, always an actress.

- Oh, I know the old saying, but what does it have to do with you?

Lola Brewster (Kim Novak) and Marina Rudd (Elizabeth Taylor) in *The Mirror Crack'd* (1980).

If God could do the tricks we can do, He'd be a happy man.

> Movie director Eli Cross (Peter O'Toole) to fugitive Cameron/Burt (Steve Railsback) in *The Stunt Man* (1980).

Lola Brewster, actress! If she read a script I'd see a blister on her finger.

> Marina Rudd (Elizabeth Taylor) speaking about Lola (Kim Novak) in *The Mirror Crack'd* (1980).

I could eat a can of Kodak and puke a better movie.

> Actress Lola Brewster (Kim Novak) to movie director Jason Rudd (Rock Hudson) in *The Mirror Crack'd* (1980).

Marty Fenn is a producer. He only lies when he speaks.

> Ella Zielinsky (Geraldine Chaplin) about Marty N. Fenn (Tony Curtis) in *The Mirror Crack'd* (1980).

Let's face it, sweetheart, without Jews, fags and Gypsies, there is no theatre.

> Frederick Bronski (Mel Brooks) to his wife Anna (Anne Bancroft) in *To Be or Not to Be* (1983).

Harry, if there's anything I know it's that nobody knows anything in this business.

> Producer Ronnie Liebowitz (Barry Miller) to director Harry Stone (Danny Aiello) who fears that his movie within a movie, *The Pickle*, will bomb in *The Pickle* (1993). Will Rogers had a similar sentiment when he went bankrupt producing silent pictures: "Movies. It's the only business in the world nobody knows anything about." This line was quoted by Dan Aykroyd in the video tribute *Will Rogers: Look Back in Laughter* (1987).

The rest of the time you're just a good-looking, sweet-talking, charm-oozing, f**k-happy fellow with nothing to offer but some dialogue. Dialogue is cheap in Hollywood, Ben.

> Virginia Hill (Annette Bening) to Ben Siegel (Warren Beatty) in *Bugsy* (1991).

I want to call CAA and my lawyer.

> Samantha Crane (Teri Hatcher) to the interrogation detectives in *Brain Smasher... A Love Story* (1993).

- Nobody comes into my dressing room uninvited. What the hell do you think that star means?

- You're Jewish?

> Claudette Cassenback (Anita Morris), the Va-Va-Va-Voom singer, and Roger Henderson (Brian Benben) in *Radioland Murders* (1994).

Name Dropping

- Look, it's got a coat of arms. It's a bonified castle.

- That's where Napoleon came from.

- Napoleon?

- Yes. Napoleon Bonified.

> George (George Burns) and Jerry Halliday (Fred Astaire) receive a letter bearing the Tutney Castle coat of arms and Gracie (Gracie Allen) supplies her own explanation in *A Damsel in Distress* (1937).

- I was reading you knocked down more passes than any man in America.

- No, Manuelito, he's second.

- Who's first?

- Ginger Rogers.

> Manuelito (Desi Arnaz) meeting a famous football player and Jojo Jordan (Eddie Bracken) setting the record straight in *Too Many Girls* (1940).

The boys are tailors and find a suit with the initials T.H. in it:

Moe-T.H.-I wonder what it means?

Shemp-Teddy Hoosevelt!

Larry-T.H.-I got it! Thomas Hedison!

> In *Sing a Song of Six Pants* (1947).

Eve would ask Abbott to give her Costello.

> Karen Richards (Celeste Holm) about Eve Harrington (Anne Baxter) in *All About Eve* (1950).

What you said all along, Clouseau, qualifies you as the greatest prophet since General Custer said he was going to surround all those Indians.

> Chief Inspector Dreyfus (Herbert Lom) to Jacques Clouseau (Peter Sellers) in *A Shot in the Dark* (1964).

First, we'll have an orgy. Then, we'll go see Tony Bennett.

> Ted (Elliott Gould) to Bob (Robert Culp), Carol (Natalie Wood) and Alice (Dyan Cannon) in *Bob and Carol and Ted and Alice* (1969).

- You ever want to be somebody else?

- I'd like to try Porky Pig!

Wyatt (Peter Fonda) and Billy (Dennis Hopper) in *Easy Rider* (1969).

May I take a page from our late great Rudy the Kip Kipling? Let our Kipling speak:

There was a young lady from Exeter

All the young men threw their sex at her

Just to be rude

She lay in the nude

While her parrot, a pervert, took pecks at her.

> Sir Guy Grand (Peter Sellers) to the Board of Directors in
> *The Magic Christian* (1969).

Find somebody pure enough for you? It won't be easy now that Albert Schweitzer is dead and Saint Francis of Assisi, I hear, is not too well either.

> Charley Nichols (Walter Matthau) to Ann Atkinson
> (Glenda Jackson) in *House Calls* (1978).

Elvis! Elvis! Let me be! Keep that pelvis far from me!

> Rizzo (Stockard Channing) sings in *Grease* (1978).

As Caesar's wife said to Sigmund Freud: You tell me yours, I'll tell you mine.

> Doctor Fell (Ed Flanders) to Colonel Hudson Kane (Stacy
> Keach) in *The Ninth Configuration* (1979).

I believe it was Wilde who said: Anyone who calls a spade a spade should be made to use one.

> Zaharov (Leo McKern), the Russian ambassador, forcing
> his victim to dig his own grave in *Reilly: The Ace of Spies*
> (1984).

"A man without a plan is not a man." Nietzsche.

> Big Boy Caprice (Al Pacino) misquoting famous people in
> *Dick Tracy* (1990).

We are for the people! "And if you ain't for the people, you can't buy the people." Lincoln.

> Big Boy Caprice (Al Pacino) misquoting famous people in
> *Dick Tracy* (1990).

If Da Vinci was alive today, he'd be eating microwave sushi naked in the back of a Cadillac with the both of us. The project of his life is now the toy of mine. History, tradition, culture, are not concepts. These are trophies I keep in my den as paper weights.

Darwin Mayflower (Richard E. Grant) in *Hudson Hawk* (1991).

I thought the Dalai Lama moved to L.A.

Celeste Talbert (Sally Field) to Rose Schwartz (Whoopi Goldberg) in *Soapdish* (1991).

The Name Game

- So, you're Ruby Carter.

- The only thing my mother ever told me. Everything else I found out for myself.

Molly Brant (Katherine De Mille) and Ruby Carter (Mae West) in *Belle of the Nineties* (1934).

- My name is Vladimir...

- My name is a couple of inches shorter than yours.

An aristocratic Russian with a family-tree name introducing himself to Cleo Borden (Mae West) in *Goin' to Town* (1935). This line was repeated by Matthew Modine, as Joe Slovak, in *Gross Anatomy* (1989): "Hi! My name's a coupla inches shorter than yours."

- I'm sorry, I didn't get your name.

- Well, it's not your fault. You tried hard enough.

An admirer, Lt. Mendoza, and Cleo Borden (Mae West) in *Goin' to Town* (1935).

- You may call me Tanka.

- Tanka?!

- You're welcome.

> Countess Scharwenka (Ginger Rogers) and Huck Haines (Fred Astaire) in *Roberta* (1935). Stan Laurel has a similar line in *Great Guns* (1941). As a soldier, in a mess hall, he's being served cofffee. Stan: "Sanka?" Soldier: "You're welcome."

Curly passing out after being kissed by a beautiful actress:

Larry-Say, he's passing out.

Moe-Tell me your name, kid, so I can tell your mother.

Curly-My mother knows my name.

> In *Movie Maniacs* (1936).

Sounds like a bubble in a bubblebath.

> Egbert Sousé (W.C. Fields) when introduced to Og Oggilby (Grady Sutton) in *The Bank Dick* (1940).

Manuel-I want you to meet Rosita, Bonita, Conchita and Pepita.

Curly-They must be hungry. They all end in "ita" (eat-a).

> Manuel Gonzales introducing his chorus girls to the Stooges, now hair-dressers and beauticians in *Cookoo Cavaliers* (1940).

So, they call me concentration camp Ehrhardt!

> Joseph Tura (Jack Benny) impersonating the colonel and later, Colonel Ehrhardt himself (Sig Ruman) in *To Be or Not to Be* (1942). Mel Brooks has the same line as F. Bronski in the 1983 remake.

- I don't believe I got your name?

  - Of course not. If you had my name you'd be my sister.

Mrs. Winthrop (Margaret Irving) and Albert (Lou
Costello) in In Society (1944).

Barnaby-Hello. Griffith Park Zoo. Snakes Department. Ssssst!

Oxley-Hello! Hello! What is this? This is Mr. Oxley speaking.

Barnaby-I'll see if he's here.

Oxley-No, no, no. I said this is Oxley speaking.

Barnaby-Who is?

Oxley-I am speaking.

Barnaby-Oh, you're Mr. Speaking.

Oxley-This is Mr. Oxley speaking.

Barnaby-Oxley Speaking. Any relation to Oxley?

Oxley-Barnaby Fulton, is that you?

Barnaby-Who's calling?

Oxley-I am, Barnaby.

Barnaby-Oh, no. You're not Barnaby. I'm Barnaby. I oughta know who I am.

Oxley-This is Oxley speaking Barnaby.

Barnaby-Well now, that's ridiculous. You can't be all three. Figure out which one you are then call me back.

Barnaby Fulton (Cary Grant), a chemist under the
influence of a rejuvenating drug, having a phone
conversation with his boss, Mr. Oliver Oxley (Charles
Coburn) in Monkey Business (1952).

- Do you have a brother who's first name is Sherlock?

  - I do not!

- You do have a brother?

- I do.

- Might I inquire as to his first name?

- Sheer Luck!

> Orville Sacker (Marty Feldman) trying to deliver a message to Sigerson Holmes (Gene Wilder) in *The Adventure of Sherlock Holmes' Smarter Brother* (1975).

Ah! Ah! Nobody says the B-word.

Beetlejuice (Michael Keaton) who gets to marry Lydia Deetz (Winona Ryder) unless his name is pronounced three times in *Beetlejuice* (1988).

My name is Jonathan Levinson Siegel. I own Jonathan of Paris here in New York. I have information which could determine the fate of the entire world and civilization as it is known today. Have you got a minute?

> Fashion designer Jonathan Levinson Siegel (Bill Dana) (a name mocking the 1973 movie *Jonathan Livingston Seagull* calling Maxwell Smart (Don Adams) in *The Nude Bomb* (1980).

- You know, when I first read about it I thought it was pronounced cli-TO-ris.

- I think it sounds nicer that way.

- Then it sounds like it could be a name. Oh, hi, Clitoris. How are you?

- That makes it sound a bit crude somehow.

- No. Why not? Plenty of men walking around called Dick. Well, anyway, that's the way I thought it was pronounced when I first mentioned it to Joe, you know, sitting in the front room one night. I said: Joe, have you ever heard of the clitoris? He didn't even look up from his paper. Yeah, he said, but it doesn't go as well as the Ford Escort.

> Shirley (Pauline Collins) talking with her mates in *Shirley Valentine* (1989).

I have given a name to my pain: Batman!

> The Joker/Jack Napier (Jack Nicholson) in *Batman* (1989).

- He works for Mr. Casey.

 - Mr. Who?

 - No, Mr. Casey

> Faith Thomas (Camille Coduri) and the Triad gangsters in
> *Nuns on the Run* (1990).

Frank-Hector Savage from Detroit. Hey! I remember this pug. Ex-boxer. His real name was Joey Chicago.

Ed-Oh yeah! He fought under the name of Kid Minneapolis.

Nordberg-I saw Kid Minneapolis fight once. In Cincinnati.

Frank-No! You're thinking of Kid New York. He fought out of Philly.

Ed-He was killed in the ring in Huston by Tex Colorado. You know, the Arizona Assassin.

Nordberg-Yeah! From Dakota. I don't remember if it was North or South.

Frank-North! South Dakota was his brother, from West Virginia.

Ed-You sure know your boxing.

Frank-Well, all I know is, never bet on the white guy.

> Frank Drebin (Leslie Nielsen), Ed Hocken (George
> Kennedy) and Nordberg (O. J. Simpson) in *The Naked
> Gun 2 1/2: The Smell of Fear* (1991).

- Selina! Selina!

 - That's my name, Maximilian. Don't wear it out or I'll make you buy me a new one.

> Max Shreck (Christopher Walken) dumbfounded by the
> reappearance of Selina Kyle/Cat Woman (Michelle
> Pfeiffer) in *Batman Returns* (1992).

*Ned Ravine-*May I call you Lana?

   *Lana Ravine-*Oh, please call me Angel Tits.

   *Prosecutor-*I object!

   *Judge Shanky-*Sustain. Counselor, you will address Angel Tits as Mrs. Ravine.

> Defense attorney Ned Ravine (Armand Assante), his wife, the defendant, Lana (Kate Nelligan), the prosecutor (Susan Angelo), and Judge Shanky (Tony Randall) in an exchange typical of the script of *Fatal Instinct* (1993).

- Take me Garth.

   - Where? I'm low on gas and you need a jacket.

   - I'm gonna be frank.

   - OK. Can I still be Garth?

   - Shut up and kiss me.

> Honey Hornay (Kim Basinger) and Garth Algar (Dana Carvey) in *Wayne's World 2* (1993).

*Jo Dee-*Doctor Animal...

   Animal-Call me A.

   *Jo Dee-*A?

   *Animal-*Also, call me doctor.

   *Jo Dee-*A doctor?

   *Animal-*Doctor A.

   *Jo Dee-*Excuse me. Doctor A.

   *Animal-*Bingo!

   *Jo Dee-*Doctor A. Bingo?

> FBI agent Jo Dee Fostar (Billy Zane) and Dr. Animal Cannibal Pizza (Dom DeLuise) in *Silence of the Hams* (1994).

Michelle Pfeiffer in *Batman*

Animal-Is Miss Fostar here yet?

Cop-Mister.

Animal-Call me doctor, please.

Cop-Not yet Doctor Please.

> Dr. Animal Cannibal Pizza (Dom DeLuise) being
> corrected by the cop while waiting for FBI agent Mister Jo
> Dee Fostar (Billy Zane) in *Silence of the Hams* (1994).

What's Your Number?

- Where'd you learn to cook?

- My first wife was a second cook in a third-rate joint on Fourth Street.

> Jeff (William Bendix) and Rusty (Eddie Marr) in *The Glass Key* (1942).

13-I didn't know 22 was your backup. She's really something, isn't she?

86-Yes, she's very nice.

13-I knew her when she was married to Agent 78.

86-22 was married to the late great 78? Wasn't he a little old for her?

13-Well, let's see. 22 was 21 when she married 78 in '72. 78 was 46. That means 78 was 22, 32, 42, 25 years older when he married 22. 22 joined PITS when 78 died in '75.

86-Tell me, 13, how was 78 killed?

13-Investigating the numbers racket.

> Agents 13 (Joey Forman) (who hides in toilets, desk
> drawers, etc.) and Agent 86, Maxwell Smart (Don

Adams) speaking of Disappearing Agent 22 (Andrea Howard) in *The Nude Bomb* (1980).

This one goes to eleven.

Nigel Tufnel (Christopher Guest) bragging about his amp in *This Is Spinal Tap* (1984).

Ronnie, may I have fifty-five words with you?

Beldar Conehead (Dan Aykroyd) to his daughter's date on prom night in *Coneheads* (1993).

Dad, eight percent of all household accidents involve ladders, another three percent involve trees. I'm looking at an eleven percent probability here.

Richard Tyler (Macaulay Culkin) refusing the climb to the tree house that his father is building for him in *The Pagemaster* (1994). Richard's fears are confirmed when his father falls out of the tree: Can't argue with statistics, dad.

Talk Talk

Now cut out the high-sounding talk and answer me!

Louis Shemaly (Edward G. Robinson) in *Barbary Coast* (1935).

That's my nature, Godfrey. I never say anything behind your back that I won't say in public.

Mrs. Bullock (Alice Brady) to Godfrey Parke (William Powell), the butler, in *My Man Godfrey* (1936).

You have a way of saying things that make me want to call for help.

Terry Havelock Allen (Lucille Ball) on a date with Private Johnny Grey (Victor Mature) in *Seven Days' Leave* (1942).

John Wayne

Everytime I opened my mouth he talked. I felt like Charlie McCarthy.

> Elizabeth Lane (Barbara Stanwyck) after a meeting with her overbearing boss Alexander Yeardley (Sidney Greenstreet) in *Christmas in Connecticut* (1945).

You said a mouthful and you sounded like you had one.

> Slip Mahoney (Leo Gorcey) in *Blues Busters* (1950).

If you've nothing more to say, pray scat.

> Lorelei Lee (Marilyn Monroe) in *Gentlemen Prefer Blondes* (1953).

You're gonna have to bend down a little with them words if you want me to understand.

> Nella Turner (Jane Russell) to Mr. Stack (Robert Ryan) about "the wine of a connoisseur" (champagne) in *The Tall Men* (1955).

Cigarette me, then I'll talk. (...) No smoky, no talky.

Susan Vance (Katharine Hepburn) pretending to be a gangster's moll in *Bringing Up Baby* (1938).

You're talking upside down!

> Ben Allison (Clark Gable) to Nella Turner (Jane Russell) in *The Tall Men* (1955).

Put an amen to it!

> Ethan Edwards (John Wayne) to Reverend-Captain Sam Clayton (Ward Bond) praying over the graves of Ethan's family in *The Searchers* (1956).

I'm sorta like a clock. I only talk when I'm running

Former President Art Hockstader (Lee Tracy) to the
conventioners, party delegates and candidates in *The
Best Man* (1964).

- Harley, I'd like to talk to you.

- Sure, John.

- You told me that story about twice now, once last week
and then once again when we were about five hundred
miles south of here. Do you know where we are now,
Harley?

- Not exactly.

- We're in Wyoming Territory. I wouldn't mention it but
you've been talking all the way from Texas.

- I've just been keeping you company, John.

- Well, I appreciate it, Harley, and I didn't mind it too
much for the first hundred miles but Harley, you've been
talking for a thousand miles.

- I'm sorry, John. You should-a told me.

John O'Hanlan (James Stewart) and Harley Sullivan
(Henry Fonda) in *The Cheyenne Social Club* (1970).

Goddarnit, Mr. Lamarr, you use your tongue prettier than a
twenty-dollar whore.

Taggart (Slim Pickens) to Hedley Lamarr (Harvey
Korman) in *Blazing Saddles* (1974).

- By God! As long as I have tongue and tonsils and the
ability to talk, I'll defend everybody's right to speak and
every man's right to be wrong.

- I'll yield to you as the authority on that, Mr. Justice.

Justices Dan Snow (Walter Matthau) and Ruth Loomis (Jill
Clayburgh) in *First Monday in October* (1981).

Ronnie, may I have fifty-five words with you?

Beldar Conehead (Dan Aykroyd) to his daughter's date
on prom night in *Coneheads* (1993).

- They talk about me like I'm unemployed or something. I mean, I'm just a kid, you know?

  - And what do they say when you tell 'em that?

  - Well, I try, but...

  - Do you know what the first law of the theater is, Mud? TALK LOUD ENOUGH FOR PEOPLE TO HEAR YOU!

Morris 'Mud' Himmel (Jonathan Jackson) complaining to
Dennis Van Welker (Christopher Lloyd) about his
communication problem with his parents in *Camp
Nowhere* (1994).

- Shall we speak the unspoken language of love?

  - You mean the kind only dogs can hear?

  - Yes. The very same.

Julia (Geena Davis) and Kevin (Michael Keaton) in
Speechless (1994).

No Pun Intended

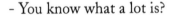

- You know what a lot is?

  - Yeah! It's too much.

  - I don't mean a whole lot, just a little lot with nothing on it.

  - Any time you've got too much, you've got a lot. Look, I'll explain it to you. Sometimes you don't got enough, you got a whole lot. Sometimes you got a little bit, you don't think it's enough. Somebody else may think it's too much, it's a whole lot too. Now, it's a whole lot, it's too much, it's too much, it's a whole lot. It's the same thing.

- Next time I see you remind me not to talk to you, will you?

Mr. Hammer (Groucho Marx) trying to explain real estate to Chico (Chico Marx) in *Cocoanuts* (1929).

- I came up to see the captain's bridge.

- I'm sorry, but he keeps it in a glass while he's eating. Would you like to see where the captain sleeps?

- Ah, I already saw it. That's the bunk.

Chicago (Chico Marx) and Groucho (Groucho Marx) in *Monkey Business* (1931).

- Anything further, father?

- Anything further, father? That can't be right. Isn't anything further, farther? The idea! I married your mother because I wanted children. Imagine my disappointment when you arrived.

Professor Quincy Adams Wagstaff (Groucho Marx) correcting his son Frank (Zeppo Marx) in *Horse Feathers* (1932).

- I changed my mind.

- Does it work any better?

Big Bill Barton (Edward Arnold) and Tira (Mae West) in *I'm No Angel* (1933).

- Wasn't you just a little nervous when he gave you all them presents?

- No, I was calm and collected.

> The maid, Jasmine (Libby Taylor), and Ruby Carter (Mae West) about her diamond jewelry in *Belle of the Nineties* (1934).

- Are you in town for good?

- I expect to be here, but not for good.

> Ruby Carter's (Mae West) answer to a group of admirers in *Belle of the Nineties* (1934).

- Won't you tell us where you are stopping during your visit here?

- Stopping at nothing.

> Ruby Carter's (Mae West) answer to her admirers in *Belle of the Nineties* (1934).

Girl-What do you take in college?

Moe-Oh, a dime here, a nickel...

> In *Three Little Pigskins* (1934).

Excuse him, ma'am, the heel has no soul.

> Moe in *Pop Goes the Easel* (1935).

- What's the excuse for a gal like you to be running around single?

- I was born that way.

> Cleo Borden's (Mae West) answer to a cowboy in *Goin' to Town* (1935).

Curly-I used to work in a bakery as a pilot.

Lady-A pilot?

Curly-Sure, I used to take the bread from one corner and pile it in another. You know, I quit that job at the bakery.

Lady-Why?

Curly-Oh, I got sick of the dough and thought I'd go on the loaf.

> Curly is Captain Dodge in *Uncivil Warriors* (1935).

Larry-Pardon me, I've got to go take care of a weak back.

Captain-How long have you had a weak back?

Larry-Oh, about a week back.

> Larry is Lieutenant Duck in *Uncivil Warriors* (1935).

Stan-Sanka?

Soldier-You're welcome.

> Pfc. Stan Laurel in a mess hall being served coffee in *Great Guns* (1941).

- That's all right. That's in every contract. That's what they call a sanity clause.

- Ah! ah! ah! You can't fool me. There ain't no Santy Claus.

> Otis B. Driftwood (Groucho Marx) and Fiorello (Chico Marx) in *A Night at the Opera* (1935).

- We'd like a room and a bath, please.

- I can give you the room but you'll have to take the bath yourself.

> Mr. Hardy (Oliver Hardy) and the hotel clerk in *Bonnie Scotland* (1935).

The boys take over the direction of a movie:

Actor-You can count me out.

Curly-One, two, three, and four is ten. The winner! (*raising Moe's hand*).

Larry-You're out! (*to the actor*).

In *Movie Maniacs* (1936).

Man-Are you sure this will be in competent hands?

Curly-Soitanly, we're all incompetent.

> Man entrusting the boys with a $50,000 cabinet for reproduction in *Slippery Silks* (1936).

Larry-Keep cool!

Moe-I can't, it's hot in here.

> *Cash and Carry* (1937).

- Say, you're pretty.

  - You know, I was going to say the very same thing.

  - Well, why don't you say it. If you think you're pretty you have as much right to say it as I have.

> Gracie (Gracie Allen) coming out of the Tunnel of Love with Reggie (Ray Noble) in *A Damsel in Distress* (1937).

- She's here.

  - Who?

  - The girl who slapped you.

  - Where?

  - On the jaw.

> Gracie (Gracie Allen) at the window warning Jerry Halliday (Fred Astaire) that Lady Alyce (Joan Fontaine) is approaching in *A Damsel in Distress* (1937).

Hotel manager showing the room to the boys:

Manager-This bed goes back to Henry the Eighth.

Curly-That's nothing, we had a bed that went back to Sears-Roebuck the Third.

> In *Healthy, Wealthy and Dumb* (1938).

Manager-What kind of fool do you take me for?

Curly-Why, is there more than one kind?

> A hotel manager and Curly in *Saved by the Belle* (1939).

Curly-Look, a rooster bar.

Moe-You mean a crowbar.

Curly-Don't roosters crow?

> Curly picking up a crowbar in *Oily to Bed, Oily to Rise* (1939).

Rummy-Now, let me tell you a little bit about Sherry.

Moe-Oh, don't bother. I'll take scotch.

Larry-Make mine rye.

Curly-I'll take gin smothered in bourbon.

> Rummy/Rumsford wishes to explain his wife's nutty condition to Drs. Ziller, Zeller and Zoller in *Three Sappy People* (1939).

Secretary-Mata Herring is here to see you.

Moe Hailstone-Marinate her and send her in.

> In *You Nazty Spy!* (1940).

Discovering Mata Herring to be a spy:

Moe Hailstone-Just think. I might have asked Mata Herring to marry me.

Larry Gallstone-Yeah! You'd been in some pickle with that Herring.

> In *You Nazty Spy!* (1940).

I was going to thrash them within an inch of their lives but I didn't have a tape measure.

S. Quentin Quale (Groucho Marx) in *Go West* (1940).

Female voice on the telephone:

Voice-Hello. Have you got anything on tonight?

Curly-No, not a thing.

Voice-You'll catch cold.

In *I'll Never Heil Again* (1941).

Moe-Hey! You nit-wit. Don't saw the wings, saw the garage.

Curly-I see the garage, but I don't saw the garage. You are speaking incorrectly the King's English, etcetera. See? Saw? See?

Moe-You saw one side and Larry will saw the other.

Curly-Oh, I see. I saw.

In order to taxi The Buzzard, an airplane, out of the garage, Curly Wrong (as opposed to the Wright Bros.) started sawing off the wings in *Dizzy Pilots* (1943).

Nazi Spy-F.B.I.?

Curly-No, I.B. Curly.

In *They Stooge to Conga* (1943).

Curly-A pelican!

Moe-That's no pelican, it's a gander.

Curly-Mahatma Gander?

Moe-A gander, a gander, a goose's husband.

Larry-Yeah, a papa goose.

Curly-Do they have papa and mama goosises?

Larry-Oh, sure. And little baby gooses too.

Curly-I read about them. They come from Germany. The Goosestapo.

> The boys bought a farm in *The Yoke's on Me* (1944).

- I'll be in the supper club tonight. Will you join me?
  - Why? Are you coming apart?

> Ronald Kornblow's (Groucho Marx) reply to the invitation of a lady in *A Night in Casablanca* (1946).

- I'm Beatrice Reiner. I stop at the hotel.
  - I'm Ronald Kornblow. I stop at nothing.

> Beatrice Reiner (Lisette Verea) and Ronald Kornblow (Groucho Marx) in *A Night in Casablanca* (1946).

I've met a lot of pin-up girls but I've never been able to pin one down.

> Ronald Kornblow (Groucho Marx) in *A Night in Casablanca* (1946).

- Gentlemen, here are your quarters.
  - Oh, boy, two bits a piece.

> Mad Professor Panser (Vernon Dent) showing Curly Howard and the boys to their room in *A Bird in the Head* (1946).

Judge-Have you got any means of support?

Larry-Sure! I've got suspenders.

> In *Shivering Sherlocks* (1948).

- You have to call back Mr. Adams.

- The Third?

- No, he only called twice.

> Gladys Glover (Judy Holliday) and her landlady in *It Should Happen to You* (1954).

In a deserted house:

Shemp-I don't like deserted houses.

Larry-Why not? Maybe we'll get dessert.

> In *Of Cash and Hash* (1955).

If you're broken, it's because you're brittle.

> Eleanor of Aquitaine (Katharine Hepburn) to King Henry (Peter O'Toole) in *The Lion in Winter* (1968).

- Look at me! I'm the greatest! I'm number one!

- To me you look like number two. Know what I mean?

> Lionel Twain (Truman Capote), claiming to be the greatest detective, and Sam Diamond (Peter Falk) in *Murder by Death* (1976).

Without them (*alarm whistle, Mace, brass knuckles*) you're a walking light bulb waiting to be screwed.

> Stella (Marilyn Sokol) to Gloria (Goldie Hawn) in *Foul Play* (1978).

- I'll have a Coke.

- Do you want that in a can?

- No, I'll have it right here.

> Clark 'Sparky' Griswald (Chevy Chase) ordering a Coke from the airline hostess in *National Lampoon's European Vacation* (1985).

Most men I know only have one gun.

> Miss Tracy (Marilu Henner) to two-gun cowboy Rex
> O'Herlihan (Tom Berenger) in *Rustlers' Rhapsody* (1985).

- You have to be the most annoying man I ever met.
  - Do I have to?

> Kendal Winchester (David O'Brien) and Arthur Bach
> (Dudley Moore) in *Arthur 2: On the Rocks* (1988).

- I think you're going around the bend.
  - Oh, I hope so. I've always wanted to travel.

> Joe (Bernard Hill) to his wife Shirley (Pauline Collins) who
> talks to 'Wall' in *Shirley Valentine* (1989).

- Chester, you keep up the good work, this time next year you'll have ten men under you.
  - Eh, Dave, can you make it women?

> Dave Mullen (Tom Parks) complimenting his salesman
> Chester Lee (Rodney Dangerfield) acting as football
> coach of the *Ladybugs* (1992).

- Got a light?
  - Sure. (*Pulls out a flashlight.*)
  - How about a match?
  - No thanks. I've got plenty.

> Lola Cain (Sean Young) failing to light Ned Ravine's
> (Armand Assante) fire by asking him to light her cigarette
> in *Fatal Instinct* (1993).

- Well, if I can't buy you a drink, how about one of those?
  - Who can say no to a wiener.

- Who's that?!

- It's just the postman. He always rings twice.

Frank Kelbo (Christopher McDonald) adulterously kissing Lana Ravine (Kate Nelligan) when the front doorbell rings twice in *Fatal Instinct* (1993), an obvious reference to the thriller: *The Postman Always Rings Twice* (1946 & 1981).

- Not me.

Lola Cain (Sean Young) treating Ned Ravine (Armand Assante) to a hot hot-dog after failing to arouse his interest with everything else in *Fatal Instinct* (1993).

- Coffee?

- Sure.

- How would you like it?

- In a cup?

- Bold choice, Mr. Flintstone.

Miss Sharon Stone (Halle Berry) and Fred (John Goodman) in *The Flintstones* (1994).

Cracking Wise

How long do you stay fresh in that can?

Zeke, the Cowardly Lion (Bert Lahr) to Hickory, the Tin Woodsman (Jack Haley) in *The Wizard of Oz* (1939).

- Henri, we're lost! Absolutely lost!

- Is there a difference?

Lt. Catherine Gates (Ann Sheridan) and Capt. Henri Rochard (Cary Grant) in *I Was a Male War Bride* (1949).

- Has there been women in his life?

- I assume he must have had a mother.

Princess Aouda (Shirley MacLaine) and Passepartout (Cantinflas) speaking of the staid Phileas Fogg (David Niven) in *Around the World in 80 Days* (1956).

- They're killing me by inches, Dudley.

- You'll outlive us all. You've got a lot of inches.

> Cyrus (John Randolph) pleading with his boyfriend
> Dudley (Hume Cronyn) in *There Was a Crooked Man*
> (1970).

You know her problem? She wants balls.

> Jonathan (Jack Nicholson) speaking of Cindy (Rita
> Moreno) in *Carnal Knowledge* (1971).

Why don't you tell me the story of your life? Just skip everything except the last few minutes.

> Luke Matthews (James Coburn) to Carbo (Jan-Michael
> Vincent) in *Bite the Bullet* (1975).

Don't forget your trenchcoat. How is anybody going to recognize you without your disguise?

> Jonathan Hemlock (Clint Eastwood) in *The Eiger Sanction* (1975).

Getting to the bottom of things, Charleston?

> Sidney Wang (Peter Sellers) noticing Dick Charleston's
> (David Niven) hand on the bottom of his wife in *Murder
> by Death* (1976).

- Bond! What do you think you're doing?

- Keeping the British end up, Minister.

> James Bond's (Roger Moore) explanation to the British
> Minister about being naked in the survival bubble with
> the Russian agent Major Anya Amasova (Barbara Bach)
> in *The Spy Who Loved Me* (1977).

If you need me, just call. You know how to dial, don't you? You just put your finger in the hole and make tiny little circles.

> Juliet Forrest (Rachel Ward) to Rigby Reardon (Steve
> Martin) in *Dead Men Don't Wear Plaid* (1982).

- Look at you, with that silly smirk on your face.

- I tried a serious smirk but it didn't feel right.

Glenda Park (Goldie Hawn) and her ex-husband Nick Gardenia (Chevy Chase) in *Seems Like Old Times* (1980).

- I changed my life today. What did you do?

   - I changed my room at the hotel.

> Frank Galvin (Paul Newman) and Laura Fischer
> (Charlotte Rampling) in *The Verdict* (1982).

- I didn't hear you knock.

   - What a relief. I thought I was going deaf.

> Mike Murphy (Burt Reynolds) and Lt. Speer (Clint Eastwood),
> who enters without knocking in *City Heat* (1984).

- Assume the position.

   - Which one did you have in mind?

> FBI agent John Buckner (Kiefer Sutherland) and middle-
> aged activist hippie Huey Walker (Dennis Hopper) in
> *Flashback* (1990).

- I do not particularly like this side of you.

   - I'm not a box. I don't have sides. This is it: one side fits all.

> Jack Falkner (Dennis Quaid) and a furious Suzanne Vale
> (Meryl Streep) in *Postcards from the Edge* (1990).

In Other Words...YES!

You can chisel it in granite.

> Marshal Anderson (Arch Johnson) in *The Cheyenne
> Social Club* (1970).

Does oatmeal have lumps?

> Pepe Demascus (Dom DeLuise) in *The Cheap Detective* (1978).

Do birds fly, do ducks duck?

> David Addison (Bruce Willis) in the movie pilot for the
> television series *Moonlighting* (1985).

Do flies fly, do Spocks beam up?

> David Addison (Bruce Willis) in the movie pilot for the
> television series *Moonlighting* (1985).

Is a frog's ass watertight?

> Rosie (Lily Tomlin) in *Big Business* (1988).

Does a hobby horse have a wooden dick?

> Red Webster (Red West) in *Road House* (1989).

There you go! Does the pope wear a hat, was Sergeant York's mother an angel and will a banker grope for money?

> Judge Alvin Valkenheiser (Dan Aykroyd) in *Nothing but
> Trouble* (1991).

- Can you do it?

  - Is the earth flat?

> Barney (Rick Moranis) and Fred (John Goodman) in *The
> Flintstones* (1994).

- What is it that has four pair of pants, lives in Philadelphia and it never rains but it pours?

  - That's a good one. I give you three guesses.

Does Madonna take her clothes off? Does Saddam Hussein and Mohammar Kadafi pull each other's toffee? Yes, but I don't do windows.

Simon B. Wilder (Joe Pesci) when asked if he can cook in *With Honors* (1994).

Riddle Me This...

- Now let me see. Has four pairs of pants... Is it male or female?

- Oh I don't think so.

- Is he dead?

- Who?

- I don't know. I give up.

- I give up too.

Rufus T. Firefly (Groucho Marx) and Chicolini (Chico Marx) in *Duck Soup* (1933).

Tenny-You rang, Sir?

Hugh-Yes I rang. Why didn't you come the first time I called?

Tenny-Because the cook is deaf, Sir.

Hugh-Are we playing games, Tenny?

Tenny-No, Sir.

Hugh-Then riddle me the reason why you didn't come because the cook is deaf.

Tenny-Because if she were not deaf, Sir, she would have heard you, and if she had heard you she would have called me.

Hugh-And if she had called you, you would have heard her.

Tenny-I would have heard her and I would have come to you, Sir.

Hugh-You win, Tenny.

Tenni-What, Sir?

Hugh-Here. (*Gives him a cigar.*)

Captain Hugh C. Drummond (John Howard) and Tenny/Tennyson (E.E. Clive), who was in the garden, in *Bulldog Drummond Comes Back* (1937).

Moe-Take it easy! I just want to ask you a question. What would you rather have: a shoe full of dollar bills or two socks of fives?

Shemp-I'll take the two socks.

Moe-Got 'em! (*Socks him.*)

In *The Hot Scots* (1948).

- Alex, how can you tell if someone is lying?

- You can't.

- There must be a way.

- No. There's an old riddle about two tribes of Indians. The Whitefeet always tell the truth and the Blackfeet always lie. So one day you meet an Indian. You say: Hey, Indian, what are you? A truthful Whitefoot or a lying Blackfoot? He says: I'm a truthful Whitefoot. So, which is he?

- Why couldn't you just look at his feet?

- Because he's wearing moccasins.

- Well, then, he's a truthful Whitefoot of course.

- Why not a lying Blackfoot?

- Which one are you.

- A truthful Whitefoot.

- Come in. Sit down.

- Why? You want to look at my feet?

- Yes.

Eugenia Lampert/Regina (Audrey Hepburn) about to try
out her own lie-detector test (kissing) on Peter Joshua,
alias Carson Dyle, alias Alexander Dyle, alias Adam
Caulfield, alias Brian Crookshank (Cary Grant) in
Charade (1963).

- Do you know why six is afraid of seven?

- No.

- Because seven eight (ate) nine.

Steven Gold (Tom Hanks) and Lilah Krytsick (Sally Field)
in *Punchline* (1988).

Why is it that we don't always recognize the moment when love begins but we always know when it ends?

Harris K. Telemacher (Steve Martin) in *L.A. Story* (1991).

Look It Up!

Lady-I'm in a terrible dilemma.

Moe-I don't care for these foreign cars myself.

In *Punch Drunks* (1934).

Upset? Why, I'm housebroken!

Stannie Dum (Stan Laurel) in *March of the Wooden
Soldiers* (Original title: *Babes in Toyland*) (1934).

Gentlemen, I want to apologize. I'm at a loss for adjectives.

Moe and the boys caught leaving the restaurant with the
cutlery and other things in *Playing the Ponies* (1937).

The perambulation of the pedal extremity is impeded by the insertion of a foreign offshoot.

Doctor Moe's diagnostic for a thorn in a dog's paw in
Calling All Curs (1939).

Not only verbatim, but word for word.

- I have a Chippendale.

  - Does he sit up?

Effie, the bearded Lady-I love you!

  Curly- Don't be superstitious.

Are you casting asparagus on my cooking?

Moe-We eluded him.

  Curly-Yeah, and we got away too.

Brothers, you all ejaculated a mouthful.

Moe-It's tremendous!

  Larry-It's colossal!

  Shemp-It's putrid!

Mr. Oxley told me to be careful about my punctuation so I'm trying to get here before nine.

Miss Lois Laurel (Marilyn Monroe) in *Monkey Business* (1952).

Larry-He couldn't fool me that way.

Moe-No, you're too much of an ignoramus.

Larry-Yeah, and that goes for my whole family, too.

In *Baby Sitters Jitters* (1951).

Larry-We work as a unit.

Shemp-Yeah, we're Unitarians.

The boys are babysitters in *Baby Sitters Jitters* (1951).

I'm a chantooze.

Cherie (Marilyn Monroe), a singer or *chanteuse*, in *Bus Stop* (1956).

- A toast to the most ravishing creature in this cabin. You are ravishing, aren't you?

- Half ravishing, half Lithuanian.

Jeff (Tommy Noonan) and Sandra (Jayne Mansfield) in *Promises! Promises!* (1963).

I love to take pictures. I'm very photogenic.

Brofy (Ron Carey) in *High Anxiety* (1977).

34-Oh, oh.

Max-Just our luck! We had to run into a poisonous ACHTUNG.

34-That means ATTENTION.

Agent 34 (Sylvia Kristel) and Maxwell Smart (Don Adams) running their car into a snow bank marked by a German sign bearing the word ACHTUNG with a skull and cross-bones in *The Nude Bomb* (1980).

- Your bogusing generousness is straining my equinimity.

- Could you put that another way?

- You're pissing me off.

> KAOS fiend Norman Saint Savage, the clone of Nino Salvatore Sebastini (Vittorio Gassman) to his prisoner Maxwell Smart (Don Adams) who offers him a quick execution if he surrenders himself, his men and his arsenal of nude bombs in *The Nude Bomb* (1980).

John Candy

Oh, Shirley, we haven't had meat in this house for years. Didn't you know we'd become vegans?

- No, I thought you were still Church of England.

> Gillian (Julia McKenzie) and her neighbor Shirley (Pauline Collins) in *Shirley Valentine* (1989).

You've got the right ta-ta but the wrong ho-ho.

> Dean Andrews (John Candy) in *JFK* (1991).

Mangled Metaphors

Mrs. Rittenhouse, ever since I met you, I've swept you off my feet.

> Captain Jeffrey Spaulding (Groucho Marx) to Mrs. Rittenhouse (Margaret Dumont) in *Animal Crackers* (1930).

A man in the house is worth two in the streets.

Ruby Carter (Mae West) in *Belle of the Nineties* (1934).

Remember the old adage: You can lead a horse to water but a pencil must be lead.

Stan Laurel explaining to Oliver Hardy that he shouldn't threaten the *Brats* (1930).

The man that hesitates is last.

Ruby Carter (Mae West) to an admirer in *Belle of the Nineties* (1934).

You're right, Ollie. You can't turn blood into a stone.

Stannie Dum (Stan Laurel) to Ollie Dee (Oliver Hardy) in *March of the Wooden Soldiers* (Original title: *Babes in Toyland*) (1934).

Larry-All for one!

Moe-One for all!

Curly-All for me!

(or)-I'll take care of myself!

(Larry) Duke of Durum, (Moe) Count of Fife, (Curly) Baron of Greymanor in *Restless Knights* (1935).

- I can feel the noose around my neck now.

- Don't worry. No noose is good noose.

The lackeys (The Ritz Brothers) impersonating King's musketeers in *The Three Musketeers* (1939).

Someday this bitter ache will pass, my sweet. Time wounds all heels.

S. Quentin Quale (Groucho Marx) in *Go West* (1940).

Two black eyes won't make a white one, Bill.

Major Barbara (Wendy Hiller) to Bill Walker (Robert Newton) in *Major Barbara* (1941).

Absence makes the heart grow fainter.

> Molly McGee (Marion Jordan) to Julie Patterson (Lucille Ball) in *Look Who's Laughing* (1941).

The way to a woman's heart is to get her out of the kitchen.

> Warrick (Sir Cedric Hardwicke) in *Valley of the Sun* (1942).

You've been bossing me long enough. Now the worm has turned and every dog had his day.

> Sheriff Chester Wooley (Lou Costello) to his new deputy Duke Egan (Bud Abbott) in *The Wistful Widow of Wagon Gap* (1947).

Keep a stiff upper plate, kid.

> Moe to Shemp in *Studio Stooges* (1950).

Up here, boys! They're starving an artist.

> Gulley Jimson (Alec Guinness) to the cops coming not to his rescue but to arrest him from stealing Lord Hickson's property in *The Horse's Mouth* (1958).

I don't know how fast he moves but it takes an early bird to get the best of a worm like me.

> Jonathan Forbes (Tony Randall) bungling his metaphors in *Pillow Talk* (1959).

Cross my heart and kiss my elbow.

> Holly Golightly (Audrey Hepburn) in *Breakfast at Tiffany's* (1961).

Well, just don't do something! Sit there!

> Professor Julius Kelp (Jerry Lewis) in *The Nutty Professor* (1963).

What in the wide, wild world of sport is going on here?

> Taggart (Slim Pickens) to his dancing railroad workers in *Blazing Saddles* (1974).

I have friends in low places.

> James Bond (Roger Moore) in *Moonraker* (1979).

When the going gets tough, the tough go to Greece.

> Jack Conton (Michael Douglas) in *The Jewel of the Nile* (1985).

Without me there would be nothing. Not even you. *Cogito ergo est:* I think, therefore you is.

> The King of the Moon (Robin Williams) in *The Adventures of Baron Munchausen* (1989). A variation on *cogito ego sum:* "I think therefore I am."

Moonraker

Daddy always says an once of pretention is worth a pound of manure.

> Shelby Eatenton (Julia Roberts) in *Steel Magnolias* (1989).

Ouiser could never stay mad at me. She worships the quicksand I walk on.

> Clairee Belcher (Olympia Dukakis) speaking of Ouiser Boudreaux (Shirley MacLaine) in *Steel Magnolias* (1989).

- My God! What have I done?

- I'll tell you what you've done. You've realized something it takes most people a whole lifetime to figure out and some people never figure it out at all: that a bird in the hand is always greener than the grass under the other guy's bushes... It's a metaphor used mostly by gardeners and landscape people in general.

> North (Elijah Wood) and Joey Fingers (Bruce Willis) mixing his metaphors in *North* (1994).

Remember, kid, if you can't stand the heat stay out of Miami.

> Joey Fingers (Bruce Willis) to North (Elijah Wood) in *North* (1994).

Who am I? What am I? Where do I come from? As I remember it I started life down the road most travelled.

> Pat's (Julia Sweeney) opening monologue in *It's Pat—The Movie* (1994).

Bruce Willis and Elijah
Wood in *North*

Petey! What's up, pup?

> Stymie (Kevin Jamal Woods) to Petey, the dog, paraphrasing Bugs Bunny's famous line: What's up, doc? in *The Little Rascals* (1994).

Like a midget at a urinal I was going to have to stay on my toes.

> Lt. Frank Drebin (Leslie Nielsen) posing, in prison, as Mike "The Slasher" McGurk in *The Naked Gun 33 1/3: The Final Insult* (1994).

- Oh, Darla, we're two hearts with but one beat, two brains with but one thought, two souls with but one... shoe.

- Oh, Alfalfa, you're a sweety-poo.

Alfalfa (Bug Hall) romancing Darla (Brittany Ashton Holmes) in *The Little Rascals* (1994).

Joe, you're the longest boyfriend I've ever had in Los Angeles, but I can't take it anymore. I want respectability. I want a house with a picket fence. I want children parked in the garage. I want a station wagon playing in the yard.

Jane Wine (Charlene Tilton) to FBI agent Jo Dee Fostar (Billy Zane) in *Silence of the Hams* (1994).

Tongue Twisters

I now take great pleasure in presenting to you the well-preserved and partially pickled Mrs. Potter.

Mr. Hammer (Groucho Marx) introducing Mrs. Potter (Margaret Dumont) in *Cocoanuts* (1929).

You dare to come to me for a heart, do you? You clinking, clanking, clattering collection of collisonous junk?

The Wizard (Frank Morgan) to Hickory, the Tin Woodsman (Jack Haley) in *The Wizard of Oz* (1939).

- You are the epitome of erudition; a double superlative. Can you handle it?

- Yeah! And I can kick it around too.

Cuthbert J. Twillie (W.C. Fields) and Flower Belle Lee (Mae West) in *My Little Chickadee* (1940).

- Big Stinker McGee I was know'ed as in those days. Big Stinker McGee, the brawny and branny Bonaparte of the benzine buggy blacksmith, busy as a beaver and bright as a beacon at bolting bumper brackets on big bus bodies bringing back the bacon as boss of the Biggs band of bumblebees of the brace and bit and big bullfrog of the brass bicycle bell bongers; a breezy brilliant so-so beginning for a bright boy... but here's my pride and joy, a dish-washing jalopy.

   - Would you mind repeating that again?

> Fibber McGee (Jim Jordan) to Edgar Bergen (as himself)
> about the old days at the Biggs Machine Shop and
> showing off his invention, The McGee Wife Saver, in
> Look Who's Laughing (1941).

Gildy-Why you anemic little anthropological aberration!

Fibber-Who's an anthological abbreviation?

Gildy-You are!

Fibber-I am not.

Molly-You are too!

Gildy-He is not!

Molly-Well, make up your mind.

> Gildy/Gildersleeve (Harold Peary), Fibber McGee (Jim
> Jordan) and Molly McGee (Marion Jordan) reversing the
> argument in Fibber's favor in Look Who's Laughing (1941).

- What I want to do is, get in, get on with it, get it over with, and get out. Get it?

   - Got it!

   - Good.

> Hawkins (Danny Kaye) and Sir Ravenhurst (Basil
> Rathbone) in The Court Jester (1956).

The sleaziest sleaze of the seven seas, Captain James Hook.

> Smee (Bob Hoskins) complimenting Captain James Hook
> (Dustin Hoffman) in Hook (1991).

Tall Tales

I can start a fire by rubbing two boyscouts together and I can even cross a river in a paper bag when I'm in a good form.

> McCool (David Niven) trying to convince Dr. Bill Canavan (Gary Cooper) to take him along on his mission in *The Real Glory* (1939).

Where did you pick up them five-gallon words?

> Andy Brock (Raymond Massey) to the Nazi officer in *49th Parallel* (U.S. title: *The Invaders*) (1941).

I wouldn't come back two inches to get her.

> Billy the Kid (Jack Beutel) speaking of Rio MacDonald (Jane Russell) in *The Outlaw* (1943).

What a story! Everything but the bloodhounds snapping at her rear end.

> Birdie (Thelma Ritter) commenting on Eve Harrington's (Anne Baxter) hard-luck story in *All About Eve* (1950).

Mind you, my throat was only slightly cut from ear to ear.

> Actor-valet Humphrey/Earl of Brinstead (Bob Hope) telling the story of his adventures as a British officer in *Fancy Pants* (1950).

I wouldn't believe anything you say if it was tattooed on your forehead.

> Dorothy Shaw (Jane Russell) to Malone (Elliott Reid) in *Gentlemen Prefer Blondes* (1953).

Compared to Clouseau, Attila the Hun was a Red Cross volunteer.

> Chief inspector Dreyfus (Herbert Lom) in *The Return of the Pink Panther* (1982).

Missed it by that much.

One of Maxwell Smart's (Don Adams) catch-phrases in the *Get Smart* television series and in the movies *Nude Bomb* (1980) and *Get Smart, Again!* (1989). Usually he was shot at (Missed me by that much) or shoots at something and misses. In *The Nude Bomb* (1980) he accidentally fires his gun while slipping it into his belt, turns around, peeks a look, turns back to the camera and spreads the thumb and forefinger.

You want to play games, I can play games. I can play ventriloquist with my underwear, I can play darts while maintaining an erection, I can gargle dishwater and fart "O Canada" at the same time, I can play the piano without being popular. I once had this dream I was dancing on a streetcorner with a jackhammer up my ass. Now let's see. It's either a sex dream or I need more fiber in my diet. If any of this is turning you on just let me know.

Steven Gold (Tom Hanks) to a
female talent scout in *Punchline*
(1988).

Bob Hope and
Bing Crosby

- Dementi, your demented plan will not work.

- Why not?

- Because at this very moment this warehouse is surrounded by one-hundred cops with Doberman pinschers. Would you believe it? One-hundred cops with Doberman pinschers.

- I find that hard to believe.

- Would you believe ten security guards and a bloodhound?

- I don't think so.

- How about a Boy Scout with rabies?

Maxwell Smart (Don Adams) and KAOS fiend Dementi
(Harold Gould) in *Get Smart, Again!* (1989).

- Now, Smart, I want an honest evaluation. Are you in good enough physical condition to return to active duty as a counter-intelligence agent? You appear to be in pretty good shape. Do you work out?

- Commander, I jog one hundred miles every day. Would you believe it? One hundred miles.

- I find that hard to believe.

- Would you believe fifty?

- No.

- How about two push-ups and a deep breath?

> Commander Drury (Kenneth Mars) and Maxwell Smart
> (Don Adams) in *Get Smart, Again!* (1989).

Express Yourself

Well, strike me pink!

> Guy Holden (Fred Astaire) in *The Gay Divorcee* (1934).

Well, dog my cats!

> Colonel Buffalo Bill's (Moroni Olsen) catch-phrase in
> *Annie Oakley* (1935). This exclamation was repeated by
> Uncle Jed (Jim Varney) in *The Beverly Hillbillies* (1993).

Well cut off my legs and call me shorty!

> Brogan (Edward Brophy) greeting Nick Charles (William
> Powell) in *The Thin Man Goes Home* (1944).

It's so drafty!

> Jerry (Jack Lemmon) dressed as a woman in *Some Like It
> Hot* (1959).

Ni!

> The Knights who say the above
> in *Monty Python and the Holy
> Grail* (1975).

Butler did it!

> Sidney Wang (Peter Sellers) in
> *Murder by Death* (1976).

Holy merde!

> Milo Perrier's (James Coco)
> Belgian version of holy shit in
> *Murder by Death* (1976).

May the Force be with you.

> Luke Skywalker (Mark Hamil), Han Solo
> (Harrison Ford), Ben 'Obi-Wan' Kenobi
> (Alec Guinness) in *Star Wars* (1977), *The
> Empire Strikes Back* (1980), *Return of the
> Jedi* (1983). Parodied by: (1) Mel Brooks, as
> Yogurt, in *Spaceballs* (1987): "May the Schwartz be with you." (2)
> Leslie Nielsen, as Father Jedediah Mayii, to Anthony Starke, as Father
> Luke Brophy in *Repossessed* (1990): "May the Faith be with you." (3)
> Eddie Murphy, as Axel Foley, to Judge Reinhold, as Billy Rosewood,
> in a 'hot pursuit' in *Beverly Hills Cop II* (1987): "Are you driving with
> your eyes open or are you, like, using the Force?"

Are we having fun yet?

> Kate (Carol Burnett) repeatedly in *The Four Seasons* (1981). Steve
> Martin, as C.D. Bales, has the same line in *Roxanne* (1987).

He slimed me!

> Dr. Peter Venkman (Bill Murray) meeting a slimy ghost in
> *Ghostbusters* (1984).

Chilly Jack Lemmon
and Tony Curtis in
Some Like it Hot

Julia Roberts and
Richard Gere in
Pretty Woman

Now! Let's turn on
the juice and see what
shakes loose.

Betelgeuse (Michael
Keaton) in *Beetlejuice*
(1988).

Well, color me happy!

Vivian Ward (Julia Roberts)
in *Pretty Woman* (1990).

Hasta la vista, baby!

The Terminator (Arnold
Schwarzenegger) learns
1990s American English from the kid and repeats the
line when shooting bad guys in *The Terminator 2-
Jugement Day* (1990). (1) Rephrased by Antonio Motel
(Ezio Greggio) in *The Silence of the Hams* (1994): "Hasta
la baby, vista!"

Dirty-pool old man! I like it!

Gomez (Raul Julia) to his lawyer Tully Alford (Dan
Hedaya) in *The Addams Family* (1991).

Great gobs of goose shit!

Rancher Clay Stone (Noble Willingham) in *City Slickers*
(1991).

Holy testicle Tuesday!

Ace Ventura (Jim Carrey) in *Ace
Ventura, Pet Detective* (1994).

We are scrapnoids!

Alien (from outer-space) Beldar Conehead (Dan
Aykroyd) when their house is besieged by immigration
agents in *Coneheads* (1993).

Eat my shorts!

Max Goldman (Walter Matthau) to John Gustafson (Jack
Lemmon) in *Grumpy Old Men* (1993).

Why don't you bore a hole in yourself and let the sap run
out.

Professor Quincy Adams Wagstaff (Groucho Marx) to
student Baravelli (Chico Marx) in *Horse Feathers* (1932).

Remember! We're fighting for this woman's honor, which is
probably more than she ever did.

Rufus T. Firefly (Groucho Marx) in *Duck Soup* (1933).

- Don't make me laugh.

- If I could make you laugh I'd go out and get drunk.

- You couldn't make a hyena laugh.

Happy (Ned Sparks) and Missouri Martin (Glenda
Farrell) in *Lady for a Day* (1933).

Hey! you big bully. What's the idea of hitting that little
bully?

Otis B. Driftwood (Groucho Marx) to Rodolfo Lassparri
(Walter King) in *A Night at the Opera* (1935).

- We're intellectual opposites.

- What do you mean?

You're a social disease. I don't like your disposition, I don't like your friends, I don't like your politics, and I don't like your hat. Your faithful denizens may stick to you but you're still a small noise at the end of a parade.

O'Hara (Gary Cooper) to General Yang (Akim Tamiroff) in *The General Died at Dawn* (1936).

- I'm intellectual and you're opposite.

Cleo Borden (Mae West) and gigolo Ivan Valadov (Ivan Lebedeff) in *Goin' to Town* (1935).

- I'm an aristocrat and the backbone of my family.

- Your family should see a chiropractor.

Ivan Valadov (Ivan Lebedeff) and Cleo Borden (Mae West) in *Goin' to Town* (1935).

- I'll send you a postcard, Granny.

- Who are you going to get to write it for you? The horse?

Blossom (Nat Pendleton), going to the races in Virginia, and Granny (May Robson) in *Reckless* (1935).

Don't just stand there like a petrified forest.

Tempermental actress Cherry Chester (Margaret Sullavan) to her servants in *The Moon's Our Home* (1936).

A bit fond of yourself, aren't you?

Edgar Brodie/Richard Ashenden (John Gielgud) to Elsa Carrington (Madeleine Carroll) who responds by slapping his face in *Secret Agent* (1936).

Don't look at me! What do you think I am? A peep show?

Dr. Hugo Hackenbush (Groucho Marx) in *A Day at the Races* (1937).

- Well, I've never been so insulted in my life.

- Well... (*looking at his watch*) it's early yet.

Flo (Esther Muir) and Dr. Hugo Z. Hackenbush (Groucho Marx) in *A Day at the Races* (1937).

Now that you've got the mine, I'll bet you'll be a swell gold digger.

> Stan Laurel to Mary Roberts (Rosina Lawrence) in *Way Out West* (1937).

You oughta be stuffed with nails.

> Eliza Doolittle (Wendy Hiller) to Professor Henry Higgins (Leslie Howard) in *Pygmalion* (1938). Audrey Hepburn to Rex Harrison in the musical version *My Fair Lady* (1964).

Why don't you trade in your head for a bowling ball?

> J. Cheever Loophole (Groucho Marx) to Tony (Chico Marx) in *At the Circus* (1939).

I'll bet your father spent the first year of your life throwing rocks at the stork.

> J. Cheever Loophole (Groucho Marx) to Tony (Chico Marx) in *At the Circus* (1939).

You're a conceited black-hearted varmint, Rhett Butler!

> Scarlett O'Hara (Vivien Leigh) to Rhett Butler (Clark Gable) in *Gone with the Wind* (1939).

You're half brother to a weasel.

> Moe to Curly in *Oily to Bed, Oily to Rise* (1939).

Curly-Wait a minute! You know I'm temperamental.
  Moe-Yeah! 90% temper, 5% mental.

> In *Saved by the Belle* (1939).

Why don't you get a toupee with some brains in it?!

> Moe to Larry in *Three Sappy People* (1939).

You must come down with me after the show to the lumber yard and ride piggy-back on the buzz-saw.

> Larson E. Whipsnade (W.C. Fields) to Charlie McCarthy (voice of Edgar Bergen) in *You Can't Cheat an Honest Man* (1939).

Are you eating a tomato, or is that your nose?

> Charlie McCarthy (voice of Edgar Bergen) to Larson E. Whipsnade (W.C. Fields) in *You Can't Cheat an Honest Man* (1939).

Shut up or I'll throw a woodpecker at you.

> Larson E. Whipsnade (W.C. Fields) to Charlie McCarthy in *You Can't Cheat an Honest Man* (1939).

We think you're the softest hard-boiled egg in the world.

> Charlie McCarthy (voice of Edgar Bergen) to Larson E. Whipsnade (W.C. Fields) in *You Can't Cheat an Honest Man* (1939).

- Shall I bounce a rock off his head?

- Show respect for your father, darling. What kind of rock?

> Elsie Mae Adele Sousé (Evelyn Del Rio) and her mother Agatha Sousé (Cora Witherspoon) speaking of Egbert Sousé (W.C. Fields) in *The Bank Dick* (1940).

I've seen better specimens in a glass jar.

> Marc (James Craig) commenting on Kitty's (Ginger Rogers) roommate in *Kitty Foyle* (1940).

Moe-You've got brains like Napoleon.

Larry-Napoleon is dead.

Moe-I know it.

In *No Census, No Feeling* (1940).

Remember this, Pig, you're the one man in the world I can never get low enough to touch.

Julie (Joan Crawford) to M'sieu Pig (Peter Lorre) in
Strange Cargo (1940).

Larry-What's the matter with him?

Curly-He's a little grouchy. Got up on the wrong side of the gutter this morning.

Speaking of dictator Moe Hailstone in *You Nazty Spy!*
(1940).

You look like the last grave over near the willow.

Jean (Barbara Stanwyck) to Charlie/Hopsie (Henry
Fonda) in *The Lady Eve* (1941).

- Watch me, Charlie. I'll make a perfect three point landing.

- Yeah, two trees and a fence.

Edgar Bergen (as himself) landing his private plane with
Charlie McCarthy in *Look Who's Laughing* (1941).

He gets a cold just from reading a weather report.

> Julie Patterson (Lucille Ball) about her boss Edgar Bergen
> (as himself) in *Look Who's Laughing* (1941).

I don't mind a parasite; I object to a cut-rate one.

> Rick/Richard Blain (Humphrey Bogart) to Ugarte (Peter
> Lorre) in *Casablanca* (1942).

You are sort of attractive, in a corn-fed sort of way. I can imagine some poor girl falling in love with you if, well, you throw in a set of dishes.

> Maggie Cutler (Bette Davis) to Bert Jefferson (Dick Travis)
> in *The Man Who Came to Dinner* (1942).

- I want to talk to you, man to man.

  - Yeah? Who's going to hold up your end?

> Jeff Peters (Bing Crosby) and Orville 'Turkey' Jackson
> (Bob Hope) in *The Road to Morocco* (1942).

Oh, a termite with dandruff.

> Curly examining Moe's head after pulling it through a
> wall in *They Stooge to Conga* (1943).

Moe-We're rich!

  Larry-We're filthy with dough.

  Moe-You're filthy without it.

> In *If a Body Meets a Body* (1945).

- It seems to me we've met somewhere before.

  - I don't think so.

- Perhaps in your dreams?

- You wouldn't be seen in those kind of places.

> Sal (Dorothy Lamour) and Chester Hooton (Bob Hope) in
> *The Road to Utopia* (1945).

The world speaks of one missing link but I swear I see three.

> Professor Quackenbush looking at The Three Stooges in
> *Half-Wit's Holiday* (1947).

Shemp-She's fainted! Fellahs, help!

  Moe-Get some water, quick.

  Shemp-What happened?

  Moe-She musta got a good look at you.

> A woman faints in Shemp's arms in *Crime on their Hands*
> (1948).

Mr. Mitchum, you're a blackguard, a liar, a hypocrite and a stench in the nostril of honest men.

> Colonel Thursday (Henry Fonda) to a corrupt Indian
> agent in *Fort Apache* (1948).

What are you doing out in broad daylight?

> Slip Mahoney (Leo Gorcey) to Rick Martin (Craig
> Stevens) in *Blues Busters* (1950).

- I warn you, you're driving me crazy

  - That's no drive, that's a short put.

> Pfc. Korwin (Jerry Lewis) and Sgt. Puccinelli (Dean
> Martin) in *At War with the Army* (1950).

Jerry Lewis and
Dean Martin

Well I ain't sorry no more, you crazy,
psalm-singing, skinny old maid.

Charlie Allnut (Humphrey Bogart) furious at Rosie
Sayer (Katharine Hepburn) in *The African Queen*
(1951).

Last night you were a small annoyance
but today you are growing into a large
nuisance.

Lise Bouvier (Leslie Caron) to Jerry Mulligan (Gene
Kelly) in *An American in Paris* (1951).

I wouldn't want him if he was dipped in
gold dust.

Angel (Gloria Grahame) about Sebastian (Cornel
Wilde) in *The Greatest Show on Earth* (1952).

I wouldn't take you if you were covered
with diamonds, upside down.

Lynn Markham (Joan Crawford) to Drummond Hall (Jeff
Chandler) in *Female on the Beach* (1955).

You know, Russ, aside from your ruthlessness, there aren't
many things about you I admire.

Jeremiah McDonald (Lee J. Cobb) to producer Russell
'Russ' Ward (Clark Gable) in *But Not For Me* (1959).

He's so low when they bury him they'll have to dig up.

Connie (Audrey Meadows) in *That Touch of Mink* (1962).

- I'll be waiting in the car, Angie.

- If it's a compact you'll never get your head in.

Stage director Dion Kapakos (Rip Torn) and critic Parker Ballantine (Bob Hope) in *Critic's Choice* (1963).

Filthy swine!

Pronounced with a French accent, *svine*, it is Inspector Clouseau's (Peter Sellers) favorite insult in *A Shot in the Dark* (1964) and other Pink Panther movies. Even animals are not spared: "Swine parrot!" in *The Return of the Pink Panther* (1982).

Peters Sellers and Herbert Lom in *The Pink Panther Strikes Again*

- How do you want your eggs? Poached, fried or raw?

- Scrambled, like your head.

The maid (Phyllis Diller) and Tom Meade (Bob Hope) in *Boy! Did I Get a Wrong Number!* (1966).

You fish-faced enemy of the people.

Max Bialystock (Zero Mostel) to Leo Bloom (Gene Wilder) in *The Producers* (1967).

Howard, you're the largest pocket of untapped natural gas known to man.

Mark Wallace (Albert Finney) to Wallace/Howie/Rooty (William Daniels) in *Two for the Road* (1967).

All the facts about you are insults.

> Horace Vandergelder (Walter Matthau) in *Hello, Dolly!*
> (1969).

- Isn't it a little past your bedtime?

- It used to be. In those days I didn't have much to keep me awake.

- In those days it wasn't easy to tell when you were awake.

> Frank Benson (Bob Hope) meeting his ex-wife Elaine
> (Jane Wyman) in a nightclub in *How to Commit
> Marriage* (1969).

You look like a hog on ice.

> Rooster Cogburn (John Wayne) to Mattie Ross (Kim
> Darby) in *True Grit* (1969).

Shut up, you Teutonic twat!

> Hedley Lamarr (Harvey Korman) to Lili Von Shtup
> (Madeline Kahn) in *Blazing Saddles* (1974).

They couldn't find a fart in a rain barrel.

> Murphy (Charles Durning) speaking of the prison guards
> in *The Front Page* (1974).

It's a statement of fact, Miss Twain, that as a man you are barely passable but as a woman, you are a dog.

> Milo Perrier (James Coco) in *Murder by Death* (1976).

You're a cliché. Nowhere, on your way to no place.

> Stephanie (Karen Lynn Gorney) to Tony (John Travolta) in
> *Saturday Night Fever* (1977).

- Up yours, Mister.

  - Same to you, with ear flaps.

> Ann Atkinson (Glenda Jackson) and Charley Nichols
> (Walter Matthau) in *House Calls* (1978).

You're just walking around to save funeral expenses.

> Charlotta (Valerie Perrine) to the down and out
> anachronistic cowboy Sonny Steele (Robert Redford) in
> *The Electric Horseman* (1979).

Eat lead, Sled!

> Captain Wild Bill Kelso (John Belushi) in *1941* (1979).
> The television series *Police Squad* (1982) had a good
> variation: "Eat lead, copper!"

You're a wuss, part wimp and part pussy.

> Mike Damone (Robert Romanus) to his girl-shy friend
> Mark 'Rat' Ratner (Brian Backer) in *Fast Times at
> Ridgemont High* (1982).

What the hell happened to you anyway? You look like forty
miles of rough road.

> Walt (Dean Stockwell) meeting his brother Travis (Harry
> Dean Stanton) after four years of absence in *Paris, Texas*
> (1984).

- May I suggest something?

  - You do suggest something. A baboon.

> Gil Turner (Ed Begley, Jr.) and Jack Harrison (Jeff
> Goldblum) in *Transylvania 6-5000* (1985).

You know what you are? You're an ass-half. It takes two of
you to make an ass-hole.

> Joey O'Brien (Robin Williams) in *Cadillac Man* (1990).

- Tell him, Ray.

- K-Mart sucks.

Charlie Babbitt (Tom Cruise) and his brother Raymond's (Dustin Hoffman) commentary on K-Mart after making quite a fuss about his boxer shorts and suit having to be from K-Mart in *Rain Man* (1988).

You would-be smoothie!

> Mickey Cohen (Harvey Keitel) to Ben Siegel (Warren Beatty) in *Bugsy* (1991).

I crap bigger than you!

> Trail boss Curly (Jack Palance) to Mitch Robbins (Billy Crystal) in *City Slickers* (1991).

I doubt you know crap from Crisco.

> Old Dr. Hogue (Barnard Hughes) to young Dr. Ben Stone (Michael J. Fox) in *Doc Hollywood* (1991).

Hey! You want a personality? Try this on for size. You can be a real bitch.

> Ann Napolitano (Mercedes Ruehl) to Lydia Sinclair (Amanda Plummer) in *The Fisher King* (1991).

Go suck a bug!

> Alvin Valkenheiser (Dan Aykroyd) to Dennis (John Candy) in *Nothing But Trouble* (1991).

You're a real Blue Flame Special, aren't you, son? Young, dumb and full of come!

> Ben Harp (John McGinley) to Johnny Utah (Keanu Reeves) in *Point Break* (1991).

Don't you know a kid always wins against two idiots?

> Kevin McCallister (Macaulay Culkin) to Marv (Daniel Stern) in *Home Alone 2: Lost in New York* (1992).

Grow feathers and shit in a tree.

> Gwen (Goldie Hawn) to Newton (Steve Martin) in *Housesitter* (1992).

You're interesting. You're sooo... average.

> Gwen (Goldie Hawn) to Newton (Steve Martin) in
> *Housesitter* (1992).

What a lady! When she walks into a room mice jump on chairs.

> Chester Lee (Rodney Dangerfield) speaking about Coach
> Annie (Nancy Parsons) in *Ladybugs* (1992).

Boy, you're getting on my last nerve.

> Diane Sway (Marie-Louise Parker) to her son Mark (Brad
> Renfro) in *The Client* (1994).

- Warden, why are you doing this?

- Edie, if I had my way you'd be under lock and key for the rest of your sorry days. As far as I'm concerned you are living proof that on occasions God makes mistakes. You don't deserve oxygen, let alone freedom.

> Edie (Beverly D'Angelo) being thrown out of jail by the
> Warden (Nell Carter) in *The Crazy Sitter* (1994).

Say AHHH! (*Puts a gun into his mouth.*) Don't act like it's the first time.

> Shame (Keenen Ivory Wayans) to a bad guy in *A Low
> Down Dirty Shame* (1994).

- One day, we will meet again.

- Next time bring some mouthwash.

> The bad guy, Chan Yung Fat (Craig Ryan Ng), and the
> good guy, Shame (Keenen Ivory Wayans), in *A Low
> Down Dirty Shame* (1994).

- Well, if it isn't Waldo. All the money in the world is no substitute for hard work and ingenuity.

- You lead a rich fantasy life.

- Thank you.

- Moron.

Spanky (Travis Tedford) comparing his makeshift go-cart to Waldo's (Blake McIver Ewing) fancy racer in *The Little Rascals* (1994).

You're scum between my toes.

Alfalfa (Bug Hall) pretending to write a hate letter to Darla in *The Little Rascals* (1994).

- You snod-wads stole our racer.

- Finders keepers, losers suck.

- Ahhhh, bite me!

Spanky (Travis Tedford), Butch (Sam Saletta), and Alfalfa (Bug Hall) in *The Little Rascals* (1994).

See Ya, Wouldn't Wanna Be Ya!

I wouldn't go for that dame if she was the last woman on earth... and I'd just got out of the navy.

Matt Nolan (James Cagney) in *Taxi!* (1932).

- Wait 'til you see how I'll grow on you.

- Yeah, like a carbuncle.

E. 'Eddy' Huntington Hall (Clark Gable) and Rudy Adams
(Jean Harlow) in Hold Your Man (1933).

- I'm a man of few words.
  - I'm a man of one word: scram!

Ambassador Trentino (Louis Calhern) and Rufus T. Firefly
(Groucho Marx) in Duck Soup (1933).

I wouldn't take that woman back if she and I were the last people in the world... and the future of the human race depended on it.

Producer-director Oscar Jaffe (John Barrymore) about
stage star Lily Garland/Mildred Plotka (Carole Lombard)
in Twentieth Century (1934).

- Molly Monahan!

- Dick! Sure, Dick, they told me you'd not be back this year.

- Did you think you'd get rid of me that easy? (...) Every minute that passed had your name on it.

- Oh, oh, that's easy to listen to but hard to believe. Me father says...

- That he doesn't like gamblers.

- Neither do I. Here you are practicing to fleece the poor lambs at the end of track.

- Marry me, Molly, and I'll reform.

- You haven't changed a bit except maybe for the worst. You're in love with her and her three sisters. You've got cards in your blood.

- And you in my heart.

- Go along with your soft talk. You'll die with your boots on and your four ladies won't be walking behind you.

- Would you walk behind me?

- Hmmm, it would be safer than walking besides you to the altar.

- All the pasteboard ladies in the world aren't worth one of your little fingers... with a ring on it.

- I'd better be getting back to the caboose.

> Gambler Dick Allan (Robert Preston) and Molly Monahan (Barbara Stanwyck), with an Irish brogue, meeting on the train in *Union Pacific* (1939).

- What about our date? Aren't you going to see me?

- The next time I see you I hope you're stuffed with cloves in a delicatessen window.

> Don Bolton (Bob Hope) and Tony Fairbanks (Dorothy Lamour), calling him a ham, in *Caught in the Draft* (1941).

If you come to New York, Doctor, try and find me.

> Sheridan 'Sheri' Whiteside (Monty Woolley) to the boring Dr. Bradley (George Barbier) in *The Man Who Came to Dinner* (1942).

I wish I had a laugh left in me. Shall I tell you something, Sheri? I think you're a selfish, petty egomaniac who would just as soon see his mother burning at the stake if that was the only way he had of lighting a cigarette. I think you'd sacrifice your best friend without a moment's hesitation if he interrupted the sacred ritual of your self-centered, paltry little life. I think you're incapable of any emotion higher up than your stomach and I was a fool of the world for ever trusting you.

> Maggie Cutler (Bette Davis) to her boss and friend Sheridan 'Sheri' Whiteside (Monty Woolley) in *The Man Who Came to Dinner* (1942).

You know, you don't have to act with me, Steve. You don't have to say anything. You don't have to do anything. Not a thing. Oh! maybe just whistle. You know how to whistle, don't you, Steve? You just put your lips together and blow.

Slim (Lauren Bacall) to Harry (Steve to her) (Humphrey Bogart) in *To Have and Have Not* (1944).

Humphrey Bogart and Lauren Bacall

- Looks like we're in the cold.

 - Perhaps we should keep each other warm.

 - Listen, buster, the only way you can keep me warm is to wrap me up in a marriage license.

Angel (Gloria Grahame) and Sebastian (Cornel Wilde), old lovers abandoned by their new ones in *The Greatest Show on Earth* (1952).

Try to get this straight. There is nothing between us. There never was anything between us. Just air.

Don Lockwood (Gene Kelly) to Lena Lamont (Jean Hagen) in *Singing in the Rain* (1952).

- Just how many kinds of fool are you?

 - Not your kind.

Matt Calder (Robert Mitchum) and Kay Weston (Marilyn Monroe) in *River of No Return* (1954).

- I adore you.

- Save your aching arteries. That road's closed.

Eleanor's (Katharine Hepburn) reply to King Henry's (Peter O'Toole) attempt at diversion in *The Lion in Winter* (1968).

I wouldn't take you if you were covered with diamonds, upside down.

Lynn Markham (Joan Crawford) to Drummond Hall (Jeff Chandler) in *Female on the Beach* (1955).

- I love you!

- Oh Harold! That's wonderful! Go and love some more.

Harold (Bud Cort) and Maude's (Ruth Gordon) dying words in *Harold and Maude* (1971).

Don't! Not here.

Sonja (Diane Keaton) to Boris (Woody Allen) who is reaching for her in the marital bed in *Love and Death* (1975).

- But James, I need you!

- So does England!

James Bond's (Roger Moore) reply to a female agent in *The Spy Who Loved Me* (1977).

If I choose to attempt to have carnal knowledge of that gorgeous bod, that will be her option, my problem and none of your business.

Elliot Garfield (Richard Dreyfuss) to Paula McFadden (Marsha Mason) in *The Goodbye Girl* (1977).

- Would you like to come in?

- I'd rather stick needles in my eyes.

Aurora (Shirley MacLaine) and Garrett (Jack Nicholson) coming home after a very bad dinner date in *Terms of Endearment* (1983).

I'm not that kind of girl!

Willie Scott (Kate Capshaw) when Indy (Harrison Ford) slips a hand in her blouse to get at the antidote to a poison in *Indiana Jones and the Temple of Doom* (1984).

By the way! I never liked your dog, and I think jazz is stupid, and I faked all those orgasms.

> Peggy Schuyler (Madolyn Smith) breaking off her engagement with Roger Cobb (Steve Martin) in *All of Me* (1984).

The only way you'll ever wind up lying next to me, Max, is if we're runned down by the same car.

> Monique (Kathryn Harrold) to Max (Robert Davi) in *Raw Deal* (1986).

By the way, I faked every orgasm.

> Lt. Frank Drebin (Leslie Nielsen) breaking up with Jane (Priscilla Presley) in *The Naked Gun: From the Files of Police Squad!* (1988).

- This isn't right! We are breaking all the rules of propriety.

- Rules! Rules are made to be broken. Oh, kiss me!

- What about the girls?

- They can't have you.

- I never met your family. I never asked your father.

- My father is a dottering old man.

- Well then, there's something I have to tell you. I'm impotent.

- Oh, I find that so charming in a man.

- Mrs. Lomax...

- Oh, shut up and take me.

> Peter (Tom Selleck) trying to extricate himself from the arms of Mrs. Lomax (Fiona Shaw), the headmistress of a girls school, in *Three Men and a Little Lady* (1990).

Why don't you run outside and jerk yourself a soda?

Virginia Hill (Annette Bening) to Ben Siegel (Warren Beatty) in *Bugsy* (1991).

I have feelings ABOUT you, not FOR you. There's a difference.

Celeste Talbert (Sally Field) to Jeffrey Anderson (Kevin Kline) in *Soapdish* (1991).

How about doing to yourself what you normally do to Wendy?

Francine (Rhea Pearlman) to her boss after being passed over for a promotion in *The Mogul* (1991).

Here's a quarter, call somebody who cares!

Emily (Melanie Griffith) in *A Stranger Among Us* (1993).

You are like wet sand in my underwear.

Cindy (Rosie Perez) to her flirting boss in *Untamed Heart* (1993).

If you're ever in Bulka, don't look me up.

T. R. Polk (M. Emmet Walsh) to a cop in *Camp Nowhere* (1994).

I'd rather do it with Donald Duck.

Molly McKenna (Frances Fisher) turning down an offer by Sergeant Mike Pamer in *Molly & Gina* (1994).

- What do you do?

 - Why do you care?

 - I don't. I was just making polite conversation.

 - I'd rather not discuss what I do.

 - You know, I think I understand what you're like now. You're very beautiful and you think men are only interested in you because you're beautiful, but you want them to be

---

interested in you because you're you. The problem is, aside from all that beauty, you're not very interesting. You're rude, you're hostile, you're sullen, you're withdrawn. I know you want someone to look past all that at the real person underneath but the only reason that anyone would bother to look past all that is because you're beautiful. Ironic, isn't it? In an odd way you're your own problem.

- Sorry. Wrong line. I am not taken aback by your keen insight and suddenly challenged by you.

Will Randall (Jack Nicholson) and Laura Alden (Michelle Pfeiffer) in *Wolf* (1994).

- What do you need, sergeant?

- You want the big answer or the little answer?

- The little one.

- Oh, your loss.

- Sensitive and shallow to the end, aren't you, Pamer? What do you want?

- I don't know. How about a drink later; just some comfort and kindness from a caring cop?

- I'd rather guzzle battery acid.

- Grief can't keep a good tongue down, eh?

- Goodbye, Pamer. You're out of my life now too.

Molly McKenna (Frances Fisher) and Sergeant Mike Pamer (Bruce Weitz) in *Molly & Gina* (1994).

Duh!

Stan-You know, if I had any sense, I'd leave.

Ollie-Well, it's a good thing you haven't.

Stan-It certainly is.

> Oliver Hardy and Stan Laurel who reflects on his last comment while scratching his head in *Helpmates* (1932).

- Oh, George, imagine meeting a deep-sea diver here of all places.

- That's a suit of armor.

- Oh. Mr. Armor must be around somewhere in his underwear.

- Probably slipped out for a smoke.

> Gracie (Gracie Allen) and George (George Burns) in *A Damsel in Distress* (1937).

- What's today?

- I don't know.

- You could tell if you looked at that newspaper on your desk.

- Oh, that's no help, George. That's yesterday's paper.

> Jerry Halliday (Fred Astaire), Gracie (Gracie Allen) and George (George Burns) in *A Damsel in Distress* (1937).

- I can't go now, she needs me. She's in trouble.

- Oh, Jerry, don't be so pessimistic. Maybe she'll still be in trouble when you get back.

> Jerry Halliday (Fred Astaire) and Gracie (Gracie Allen) in *A Damsel in Distress* (1937).

- That's for children. I don't like these things. I never did and I never will. Jerry, don't get me a ticket.

- Why not?

- Because I've got a weak heart.

- Oh, don't be silly, George. If Jerry pays for the ticket how can that affect your heart?

- I don't get any pleasure out of these things.

- Oh, come along, George. For the fun of it. It's lots of fun having fun even if you don't enjoy it.

George (George Burns), Jerry Halliday (Fred Astaire) and Gracie (Gracie Allen) at the fair in *A Damsel in Distress* (1937).

- Shouldn't you have been in two hours ago?

- Why? What happened?

- If you're not on time I'll have to get myself another stenographer.

- Another stenographer? Do you think there's enough work for the two of us?

George (George Burns) and Gracie (Gracie Allen) in *A Damsel in Distress* (1937).

Jerry-Good old Tutney Castle.

Gracie-Oh, isn't it beautiful. It's almost pretty enough to be a filling station.

George-Filling station!? Why this castle is over three hundred years old.

Jerry-Oliver Cromwell went through here in 1628.

Gracie-Well, that was pretty fast time in those days.

Jerry-I mean he went through the castle, Gracie.

Gracie-Oh, couldn't stop the car, hey?

Jerry Halliday (Fred Astaire), Gracie (Gracie Allen) and George (George Burns) in *A Damsel in Distress* (1937).

We've got to dig a hole to put that dirt in.

Moe, the clever one, in *Cash and Carry* (1937).

- What's today?

- I don't know.

- You could tell if you looked at that newspaper on your desk.

- Oh, that's no help, George. That's yesterday's paper.

Jerry Halliday (Fred Astaire), Gracie (Gracie Allen) and George (George Burns) in *A Damsel in Distress* (1937).

Curly-I can't see! I can't see!

Moe-Why not?

Curly-I got my eyes closed.

In Calling All Curs (1939).

- I'm looking for the Eiffel Tower?

- Good heavens! Is that thing lost again?

Lena Yakushova 'Ninotchka' (Greta Garbo) and Count
Leon Bressart (Melvyn Douglas) in Ninotchka (1939).

Insomnia! I know a good cure for that. Get plenty of sleep.

Bill (W.C. Fields) in Never Give a Sucker an Even Break
(1941).

Centurion-What's behind those drapes?

Curlycue-The back of the drapes.

(Moe) Mohicus, (Larry) Larrycus, (Curly) Curlycue in
Matri-Phony (1942).

- I have a Chippendale.

- Does he sit up?

Gildersleeve (Harold Peary) and Private Johnny Grey
(Victor Mature) in Seven Days' Leave (1942).

Moe-Did you lock the door?

Curly-Yeah, twice. Once this way and once that way.

Curly flips his wrist on and off in Idle Roomers (1944).

Larry-It's getting late. (...)

Moe-What does your watch say?

Shemp-Tick, tick, tick, tick.

In *Fright Night* (1947).

The boys are locked up. They hear knocking sounds from the room below: knock, knock, ka-knock, knock

Larry-What's that?

Shemp-It's a message.

Moe-Yes.

Shemp-It's in code.

Moe-What does it say?

Shemp-Knock, knock, ka-knock, knock.

In *Fuelin' Around* (1949).

Moe-What does your watch say?

Shemp-It don't say nothin'. You've got to look at it.

In *Who Done It?* (1949).

I seem to have misplaced my buttonhole.

Elwood P. Dowd (James Stewart) in *Harvey* (1950).

Is that a new dress? I like it. I like the way it sticks out... or is it you?

Absent-minded chemist Barnaby Fulton (Cary Grant) to his wife Edwina (Ginger Rogers) in *Monkey Business* (1952).

Ladies and gentlemen, I can't tell you how thrilled we are at your reception for the Dancing Cavalier, our first musical picture together. If we bring a little joy in your humdrum

Marilyn Monroe

life it makes us feel like our hard work ain't been in vain for nothing.

Lena Lamont (Jean Hagen) in *Singing in the Rain* (1952).

Does this boat go to Europe, France?

Lorelei Lee (Marilyn Monroe) in *Gentlemen Prefer Blondes* (1953).

If you find the man who killed Dr. Zoomer you've found the murderer.

Freddie Franklin (Lou Costello) to Pete Patterson (Bud Abbott) in *Abbott and Costello Meet the Mummy* (1955).

- Is there any gas left?

- The arrow points halfway. I don't know if its half empty or half full.

Moe Howard and Curly Howard in the Three Stooges comedy *Dizzy Pilots* (1934).

- Call me a taxi.

- You're a taxi.

Jean-Marc Clement (Yves Montant) and the doorman in *Let's Make Love* (1960).

- Lascivious adulterer!

- Don't you dare call me that again until I have looked it up.

Anna (Edra Gale) and her husband Dr. Fritz Fassbender (Peter Sellers) in *What's New Pussycat?* (1965).

I only yesterday said: I want you for my wife. And she said: Your wife, what would she want with me?

The Emcee (Joel Grey) in *Cabaret* (1972).

- Do you know what kind of bomb it was?

- The exploding kind.

Inspector Jacques Clouseau's (Peter Sellers) answer to his aide François in *The Pink Panther Strikes Again* (1976).

Animal House

Over? Did you say over? Nothing is over until we say it is. Was it over when the Germans bombed Pearl Harbor? Hell no! And it ain't over now!

John 'Bluto' Blutarsky (John Belushi) motivating the members of the Delta House Fraternity for one last assault on their school and town in *National Lampoon's Animal House* (1978).

- Cigarette?

- Yes, I know. (or: Yes, it is.)

A recurring joke in the *Police Squad/Naked Gun* series. Lt. Frank Drebin (Leslie Nielsen) offers a cigarette or coffee to someone but the question is misunderstood and answered inappropriately, in this case by Mimi Du Jour (K.T. Sullivan) in *More! Police Squad* (1982). Also in: *The Naked Gun 33 1/3: The Final Insult* (1994).

Oh, I have the napkins that match your hats.

Protocol hostess Sunny Davis (Goldie Hawn) to visiting Arab royalty wearing checkered head scarfs in *Protocol* (1984).

- I'll have a Coke.

    - Do you want that in a can?

    - No, I'll have it right here.

> Clark 'Sparky' Griswald (Chevy Chase) ordering a Coke from the airline hostess in *National Lampoon's European Vacation* (1985).

I love history. So old! So full of events!

> Elliott James (Michael Caine) in *Sweet Liberty* (1986).

- Now, Smart, I want you to listen to me because I'm going to say what I have to say once and only once. One: KAOS has a weather machine. It is capable of changing the world as we know it.

    - Changing the world as we know it!? That's a very hopeful sign, sir.

    - Two: they can produce acid rains, destroy our crops, and pollute our water.

    - You mean they can do that better than we're doing it now?

    - Three: there is a mole in our outfit and he turned Dr. Hottentot.

    - Into what?

> Commander Drury (Kenneth Mars) and Maxwell Smart (Don Adams) in *Get Smart, Again!* (1989).

- I'd also like to look into the Hottentot file. There may be something in there that I can use.

    - Our records are in a warehouse at nine-oh-four-twenty-seven-forty-third street. Got that?

    - Everything but the address.

> Maxwell Smart (Don Adams) and Commander Drury (Kenneth Mars) in *Get Smart, Again!* (1989).

Somebody get me the number for 911!

Ruby Lin (Jedda Jones) in *Talkin' Dirty After Dark* (1991). Rephrased by Buckwheat (Ross Elliot Bagley) to Porky (Zachary Mabry) when their club house is on fire in *The Little Rascals* (1994): "Quick! What's the number for 911?"

- The face is familiar.

  - It's mine!

> Roland T. Flakfizer (John Turturro) and Jacques (Bob
> Nelson) in *Brain Donors* (1992).

- Do you sleep in the nude?

  - Only when I'm naked.

> Becker (Jon Lovitz) interrogating Destiny Demeanor
> (Kathy Ireland) in *National Lampoon's Loaded Weapon I*
> (1993).

Say, What?

There's a picture I want to show you. That's a gondola going through the Panama Canal... in Venice.

> Ollie (Oliver Hardy) to Sir Leopold Ambrose Plumtree
> (Charles Gerrard) in *Another Fine Mess* (1930).

If you must make a noise, make it quietly.

> Stan Laurel to the *Brats* (1930). The same line is told by
> Oliver Hardy to Stan in *Great Guns* (1941).

How happy I could be with either of these two if both of 'em went away.

> Captain Jeffrey Spaulding (Groucho Marx) speaking of
> Mrs. Rittenhouse (Margaret Dumont) and Mrs.
> Whitehead (Margaret Irving) in *Animal Crackers* (1930).

- You can't stay in that closet!

- Oh I can't, can I? That's what they said to Thomas Edison, mighty inventor, Thomas Lindberg, mighty flyer, and Tommy Shelfsky, mighty like a rose. Just remember, my little cabbage, that if there weren't any closets, there wouldn't be any hooks, and if there weren't any hooks, there wouldn't be any fish, and that would suit me fine.

> Lucille (Thelma Todd) and Groucho (Groucho Marx) in
> *Monkey Business* (1931).

- Well, you read it, didn't you?
  - Yes, but I didn't listen.

> Oliver Hardy asking Stan Laurel about the contents of a
> letter containing bad news in *Beau Chumps* (1931).

- You never met my wife, did you?
  - Yes, I never did.

> Ollie (Oliver Hardy) and Stan (Stan Laurel) in *Helpmates* (1932).

I'm very quick, in a slow way.

> Tira (Mae West) in *I'm No Angel* (1933).

I'm just an old-fashioned girl... like Mae West.

> Kitty (Patsy Kelly) in *The Girl from Missouri* (1934).

If I'd forgotten myself with that girl, I'd remember it.

> Jerry Travers (Fred Astaire) about Dale Tremont (Ginger
> Rogers) in *Top Hat* (1935).

Shttt! Don't wake him up! He's got insomnia and he's trying to sleep it over.

> Fiorello (Chico Marx) speaking of Tomasso (Harpo Marx)
> sleeping in a drawer of Groucho's trunk in *A Night at the
> Opera* (1935).

I'm still blind in this ear!

> The General (Peter Lorre) after being trapped in the bell
> tower in *Secret Agent* (1936).

Let's get something to eat. I'm thirsty.

> Nick (William Powell) to Nora (Myrna Loy) in *After the*
> *Thin Man* (1936).

Keggs-Admission is one shilling.

Gracie-Oh, well, we usually get more than that but give us our shilling and we'll go in.

Keggs-Oh, but I don't pay the people, the people pay me.

Gracie-Well, then, give me my money back.

Keggs-But you didn't give me any money.

Gracie-Well, that's not my fault.

George-Here's your money, mister.

Gracie-How much did he give you?

Keggs-Two shillings.

Gracie-And how much is the admission?

Keggs-One shilling.

Gracie-Oh, well then, give me back my change.

Keggs-Oh, I beg your pardon, madam. I was a little confused for a moment.

> Keggs (Reginald Gardiner), charging admission for
> visiting Tutney Castle, is even more confused once he
> figures out Gracie's (Gracie Allen) special kind of logic in
> *A Damsel in Distress* (1937).

- I say, I'm with the lady in the car ahead.

  - My, you must be a magician.

- No, but really, aren't you with the gentleman in the car ahead?

- So I am. Well, if we're both in the car ahead then who could the people be in this car?

- Yes, that's right. There must be some mix-up. (*The Tunnel of Love darkens.*) Shall I strike a match?

- Well, why hit a poor little match? It isn't its fault.

> Reggie (Ray Noble) sharing a car (swan) with Gracie (Gracie Allen) in the Tunnel of Love while their respective dates (Fred Astaire, Joan Fontaine) are in the car ahead in *A Damsel in Distress* (1937).

I'll show him who he thinks we are!

> House detective Casey (Eugene Pallette) to the hotel manager in *Topper* (1937).

- Yes, it's funny that everything is the way it is on account of the way you feel. I mean if you didn't feel the way you do, things wouldn't be the way they are, would they? I mean things could be the same if things were different.

- But things are the way you made them.

- Oh no! Things are the way you think I made them. I didn't make them that way at all. Things are just the same as they always were only you're the same as you were too so I guess things will never be the same again. Goodnight.

- You're wrong about things being different because they aren't the same. Things are different except in a different way. You're still the same, only I've been a fool. But I'm not now. So long as I'm different don't you think, well, maybe things could be the same again only a little different, hmm?

> Lucy Warrimer (Irene Dunne) explaining to Jerry Warrimer (Cary Grant) that their divorce was caused by Jerry's suspicions and jealousy, and Jerry's attempt at reconciliation in *The Awful Truth* (1937).

Moe-We're terrific!

Larry-We're colossal!

Curly-We're even mediocre!

> The boys claiming to be great actors and animal
> imitators in *Three Missing Links* (1938).

Larry-Do you think it's serious, Doctor Curly?

Curly-Yes indeed, to say the least, if not less.

> The boys are vets in *Calling All Curs* (1939).

Moe-I'll take that end.

Larry-I'll take this end.

Curly-I'll take the end in the middle.

> The boys have a special way of carrying boxes in *We
> Want Our Mummy* (1939).

Take your hat off when I'm talking to a lady.

> Michael O'Leary (Humphrey Bogart) to the stable boy
> while talking to Judith Traherne (Bette Davis) in *Dark
> Victory* (1939).

Psychologically, I'm very confused, but personally, I don't
feel bad at all.

> Klara Novak (Margaret Sullavan) upon learning that her
> secret correspondent and her co-worker Alfred Kralik
> (James Stewart) are one and the same man in *The Shop
> Around the Corner* (1940).

- You're just a mass of prejudices, aren't you? You're so much
thought and so little feeling, professor.

  - I am, am I?

- Yes, you am I, you!

Tracy Lord (Katharine Hepburn) and Macaulay Connor
(James Stewart) in *The Philadelphia Story* (1940).

To hardly know him is to know him well.

C.K. Dexter-Haven (Cary Grant) about George Kitteridge
(John Howard), his ex-wife's (Katharine Hepburn) new
fiancé in *The Philadelphia Story* (1940).

Tell me, is it as warm in the summer as it is in the country, or vice versa?

Larry to a block of ice he's about to shave in *An Ache in*
Every Stake (1941).

In former years we travelled incognito, then, by freight. Now we just stomach.

Moe to society people in *In the Sweet Pie and Pie* (1941).

4000 miles and I rowed every step of the way.

Moe rowing a boat to the Island of Rhum Boogie where
the natives live in bamboo huts on milk from concentrated
cocoanuts in *Some More of Samoa* (1941).

You know, I'd like to show you my chateau in Brooklyn. It's on the right as you go in. It's on the right as you come out too. Every one enters through an exit.

Curly Pebble to the lady spy-astrologer in *I'll Never Heil*
Again (1941).

I've got her just where she wants me.

Private Johnny Grey (Victor Mature) in *Seven Days'*
Leave (1942).

- You want my opinion, Mr. Dobosh?

- No, Mr. Greenberg, I do not want your opinion.

- Alright, let me give you my reaction then. A laugh is nothing to sneeze at.

> Actor Greenberg (Felix Bressart) and producer Dobosh (Charles Halton) furious at Bronski for trying to fatten his part with "Heil myself!" in *To Be or Not to Be* (1942).

Moe-Go get my fishing rod.

Curly-Is this gonna hurt?

Moe-Of course not. I won't even feel it.

> Planning to pull Curly's tooth in *I Can Hardly Wait* (1943).

When I come back I expect to find you gone. Wait for me.

> Mortimer Brewster (Cary Grant) giving warning, of sorts, to his murdering brother Jonathan (Raymond Massey) and his sidekick Dr. Einstein (Peter Lorre) in *Arsenic and Old Lace* (1944).

- Some people say 'yes' and some people say 'no'.

- But what do you say?

- I'm inclined to agree with them.

> Elizabeth Lane (Barbara Stanwyck) and the butler on the value of bottom land for farming in *Christmas in Connecticut* (1945).

Bacall-Hello. Police department, please.

Bogart-(Grabs the phone.) Hello. What do you want, please?

Police-What do I want? You called me.

Bogart-I called you!? Say, who is this?

Remember, Gritto spelled sideways is agraggo...

Moe on the radio in *Micro-Phonies* (1945).

Police-This is Sergeant Riley at headquarters.

Bogart-Sergeant Riley? There isn't any Sergeant Riley here.

Police-I know that!

Bogart-Wait a minute. You better talk to my mother.

Police-I don't want to talk to your mother...

Bacall-Hello. Who is this?

Police-This is the police.

Bacall-The police! Well, this isn't a police station.

Police-I know that! This is silly...

Bacall-What was that you said? My father should hear this.

Police-I don't want to talk to your father...

Bogart-Hello. Who is this?

Police-This is the police talking.

Bogart-But she just told you that this isn't...

Police-No! I'm the police!

Bogart-Oh, you're the police. Well, that's different. What can I do for you?

Police-You can...

Bogart-I can what? When? Oh, no. I wouldn't like that, neither would my daughter. (*Hangs up the phone.*) I hope the sergeant never traces that call.

> Vivian Sternwood Rutledge (Lauren Bacall) and Philip Marlowe (Humphrey Bogart) changing their minds about calling the police in *The Big Sleep* (1946).

As far as I'm concerned, the rattlesnake on his stomach is higher than a giraffe on a pair of stilts, compared to a sheepherder.

> Whittaker (George 'Gabby' Hayes), a cattle-rancher who hates sheep and sheepherders in *Roll on Texas Moon* (1946).

I hate the dawn. The grass always looks as though it's been left out all night.

Hardy Cathcart (Clifton Webb) in *The Dark Corner*
(1946).

- I had a terrible time getting here, Nora. I got lost east of West Point and I was held up north of South Ferry. And not only that, at Barton's Barn, I had binish with a buttush.

- A what?

- A British with a brush, a brush with a British. And I was shot.

- Where?

- Right through the saddle. Nora, I would never go through that for anyone except you.

Horatio Primm (Lou Costello) to his love Nora (Anne
Gillis) in *The Time of Their Lives* (1946).

- Hey, you remind me of a man.
  - What man?
  - The man with the power.
  - What power?
  - The power of hoo-doo.
  - Hoo-doo?
  - You do.
  - Do what?
  - Remind me of the man.
  - What man?
  - The man with...

Richard Nugent (Cary Grant) and Susan Turner (Shirley
Temple) in *The Bachelor and the Bobby-Soxer* (1947).

Shemp-(*on the phone*) Yes? Yes. Yes-yes-yes. No. No.

Moe-What was it?

Shemp-Wrong number.

In *Crime on Their Hands* (1948).

There is one reassuring thing about airplanes. They always come down.

August (Rudy Vallee) in *Unfaithfully Yours* (1948).

It looks like a cold winter ahead, so she's knitting herself an electric blanket.

Detective Sam Grunion (Groucho Marx) in *Love Happy* (1949).

- I'm sure that we won't have to have another little talk like this again. Am I correct in assuming that?

- Without question, yes, we'll never have to correct our talk, we won't ever speak, that is, we'll never have to talk again, we'll just never discuss talking, we should really converse about speaking.

Mortimer Warfield (Del Moore) reprimanding Professor Julius Kelp (Jerry Lewis) for blowing up his lab in *The Nutty Professor* (1963).

Don't shake your head at me in that tone of voice.

Junior (Bob Hope) in *Son of Paleface* (1952).

Believe me, I don't like her half as much as I hate you.

Don Lockwood (Gene Kelly) to Lena Lamont (Jean Hagen) in *Singing in the Rain* (1952).

You are a fool but not a silly fool.

Gregory Arkadin (Orson Welles) to Guy Van Stratten (Robert Arden) in *Confidential Report* (also known as *Mr. Arkadin*) (1955).

You're defending yourself, you coward!

Dr. Bedlo (Peter Lorre) to Dr. Sacabus (Boris Karloff) in a duel of magicians in *The Raven* (1963).

- Who is she?

- Sir, you may well ask. Who is she, ask, as well you may?

Senex (Michael Hordern) and Pseudolus (Zero Mostel) in *A Funny Thing Happened on the Way to the Forum* (1966).

Remember! Forget everything I tell you!

Polo (Ronnie Corbett) to Mata Bond (Joanna Pettit) (daughter of Sir James Bond and Mata Hari) in *Casino Royale* (1967).

- There, there...
- Where? Where?

Max Bialystock (Zero Mostel) comforting the paranoid ex-Nazi Franz Liebkind (Kenneth Mars) in *The Producers* (1967).

Insomnia is nothing to lose sleep about.

Psychiatrist Dr. Hieronimous Taylor (Bob Monkhouse) to Robert Blossom, Esq. (Richard Attenborough) in *The Bliss of Mrs. Bloom* (1968).

- Impresario, it is written: When the most humble enjoy the fruits of wealth then the wealthy become richer and the poor poorer, giving indigence to those who sublime the attitude with all the benevolence upon which tranquility is based and therefore to substantiate tranquility give them the omnipotence wherefore we provide, then the development of those who retrogress feel that the umbilicals upon those who tranquilitize and therefore, many times over.
- Superior wisdom from a superior mind.

The guru, Baba Ziba (Irwin Corey) explaining to Oliver Poe (Jackie Gleason) why he gave the star dressing room to a 'minion' in *How to Commit Marriage* (1969).

I warn you, gentlemen, I am not to be trifled with. To pull the tail of a lion is to open the mouth of trouble and reveal the teeth of vengeance biting the tongue of dissent.

> Duke D'Escargot (Vicor Spinetti) to the Coupet brothers impersonating the Corsican brothers Philippe de Sisi (Gene Wilder) and Pierre (Donald Sutherland) in *Start the Revolution Without Me* (1970).

Escargot-What brings you to Paris?

Philippe-Oh, you might say a little business...

Pierre-And a little pleasure.

Escargot-Which do you prefer? Business or pleasure?

Philippe-Well, that depends on what you regard as business...

Pierre-And what you may regard as pleasure.

Escargot-In Paris we say business is pleasure.

Philippe-Then your business should be a pleasure making my pleasure a business.

Pierre-Unless some mistake business for pleasure while others know no business but pleasure.

Escargot-In that case, sir, I will show you my business.

> Duke D'Escargot (Victor Spinetti) and the Corsican brothers Philippe de Sisi (Gene Wilder) and Pierre (Donald Sutherland) in Paris in 1789 in *Start the Revolution Without Me* (1970).

Well, you've heard it with your own eyes.

> Howard Cosell (as himself) reporting on the scene of the assassination of El Presidente in *Bananas* (1971).

You should never, never doubt what nobody is sure about.

> Willy Wonka (Gene Wilder) to the kid in *Willy Wonka and the Chocolate Factory* (1971).

Insinuendo is insinuation towards innuendo brought about by increased negativism out of a negative reaction to your father's positivism.

> Jack, 14th Earl of Gurney/God/J.C. (Peter O'Toole) to young Dinsdale Gurney (James Villiers) who is trying to show J.C. the light of his father's true intentions in marrying Him to his mistress in *The Ruling Class* (1972).

- May I ask what made you change your mind about seeing me?

   - Yes, you may.

> Sigerson Holmes (Gene Wilder) and Jenny Hill (Madeline Kahn) in *The Adventure of Sherlock Holmes' Smarter Brother* (1975). Siggy eventually has to repeat the question to get an answer.

Room filled with empty people.

> Sidney Wang (Peter Sellers) entering a room no longer filled with people in *Murder by Death* (1976).

I have a headache in my entire body.

> Glenda Park (Goldie Hawn) in *Seems Like Old Times* (1980).

Good Sharky Colonel God. We were just talking about you. Well, as you can see I've got the whole case buttoned up, everything is sown up. This is Sir Charles Phantom, the famous Pink Lytton...

> Inspector Jacques Clouseau (Peter Sellers) to Colonel Sharky of the Lugash secret police in *The Return of the Pink Panther* (1982).

Us loners gotta stick together.

> Niki (Molly Ringwald) in *Spacehunter* (1983).

Of course it won't be easy! That is why I have always failed where others have succeeded.

Inspector Jacques Clouseau (Peter Sellers) in *The Pink Panther Strikes Again* (1976).

I can kick myself out, thanks.

> Terry Brogan (Jeff Bridges) to Ben Caxton (Richard Widmark) in *Against All Odds* (1984).

He's world-famous in Poland.

> Anna Bronski (Anne Bancroft) speaking of her husband, the famous actor Frederick Bronski (Mel Brooks), in *To Be or Not to Be* (1983).

- Lyle, are you disappointed in me?

  - No!

  - I mean because I'm not the kind of guy you thought I was.

  - You are the kind of guy I thought you were.

  - I'm not, Lyle. I lived with my parents 'til I was thirty-two. I just threw my life away.

  - Hey, it takes a lot of nerve to have nothing at your age. Don't you understand that? Most guys would be ashamed but you got the guts to just say the hell with it. You say you'd rather have nothing than settle for less. Understand?

  - I've never thought of it that way.

> Chuck Clark (Dustin Hoffman) contemplating suicide on the ledge of his apartment building is being rescued by his friend Lyle Rogers (Warren Beatty) in *Ishtar* (1987).

I like you as much as I can like anyone who thinks I'm an asshole.

> Tom Grunick (William Hurt) to Aaron Altman (Albert Brooks) in *Broadcast News* (1987).

I'm going to miss you. You're a prick... in a great way.

> Tom Grunick (William Hurt) to Aaron Altman (Albert Brooks) in *Broadcast News* (1987).

- It's simple double entry bookkeeping, Einstein. In the right column you write what's left out.

- Left out.

- In the left column you write what's left in.

- Left in.

- So, all that's left in is left, right?

- Left right.

- And all that's left out you write in the right column, right? So nothing is left out, right.

- Left out right.

> Preston Preston (John Howard) teaching Albert Einstein (Yahoo Serious) simple bookkeeping in *Young Einstein* (1988).

- Max... You've been reactivated!

- Yes. I'm so glad I don't have to lie to you anymore, 99. I can finally tell you the truth.

- What is the truth?

- I can't tell you that!

> Agent 99 (Barbara Feldon) and her husband, Agent 86, Maxwell Smart (Don Adams) who is on a secret mission in *Get Smart, Again!* (1989).

Sammy is so confused he doesn't know whether to scratch his watch or wind his butt.

> Truvy Jones (Dolly Parton) in *Steel Magnolias* (1989).

You're the realest person I ever met in the abstract.

> Jack Falkner (Dennis Quaid) to the actress Suzanne Vale (Meryl Streep) in *Postcards from the Edge* (1990).

- All I want is for this lady to watch over my affairs.

I was deeply unhappy but didn't know it because I was so happy at the time.

Harris K. Telemacher's (Steve Martin) opening monologue. His life is about to change in *L.A. Story* (1991).

- Me!? You want me!?

- Well, I reckon you done what you done 'cause you didn't know we was who we was. If we hadn't been who we was we'd a-still been much obliged for you done what you done.

Uncle Jed (Jim Varney) and Mrs. Hathaway (Lily Tomlin), who had the Clampett family arrested for trespassing on their own property in *The Beverly Hillbillies* (1993).

I couldn't save a life if my life depended on it.

Phillip (Steve Martin) of Lifesavers in *Mixed Nuts* (1994).

- What day is this?

- Fifth.

- It's not the fourth?

- Fifth.

- Wednesday the fifth?

- Tuesday the fifth.

- Is this the beginning of Tuesday or was it Tuesday? What I'm saying is, is this last night or is it now tomorrow the fifth?

- This day is the fifth. It has begun the fifth, it's now ending the fifth.

- The sixth I've got to get my head checked out. Accident.

William (Christian Slater), who has a memory problem, and Jimmy Alto (Joe Pesci) in *Jimmy Hollywood* (1994).

- So, do I get the records?

- No.

- Come on. Is that all you ever say?

- No.

- Hmmm. A window of opportunity.

Bill Rago (Danny DeVito), pretending to be CID, and Marie (Isabella Hofmann), the records officer, in *Renaissance Man* (1994).

- I am delighted. I have heard so much about you.

- Yeah, but you can't prove it.

> Serge Stanieff (Gilbert Roland) being introduced to Lady Lou (Mae West) in *She Done Him Wrong* (1933). The answer she gave Connie Hines on the *Mister Ed* television show is usually the one best remembered: "Yeah, honey, but you can't prove a thing."

- Heil Hitler!

- Heil myself!

> Bronski (Tom Dugan), as Hitler, answering the chorus of actors in a play in *To Be or Not to Be* (1942). Mel Brooks has the same line as F. Bronski in the 1983 remake.

- Hello, Johnny.

- You've been eating vitamins again.

> Captain Johnny Angel (George Raft) to a dance hall girl jumping into his arms in *Johnny Angel* (1945).

Larry-Delighted.

Moe-Devastated.

Curly-Dilapidated.

> The boys being introduced to Mrs. Gottrocks in *Half-Wit's Holiday* (1947).

Moe-Enchanted.

Larry-Enraptured.

Curly-Embalmed.

> The boys are introduced to society ladies in *Half-Wit's Holiday* (1947).

Pardon me, I didn't quite catch your name. Would you mind spraying it again?

George M. Cohan (James Cagney) to Eddie Foy (Eddie Foy, Jr.) in *Yankee Doodle Dandy* (1942).

Moe-Top of the morning to you, Captain.

Shemp-And the rest of the day for me.

> Moe and Shemp saluting the captain in *Fuelin' Around*
> (1949).

- Do we know each other?

  - Why? Do you think we're going to?

  - I don't know. How would I know?

  - Because I already know an awful lot of people and until one of them dies I couldn't possibly meet anyone else.

  - Hum! Well, if anyone goes on the critical list, let me know.

  - Quitter.

  - Hum?

  - You give up awfully easy, don't you?

> Peter Joshua (Cary Grant) meeting Eugenia Lampert
> (Audrey Hepburn) in *Charade* (1963).

Is that a gun in your pocket or are you just glad to see me?

> Marlo Manners (Mae West) to ex-husband gangster Vance
> Norton (George Hamilton) in *Sextette* (1978). She first spoke
> that line in her Broadway play *Catherine Was Great* (1944).
> Imitations: (1) "Hello handsome. Is that a ten-gallon hat or
> are you just happy to see the show?" Lili Von Shtupp
> (Madeline Kahn) in *Blazing Saddles* (1974). (2) "Hey! Are
> you glad to see me or is this a shotgun in your pocket?"
> Frank Cross (Bill Murray) to Elliot Loadermilk (Bobcat
> Goldthwait) in *Scrooged* (1988). (3) "What's that in your
> pocket, big boy?" "It's a compass." A young girl meeting
> Albert Einstein (Yahoo Serious) in *Young Einstein* (1988). (4)
> "Is that a rabbit in your pocket, or are you just happy to see
> me?" Dolores (Joanna Cassidy) to Eddie Valiant (Bob
> Hoskins) who is hiding Roger under his coat in *Who Framed
> Roger Rabbit* (1988).(5) "Is that a cowlick or are you just
> happy to see me?" A.J. Ferguson (Reba McEntire) kissing

Alfalfa (Bug Hall), winner of the go-cart race, in *The Little Rascals* (1994). (6) "Whoa, Pat! Is that a banana in your pocket or are you just happy to see me?" "It's a banana." Kyle (Charles Rocket) always looking for ways to solve the riddle of Pat's (Julia Sweeney) true gender in *It's Pat—The Movie* (1994). (7) "Hi, Lelaina. Was there a frog in your throat or are you just glad to see me?" Troy Dyer (Ethan Hawke) to a surprised and choked up Lelaina Pierce (Winona Ryder) in *Reality Bites* (1994). (8) "So, listen, is that a gun in your pocket?" Carla Duvall (Shannon Tweed) to her husband (Wings Hauser) in *Victim of Desire* (1994).

He's a member of my staff. Lilian Oglethorpe, Rocco Meloncheck, Rocco Meloncheck, Lilian Oglethorpe. In order to tell you apart one of you will have to wear a mustache.

Shyster lawyer Roland T. Flakfizer (John Turturro) introducing Lilian (Nancy Marchand) to his cab driver and assistant Rocco (Mel Smith) in *Brain Donors* (1992).

Let's give 'em a California howdy.

Uncle Jed (Jim Varney) and the Clampetts giving the birdie to passing motorists in *The Beverly Hillbillies* (1993).

- Guess who?

  - Bob!

  - Hi.

  - What are you doing here?

  - Are you glad to see me? Surprised to see me? Little less than thrilled to see me?

  - What was the middle one?

Bagdad Bob/Baggy (Christopher Reeve) arriving unexpectedly during the campaign to surprise Julia Mann (Geena Davis) in *Speechless* (1994).

Threats or Why I Oughta...

Would you mind going out and crossing the boulevard while the light is against you?

> Captain Jeffrey Spaulding (Groucho Marx) to Signor Ravelli (Chico Marx) in *Animal Crackers* (1930).

- Don't you think he's handsome, father?

- Yes, but I'll take care of that.

> Angela (Susan Fleming) and her father (W.C. Fields), the tyrannical President of Klopstokia, about her suitor (Jack Oakie) in *Million Dollar Legs* (1932).

- Oh! Fresh guy, hey? What you need is a sock on the nose.

- Listen partner, you may not like my nose but I do. I always wear it out in the open where everyone who wants to take a poke at it can do it.

- Oh yeah?!

- Now that's a brilliant answer. Why didn't I think of it?

- Oh yeah?!

- If you keep that up we're not going to get anywhere.

- Oh yeah?!

- You got me. Yeah!

> The bus driver (Ward Bond) and Peter Warne (Clark Gable) in *It Happened One Night* (1934).

I'll squeeze the cider out of your Adam's apple.

> Moe putting Curly's head in a press in *Disorder in the Court* (1936).

Moe-Remind me to kill you later.

   Curly-I'll make a note of it.

In Cash and Carry (1937).

You know, if I wasn't so weak from hunger, I'd bash your brains out—if you had brains.

Moe to Curly in Oily to Bed, Oily to Rise (1939).

- You're through!

   - The last man who said that to me was Archie Leach, just a week before he cut his throat.

Walter Burns (Cary Grant, whose real name is Archibald 'Archie' Leach) in His Girl Friday (1940).

Show them in. I'll show these Axis partners a two or thing or three or four.

Moe Hailstone in I'll Never Heil Again (1941).

He can't call me that and get away with it. I'll sock his face so far down into his oxfords he'll be known as Puss & Boots.

Fibber McGee (Jim Jordan) threatening The Great Gildersleeve (Harold Peary) in Look Who's Laughing (1941).

Two black eyes won't make a white one, Bill.

Major Barbara (Wendy Hiller) to Bill Walker (Robert Newton) in Major Barbara (1941).

You leave me alone or I'll do you a mischief.

Bill Walker (Robert Newton) threatening a man in Major Barbara (1941).

Remind me to have you stuffed.

> Moe to Curly in *So Long, Mr. Chumps* (1941).

Curly-Hey Moe, what happened? Say a few words.

Moe-I'll annihilate you! I'll murder you!

Curly-Wrong words.

> Curly inadvertently hammers Moe's head in *Loco Boy Makes Good* (1942).

Mingle or I'll mangle.

> Moe to Curly and Larry in *Loco Boy Makes Good* (1942).

You'll pay for this with every drop of your anemic blood.

> Eduardo Acuna (Adolphe Menjou) to his secretary in *You Were Never Lovelier* (1942).

I'll knock your head right down to your socks.

> Moe to Curly in *Spook Louder* (1943).

Curly-I'll give you...

Moe-What?

Curly-The meanest look.

> Curly's threat falls short of impressing Moe in *No Dough, Boys* (1944).

I'll tear your tonsils out and tie them around your neck for a bow tie.

> Moe in *If a Body Meets a Body* (1945).

I'm going to kick you bowlegged!

> Capt. Henri Rochard (Cary Grant) to Lt. Catherine Gates (Ann Sheridan) in *I Was a Male War Bride* (1949).

I may as well warn you, bubble-mouth, that I'm going to carry a revolver and a trench knife and if you so much as lay a finger on me this trip, you're going back to France minus a lot of parts you probably value.

> Lt. Catherine Gates (Ann Sheridan) to Capt. Henri Rochard (Cary Grant) in *I Was a Male War Bride* (1949).

If you ever try to cross me again, you'll wind up with a lead girdle.

> Ellen Grant (Lucille Ball) to Peggy Donato (Janis Carter) in *Miss Grant Takes Richmond* (1949).

I oughta take this pencil and make a circle around you.

> Billie Dawn (Judy Holliday) to her tutor Paul Verrall (William Holden), who asked her to circle words and paragraphs she didn't understand in the newspaper in *Born Yesterday* (1950).

You have the money for me by Christmas Eve, or Christmas morning you'll find your head in a Christmas stocking.

> Mob boss Moose Moran (Fred Clark) to the Kid (Bob Hope) in *The Lemon Drop Kid* (1951).

He'll regret it to his dying day... if ever he lives that long.

> Red Will Danaher (Victor McLaglen) muttering threats against Sean Thornton (John Wayne) in *The Quiet Man* (1952).

Pickering, should we ask this baggage to sit down or should we throw her out the window?

> Professor Henry Higgins (Rex Harrison) speaking of Eliza Doolittle in *My Fair Lady* (1964).

Rosie, if this is a shim, I'm coming back and I'll iron your face.

Lon McQ (John Wayne) to an informer in *McQ* (1974).

I'd like to introduce Robbo. Here's a man who was very close to Big Jim in the past and he might be even closer to him in the future.

Guy Gisborne (Peter Falk) introducing Robbo (Frank Sinatra) at Big Jim's burial in *Robin and the Seven Hoods* (1964).

Stringbean, if you so much as lay a hand on this automobile, I'm gonna jump down your throat and tap dance on your lungs.

Boone (Steve McQueen) to Ned (Rupert Crosse) in *The Reivers* (1969).

I'll have his guts for garters.

Grace Shelley Gurney (Carolyn Seymour) about her ex-lover Charles in *The Ruling Class* (1972).

We make a deal now or you're gonna be wearing wings.

Silky Slim (Calvin Lockhart) to Geechie Dan Beauford (Harry Bellafonte) in *Uptown Saturday Night* (1974).

Get back to the stands before I shave off half your mustache and shove it up your left nostril.

Morrie Buttermaker (Walter Matthau) in *The Bad News Bears* (1976).

You can end up with your balls in spaghetti sauce.

A pimp, Buchinski (Robert Hoy), to Dirty Harry Callahan (Clint Eastwood) in *The Enforcer* (1976).

Make like that's a nipple!

John Bernard 'J.B.' Brooks (John Wayne) shoving a gun barrel into the mouth of a journalist in *The Shootist* (1976).

Keep riding me, Mack, and they'll bury you in 42 different cemeteries.

> Boy (Paul Williams) to Lou Peckingpaugh (Peter Falk) in
> *The Cheap Detective* (1978).

You're gonna look pretty silly eating corn on the cob without teeth.

> Tucker (Charles Napier) to Joliet Jake (John Belushi) in
> *The Blues Brothers* (1980).

Open your mouth, Willard, and I'll smear Crazy Glue on your bed pan.

> Polly Reed (Loretta Swit) to her husband Willard (Craig
> Stevens), in the adjoining hospital bed in *S.O.B.* (1981).

I'll hit you so hard I'll kill your whole family.

> Billy (Timothy Daly) to a cellmate in *Diner* (1982).

You're not worth killing, but if you come at me again I'll put a window through your head.

> Bill Miner (Richard Farnsworth) to a young hoodlum in
> *The Grey Fox* (1982).

He'll have you skewed, tattooed and served with an apple in your mouth.

> Ben Pease (Max Phipps) speaking to the Count (Brant
> Tilly) in *Nate and Hayes* (1983).

I'll blow you away like lint.

> Donald Quinelle (Robin Williams) to Jack Locke (Jerry
> Reed) in *The Survivors* (1983).

Hey, back off! I'll rip out your eyes and piss on your brain.

> C. Deeks (Paul Gleason) in *Trading Places* (1983).

It's either me or your balls, Roger. You can't have both.

> Peggy Schuyler (Madolyn Smith) to Roger Cobb (Steve
> Martin) in *All of Me* (1984).

Back off, man! I'm a scientist!

> Dr. Peter Venkman (Bill Murray) in *Ghostbusters* (1984).

All right! This chick is toast!

> Dr. Peter Venkman (Bill Murray) to the ghostbusters about
> zapping Gozer the Gozerian in *Ghostbusters* (1984).

Cross me and you're snail food.

> Leon Coll (Tony Lo Bianca) to Mike Murphy (Burt
> Reynolds) in *City Heat* (1984).

Next time I see you I'm gonna hit you so hard, I'm gonna
knock you back into the Stone Age where you come from.

> Mike Murphy (Burt Reynolds) to Lt. Speer (Clint
> Eastwood) in *City Heat* (1984).

Gophers are gonna be delivering your mail if you keep that
up.

> Slam Dunk (Anna Maria Horsford) to her pimp,
> Boardwalk (Larry Riley), in *Crackers* (1984).

Move, boys, unless you want to look like boxes of Cheerios.

> Harry (Robert Forster) to the bad guys in *Hollywood
> Harry* (1985).

I'll give you a one-way ticket to harp-land.

> Ralph (Danny DeVito) to Jack
> (Michael Douglas) in *The Jewel
> of the Nile* (1985).

All right, but when we get outta this alive I'm gonna kill you!

> Jack (Michael Douglas) to Joan
> (Kathleen Turner) in *The Jewel of
> the Nile* (1985).

Back off, Mister, or these walls will be getting a free paint job.

> Willie Brown (Joe Senaca)
> pointing a gun in *Crossroads*
> (1986).

Michael Douglas and
Kathleen Turner

You cross me, I'll personally grease the pole that slides you into a tub of shit.

> Lt. Hall (Bruce McGill) to Eddie Jillette (Richard Gere) in
> *No Mercy* (1986).

The plague on your scurvy end.

> Captain Red/Thomas Bartholomew Red's (Walter
> Matthau) curse in *Pirates* (1986).

You'll be dancing a jig on air, come daybreak.

> Captain Red/Thomas Bartholomew Red (Walter Matthau) to the
> Spanish captain in *Pirates* (1986).

And if you f**k this up, I'm going to take your nuts and tie 'em into a knot and run them through my shredder.

> Captain Al Giles (Earl Billings) to Chris (Richard Dreyfuss) and Bill (Emilio Estevez) in *Stakeout* (1987).

Get out, cupcake, unless you want your neck separated from your face.

> Alonzo (Harvey Keitel) to Jack (Robert Downey, Jr.) in *The Pick-Up Artist* (1987).

You poke me one more time I'm gonna have to redefine your face.

> Ernest Tilley (Danny DeVito) to Bill 'B.B.' Babowsky (Richard Dreyfuss) in *Tin Men* (1987).

You forgot your fortune cookie. It says: you're shit out of luck.

> Dirty Harry Callahan (Clint Eastwood) to a bad guy before shooting him in *The Dead Pool* (1988).

If you don't cooperate you'll also suffer from fistophobia!

> Jack Walsh (Robert De Niro) to Jonathan Mardukas/The Duke (Charles Grodin) who claims to suffer from aerophobia, acrophobia and claustrophobia in *Midnight Run* (1988).

Are you an organ donor, Alex?

> Tommy Novak (Clint Eastwood) holding a gun to the head of a white supremacist in *Pink Cadillac* (1989).

Because if you lie to me (...) you'll be doing a little East River snorkeling.

> Joey O'Brien (Robin Williams) in *Cadillac Man* (1990).

One f**king word and your head is everywhere.

> Eddie (Whoopi Goldberg) robbing people at gun point in
> *Homer & Eddie* (1990).

You f**k with me, better you piss a kidney stone through your hard-on.

> Mike Brennan (Nick Nolte) to Luis Valentin (Luis Guzman)
> in *Q & A* (1990).

You guys give up, or are you thirsty for more?

> Kevin McCallister's (Macaulay Culkin) ultimatum to Harry
> (Joe Pesci) and Marv (Daniel Stern) in *Home Alone*
> (1990).

Keep it up and you'll be carrying your face home in a doggy bag.

> Topper Harley (Charlie Sheen) to Kent Gregory (Cary
> Elwes) in *Hot Shots!* (1991).

I'll torture you so slowly you'll think it's a career. I'll kill your friends, your family and the bitch you took to the prom.

> Darwin Mayflower (Richard E. Grant) to Eddie (Bruce
> Willis) in *Hudson Hawk* (1991).

You keep looking at me, you'll see me kill you.

> Dining tough guy (Tony Epper) to Alex Furlong (Emilio
> Estevez) in *Freejack* (1992).

I've got a gun in my pocket. You open your mouth and you'll be spitting gum out through your forehead.

> Harry (Joe Pesci) to Kevin McCallister (Macaulay Culkin)
> in *Home Alone 2: Lost in New York* (1992).

You bop me with one more can, kid, and I'll snap off your cojones and boil them in motor oil.

Harry (Joe Pesci) to Kevin (Macaulay Culkin) in *Home Alone* (1990).

- What's in it for me?

- You get to keep all your teeth.

> Gee Q's (Omar Epps) answer to his brother in *Juice*
> (1992).

One word about this and you'll never see 15.

> Chester Lee (Rodney Dangerfield) to his son-in-law
> Matthew (Jonathan Brandis) in *Ladybugs* (1992).

- What are you going to do now, Mr. Pig?

- Well, I'm thinking about taking your head off and shitting in it and then hiding it and see how long it takes you to find it.

> Det. Harry 'Nails' Niles's (Dennis Hopper) answer to a
> bad guy in *Nails* (1992).

You'll regret this for the rest of your life—both seconds of it.

> John Spartan (Sylvester Stallone) in *Demolition Man* (1993).

No sequel for you!

> Jack Slater (Arnold Schwarzenegger) before shooting the
> bad guy, Benedict (Charles Dance), in *Last Action Hero*
> (1993).

I snap my fingers and sometime tomorrow you emerge from several canine rectums.

> Benedict's (Charles Dance) threatening to have Danny
> (Austin O'Brien) and Jack Slater (Arnold
> Schwarzenegger) eaten alive by guard dogs in *Last
> Action Hero* (1993).

Lose the guns or I redecorate in brain-matter grey, got it?

> Whitney/Meredith (Bridgette Wilson) in *Last Action Hero* (1993).

If you ever show your faces around here again, I'll have you arrested for trying to visit.

> Debbie (Joan Cusack) to the
> visiting Addams family in
> *Addams Family Values* (1993).

One more push and I'm gonna smack his face so hard he'll have to stick his toothbrush up his ass to clean his teeth.

> Bernadette (Terence Stamp)
> about Felicia (Guy Pearce) in
> *The Adventures of Priscilla,
> Queen of the Desert* (1994).

- Are you cheating on me, Gunther?
- Cheating!? Are you crazy? You would kill me.
- Worse. I would grab your scrotum, I would stretch it over your head and I would use you as a puncher bag.

> Lucille Toody (Rosie O'Donnell) and her husband Gunther
> (David Johansen) in *Car 54, Where Are You?* (1994).

Last Action Hero

You ever talk to me like that again and I'll turn your balls into earrings.

> Duke (Jack Palance) to Mitch Robbins (Billy Crystal) in
> *City Slickers II: The Legend of Curly's Gold* (1994).

Brother, you better show me some tits or die.

> Shame (Keenen Ivory Wayans) waking up in bed with a transvestite in
> *A Low Down Dirty Shame* (1994).

Blink and black is the last thing you'll see.

Shame (Keenen Ivory Wayans) to Luis in *A Low Down Dirty Shame* (1994).

- Shame, just promise me you'll smoke his ass.

  - Like a motherf**king pack of Kools.

Angela (Salli Richardson) and Shame (Keenen Ivory Wayans) in *A Low Down Dirty Shame* (1994).

- You can't hang me. I was framed!

  - In a minute you're gonna be in a box.

Fred (John Goodman) and a lynch mob in *The Flintstones* (1994).

- I've got half a mind...
    - Don't flatter yourself.
    - That's it! Where's my club, Wilma?

Fred (John Goodman) and his mother-in-law Pearl (Elizabeth Taylor) in *The Flintstones* (1994).

"Punch" Lines

- You drink coffee?

  - Yeah.

  - You like sugar in your coffee?

  - Sure.

  - Here's a lump. (*Smacks him.*)

Ted Healy and Curly Howard in the early days of Ted Healy and His Stooges in *Meet the Baron* (1933).

Moe-Pick out two. (*Shows an open hand.*)

Curly-One, two.

Moe-Here. (*Pokes him in the eye with the two he picked.*)

In *Slippery Silks* (1936).

Moe-I'm taking census.

Man-Well, have some.

Man breaks his cane on Moe's head in *No Census, No Feeling* (1940).

He can't call me that and get away with it. I'll sock his face so far down into his oxfords he'll be known as Puss & Boots.

Fibber McGee (Jim Jordan) threatening The Great Gildersleeve (Harold Peary) in *Look Who's Laughing* (1941).

The Three Stooges

I've a mind to carve you to ribbons.

The Hook (Victor McLaglen) to Sylvester Crosby/Sylvester the Great (Bob Hope) in *The Princess and the Pirate* (1944).

Moe-If you don't stop, I'll give you a pop.

   Curly-What flavor?

   Moe-Five delicious flavors. (Slaps him.)

In *The Yoke's On Me* (1944).

A girl's best friend is a good looping right.

Pearl White (Betty Hutton) after knocking down her boss in *The Perils of Pauline* (1947).

- Why don't you take that chip off your shoulder?

   - Every time I do, someone hits me over the head with it.

Nick Cochran (Robert Mitchum) and Julie Benton (Jane Russell) in *Macao* (1952).

We came, we saw, we
kicked its ass.

Dr. Peter Venkman (Bill Murray)
paraphrasing Julius Caesar
(*Veni, vidi, vici* = I came, I saw,
I conquered) after defeating
their first ghost in *Ghostbusters*
(1984).

Life with Mary was like being in a phone booth with an opened umbrella; no matter which way you turned you got hit in the eye.

Bob McKellaway (Barry Nelson) speaking of Mary McKellaway (Debbie Reynolds) in *Mary, Mary* (1963).

When I was a kid my father told me: never hit anyone in anger unless you're absolutely sure you can get away with it.

Russell (Harold Ramis) in *Stripes* (1981).

- Last year I got a sweater with a big bird knitted on it.
  - That's nice.
  - Not if you're in the second grade. You can get beat up for wearing something like that.

Kevin McCallister (Macaulay Culkin) and the old man in the church in *Home Alone* (1990).

Big City, Bright Lines

Just a New York cowboy, aren't you? Passing through and giving the little small town girl her big moment. You'd be lovely to have around just to sprinkle the flowers with your personality.

Connie Randall (Carole Lombard) to Jerry 'Babe' Stewart (Clark Gable) in *No Man of Her Own* (1932).

I don't want to live in a city where the only cultural advantage is you can make a right turn on a red light.

Alvy Singer (Woody Allen) about living in Los Angeles in *Annie Hall* (1977).

It's like living in Munchkinland.

> Alvy Singer (Woody Allen) about Los Angeles in *Annie Hall* (1977).

- It's so clean out here.

- That's because they don't throw their garbage away. They turn it into television shows.

> Alvy Singer (Woody Allen) about Los Angeles in *Annie Hall* (1977).

The rest of the country looks upon New York like we're left-wing, communist, Jewish, homosexual pornographers. I think of us that way sometimes and I live here.

> Alvy Singer (Woody Allen) in *Annie Hall* (1977).

Let's give 'em a California howdy.

> Uncle Jed (Jim Varney) and the Clampetts giving the birdie to passing motorists in *The Beverly Hillbillies* (1993).

Being miserable and treating other people like dirt is every New Yorker's God-given right.

The Mayor (David Margulies) in *Ghostbusters II* (1989).

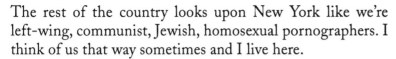

The Grass Is Always Greener

- You can pass away your holidays right here in Glendale.

- Yeah, you can pass away any day in Glendale.

> Jerry 'Babe' Stewart (Clark Gable) to the hotel clerk of small town Glendale in *No Man of Her Own* (1932).

Chicago! What a town! They should never have taken it from the Indians.

> Owen O'Malley (Roscoe Karns) in *Twentieth Century* (1934).

Vermont! You don't mean that narrow, pinched-up, little state on the wrong side of Boston? (...) What are you going to do there between yawns?

Judith Traherne (Bette Davis) to Doctor Frederick Steele (George Brent) in *Dark Victory* (1939).

Lady-I've heard you travelled a lot. Are you familiar with the Great Wall of China?

Curly-No, but I know a great fence in Chicago.

In *In the Sweet Pie and Pie* (1941).

- Here's to Nevada. The Leave It State.

- The what state?

- The Leave It State. You got money you want to gamble, leave it here. You got a wife you want to get rid of, get rid of her here. Extra atom bombs you don't need, blow it up here. Nobody is gonna mind in the slightest. The slogan of Nevada is: Anything goes but don't complain if it went. (...) I even left my southern accent here.

Isabelle Steers (Thelma Ritter) and Roslyn Taber (Marilyn Monroe) in *The Misfits* (1961).

Poland, the doormat of Europe. Everybody steps on us.

Frederick Bronski (Mel Brooks) in *To Be or Not to Be* (1983).

Only a Carpathian would come back to life now and choose New York.

Dr. Peter Venkman (Bill Murray) to Vigo in *Ghostbusters II* (1989).

I prefer Russia. It's as corrupt as America but there's less bullshit.

Barley Blair (Sean Connery) in *The Russia House* (1990).

This town needs an enema.

The Joker/Jack Napier (Jack Nicholson) in *Batman* (1989).

Don't be getting so uppity. Even if you is the last chicken in Atlanta.

(Eddie 'Rochester' Anderson) in *Gone with the Wind* (1939).

Away Down South

Wait you alll! It's me alll.

Curly, a southerner in *Uncivil War Birds* (1946).

Well corn my porn and chit my chitlins.

The Kid (Bob Hope) affecting a thick southern accent in *The Lemon Drop Kid* (1951).

Jackson comes from a good southern family with good old southern values: either shoot it, stuff it or marry it.

M'lynn Eatenton (Sally Field) in *Steel Magnolias* (1989).

I'm in the Twilight Zone!

Ben Stone (Michael J. Fox) arriving in Grady, South Carolina, "the buckle of the Bible Belt," in *Doc Hollywood* (1991).

Foreign Correspondence

Pretending to be Scotsmen and dressed appropriately, Curly is McSniff, Moe is McSnuff, Larry is McSnort.

Scotchman-Are you laddies by any chance from Loch Lomond?

Julia Roberts and Sally
Field in *Steel Magnolias*

Curly-No, we're
from Lockjaw.

In *Pardon My Scotch*
(1935).

If only I could teach
you English. It's the
only language low
enough to describe you.

Batouch (Joseph
Schildkraut) to his Arab
cousin in *The Garden of
Allah* (1936).

How cursed is the
man with relatives!

Do you have them in Europe too?

Batouch (Joseph Schildkraut) to Domini Enfilden (Marlene
Dietrich) in *The Garden of Allah* (1936).

- I'm pretty glad I came to the Riviera.

- Oh, yes, it's a lovely place, beautiful, but the class of
people who come here gets worse every year and this year
we seem to have next year's crowd already.

Mike Brandon (Gary Cooper) trying, unsuccessfully, to
flirt with Nicole de Loiselle (Claudette Colbert) in
Bluebeard's Eighth Wife (1938).

Moe-How about you and me making with the conversation?

Lorna-Aie!?

Moe-Oh, me too.

Lorna-You too?

Moe-Aie!?

MacMoe flirting with a Scottish lassie, Lorna (Christine
McIntyre), in *The Hot Scots* (1948).

Some of us prefer Austrian voices raised in song to ugly German threats.

> Captain Von Trapp (Christopher Plummer) in *The Sound of Music* (1965).

The problem with these international affairs is they attract foreigners.

> Lord Rawnsley (Robert Morley) to his daughter Patricia (Sarah Miles) in *Those Magnificient Men in Their Flying Machines* (1965).

Shall I get dressed or is it foreign movie time?

> Carole Werner (Romy Schneider) to Michael James (Peter O'Toole) in *What's New Pussycat?* (1965).

My father flew with the RAF. He said there were three things wrong with the Yanks: overpaid, oversexed, and over here.

> Scotland Yard Sgt. Jenny Thatcher (Judy Geeson) to Chicago Police Lt. James Brannigan (John Wayne) in *Brannigan* (1975).

- Hey! America was discovered by an Italian and it was named after another.

  - So what? What does that prove?

  - It proves that America is an Italian country.

> Joey Boca (Kevin Kline) to Lacey in *I Love You To Death* (1990).

- Are you finished?

  - No, are you Swedish?

> Neil (James Belushi) in *Once Upon a Crime* (1991).

Now let me ask you, gentlemen, is it true that in China, you drown middle-aged businessmen at birth?

Sheridan 'Sheri' Whiteside (Monty Woolley) to his unilingual Chinese guests in *The Man Who Came to Dinner* (1942).

Francophiles & Francophobes

Queen-From whence came you?

Larry-From Paris.

Queen-What were you doing there?

Moe-Oh, looking over the parasites.

In *Restless Knights* (1935).

Devilishly clever race the French. How they speak that unspeakable language of theirs defeats me.

Sir Percy Blakeney (Leslie Howard) to French spy-master Chauvelin (Raymond Massey) in *The Scarlet Pimpernel* (1935).

Ninotchka! It's midnight. One half of Paris is making love to the other half.

Count Leon (Melvyn Douglas) to Ninotchka (Greta Garbo) in *Ninotchka* (1939).

I am not a Frenchie! I am a Belgie!

Milo Perrier (James Coco) in *Murder by Death* (1976).

- Look, a sink in the living room.

- That's what the French call a bidet.

Two country girls, Rosie (Lily Tomlin) and her sophisticated sister Sadie (Bette Midler) in a fancy hotel room in *Big Business* (1988).

It's About Time

- I guess I'm taking your time.

- What do you think my time is for?

> Captain Cummings (Cary Grant) and Lady Lou (Mae West) in *She Done Him Wrong* (1933).

- To catch a Hardy you have to get up pretty early in the morning.

- What time?

- Oh, about half past...

> Ollie (Oliver Hardy) and Stan (Stan Laurel) in *Sons of the Desert* (1933).

- I'm afraid I was born a hundred years before my time.

- I was born ten days ahead of mine.

> Richard Miller (Eric Linden) and Muriel McComber (Cecilia Parker) in *Ah, Wilderness* (1935).

Wilkins, after all these years, are you trying to be funny?

> Henrietta Topper (Billie Burke) to her butler Wilkins (Alan Mowbray) in *Topper* (1937).

The age of chivalry is dead and when I come back I'll take you to the funeral.

> Jim Trevor (Douglas Fairbanks, Jr.) locking Nicole De Cortillon (Danielle Darrieux) in his apartment in *The Rage of Paris* (1938).

It's been so long since you've been up here I was beginning to commence to forget what you look like.

> Pop (Harry Davenport), the caretaker, to Jim Trevor (Douglas Fairbanks, Jr.) in *The Rage of Paris* (1938).

- This is Miss Judith Traherne of the sleepy Trahernes.

- Is it now? Well, this Mr. Michael O'Leary of the wide-awake O'Learys.

Judith (Bette Davis) and Michael (Humphrey Bogart)
having an early, in Judith's opinion, phone conversation
in *Dark Victory* (1939).

Moe-What time is it?

Shemp-I'll give you the time, old timer.

Moe-What's the idea of the three watches?

Shemp-That's the way I tell time.

Moe-How do you tell time?

Shemp-This one is ten minutes slow, this one is twenty minutes fast, the one in the middle is broke; it stopped at two o'clock.

Moe-How do you tell the time?

Shemp-I take the ten minutes slow, subtract it from the twenty minutes fast and divide it by the two in the middle.

Moe-What time is it now?

Shemp-(*Pulls out a fourth clock.*) Nine-thirty.

In *Studio Stoops* (1950). Moe had the same routine with
Curly in an earlier movie.

Every day, up at the
crack of noon.

Mame (Lucille Ball) in *Mame*
(1974).

I know we've only known each other for four weeks and three days, but to me it seems like nine weeks and five days. The first day seemed like a week; and the second day seemed like five days; and the third day seemed like a week again; and the fourth day seemed like eight days; and the fifth day you went to see your mother and that seemed just like a day and then you came back and later, on the sixth day, in the evening, when we saw each other, that started seeming like two days, so in the evening it seemed like two days spilling over into the next day and that started seeming like four days so at the end of the sixth day on into to seventh day, it seemed like a total of five days; and the sixth day seemed like a week and a half. I have it written down. I can show it to you tomorrow if you want to see it.

Navin Johnson (Steve Martin) to the sleeping Marie
(Bernadette Peters) in The Jerk (1979).

- You're not the man I knew ten years ago.

- It's not the years, honey, it's the mileage.

Marion Ravenswood (Karen Allen) and Indiana Jones
(Harrison Ford) in Raiders of the Lost Ark (1981).

- What time is it?

- I don't know.

- Don't you have a watch?

- No. I'm not allowed to wear a watch.

- Why not?

- I don't trust them.

- Why?

- One hand is shorter than the other.

Alan Swan (Peter O'Toole) and a stewardess (in the
morning) in My Favorite Year (1982).

- What the hell am I looking at? When does this happen in the movie?

- Now! You're looking at now, sir. Everything that happens now is happening now.

- What happened to then?

- We passed that.

- When?

- Just now. We're at now, now.

- Go back to then.

- When?

- Now.

- Now?

- Now.

- I can't.

- Why?

- We missed it.

- When?

- Just now.

- When will then be now?

- Soon.

> Lord Dark Helmet (Rick Moranis) and Colonel Sanderz
> (George Wyner) watching a videocassette of the movie
> *Spaceballs* (1987) while it is being filmed.

- What time is it?

- It's time to get your big, fat, extra-crispy-bucket-of-chicken, two-liter-Pepsi-Cola drinking ass out of bed.

> Jack Moony (Bob Hoskins), who inherited his heart from
> murdered lawyer Napoleon Stone (Denzel Washington),
> gets told off by Napoleon's ghost in *Heart Condition* (1990).

It's 1948. The future is here. If you don't wise up you're gonna be left so far behind it's gonna cost thirty cents just to send you a postcard.

> Harry Gordon (Clancy Brown) to P.I. Philip Lovecraft
> (Fred Ward) in *Cast a Deadly Spell* (1991).

Doin' Time

- I suggest we give him ten years in Leavenworth or eleven years in Twelveworth.

- I tell you what I'll do. I'll take five and ten in Woolworth.

> Rufus T. Firefly (Groucho Marx) and Chicolini (Chico Marx) at Chicolini's trial in *Duck Soup* (1933).

The prison hasn't been built that can hold me. I'll get out of this if it means spending my entire life here.

> Conman (Woody Allen) in *Take the Money and Run* (1969).

- I'm entitled to one phone call.
  - Well, if somebody phones you I'll let you know.

> Dan Bartlett (Bob Hope) and Sheriff Riley (Keenan Wynn) in *Cancel My Reservation* (1972).

Do you have a cell for beginners?

> Freddy Shoop (Mark Harmon) at the jailhouse in *Summer School* (1987).

I want to call CAA and my lawyer.

> Samantha Crane (Teri Hatcher) to interrogation detectives in *Brain Smasher... A Love Story* (1993).

I guess one bad habit is as good as another.

> Ruby Carter (Mae West) in *Belle of the Nineties* (1934).

When caught between two evils, I usually take the one I never tried.

> Mavis Arden (Mae West) makes a choice in *Go West, Young Man* (1936).

Hey, you said I was allowed one call. (*Fiyafit.*) A bluejay.

Jack Monicker (Robin Williams) in prison in *Club Paradise* (1986).

Sin & Vice

The boys are working on a plane:

Moe-Where's the vice?

Curly-Vice? I have no vice. I'm as pure as the driven snow.

Moe-But you drifted.

In *Dizzy Pilots* (1943). Taken from Mae West: "I was snow white, but I drifted."

Moe-You want to burn the scenery down? Read the sign.

Curly-HEY, YOU, NO SMOKING.

Moe-Well?

Curly-It says you, not me.

In *No Dough, Boys* (1944).

This is serious business, Father O'Malley. As you're more familiar with the case, I think you should handle it. I'll handle the little sins.

Old Father Fitzgibbons (Barry Fitzgerald) to Father O'Malley (Bing Crosby) in *Going My Way* (1944).

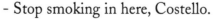

Good gracious! Water!

Professor Quail (W.C. Fields) drinking from the wrong glass in *International House* (1933). One of W.C. Fields catch-phrases was: "Don't drink water, fish f**k in it." Later in life, when his abdomen was water-swollen from cirrhosis of the liver, he told his doctor: "I knew that abominable, tasteless liquid would some day poison me."

- Stop smoking in here, Costello.

 - Who's smoking?

- You are.

- What makes you think that?

- You have a cigar in your mouth.

- I've got shoes on but I'm not walking.

Peter (Bud Abbott) and Jack (Lou Costello) in *Abbott and Costello Meet Frankenstein* (1948).

In my family the biggest sin was to buy retail.

Howard Prince (Woody Allen) in *The Front* (1976).

I need a valium the size of a hockey puck.

> Danny Rose (Woody Allen) in *Broadway Danny Rose* (1984).

- Do you smoke after you make love?

- I don't know. I never looked... but I'll tell you one thing, my smoke alarm never went off.

> Joey Fingers (Bruce Willis), a stand-up comic, in *North* (1994). The public laughs on the wrong line. Reminds us of words sung by Missouri Martin (Glenda Farrell) in *A Lady for a Day* (1933): "I'm so hot I'm smoking."

Make That a Double!

I never drink... wine!

> Count Dracula (Bela Lugosi) to Renfield (Dwight Frye) in *Dracula* (1931).

- You're drunk!

- Yeah! and you're crazy. I'll be sober in the morning, you'll be crazy the rest of your life.

> A land promoter and Harold Bissonette (W.C. Fields) in *It's a Gift* (1934). Sir Winston Churchill gave a similar reply to Bessie Braddock when she accused him of being drunk at a dinner party: "And you, madam, are ugly. But I shall be sober tomorrow."

I feel as though the Russian army'd been walking over my tongue in their stocking feet.

> Sheriff 'Honest John' Hoxley (W.C. Fields) the morning after in *Six of a Kind* (1934). Compare: *My Little Chickadee* (1940) and *Never Give A Sucker an Even Break* (1941).

Your ice is not cold enough.

> Fiorello (Chico Marx) drinking Gottlieb's (Siegfried Rumann) booze in *A Night at the Opera* (1935).

- I'm hot, soaked all over.

- You oughta get out of those wet clothes and into a dry martini.

> Van Reighle Van Pelter Van Doon (Charles Winninger) and his butler Larmadou Graves (Charles Butterworth) at the theater in *Every Day's a Holiday* (1937). See also *The Major and the Minor* (1942).

- My wife objects to drinking.

- Then she shouldn't drink.

- She doesn't.

- Then what's her objection?

> Topper (Roland Young) and George Kerby (Cary Grant) in *Topper* (1937).

There's lots of women has to make their husband drunk to make them fit to live with.

> Eliza Doolittle (Wendy Hiller) in *Pygmalion* (1938).

Gin was mother's milk to her.

> Eliza Doolittle's (Wendy Hiller) scandalizing anecdote about her alcoholic aunt in *Pygmalion* (1938).

- Will you stop drinking? For my sake?

- Who said I was drinking for your sake?

> Minerva Garrett (Alice Brady) and her husband Dennis (Guy Kibbee) in *Joy of Living* (1938).

My dear, I've been drinking for over forty years and I've never acquired the habit yet.

> Dennis Garrett (Guy Kibbee) to his wife Minerva (Alice Brady) in *Joy of Living* (1938).

Keep your hands off my lunch!

> Larson E. Whipsnade (W.C. Fields) about his bottle of whisky in *You Can't Cheat an Honest Man* (1939).

Some weasel took the cork out of my lunch.

> Larson E. Whipsnade (W.C. Fields) speaking of his whisky bottle in *You Can't Cheat An Honest Man* (1939).

During one of my trips through Afghanistan, we lost our corkscrew. Had to live on food and water for several days.

> Cuthbert J. Twillie (W.C. Fields) in *My Little Chickadee* (1940).

- What are you having?

  - I think I'll start with an old fashioned and bring it up to date.

> Mary Carter (Paulette Goddard) and Larry Lawrence (Bob Hope) in *The Ghost Breakers* (1940).

I'm not drunk, but what's the ceiling doing on the floor?

> S. Quentin Quale (Groucho Marx) in *Go West* (1940).

What a conk! The two-headed boy at the circus never had such a headache.

> Cuthbert J. Twillie (W.C. Fields) waking up with a drunk's headache in *My Little Chickadee* (1940).

I feel as though a midget with muddy feet had been walking over my tongue all night.

> Cuthbert J. Twillie (W.C. Fields) the morning after in *My Little Chickadee* (1940). See: Six of a Kind (1934), *Never Give a Sucker an Even Break* (1941).

- Are you airsick?

- No, dear, somebody put too many olives in my martinis last night.

- Shall I get you a Bromo?

- No, I couldn't stand the noise.

> The stewardess and Bill (W.C. Fields) in *Never Give a Sucker an Even Break* (1941).

I feel as though somebody stepped on my tongue with muddy feet.

> Uncle Bill (W.C. Fields) in *Never Give a Sucker an Even Break* (1941). See also: *Six of a Kind* (1934), *My Little Chickadee* (1940).

Why don't you get out of that wet coat and into a dry martini?

> Mr. Osborne (Robert Benchley) to Susan Applegate (Ginger Rogers) in *The Major and the Minor* (1942). See also *Every Day's a Holiday* (1937).

- Shall we drink to a blitzkrieg?

- No, I prefer a slow encirclement.

> Nazi professor Alexander Siletsky (Stanley Ridges) and Polish actress Maria Tura (Carole Lombard) in *To Be or Not to Be* (1942).

Champagne?! I love it. It tastes like your foot's asleep.

> Joan Mason (Joan Davis) in *George White's Scandal* (1945).

- Champagne?

   - Oh! What big bubbles.

   - Yes, they had big grapes that year.

> Eve Floogle (Binnie Barnes), Mr. Parker (Robert Benchley)
> and Fred Floogle (Fred Allen) in *It's in the Bag* (1945).

I always start around noon, in case it gets dark early.

> Rose Hopkins (Peggy Lee) about her drinking habit in
> *Pete Kelly's Blues* (1955).

- What are you trying to do? Drown your troubles?

   - Naw, I'm just teaching 'em how to swim.

> The bartender (Stanley Adams) and Parker Ballantine
> (Bob Hope) in *Critic's Choice* (1963).

I never drink when I fly!

> Superman (Christopher Reeve) to Lois Lane (Margot
> Kidder) in *Superman* (1978).

- How many gins and tonic have you had?

   - Three gins and one tonic.

   - Catch up on the tonic. We don't want to be disgusting
tonight, do we?

> Diana Barrie (Maggie Smith) and Sidney Cochran
> (Michael Caine) in *California Suite* (1978).

- I don't drink because drinking affects your decision making.

   - You may be right, I can't decide.

> Burt Johnson (Stephen Elliott) and Arthur Bach (Dudley
> Moore) in *Arthur* (1981).

**Martha, rubbing
alcohol for you?**

George (Richard Burton)
offering to replenish Martha's
(Elizabeth Taylor) drink in
*Who's Afraid of Virginia
Woolf?* (1966).

- A real woman could stop you from drinking.

- It would have to be a real big woman.

> Susan Johnson (Jill Eikenberry) and Arthur Bach (Dudley
> Moore) in *Arthur* (1981).

- Trust me about this one thing. You need a lot of drinks.

- To break the ice?

- To kill the bug that you have up your ass.

> Garrett Breedlove (Jack Nicholson) and Aurora
> Greenway (Shirley MacLaine) in *Terms of Endearment*
> (1983).

I need two aspirins, some tomato juice and some Worcestershire sauce, some goat cheese and some chicken fat.

> The Danny Rose (Woody Allen) formula for sobering up
> drunk performers in *Broadway Danny Rose* (1984).

- With women I never cry, never. I beg.

- If we finish this bottle of wine, you won't have to beg.

> Thornton Melon (Rodney Dangerfield) and Diane (Sally
> Kellerman) in *Back to School* (1986).

It's true. I am a vegetarian, but I hear vodka comes from a potato.

> Barbara Whiteman (Bette Midler) to her husband Dave
> (Richard Dreyfuss) in *Down and Out in Beverly Hills*
> (1986).

Fact! Alcohol kills brain cells. You lose one more, you're a talking monkey.

> Freddy Shoop (Mark Harmon) to Chainsaw (Dean
> Cameron) in *Summer School* (1987).

- An occasional libation enables me to stiffen my resolve.

   - Your resolve should be pickled by now.

> Sherlock Holmes/Reginald Kinkaid (Michael Caine) and
> Mrs. Hudson in *Without a Clue* (1988).

Sorry, guys. The Brothers Against Drunk Driving, they've been busting my ass. You've gotta perform a sobriety test. (...) Close your eyes. Real tight. No peeking. Now, recite the alphabet backward, skipping all the vowels, and give me the sign language for each letter as you pass by.

> The bartender (Sy Richardson) to Josh (Tim Robbins) and
> Ivan (John Cusack) when they order two extra beers in
> *Tapeheads* (1988); they pass.

- You're drunk!

   - On the contrary. I've never been more intoxicated in my life.

> Stanford Bach (Thomas Barbout) and his son Arthur
> (Dudley Moore) in *Arthur 2: On the Rocks* (1988).

Look at him! Drunk as a skunkasaurus.

Wilma (Elizabeth Perkins) about her hubby Fred (John Goodman) in *The Flintstones* (1994).

What Are the Odds? or Roll Dem Bones

- Is this a game of chance?
- Not the way I play it.

> Cousin Zeb (Fuzzy Knight) playing poker with Cuthbert J.
> Twillie (W.C. Fields) in *My Little Chickadee* (1940).

What's that you're playing, boys? Poker?

> Card sharp Sniper (Chill Wills) playing the innocent
> everytime he sits at a gambling table in *Honky Tonk* (1941).

*Butch Cassidy and the
Sundance Kid*

Anyone knows that a hunch can make a dollar faster than an expert.

Professor B (Ray Collins) about betting on the horses in *The Big Street* (1942).

Moe-Why you cheap crook. Stealing a baby's bank.

Curly-It's only a lend-lease. I figured I'd bet on a fifty to one shot and double the baby's money.

Moe-Why you imbecile! Why don't you pick a hundred to one shot and triple it?

Moe, always the bright one, in *Even as I.O.U.* (1942).

I'll lay you ten to one I never took a bet in my life.

Sorrowful (Bob Hope) to a detective in *Sorrowful Jones* (1949).

- I begged him not to bet. He always loses.

- I do not!

- Of course you do. Never mind. Hand me that chair.

- What chair?

- That one. Hurry.

- There's no chair there.

- Of course there is. Don't be ridiculous... Look, you say there's no chair there and I say there is. You give me a buck if I'm wrong?

- You got a bet.

- Okay, I'm wrong. (*Grabs the buck.*)

> Raymond Paine (Jason Robards) and Chick Williams
> (Norman Wisdom) in *The Night They Raided Minsky's*
> (1968).

- What's the secret of your success?

  - Prayer.

> The Sundance Kid's (Robert Redford) answer to the losing
> gambler in *Butch Cassidy and the Sundance Kid* (1969).

Holy Quotes!

Until you stirred Him up, I had no trouble with God.

> Clarence 'Clare' Day (William Powell) to his wife Vinny
> (Irene Dunne) who discovered that he wasn't baptised in
> *Life with Father* (1947).

I can't go to heaven in a cab!

> Clarence 'Clare' Day (William Powell) to his wife Vinny
> (Irene Dunne) in *Life with Father* (1947).

King Solomon had the right idea about work: Whatever thy hand findeth to do, Solomon said, do thy doggonedest.

> Clarence 'Clare' Day (William Powell) to his son
> Clarence, Jr. (James Lydon) in *Life with Father* (1947).

Joe couldn't find a prayer in the Bible.

> Mobster Whit Sterling (Kirk Douglas) speaking of his
> henchman in *Out of the Past* (1947).

You two guys must have been born in revival meetings.

> Fred C. Dobbs/Dobbsy (Humphrey Bogart) to Howard
> (Walter Huston) and Curtin (Tim Holt), who want to give

a fourth of the take to Cody's widow in *The Treasure of the Sierra Madre* (1948).

Oh, Moses, Moses, you stubborn, splendid, adorable fool.

Nefretiri (Anne Baxter) to Moses (Charlton Heston) in *The Ten Commandments* (1956).

God opens the sea with a blast of his nostrils!

Old man in *The Ten Commandments* (1956).

- God meant us to find each other.

- His will be done.

Major Frank Burns (Robert Duvall) and Major 'Hot Lips' Houlihan (Sally Kellerman) in the heat of passion in *M*A*S*H* (1970).

- My God!!!

- Yesss?

Sir Charles Gurney/Uncle Charles (William Mervyn), outraged by Jack, 14th Earl of Gurney (Peter O'Toole), who believes Himself to be God in *The Ruling Class* (1972).

- How did you come to be in this state... of grace?

- Like every prophet I saw visions, I heard voices, I ran, but the voices of Saint Francis, Socrates, General Gordon and Timothy O'Leary all told me I was God.

Lady Claire Gurney/Aunt Claire (Coral Browne) and Jack, the 14th Earl of Gurney (Peter O'Toole), who believes Himself to be God, J.C., or 'any of the nine billion names of God' all rolled into one in *The Ruling Class* (1972).

- What does it feel like to be God?

- Like a river flowing everywhere. I pick up a newspaper and I'm everywhere: conducting a summit conference, dying of hunger in a Peruvian gutter, accepting the Nobel Prize for literature, raping a nun in Sumatra. Under this protective outer shell I'm God-filled.

> Lady Claire Gurney/Aunt Claire (Coral Browne) and
> Jack, 14th Earl of Gurney (Peter O'Toole), who believes
> Himself to be God in *The Ruling Class* (1972).

For what I am about to receive may I make Myself truly thankful.

> Jack, 14th Earl of Gurney/God/J.C. (Peter O'Toole)
> breaking toasted muffin in *The Ruling Class* (1972).

- J.C., we were just talking about you and marriage. We think you should take a wife.

  - Who from?

> Sir Charles Gurney/Uncle Charles (William Mervyn) and
> Jack, 14th Earl of Gurney (Peter O'Toole), who believes
> Himself to be God and insists upon being called J.C., in
> *The Ruling Class* (1972).

All right! If you're God reveal your godhead.

> Lady Claire Gurney (Coral Browne) to Jack, the lunatic
> 14th Earl of Gurney (Peter O'Toole), who believes He's
> God and unzips his fly to prove it in *The Ruling Class*
> (1972).

- You deserve a big kiss.

  - Not here in the garden. The last time I was kissed in a garden it turned out rather awkward.

  - But Judas was a man.

  - Yes, strange business. Who are you?

  - A woman.

The Ruling Class

- Descended from Eve?

- No, a doorstep. I'm an orphan.

- We'll be orphans together, Marguerite.

- Call me Grace.

> Marguerite/Grace Shelley (Carolyn Seymour) and Jack,
> 14th Earl of Gurney/God/J.C. (Peter O'Toole), in *The
> Ruling Class* (1972).

- Do you believe in God?

- Do I believe in God? I'm what you'd call a theological existential atheist. I believe that there is an intelligence to the universe with exception to certain parts of New Jersey.

> Luna Schlosser (Diane Keaton) to the recently defrosted
> Miles Monroe (Woody Allen) after 200 years in a
> cryogenetic capsule in *Sleeper* (1973).

- Do you believe in God?

- Well, I believe that there's somebody out there who watches over us.

- Unfortunately, it's the government.

> Miles Monroe (Woody Allen) and Luna Schlosser (Diane
> Keaton) in *Sleeper* (1973).

I was walking through the woods thinking about Christ. If He was a carpenter I wondered how much He charged for bookshelves.

> Boris Grushenko (Woody Allen) in *Love and Death*
> (1975).

- Of course there's a God. We're made in his image.

- You think I was made in God's image? Take a look at me. Do you think He wears glasses?

- Not with those frames.

Sonja (Diane Keaton) and Boris (Woody Allen) in *Love and Death* (1975).

If it turns out that there is a God, I don't think that He's evil. I think that the worst you can say about Him is that He's an underachiever.

Boris Grushenko (Woody Allen) in *Love and Death* (1975).

- Boris, we must believe in God.

- If I could just see a miracle. Just one miracle. If I could see a burning bush or the seas part or my Uncle Sacha pick up a check.

Sonja (Diane Keaton) and Boris (Woody Allen) in *Love and Death* (1975).

- My God!

- Mine too!

Simone (Dyan Cannon) and Jacques Clouseau (Peter Sellers) in *Revenge of the Pink Panther* (1978).

We're on a mission from God!

Repeatedly, preceded by: "They're not going to catch us..." or, "Me and the Lord we've got an understanding...." Joliet Jake Blues (John Belushi) and his brother Elwood (Dan Aykroyd) in *The Blues Brothers* (1980).

He's got a record a mile long and he's a Catholic.

Two good reasons for the Nazi leader (Henry Gibson) to hate Elwood Blues (Dan Aykroyd) in *The Blues Brothers* (1980).

Why me, Lord?! I mean, you made other men out of clay, mine you made out of shit?

Cholla (John Quade), gang leader of the Black Widow bikers in *Any Which Way You Can* (1981).

- Moses, this is the Lord thy God.... Do you hear me?

- I hear you, I hear you. A deaf man could hear you.

> Moses (Mel Brooks) in *History of the World: Part 1*
> (1981).

Hear me! O hear me! All pay heed. The Lord Jehovah has just given unto you these fifteen... ten commandments.

> Moses (Mel Brooks) revises his speech after dropping one
> the tablets in *History of the World: Part 1* (1981).

Jews know two things: suffering and where to find great Chinese food.

> Benjy Stone (Mark Linn-Baker) to K.C. Downing (Jessica
> Harper) in *My Favorite Year* (1982).

Why do you think God invented credit? He values people like me.

> Jules (Demi Moore) in *St. Elmo's Fire* (1985).

She's not just a girl. She's the only evidence of God that I can find on this entire planet, with the exception of the mystical force that removes one of my socks from the dryer every time I do the laundry.

> Kirbo (Emilio Estevez) in *St. Elmo's Fire* (1985).

Jesus said: It is easier for a camel to pass through the eye of a needle than for an officer to enter the kingdom of heaven.

> Captain Red/Thomas Bartholomew Red (Walter Matthau)
> to the mutineers in *Pirates* (1986).

I'm attracted to you (...) and if we made love you could give absolution.

> Holly Parish (Sally Kellerman) to Father Baragone (Robert Loggia) in *That's Life!* (1986).

This guy knows God personally. I hear they play racketball together.

> Pep Streebek (Tom Hanks) speaking of Reverend Whirley (Christopher Plummer) in *Dragnet* (1987).

- I don't hear God laughing.

  - He will, once he sees your haircut.

> Joe Friday (Dan Aykroyd) and Pep Streebek (Tom Hanks) in *Dragnet* (1987).

- Jesus Christ!

  - Guess again!

> Amber Mendez (Maria Conchita Alonso) and Ben Richards (Arnold Schwarzenegger) when Fireball (Jim Brown) jumps in the arena in *The Running Man* (1987).

- What if it isn't funny? You tell me to talk about my life but what if my life isn't funny?

  - All of our lives are funny, babe. We're God's animated cartoons.

> Lilah Krytsick (Sally Field) and Steven Gold (Tom Hanks) in *Punchline* (1988).

No sermons please, Bosey. I'm not in the mood for the missionary position now.

> Oscar Wilde (Nickolas Grace) to Lord Alfred 'Bosey' Douglas (Douglas Hodge) in *Salome's Last Dance* (1988).

It's amazing! You look like a normal person, but actually you're the angel of death.

> Harry Burns (Billy Crystal) in *When Harry Met Sally*
> (1989).

- Do nuns wear make-up?

  - It's our day off.

> Sister Inviolata of the Immaculate Conception/Charlie
> McManus (Robbie Coltrane) to the inquisitive pharmacist
> in *Nuns on the Run* (1990).

- Explain the Trinity.

  - Hmmm. It's a bit of a bugger.

  - It can't be that difficult. You've been a Catholic all your life.

  - Yeah.... Well, here's the pitch. You've got the Father, the Son, and the Holy Ghost. The three are one, my old priest used to say, three leafs but one leaf. Now, the Father sent down the Son, who was love, and when he went away he sent down the Holy Spirit who came down in the form of a...

  - You told me already. A ghost.

  - No, a dove.

  - The dove was a ghost?

  - No, the ghost was a dove.

  - Let me try and summarize this. God is his Son and his Son is God but his Son moonlights as a Holy Spirit and a dove and they all send each other even though they're all one and the same thing.

  - Got it!

  - What?

  - You really could be a nun.

- Thanks. Wait a minute! What I said, does that make any sense to you?

- Well, no. No, but it makes no sense to anybody. That's why you have to believe it, that's why you have to have faith. I mean if it made sense it wouldn't have to be a religion, would it?

Look, I told you: with spectacles, testicles, wallet and watch.

- Charlie, some con man sells life insurance and the Church sells afterlife insurance. It's brilliant! Everyone thinks you might need it and no one can prove you don't.

- The Church isn't selling anything, Brian.

- Oh, well, if the Church isn't selling anything how did it get to be so rich? Just remember. Whenever there's a deep human need there's money to be made.

- Oh, you think so?

- Of course. Look at Kentucky Fried Chicken.

- Is that what you're saying God wanted the Church to be? Rich?

- No, but God is very busy. He can't conrol all the details. He's running a franchise operation.

> Brian Hope/Sister Euphemia of the Five Wounds (Eric Idle)
> and Charlie McManus/Sister Inviolata of the Immaculate
> Conception (Robbie Colrane) in *Nuns on the Run* (1990).

I must come clean though. I had a man in my bed last night, all night. You see, the way I see it, sex is allowed. (...) It's the doctrine of original sin. You see, we're all born sinful except for Jesus who was born perfect, of course, and he was sent to save us, but how can he save us unless were sinning? So, we have to go on sinning in order to be saved and go to heaven. That's how Christianity works. That's why it suits so many of us.

> Sister Inviolata of the Immaculate Conception/Charlie
> McManus (Robbie Coltrane) to Father Shamus (Tom
> Hickey) in *Nuns on the Run* (1990).

- God created man in His own image.
  - Oh yeah! Then how do you explain Pee Wee Herman?

> The Devil and Father Brophy (Anthony Starke) in
> *Repossessed* (1990).

Any decent church would have burned you bastards long ago.

> Barley Blair (Sean Connery) to the British intelligence
> officers in *The Russia House* (1990).

I'm the janitor of God!

> Parry (Robin Williams) in *The Fisher King* (1991).

- Jesus Christ!
  - Nah! He had nothing to do with it.

> Ritchie Madano (William Forsythe) in *Out for Justice* (1991).

- Jesus Christ!

  - Almost.

> Nick Styles (Denzel Washington) and murderer Blake
> (John Lithgow) in *Ricochet* (1991).

- Oh, Jesus! Oh, God!

  - This is no time for prayers!

> President Benson (Lloyd Bridges) to his assistant Bob, who
> is trying to extract a sharp object from his skull in *Hot
> Shots! Part Deux* (1993).

Miss(ed) Manners

John, every day you act worse, but today, you're acting like tomorrow.

> Huck Haines (Fred Astaire) to John Kent (Randolph Scott)
> in *Roberta* (1935).

What a pity her manners don't match her looks.

> Sir Robin of Locksley/Robin Hood (Errol Flynn) speaking
> of Maid Marian (Olivia de Havilland) in *The Adventures
> of Robin Hood* (1938).

Hey! Where's your Emily Post?

> Moe reprimanding Larry for not sticking out his little
> fingers when drinking soup from the bowl in *Three Sappy
> People* (1939).

- You oughta marry Bergen while you have the chance.

  - Emily Post says a lady waits until she's asked.

- Tie yourself to a post and you'll never get hitched.

> Molly McGee (Marion Jordan) and Julie Patterson (Lucille
> Ball) in *Look Who's Laughing* (1941).

Young woman, either you have been raised in some incredibly rustic community where good manners are unknown, or you suffer from the common feminine delusion that the mere fact of being a woman exempts you from the rules of civilized conduct. Possibly both.

> Waldo Lydecker (Clifton Webb) to Laura Hunt (Gene
> Tierney), who interrupts his dinner in *Laura* (1944).

You're just not couth!

> Billie Dawn (Judy Holliday) to Harry Brock (Broderick
> Crawford) in *Born Yesterday* (1950).

- I'm sorry to seem so inhospitable but in the past twelve months alone over 320 girls in the Greater London area have been attacked by persons unknowned and many of them unnecessarily mutilated. Do come in.

   - They do say it's something to do with the weather.

> Julia Finsbury (Nanette Newman) and Michael Finsbury
> (Michael Caine) in *The Wrong Box* (1966).

Bill-No!

   Hannah-No what?

   Bill-No, Sir!

> Bill Warren (Alan Alda) and his ex-wife Hannah (Jane
> Fonda) in *California Suite* (1978).

Sir! Your humor is as tasteless as your manners.

> Sara (Jane Seymour) to Lassiter (Tom Selleck) in *Lassiter*
> (1984).

He's a real gentleman. I bet he takes the dishes out of the sink before he pees in it.

Ouiser Boudreaux (Shirley Maclaine) in *Steel Magnolias* (1989).

You guys are guests in my corn.

Ray Kinsella (Kevin Costner) to Shoeless Joe Jackson and the baseball players in *Field of Dreams* (1990).

Volare, you know it's not polite to drool in public.

Rolant T. Flakfizer (John Turturro) to Roberto Volare (George De La Pena) in *Brain Donors* (1992).

Elly Mae, don't spit from a moving vehicle.... Wait 'til it stops.

Granny (Cloris Leachman) to tobacco-chewing Elly Mae (Erica Eleniak) in *The Beverly Hillbillies* (1993).

Hygiene Hijinks

Moe-Go take a bath.

Larry-But it ain't spring yet.

In *Healthy, Wealthy and Dumb* (1938).

- Shame, the least you could do is shave.

- What are you talking about? I'm clean.

- Well, you need to wear a sign that says so.

Peaches Jordan (Jada Pinkett) and Shame (Keenen Ivory Wayans) in *A Low Down Dirty Shame* (1994).

- Did you take a shower?

- Why? Is there one missing?

Willoughby (Lou Costello) to the pool attendant in *Ride 'Em Cowboy* (1942).

Shemp-Ah, money shrinks.

Moe-So do you, anytime you get near a bathtub.

In *Don't Throw That Knife* (1951).

May I make a statement, McKay? Your mouthwash ain't making it.

Dirty Harry Callahan (Clint Eastwood) to Captain McKay (Bradford Dillman) in *The Enforcer* (1976).

- I think I'll take a bath.

- I'll alert the media.

Arthur (Dudley Moore) and his valet Hobson (John Gielgud) in *Arthur* (1981).

- Do you know the worst part... the worst part of being me?

- I would imagine your breath.

Arthur (Dudley Moore) and Hobson (John Gielgud) in *Arthur* (1981).

Dudley Moore in *Arthur*

You're standing awful close, Gus. I can't tell whether it's your toes I'm smelling or mine.

Roy Hobbs (Robert Redford) to Gus in *The Natural* (1984).

- What can I do, Hobson? What would you do if you were me?

- The word bathe comes to mind. (...)

- Maybe we should go somewhere else.

- Yes, if possible somewhere upwind.

- Look at me, Hobson.

- No, thank you.

Arthur (Dudley Moore), now a destitute drunk on skid row asking advice of former butler Hobson (John Gielgud) in *Arthur 2: On the Rocks* (1988).

I'm afraid we haven't properly housebroken Miss Kyle. In the plus column though, she makes a hell of a cup of coffee.

Max Shreck (Christopher Walken) speaking of Selina Kyle/Cat Woman (Michelle Pfeiffer) in *Batman Returns* (1992).

- Wilma, how did you get rid of ring around the collar?

- I just started washing Fred's neck.

Betty (Rosie O'Donnell) and Wilma (Elizabeth Perkins) in *The Flintstones* (1994).

Auto-Rama

Drive me off this picture!

Hedley Lamarr (Harvey Korman) jumping into a yellow taxi to escape the mob of fighting cowboys in *Blazing Saddles* (1974).

- It's 106 miles to Chicago, we got a full tank of gas, half a pack of cigarettes, it's dark and we're wearing sunglasses.

- Hit it!

Elwood Blues (Dan Aykroyd) and his brother Joliet Jake (John Belushi) about to start one of the biggest car chases in the history of motion pictures in *The Blues Brothers* (1980).

Are you driving with your eyes open or are you, like, using the Force?

Axel Foley (Eddie Murphy) to Billy Rosewood (Judge Reinhold) in *Beverly Hills Cop II* (1987).

- Are those your initials?

- Yes.

- I bet you had to try a thousand dealers before you found a car with your initials on it.

Arthur (Dudley Moore) to Kendal Winchester (David O'Brien) riding the limousine next to him in the park in *Arthur 2: On the Rocks* (1988).

Charlotte, you drive like old people make love.

Mrs. Flax (Cher) to her daughter Charlotte (Winona Ryder) learning to drive in *Mermaids* (1990).

- How come you didn't knock?
- I'm using a better grade of gas.

Roland T. Flakfizer (John Turturro) and taxi driver/assistant manager Rocco Meloncheck (Mel Smith), coming into his room unannounced in *Brain Donors* (1992).

The next time you jump out of a car make sure it's moving.

Chester Lee (Rodney Dangerfield) to his young son-in-law Matthew (Jonathan Brandis) in *Ladybugs* (1992).

The Blues Brothers, Jake and Elwood Blues

- Give you a ride home, Ned?
  - No. I have my own car
  - I'll tow you.
  - Not today.

Laura (Sherilyn Fenn) and Ned Ravine (Armand Assante) in a typical scene from *Fatal Instinct* (1993).

If he so much as sniffles this afternoon I will be on your tail like a Carolina speed cop on a New York Cadillac.

Capt. Dave Anderson (Nipsey Russell) entrusting the protection of a witness to Officer Gunther Toody (David Johansen) in *Car 54, Where Are You?* (1994).

He Shoots, He Scores!

Moe-Quarterback.

Larry-Halfback.

Curly-Hunchback.

The boys stating their position to the security guard while sneaking on the football field in *No Census, No Feeling* (1940).

Larry-There oughta be plenty of shooting around here. This is game country.

Curly-How do you know?

Larry-I just saw a sign: FINE FOR HUNTING.

Curly-I think you've got something there.

In *Idiots Deluxe* (1945).

- Water polo?! Isn't that terribly dangerous?

- I'll say! I've had two ponies drown under me.

Sugar Kane (Marilyn Monroe) and Joe (Tony Curtis) pretending to be a rich playboy in *Some Like It Hot* (1959).

- My God! They shot him!

- Hot Lips, you incredible nincompoop! It's the end of the quarter.

Major 'Hot Lips' Houlihan (Sally Kellerman) and Colonel Henry Blake (Roger Bowen) at the football game in *M*A*S*H* (1970).

- Oh, Ty, what did you shoot today?

- I don't keep score, Judge.

- Well, how do you measure yourself with other golfers?

- By height.

> Judge Smalls (Ted Knight) and
> Ty Webb (Chevy Chase) in
> *Caddyshack* (1980).

Thank you for a memorable afternoon.
Usually one has to go to a bowling alley
to meet a woman of your stature.

> Hobson (John Gielgud) to Gloria
> (Liza Minnelli) in *Arthur* (1981).

I'd never sleep with a player hittin' under
.200 unless he had a lot of RBIs and was
a great glove man up the middle.

> (Susan Sarandon) to (Tim
> Robbins) and (Kevin Costner) in
> *Bull Durham* (1988).

Chevy Chase and Bill
Murray in *Caddyshack*

Frank-Hector Savage from Detroit.
Hey! I remember this pug. Ex-boxer. His real name was
Joey Chicago.

Ed-Oh yeah! He fought under the name of Kid Minneapolis.

Nordberg-I saw Kid Minneapolis fight once. In Cincinnati.

Frank-No! You're thinking of Kid New York. He fought
out of Philly.

Ed-He was killed in the ring in Houston by Tex Colorado. You know, the Arizona Assassin.

Nordberg-Yeah! From Dakota. I don't remember if it was
North or South.

Frank-North! South Dakota was his brother, from West Virginia.

Ed-You sure know your boxing.

Frank-Well, all I know is, never bet on the white guy.

> Frank Drebin (Leslie Nielsen), Ed Hocken (George Kennedy) and Nordberg (O. J. Simpson) in *The Naked Gun 2 1/2: The Smell of Fear* (1991).

Kinky, but I like my sex the way I play basketball: one on one and with as little dribbling as possible.

> Frank Drebin (Leslie Nielsen) to Tanya (Anna Nicole Smith) who offers to take him on as a second lover in *The Naked Gun 33 1/3: The Final Insult* (1994).

Purely Political

Politics!? You couldn't get into politics! You couldn't get in anywhere. You couldn't even get into the men's room at the Astor.

> Kitty Packard (Jean Harlow) to her husband Dan (Wallace Beery) in *Dinner at Eight* (1933).

- Do you believe in reincarnation, you know, that dead people come back?

- You mean, like Republicans?

> Cicily (Nydia Westman) and Wallie Campbell (Bob Hope) in *The Cat and the Canary* (1939).

- I'm just going to sit around and listen.

- That's the way to get re-elected.

> Senator Jefferson Smith (James Stewart) and a page boy on his first day in the house in *Mr. Smith Goes to Washington* (1939).

I'm going to take him to the roof and overthrow him.

Larry Gallstone speaking of dictator Moe Hailstone in
You Nazty Spy! (1940).

My good people of Moronica. I'm very happy to see this little gathering. We must throw off the yoke of monarchy and make our country safe for hypocrisy. Our motto shall be: Moronica for Morons. We will have less work and more play. Every Thursday, you will receive hamburgers and eggs. Moronica must expand. We must extend our neighbors a helping hand. We will extend them two helping hands and help ourselves to our neighbors.

Moe Hailstone, dictator of Moronica in *You Nazty Spy!*
(1940).

- A zombie has no will of his own. You see them sometimes, walking around blindly with dead eyes, following orders, not knowing what they do, not caring.

  - You mean... like democrats?

Geoff Montgomery (Richard Carlson), describing Cuban
zombies, and Larry Lawrence (Bob Hope) in *The Ghost
Breakers* (1940).

- I don't know what came over me. I found myself saying things and didn't know why I was saying them.

  - Look, why don't you just run for Congress and let us alone, eh?

Lucia de Andrade (Dorothy Lamour) and 'Hot Lips'
Barton (Bob Hope) in *The Road to Rio* (1947).

Why did God make so many dumb fools and democrats?

Clarence Day (William Powell) in *Life with Father* (1947).

- I thought it was agreed we were going to trust each other?

- Only when we're all in the same room.

Spike (Van Johnson) and Jim Conover (Adolphe Menjou)
in *State of the Union* (1948).

The world's sure changed since I was politicking. In those days we had to pour God over everything, like catsup.

Former President Art Hockstader (Lee Tracy) in *The Best Man* (1964).

T.T. Claypoole has all the characteristics of a dog, except loyalty.

William Russell (Henry Fonda) about fellow candidate T.T. Claypoole (John Henry Faulk) in *The Best Man* (1964).

I can no longer sit back and allow Communist infiltration, Communist indoctrination, Communist subversion, and the international Communist conspiracy to sap and impurify all of our bodily fluids.

General Jack D. Ripper (Sterling Hayden) in *Dr. Strangelove, or: How I Learned to Stop Worrying and Love the Bomb* (1964).

It would be difficult Mein Fuhrer, nuclear... I'm sorry, Mr. President...

Dr. Strangelove (Peter Sellers) confusing his old master with the new one in *Dr. Strangelove, or: How I Learned To Stop Worrying and Love the Bomb* (1964).

- Miles, have you ever taken a serious political stand on anything?

- Yeah, sure. For twenty-four hours once I refused to eat grapes.

> Dr. Melik (Mary Gregory) after bringing Miles Monroe (Woody Allen) out of a 200-year sleep in a cryogenetic capsule in the year 2173 in *Sleeper* (1973).

What is it with you people? You think not getting caught in a lie is the same as telling the truth?

> Joe Turner (Robert Redford) to his CIA chief Higgins (Cliff Robertson) in *Three Days of the Condor* (1975).

Lyndon Johnson is a politician. You know the ethics those guys have. It's like a notch underneath child molesters.

> Alvy Singer (Woody Allen) in *Annie Hall* (1977).

- What is this all about, Max?

- I can't tell you that, 99. I've been sworn to secrecy by the President himself.

- You met the President?! What is he like?

- Everything you'd expect him to be.

- Oh! I'm sorry to hear that.

> Agent 99 (Barbara Feldon) and her husband, Agent 86, Maxwell Smart (Don Adams) in *Get Smart, Again!* (1989).

- Is there much interaction between the two campaigns? You know, between Democrats and Republicans?

- Ah, I think this is your area.

- It's discouraged for campaigns to socialize. If one speech-writer, to use an example, were to date another they might reveal something about their campaigns. Some campaigns have spies for just that purpose. To pursue someone on the other campaign, to seduce her...

Listen, I'm a voter. Aren't you supposed to lie to me and kiss my butt?

Dr. Peter Venkman (Bill Murray) to a politician in *Ghostbusters II* (1989).

- Or him...

- And try to find out her secrets.

- On the other hand, sometimes people have a tendency to get what's called paranoid, and just because someone seems interested in them that doesn't mean they're after their 'secrets'.

- Still, it's not paranoid to be suspicious of, let's say, a relationship that moves too fast, a chance encounter that isn't really chance...

- Or somebody lying about the work she does...

- Or asks too much about the other's work.

- Of course, a speechwriter could use Miss, I'm sorry, I forgot your name.

- Mann.

- Yeah, righ, to use Miss Mann's earlier example, a speechwriter could protect herself...

- Or himself...

- From being compromised in this way by not flirting, you know, not sniffing around like cat in heat.

- Or she might actually tell the other speechwriter to his face: Peddle your shit elsewhere, scumbag.

- One thing is clear. Once the infiltrator or slut spy for lack of other words has been uncovered, well then the other speechwriter's passion for the campaign is renewed.

- And he'll need it because if he's a has-been, let's say, jumping from field to field like some f**k-happy rabbit carrying the inadequacies that come from inexperience...

- Or the total lack of creativity that comes from over-experience...

- He will need any motivation he can find, especially if he's fighting against someone who actually believes in her cause.

- I'd like to thank both Mr. Vallek and Miss Mann for their illuminating words about Politics, The Human Side.

> Once the first question is asked by a student from Mesa Junior High, knives, bullets, mud and sludge fly between Kevin (Michael Keaton) and Julia (Geena Davis), who lower their voices for the more vicious insults in *Speechless* (1994).

War...What Is It Good For?

- Now that you are Secretary of War, what kind of an army do you think we oughta have?

- Well, I tell you what I think. I think we should have a standing army.

- Why should we have a standing army?

- Because then we save on chairs.

> Rufus T. Firefly (Groucho Marx) and Chicolini (Chico Marx) in *Duck Soup* (1933).

There's a cross on the muzzle of the pistol with the bullet, there's a nick on the muzzle of the pistol with the blank.

> Told to John Kidley (Bob Hope) before a duel in *Never Say Die* (1939).

Lovely sound, but a little late.

> Beau Geste (Gary Cooper) at the sound of the bugle announcing the arrival of reinforcements in *Beau Geste* (1939).

Moe Hailstone-I want to know about my armies. Have we taken the dykes of Holland?

___ 66 ___

- I'm willing to do anything to prevent this war.

- It's too late. I've already paid a month's rent on the battlefield.

> Ambassador Trentino (Louis Calhern) and Rufus T. Firefly (Groucho Marx) in *Duck Soup* (1933).

Curly Pebble-Certainly, and the Van Dykes of Amsterdam, and the Updikes of Rotterdam, and the Hunchback of Notre Dame.

Moe Hailstone-Heil!

Curly Pebble-Heil!

Larry Gallstone-Heel!

Moe Hailstone-Heil! you say.

Larry Gallstone-Heil! you say.

Dictator Moe and the boys in I'll Never Heil Again (1941).

When we win the war we'll send you some missionaries.

Johnnie's (Laurence Olivier) dying words to the Nazi
officer in 49th Parallel (U.S. title: The Invaders) (1941).

- Throw your chest out!

  - I'm not through with it yet.

Slicker Smith (Bud Abbott) drilling Pfc. Herbie Brown (Lou
Costello) in Buck Privates (1941).

- Throw your chest out.

  - How far?

  - Alright, throw it out.

  - I'm not through with it yet.

Slats McCarthy (Bud Abbott) pushing Oliver
Quackenbush (Lou Costello) into the wrestling ring in
Here Come the Co-Eds (1945).

And what if you tracked down these men and killed them? What if you murdered all of us? From every corner of your appandance, thousands would rise to take up our places. Even Nazis can't kill that fast.

> Victor Laszlo (Paul Henreid) to Nazi Major Strasser
> (Conrad Veidt) in *Casablanca* (1942).

You and your stripes. A zebra is covered with stripes but underneath he's still a jackass.

> Private Wally Hogan (Bob Hope) to Sergeant Danzig
> (Eddie Mayeoff) in *Off Limits* (1953).

I'm not very good with swords. How about blades? How about next Tuesday?

> Pipo Papolino (Bob Hope) impersonating the great
> swordsman Casanova being challenged to a duel in
> *Casanova's Big Night* (1954).

We live in a democracy and in a democracy it's everyman's right to be killed fighting for his country.

> Brendan Byers III (Jerry Lewis) in *Which Way to the
> Front?* (1970).

- I wonder how a degenerate person like that could have reached a position of responsibility in the army medical corps?

- He was drafted.

> Major 'Hot Lips' Houlihan (Sally Kellerman) and Dago
> Red (Rene Auberjonois) in *M*A*S*H* (1970).

- Shall we say pistols at dawn?

- Well, we can say it. I don't know what it means, but we can say it.

- You have insulted the honor of Countess Alexandrovna.

- Why? I let her finish first.

Martin Sheen in
Apocalypse Now

- Her seconds will call on you.

- Seconds?! I never gave her seconds.

- As her fiancé, my seconds will call on your seconds.

- Well, my seconds will be out. Have them call on my thirds. If my thirds are out, have them call on my fourths.

Anton (Harold Gould) challenging Boris (Woody Allen) to a duel in *Love and Death* (1975).

Shit! Charging a man with murder in this place is like handing out speeding tickets at the Indy 500.

Captain Willard (Martin Sheen) in *Apocalypse Now* (1979).

I love the smell of napalm in the morning... Smells like victory.

Lt. Col. Kilgore (Robert Duvall) in *Apocalypse Now* (1979).

We're Americans, with a capital A. Do you know what that means? That means that our forefathers were kicked out of every decent country in the world. We are the wretched refuse. We're underdogs. We're mutts. Here's proof (*touches a soldier's nose*). His nose is cold. But there's no animal that's more faithful, that's more loyal, that's more lovable than the mutt. Who saw *Old Yeller*? Who cried when Old Yeller got shot at the end? I cried my eyes out. So we're all dog faces. We're all very, very different. But there is one thing that we all have in common: we were all stupid

Bill Murray in *Stripes*

Forrest Gump

enough to enlist in the army.

John Winger (Bill Murray) in *Stripes* (1981).

Excuse me, sir. Seeing as the VP is such a VIP, shouldn't we keep the PC on the QT, because if it leaks to the VC, you could end up a MIA and then we'd all be put on KP.

Adrian Cronauer (Robin Williams) speaking of the coming visit of then vice-president Richard Nixon in *Good Morning, Vietnam* (1987).

This is it! There's no going back! Another Christmas in the trenches.

Kevin McCallister (Macaulay Culkin) going to war against Harry and Marv, the Sticky Bandits (formerly: the Wet Bandits), in *Home Alone 2: Lost in New York* (1992).

- There's something between you and this General Mortars.

- He was my CO in Nam. The CIA listed him as MIA but the VA ID-ed his MO and we put out an APB.

Sgt. Wes Luger (Samuel L. Jackson) and Sgt. Jack Colt (Emilio Estevez) in *National Lampoon's Loaded Weapon I* (1993).

- It was a bullet, wasn't it?

- A bullet?

- That jumped up and bit you.

- Oh, yes, Sir. Hit me directly in the buttocks. They said it was a million dollar wound, but the army must keep that money 'cause I still ain't seen a nickel of that million dollars.

Forrest Gump (Tom Hanks) telling the story of how, when he rescued his comrades in Vietnam, something jumped up and bit him in *Forrest Gump* (1994).

- Excuse me, I'm looking for the Army Education Center, Captain Tom Murdoch.

- Captain Murdoch is not at the AEC. Captain Murdoch is at the ARC. (...) The AEC is building 2310. You want building 4475. Look, here's what you do. You go right here. You take another right at the PX. Go half a click until you see the DPTM Center, then take a left. If you hit the RFPC, you've gone too far.

- Can I buy a vowel?

Bill Rago (Danny DeVito) and a traffic MP (Gary Dewitt Marshall) in *Renaissance Man* (1994).

They're Coming to Take Me Away, Ha

I'm going crazy! I'm standing here, solidly on my own two hands, and I'm going crazy.

Macaulay Connor (James Stewart) in *The Philadelphia Story* (1940).

Don't you dare hit me. You know I ain't normal.

Curly to Moe in *Loco Boy Makes Good* (1942).

Insanity runs in my family. It practicaly gallops.

Mortimer (Cary Grant) in *Arsenic and Old Lace* (1944).

- I'm a great hero. People run when they see me coming. I kill nips with a wave of the hand. I blow them down: fuffff. I shoot them from all angles, backward, forward, while looking in mirrors. I swim in the water and drown 'em like rats. A pick up a machine gun and brrrt.

   - I got it.

   - You got what?

   - He's playing Daffodil from Dopeyville.

> Sergeant (William Demarest) claiming that Woodrow Lafayette Pershing Truesmith (Eddie Bracken) is feigning insanity to get out of his predicament in *Hail the Conquering Hero* (1944).

Oh! Oh! Her schizo's about to phrenia.

> Ronnie Jackson (Bob Hope) who believes Carlotta Montay (Dorothy Lamour) to be schizophrenic in *My Favorite Brunette* (1947).

I can no longer sit back and allow Communist infiltration, Communist indoctrination, Communist subversion, and the international Communist conspiracy to sap and impurify all of our bodily fluids.

General Jack D. Ripper (Sterling Hayden) in *Dr. Strangelove, or: How I Learned to Stop Worrying and Love the Bomb* (1964).

Judge-What's the matter with him?

   Moe-He thinks he's a chicken.

   Judge-Why don't you put him in an institution?

   Larry-We can't, we need the eggs.

> In *Listen, Judge* (1952). Woody Allen uses the same joke in *Annie Hall* to explain relationships, saying that "they're totally irrational and crazy and absurd, but I guess we keep going through it because most of us need the eggs."

- Well, Murray, to sort of return to reality for a moment...

   - I only go as a tourist.

> Sandra Moskowitz (Barbara Harris) and Murray Burns (Jason Robards) in *A Thousand Clowns* (1965).

Behavior which could be considered insanity in a tradesman is looked on as mild eccentricity in a lord.

> Jack, 14th Earl of Gurney (Peter O'Toole), who started out with a God-complex and was cured into secretly believing himself to be Jack the Ripper in *The Ruling Class* (1972).

You short madman!

> Milo Perrier (James Coco) to Lionel Twain (Truman Capote) in *Murder by Death* (1976).

- What kind of man are you?

    - A madman!

> Dreyfus' (Herbert Lom) answer to the kidnapped professor in *The Pink Panther Strikes Again* (1976).

Raising Arizona

That man's nuts. Grab 'em!

> Double entendre by crazy Marlin Borunki (Dom DeLuise) about Sonny Lawson (Burt Reynolds) running to escape from the insane asylum in *The End* (1978).

- It's a crazy world.

    - Someone oughta sell tickets.

> Glen (Sam McMurray) and Hi (Nicolas Cage) in *Raising Arizona* (1987).

- I think you're going around the bend.

- Oh, I hope so. I've always wanted to travel.

> Joe (Bernard Hill) to his wife Shirley (Pauline Collins) who talks to 'Wall' in *Shirley Valentine* (1989).

I'm not crazy, M'lynn, I've just been in a very bad mood for forty years.

> Ouiser Boudreaux (Shirley MacLaine) to M'lynn Eatenton (Sally Field) in *Steel Magnolias* (1989).

Don't listen to her, mate. She's not sailing with a full crew.

> Adventure (voice of Parick Stewart) to Richard Tyler (Macaulay Culkin) about Fantasy (voice of Whoopi Goldberg) in *The Pagemaster* (1994).

Cosmic Quips

- I see a new position for you.
  - Sitting or reclining?

> Rajah (Nigel de Brulier), the astrologer, and Tira (Mae West) in *I'm No Angel* (1933).

- I see a wonderful future. I see a man in your life.
  - What, only one?

> Rajah (Nigel de Brulier) and Tira (Mae West) in *I'm No Angel* (1933).

I see a long woman and a dark journey.

> Stan Laurel affecting to tell somebody's fortune in *The Bohemian Girl* (1936).

I always got along swell with me.

> Stan Laurel's answer when asked about reincarnation in *The Flying Deuces* (1939).

He always sees the darkest side of everything; he was born during an eclipse.

> Larry Lawrence (Bob Hope) speaking of his valet Alex (Willie Best) in *The Ghost Breakers* (1940).

Moe-Who might you be fair one?

Lady-I'm your new astrologer, the Cyrus of Robuck.

Larry-Oh?! Was your father the Sears of Roebuck?

Lary-Oh no. I was raised by Montgomery.

Curly-Oh! Montgomery's ward.

Moe-You must help me get in touch with the stars.

Larry-Yeah, me too. I'll take Lemarr.

Curly-I'll take Lamour.

Moe-I'll take lasanga with six lessons. (*They dance.*)

> In *I'll Never Heil Again* (1941).

I only hope you live up to that 'y,' professor.

> Maria Tura (Carole Lombard) analyzing Professor Siletslky's (Stanley Ridges) handwriting in *To Be or Not to Be* (1942).

- What's your sign?

  - I'm sorry, it's unlisted.

> Dr. Richard Thorndyke (Mel Brooks) and Victoria Brisbane (Madeline Kahn) in *High Anxiety* (1977).

So he says to me, 'You will receive no money, but when you die, on your deathbed, you will have total consciousness.' So I got that going for me. Which is nice.

> Carl the Assistant Greenskeeper (Bill Murray) on his golf bet with Dalai Lama in *Caddyshack* (1980).

We were doomed from the start. I'm an earth sign, she's a water sign; together we made mud.

Thornton Melon (Rodney Dangerfield) speaking of his second marriage in *Back to School* (1986).

- I seem to know instinctively when two people have the right chemistry and as far as I'm concerned, you and I, we're magic.

- Well, then, I'll just disappear.

Mark (Dabney Coleman) and Darcy (Patti D'Arbanville) in *Modern Problems* (1981).

Billy Ray Valentine-Capricorn.

Billy Ray (Eddie Murphy) introducing himself to the rich Duke brothers in *Trading Places* (1983).

Strange things are afoot at the Circle-K.

Ted Logan (Keanu Reeves) in *Bill & Ted's Excellent Adventure* (1989).

Spirits above me, give me a sign. Shall I be joyous or shall I be damned?

Gomez (Raul Julia) in *The Addams Family* (1991).

I feel I've done this before.

Detective Balsam (Martim Balsam) having a *déja vu* feeling when driving up to the house from *Psycho* in *Silence of the Hams* (1994).

Fashion Faux Pas

- They tell me that in Paris, if you don't buy your gown from Roberta, you're not dressed at all.
- I see. Nude if you do and nude if you don't.

John Kent (Randolph Scott) and Huck Haines (Fred Astaire) in *Roberta* (1935).

- Hello. How was heaven when you left it?

- Tell me, little boy, did you get a whistle or a baseball bat with that suit?

> Kitty Collins (Lucille Ball) to a flirtatious sailor in *Follow the Fleet* (1936).

Where are you going in them buzzard feathers?

> Calamity Jane (Jean Arthur) welcoming home a fancily-dressed Buffalo Bill Cody (James Ellison) in *The Plainsman* (1936).

- You look pretty smart in those pants.

- I'd look pretty silly without 'em.

> Mike McComb (Errol Flynn) trying to flirt with Georgia Moore (Ann Sheridan) in *Silver Rider* (1948).

- I'm quite proud of the earrings. Heirloom, you know. Been in the family for ages.

- You'd never know. They look just like new.

> Lady Beekman (Norma Varden) and Lorelei Lee (Marilyn Monroe) in *Gentlemen Prefer Blondes* (1953).

You know what they say: It's the clothes that make the man. And if we are going to work together, I have to know what kind of a man you are.

> Vesper Lynd (Ursula Andress) to Tremble (Peter Sellers) in *Casino Royale* (1967).

Let's face it, Roger. That dress is you.

> Max Bialystock (Zero Mostel) to Roger de Bris (Christopher Hewett) in *The Producers* (1967).

Larrabee-Max... if they decide to drop the Nude Bomb I know the answer... Well?

Maxwell-Well what?

Larrabee-Don't you want to know the answer?

Maxwell-No.

Larrabee-Food!

Maxwell-Food?

Larrabee-Sure. The whole world will start wearing food.

Maxwell-Larrabee, that's the stupidest thing I have ever heard in my entire life. The whole world will start wearing food!? I have heard you say some dumb things, Larrabee, but that's got to be the dumbest thing I have ever heard come out of your mouth. People wearing food. Forget it, just forget it.... What kind of food?

Larrabee-Fruits, vegetables, fish, but not too much red meat. You wear red meat a couple of times a week, that's plenty.

Maxwell-But this is crazy!

Larrabee-Why? We're just going back to the Bible. Now, what did Adam and Eve wear to cover up the good parts? Fig leaves! Now that's a fruit. You take a head of romaine lettuce, that will clothe a family of six. You buy a flank steak, you throw it over your shoulders and you've got a stole. Cantaloupes. You scoop out the insides and you've got a bra.

Maxwell-What holds the bra up?

Larrabee-Linguini.

Maxwell-Linguini!? Larrabee, that's insane! Do you realise the world is facing a food shortage as it is?

Larrabee-Max, this will work. For the first time people will know where their next meal is coming from. They'll be wearing it. They'll wear it two or three times and then they'll eat it.

Maxwell-Won't it spoil?

Larrabee-Not if you're neat.

Maxwell-What has neatness got to do with it?

Larrabee-Well, you can't take your clothes off and throw 'em over a chair anymore. You've got to learn to fold them neatly and put them in the refrigerator.

> Agents Larrabee (Robert Karvelas) and Maxwell Smart
> (Don Adams) in *The Nude Bomb* (1980).

22-What's that in your hand?

86-That? That's my bra.

22-Your bra?

86-Would you believe my training bra?

22-Hmm, hmm.

86-I can explain that bra in five seconds. (*Points to it with panties in his other hand.*) These panties on the other hand are going to take a little longer.

> Agent 22 (Andrea Howard) and Agent 86, Maxwell
> Smart (Don Adams) in *The Nude Bomb* (1980).

The Nude Bomb

- Is that the latest fashion?

- No, it's the oldest profession.

> Jenny Fields (Glenn Close) and her son Garp (Robin Williams) speaking of a street hooker in *The World According to Garp* (1982).

Oh, I have the napkins that match your hats.

> Protocol hostess Sunny Davis (Goldie Hawn) to visiting Arab royalty wearing checkered head scarfs in *Protocol* (1984).

- How can you not like that suit?

- It's not a K-Mart suit.

Charlie Babbitt (Tom Cruise) and his brother Raymond
(Dustin Hoffman) in *Rain Main* (1988).

Doctor–Although this appears to be an ordinary sports coat, it is in reality a size forty regular megabyte mainframe computer. The material in this jacket is composed of thousands of cotton microchips interwoven with silk spun from specially bred silk worms from the Silicon Valley. This jacket is user friendly and is compatible with almost any soft-wear shirt. The four buttons on each sleeve are computer keys. So, you are virtually a walking arsenal and communication center. Are there any questions?

Smart–Does it come in navy blue?

Lisa–Will agents Hymie and Larrabee require jackets?

Doctor–Yes.

Lisa–Gentlemen, I'll need to take your measurements: waist, neck, inseam, sleeve, nostril...

Larrabee–Nostril?

Doctor–We have perfected a mini-camera that fits right into your nose. All you have to do is press this button on your jacket and your elbow will record what your nose sees.

Smart–Wouldn't it be better if my nose recorded what my elbow sees?

Doctor–No.

Smart–No?

Doctor–No, simply because in your elbow patch compartment there is a mini-recorder plus everything else you might need: a mini-magnet, a mini-gun, and a mini-condom.

Larrabee–I'm curious. What use do we have for a mini-magnet?

Doctor-All you need to know is in your mini-manual which is in your other patch compartment.

Hymie-How do we access the elbow patches?

Doctor-Just press the first cuff button.

Larrabee-I thought the first cuff button worked your nostril.

Doctor-No, that's the third cuff button.

Smart-I thought that was the second cuff button.

Doctor-No, the second cuff button activates the cuff button phone. When this button lights up, you have an incoming call. To answer, lift the cuff to your ear, talk into your lapel.

Smart-Is that the left lapel or the right lapel?

Doctor-The right is for local calls, the left is for long distance.

Smart-Long distance!? Do I get my choice of carriers?

> Dr. Benton (Danny Goldman), Maxwell Smart (Don Adams), Lisa (Rachelle Carson), Larrabee (Robert Karvelas), and Hymie (Dick Gautier) in *Get Smart, Again!* (1989).

- Ever since I was a lad I've had this dream, a dream that I now, finally, have a chance to fulfill.

- And that is?

- To travel to the center of Australia, climb King's Canyon, as a queen, in a full length Gaultier sequin, heels, and a tiara.

- Great! That's just what this country needs; a cock in a frock on a rock.

> Felicia (Guy Pearce) explaining to Bernie/Bernadette (Terence Stamp) why she has joined the expedition in *The Adventures of Priscilla, Queen of the Desert* (1994).

Idol Worship

Jonathan is more than a man, he's an experience; and he's habit-forming. If they could ever bottle him, he'd outsell ginger ale.

Fred Amiel (Barry Sullivan) speaking of Jonathan Shields (Kirk Douglas) in *The Bad and the Beautiful* (1952).

To a New Yorker like you, a hero is some type of weird sandwich, not some nut who takes on three Tigers.

Oddball (Donald Sutherland) to Crap Game (Don Rickles) about attacking three German Tiger tanks with a Sherman in *Kelly's Heroes* (1970).

Why didn't you tell me you like heroes? I would have helped an old lady across the street.

Lou Peckingpaugh (Peter Falk) to Marlene Duchard (Louise Fletcher) in *The Cheap Detective* (1978).

- John! I'm not a nice guy. You're a nice guy. Now do your job. Be a hero. (...)

- Are you going to be alright with me receiving all the credit?

- Hey! I don't take credit. I'm a cash kind of guy.

Bernie La Plante (Dustin Hoffman) and John Bubber (Andy Garcia) sitting on the ledge in *Hero* (1992).

Now the whole world will know the splendor that is Pat.

Kyle (Charles Rocket) obsessed by Pat's (Julia Sweeney) androgynous nature (Oh! Sweet mystery that is Pat.) in *It's Pat—The Movie* (1994).

Upper Crusty

You're just nothing to me, just nothing at all. And if I was a pirate and had you on my ship, I wouldn't toss you to the crew.

> Joe Anton (George Raft) to high society Miss Healy (Constance Cummings) who, earlier in the movie, compared him to a pirate in *Night After Night* (1932).

- What's your name?

- Maudie Triplet. One of the bluebloods of Kentucky. And if you don't like the color, honey, we'll change it.

> Miss Healy (Constance Cummings) meeting Maudie (Mae West) in *Night After Night* (1932).

You can take your Bostons and Bunker Hills and your bloodlines and stuff a codfish with them. And you know what you can do with the codfish.

> Lola Burns (Jean Harlow) to her Bostonian socialite boyfriend Gifford Middleton (Franchot Tone) and his aristocratic parents in *Bombshell* (1933).

- Oh, Your Excellency!

- You're not so bad yourself.

> Rufus T. Firefly (Groucho Marx) to Gloria Teasdale (Margaret Dumont) in *Duck Soup* (1933).

Beulah, peel me a grape.

> Tira (Mae West) to her maid Beulah Thorndyke (Gertrude Howard) in *I'm No Angel* (1933).

Say! Where did you learn to dunk? In finishing school?

> Peter Warne (Clark Gable) to Ellie Andrews (Claudette Colbert) in *It Happened One Night* (1934).

You're brainless, spineless, useless, but you do know clothes.

> The Prince of Wales (Nigel Bruce) to the fop Sir Percy Blakeney (Leslie Howard) who, secretly, is *The Scarlet Pimpernel* (1935).

Madam, royalty loves an occasional roll in the gutter.

> Marie Antoinette (Norma Shearer) to Madame Du Barry (Gladys George), King Louis' mistress, in *Marie Antoinette* (1938).

This aging debutante, Mr. Jefferson, I retain in my employ only because she is the sole support of her two-headed brother.

> Sheridan 'Sheri' Whiteside (Monty Woolley) speaking of his assistant Maggie Cutler (Bette Davis) in *The Man Who Came to Dinner* (1942).

Me thinks I like Camelot a lot.

> Hank Martin (Bing Crosby) in *A Connecticut Yankee in King Arthur's Court* (1949).

You must be out of your mink-lined brain!

> Jerry Mulligan (Gene Kelly) to Milo Roberts (Nina Fotch) in *An American in Paris* (1951).

Fetch me fifty happy people immediatly.

> Wazir of Bagdad (Sebastian Cabot) to his soldiers in *Kismet* (1955).

It's good to be the king.

King Louis XVI (Mel Brooks) in *History of the World: Part 1* (1981).

- Murray, what did you get me down here for?

  - Nick, what time is it?

  - It's about 7:20.

  - Shhht! Nick, in a moment you're going to see a horrible thing.

  - What's that?

- People going to work.

Murray Burns (Jason Robards) and young Nick (Barry Gordon) in *A Thousand Clowns* (1965).

Doctor, the Queen wouldn't like it.

Sherlock Holmes (Nicol Williamson) pulling Doctor Watson (Robert Duvall) away from the bordello in *The Seven-Per-Cent Solution* (1976).

- It is said the people are revolting.

- You said it! They stink on ice.

King Louis XVI's (Mel Brooks) reply to an aristocrat in *History of the World: Part 1* (1981).

This must be His Gucci-ness.

Joe Paris (Burt Reynolds) about a yuppie investment counselor in *Physical Evidence* (1989).

I've got a galaxy to run. I don't have time for flatulence and orgasms.

King of the Moon (Robin Williams) in *The Adventures of Baron Munchausen* (1989).

History of the World: Part 1

Food, Glorious Food

- My friend and I are victims of the Depression. We haven't tasted food for three days.

- Fancy that! Not eating for three whole days.

- Yes, ma'am. Yesterday, today and tomorrow.

> Ollie (Oliver Hardy) begging a meal from an old lady (Mary Carr) and Stan (Stan Laurel) ruining his play as usual in *One Good Turn* (1931). Mr. Hardy and Mr. Laurel repeated the joke in *Great Guns* (1941): "We haven't eaten for three days." "Yesterday, today, and tomorrow."

The one without the parsley is the one without the poison.

> Eddie/Oedipus (Eddie Cantor), the royal food-taster in *Roman Scandals* (1933). Often misquoted as: "The pellet with the poison's in the pullet with the parsley."

- Coffee?

- Please.

- Now let me see. Four lumps wasn't it?

- Yes, that's me.

> Laurence Bradford (William Powell) and his ex-wife Paula (Jean Arthur) in *The Ex-Mrs. Bradford* (1936).

- Your milk, your Lordship.

- Milk! What am I? A baby or a cow?

> Keggs (Reginald Gardiner) and Lord Marshmorton (Montagu Love) in *A Damsel in Distress* (1937).

It's the first time I ever had two kinds of birds with one meal: turkey to eat and buzzards to look at.

> Bob Seton (John Wayne) invited to dinner by William Cantrel (Walter Pigeon) in *Dark Command* (1940).

Mata-I'm Mata Herring.

Moe-Ah! My favorite dish.

Curly-Mmm! (*kisses her hand*) Don't taste like herring to me.

In *You Nazty Spy!* (1940).

The boys serving a cake inflated with cooking gas:

Moe-Larry-Curly-We baked you a birthday cake.

Larry-If you get a tummy ache.

Curly-And moan, and groan, and woe.

Larry-Curly-Don't forget we told you so. (*The cake explodes.*)

In *An Ache in Every Stake* (1941).

If I were the cream for that woman's coffee, I'd curdle.

Miss Bragg (Kathleen Howard) speaking of Sugarpuss O'Shea (Barbara Stanwyck) in *Ball of Fire* (1941).

- I didn't squawk about the steak dear. I merely said I didn't see that old horse that used to the tethered outside here.

- You're as funny as a cry for help.

Bill (W.C. Fields) and the waitress in *Never Give a Sucker an Even Chance* (1941).

- I'm a Ziegfeld girl!

- You sound like a bottle of milk that just got certified.

Sheila/Red (Lana Turner) and Gilbert (James Stewart) in *Ziegfeld Girl* (1941).

Cook this thing. Make the head well done, the middle medium, the tail rare.

Moe giving a stuffed fish to Curly in *Even as I.O.U.* (1942).

- Good morning, sir. Fruit, cereal, bacon and eggs, eggs and sausage, sausage and hot cakes, hot cakes and ham, ham and eggs, eggs and bacon?

- Give me a spoonful of milk, a raw pigeon's egg and four houseflies. If you can't catch any, I'll settle for a cockroach.

Muggsy's (William Demarest) answer to the steward in *The Lady Eve* (1941). (The breakfast is for a snake.)

- What's the matter? Don't you like your steak medium?

- When I bite a steak, I like it to bite back at me.

Rusty (Eddie Marr) and Jeff (William Bendix) in *The Glass Key* (1942).

- Hey, how long do I have to wait? I ordered a strawberry sundae.

- You did? What day is today?

- Friday.

- You've got two more days to wait.

Soda jerk Mervin Milgrim (Lou Costello) and a customer in *Who Done It?* (1942).

Butler-When you're ready serve the drinks and the canapés.

Moe-Canapés! Oh, you mean the toasts with lace curtains. (...)

Curly-Now what would he want with a can-a-peas.

Moe-Not can-a-peas, canapés.

Larry-Not can-a-peas, can-a-peas. One of us is crazy and it's not you.

Moe-Right! Canapés, hors-d'oeuvres.

Curly-Which one? Can-a-peas or d'oeuvres? Make up your mind.

Moe-You put them on crackers. They give you an appetite like a horse.

Curly-Oh, animal crackers. (*Moe slugs him.*)

Moe-(*To Larry*) Go on, make the canapés.

Curly-(*To Larry*) With animal crackers.

Larry finds a can of peas and a box of dog biscuits which he serves with olives on top in *Crash Goes the Hash* (1944).

Just the smell of her is a meal.

> Mrs. Mott (Ethel Barrymore) about the fish-and-chips
> woman in *None But the Lonely Heart* (1944).

Curly-How do you like your eggs?

Moe-Sunny side down and don't turn them over.

> In *Idiots Deluxe* (1945).

There's a guy who never goes out of a girl's mind. He just stays there like a heavy meal.

> Agnes (Veda Ann Borg) infatuated with Richard Nugent
> (Cary Grant) in *The Bachelor and Bobby-Soxer* (1947).

- Sugar?

- A lump.

- Lemon?

- A squeeze.

- Cream?

- A dribble.

- Tea?

- Never touch it.

> Leza (Barbara Bates) and Georgi (Danny Kaye) in *The
> Inspector General* (1949).

Moe peeling bananas:

I hate the stuffing in these things.

> Moe peeling bananas in *Baby Sitters Jitters* (1951).

Don't look at me with those soft-boiled eggs!

> Ned Land (Kirk Douglas) to Conseil (Peter Lorre) in
> *20,000 Leagues Under the Sea* (1954).

- You know what they say about breakfast.

- Yes, they say breakfast is the most important meal of the morning.

> Cathy (Kathleen Freeman) and Herbert H. Hebert (Jerry Lewis) in *The Ladies' Man* (1961).

- You don't have to pretend it's good. I'm not a cook, I never was. I'm an interior decorator.

- I hate to think what you're doing to mine.

> Charlotte Oar (Jessie Royce Landis), the mother-in-law, and Parker Ballantine (Bob Hope) in *Critic's Choice* (1963).

- There's some nice warm milk.

- Milk! How vomitable!

> Dr. Craven (Vincent Price) and Dr. Beddo (Peter Lorre) in *The Raven* (1963).

- Lunch!!!

- Lunch?

- I thought you'd never ask.

> Rosemary Pilkington (Michele Lee) cleverly trapping J. Pierpont Finch (Robert Morse) in *How to Succeed in Business Without Really Trying* (1967).

I'm a bagel on a plate of onion rolls.

> Fanny Brice (Barbra Streisand) comparing herself to perfect chorus line hoofers in *Funny Girl* (1968).

You're a fat pudding stuffed with proverbs.

> Don Quixote (Peter O'Toole) to Sancho Panza (James Coco) in *Man of La Mancha* (1972).

- I've got a nice thick bed of hay in the stable.

- Good! Eat it.

> Aldonza's (Sophia Loren)
> answer to the travelling trader in
> *Man of La Mancha* (1972). Off-
> screen, Loren once said:
> Everything you see I owe to
> spaghetti.

- Shall we dine?

- Can we eat first?

> Boris (Woody Allen) accepting
> an invitation to dine with the
> General in *Love and Death*
> (1975).

You come in here to get sick just like everybody else.

> Joe Turner (Robert Redford) in a
> greasy spoon in *Three Days of
> the Condor* (1975).

Barbara Streisand in
Funny Girl

- What's that green slime you're eating? It looks like a dish out of Oliver Twist.

- I'm not sure. I think they run the front lawn through a blender.

> Diana Barrie (Maggie Smith) and Sidney Cochran
> (Michael Caine) in *California Suite* (1978).

Today is Navin's birthday and I cooked him up his favorite meal. Tuna fish salad on white bread with mayonnaise, a Tab and a couple of Twinkies.

> The Mother (Mabel King) to Navin R. Johnson (Steve Martin) in *The Jerk*
> (1979).

I'm not gonna waste my time arguing with a man who's lining up to be a hot lunch.

> Marine biologist Matt Hooper (Richard Dreyfuss) chides
> Mayor Hamilton (Larry Vaughn) for not believing there's
> a killer shark stalking his island's shore in *Jaws* (1975).

This steak still has the mark of the jockey's whip on it.

> Al Czervik (Rodney Dangerfield) comments on the
> country club cuisine in *Caddyshack* (1980).

He's able to eat things that would make a billy goat puke.

> Troutman (Richard Crenna) on former Green Beret
> Rambo (Sylvester Stallone) in *First Blood* (1982).

I don't know why this stuff is called Hamburger Helper. It does just fine by itself.

> Hick cousin Eddie (Randy Quaid) serves up a meal in
> *National Lampoon's Vacation* (1983).

Younger men are like fast food restaurants; it's quick, but not all that good. But with you, it's like dining at the most expensive restaurant in the world. Of course, the service may be a little slow.

> Daniella Eastman (Nastassja Kinski) gives a backhanded
> compliment to her older husband Claude (Dudley Moore)
> in *Unfaithfully Yours* (1984).

-Did anything go wrong at lunch?
  -My frog turned on me.
  -Yeah, I had some bad tuna myself.

> Joan Rivers and Miss Piggy commiserate in *The Muppets
> Take Manahtten* (1984).

Clean up your sugar and for dessert you can have some rancid trash I found in a Dumpster behind 7-11.

> Jane Applegate (Stockard Channing) makes a tempting
> offer to her insect family in *Meet the Applegates* (1991).

Can I use her underwear to make soup?

> Rigby Reardon (Steve Martin) in *Dead Men Don't Wear
> Plaid* (1982).

Chili sauce. Stay away from this baby. A couple of drops of this and your tongue dials the fire department.

> Benjy Stone (Mark Linn-Baker) to K.C. Downing (Jessica
> Harper) in *My Favorite Year* (1982).

You wouldn't know a tit from a tortilla.

> Restaurant owner (Allan Goornitz) to Ray (Raul Julia) in
> *One from the Heart* (1982).

- You will be my guests for dinner.

  - Does that mean he's going to eat us or feed us?

> Suleiman Khan (Brian Blessed) and Struts (Jack Weston)
> in *High Road to China* (1983).

I never sup after I've dined.

> Anna Bronski (Anne Bancroft) turning down an invitation
> from Colonel Ehrhardt (Charles Durning) in *To Be or Not
> to Be* (1983).

- What is it?

  - It's free. Look, it's nutritious, it's delicious. I brought it home from the diner, dad.

- I'm only asking in case I have to describe it later on to a doctor.

Ralph Marolla (Barney Martin) being served leftover meatloaf by his daughter Linda Bach (Liza Minnelli) in *Arthur 2: On the Rocks* (1988).

- You say the blessing, Arthur.

- Blessing?

- Yeah. Just tell us something you're thankful for.

- Oh. I'm thankful... I got the smallest piece of meatloaf.

Linda Bach (Liza Minnelli) and her husband Arthur (Dudley Moore) in *Arthur 2: On the Rocks* (1988).

She's got a heart like a twelve-minute egg.

Jamie Conway (Michael J. Fox) speaking of his boss in *Bright Lights, Big City* (1988).

- Who could that be?

- Dad, it's probably somebody standing in the hall, you know, knocking at the door.

- Yeah, maybe it's the mother of this meatloaf coming to kill you.

Ralph Marolla (Barney Martin) being served left-over diner meatloaf by his daughter Linda Bach (Liza Minnelli) in *Arthur 2: On the Rocks* (1988).

Do you like your chili with or without crushed Oreos in it?

Martin Riggs (Mel Gibson) to a female guest in *Lethal Weapon 2* (1989).

Cheeseball pick-me-ups accompanied by miniature franks, and for dessert, mashmallow kabobs.

Mrs. Flax (Cher), a specialist of fun finger foods, in *Mermaids* (1990).

- Would you care for some spotted...

- Dick?

> King Ralph/Ralph Jones (John Goodman) offering
> dessert (Spotted Dick) to Miranda (Camille Coduri) in
> *King Ralph* (1991).

I do wish we could chat longer but I'm having an old friend for dinner.

> Dr. Hannibal (the Cannibal) Lecter (Anthony Hopkins)
> speaking to Clarice Starling (Jodie Foster) on the phone
> on her graduation day while watching Dr. Frederick
> Chilton (Anthony Heald), the prison warden, coming onto
> the island in *The Silence of the Lambs* (1991).

The doves we serve cold.

> Linda Voss (Melanie Griffith) to the German officer after
> serving hot (instead of cold) cucumber soup in *Shining
> Through* (1992).

- Who wants Chinese take-out?
  - I'll have the cream of sum-yung-guy.

> Benjamin Oliver (Rob Lowe) and Wayne Campbell (Mike
> Myers) in *Wayne's World* (1992).

- I only drink herb tea.
  - That accounts for the green.

> Molly McKenna (Frances Fisher) comments on punk
> actress Gina King's (Natasha Gregson Wagner) hair
> color in *Molly & Gina* (1994).

From now on, you're on a low yuk diet.

> Eva (Thora Birch) to her pet monkey whose diet includes
> lizards and bugs in *Monkey Trouble* (1994).

He's so cheesy I can't watch him without crackers.

> Lelaina Pierce (Winona Ryder) about a television show
> host in *Reality Bites* (1994).

Animal Crackers

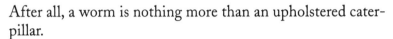

After all, a worm is nothing more than an upholstered caterpillar.

> One of Patricia Harrington's (Marion Davies) catch-
> phrases in the silent movie *The Patsy* (1928).

I wish I was back in the jungle where men are monkeys.

> Captain Jeffrey Spaulding (Groucho Marx) in *Animal
> Crackers* (1930).

I just saw MGM!

> Stan (Stan Laurel) scared witless thinking he's seen
> MGM's Leo the Lion in *The Chimp* (1932).

Snakes like you usually die of their own poison.

> Chris Morel (John Wayne) in *'Neath the Arizona Skies*
> (1934).

One morning I shot an elephant in my pajamas. How he got in my pajamas I'll never know.

Capt. Jeffrey Spaulding (Groucho Marx) *Animal Crackers* (1930).

The mosquitos around here carry tomahawks.

> Capt. Richard Warrington (Nelson Eddy) in Colonial
> America in *Naughty Marietta* (1935).

You know Effie. When she gets riled up, she'll fight a rattlesnake and give it the first two bites.

> Egbert Floud (Charlie Ruggles) speaking of his wife in
> *Ruggles of Red Gap* (1935).

A yap like you hasn't got any more conscience than a coyote.

> Boze Hertzlinger (Dick Foran) to a gangster in *The Petrified Forest* (1936).

Love at first sight is rather like a mule, Miss Clavering. It kicks backward.

> Tenny/Tennyson (E.E. Clive) to Phyllis Clavering (Louise Campbell) in *Bulldog Drummond Comes Back* (1937).

Why don't catfish have kittens?

> Moe answering one stupid question with another in *Playing the Ponies* (1937).

There goes a couple of rats I raised from mice.

> Matt Libby (Jack Carson), the publicist in *A Star Is Born* (1937).

Lady-We're looking for our pet monkey. Have you seen him?

Curly-Hey, what's that monkey got that I ain't got?

Moe-A longer tail.

> The boys won $50,000 and three fortune hunters are hoping to take it away from them in *Healthy, Wealthy and Dumb* (1938).

- Well, we're off. (...) You see, we're going to ride to the hounds in the morning. It's tallyho at dawn.

- Yes, you have to get up very early in the morning to catch the fox.

- Yes, and stay up late at night to catch a minx.

> Gloria Patterson (Helen Broderick) and Mr. Duncan (Samuel S. Hinds) in *The Rage of Paris* (1938).

Moe-Here's a peculiar case.

   Visitor-What does G.C.M. mean? (*Reading the chart.*)

Moe-Garbage Can Moocher.

Larry-He's got a bad case of scavengeritis.

Speaking of a dog in Calling All Curs (1939).

This cat suffers from operatic tendencies—likes to sing opera on back fences.

Doctor Moe about one of their patients in Calling All Curs (1939).

Who am I to cost the Russian people seven cows?

Lena 'Ninotchka' Yakushova (Greta Garbo) a Russian trade delegate occupying the royal suite at 2000 francs a day, the price of a cow, in Ninotchka (1939). This film was advertised as: "Garbo laughs."

- He's got a lot of charm.

   - He comes by it naturally. His father was a snake.

Bruce Baldwin (Ralph Bellamy) and Hildy Johnson (Rosalind Russell) speaking of Walter Burns (Cary Grant) in His Girl Friday (1940).

I'm as gentle as a forest bred lion.

Cuthbert J. Twillie (W.C. Fields) knocking at the door (without success) of his new bride Flower Belle Lee (Mae West) in My Little Chickadee (1940).

Men die all the time, and pigs live on and on when you'd think that their own smell would kill them.

Julie (Joan Crawford) to M'sieu Pig (Peter Lorre) in Strange Cargo (1940).

The stork that brought you must have been a vulture.

Nightclub singer Lee Donley (Ann Sheridan) to plantation
owner Steve Case (Pat O'Brien) when he has her tossed
into the local jail in Torrid Zone (1940).

- The stork came to your house this morning?

  - Wonderful! Boy or girl, deary?

  - They don't know. They've got it tied up and if it lays an egg it's a girl.

Fibber McGee (Jim Jordan) and Molly (Marion Jordan)
speaking to the telephone operator in Look Who's
Laughing (1941).

Will you take your clammy hands off my chair? You have the touch of a love-starved cobra.

Sheridan 'Sheri' Whiteside (Monty Woolley) to his nurse
in The Man Who Came to Dinner (1942).

- B milk?! Do bees give milk?

  - No. Honey.

  - Thanks, dear.

Willoughby (Lou Costello) and Duke (Bud Abbott) in Ride
'Em Cowboy (1942).

- Do I have to milk that bunch of cows?

  - No. Not bunch, herd.

  - Heard what?

  - Herd of cows.

  - Sure I've heard of cows. What do you think I am? A dummy?

  - No. A cow herd.

- What do I care if a cow heard. I didn't say anything to be ashamed of.

- No, please. Do you know what a cow gives?

- No she don't. You've got to take it away from her.

> Willoughby (Lou Costello) and Duke (Bud Abbott) are sent to the barn to milk the cows in *Ride 'Em Cowboy* (1942).

- It's only a bear skin. Look.

- Don't tell me about those things, I use to hunt them.

- You hunted bear?

- Oh, no. I had my clothes on.

> Flash (Bud Abbott) and Weejie (Lou Costello) in *Hit the Ice* (1943).

Larry-I don't see a single cow.

Curly-I don't even see a married one.

> The boys bought a farm and are looking for the livestock in *The Yoke's On Me* (1944).

What's the trouble, Benny? You're lower than a caterpillar with fallen arches.

> Rudy (Brenda Joyce) to Benny Miller (Lou Costello) in *Little Giant* (1946).

You double-crossing buzzard.

Alicia (Ingrid Bergman) to Devlin (Cary Grant) in
Notorious (1946).

- Let me tell you a bedtime story. Now, let me see. Once upon a time there were three little bears. Max Bear, Bud Bear and Bugs Bear. Now, bear in mind these bears were never bare because they ran around in their bear skins, but with bare feet. So, the three little bears went skipping and frolicking hither, tither and yither without their mither and fither. Skip, skip, skip...

- How'd that baby get in here?

Larry tells a bedtime story to a baby abandoned in their pawnshop in *Three Loan Wolves* (1946).

Larry-We're trapped like rats!

Moe-Speak for yourself.

In *Crime on their Hands* (1948). In *Nutty but Nice* (1940) Moe added 'rodent' to the routine: "Speak for yourself, Rodent."

What's the matter with you? You're acting like a crocodile with a toothache.

Daphne (Linda Darnell) to her husband Alfred (Rex Harrison) in *Unfaithfully Yours* (1948).

Trust a frog before a rat, and a rat before a snake, and a snake before a Red Beard.

Kim (Dean Stockwell) to Muhbud Ali/Red Beard (Errol Flynn) in *Kim* (1950).

- You're a dear.

- You're an antelope. Later around we'll go in the plains and play. Okay?

> Mike (Jane Russell) and Junior (Bob Hope) in *Son of Paleface* (1952).

Take back your mink from whence it came!

> Miss Adelaide (Vivien Blaine) to Nathan Detroit (Frank Sinatra) in *Guys and Dolls* (1955).

Two beds madam, without fleas.

> Alexis Zorba (Anthony Quinn) to the aubergiste Mme. Hortense (Lila Kedrova) in *Zorba the Greek* (1964).

I didn't surrender either, but they took my horse and made him surrender. They have him pulling a wagon in Kansas, I bet.

> Lone Watie (Chief Dan George) to Josey (Clint Eastwood) in *The Outlaw Josey Wales* (1976).

Softy, softy, catchy monkey.

> Fu Manchu (Peter Sellers) in *The Fiendish Plot of Dr. Fu Manchu* (1980).

I believe he suffers from nipple anxiety. Probably came from a nine-dog litter.

> Dog psychiatrist's (Donald F. Muhich) analysis of Matisse to Barbara (Bette Midler) in *Down and Out in Beverly Hills* (1986).

He's going to give that dog fleas.

> Barbara Whiteman (Bette Midler) speaking of Jerry
> Baskin (Nick Nolte) in *Down and Out in Beverly Hills*
> (1986).

You've got all the warmth of a penguin on an iceberg.

> Jack (Steve Guttenberg) to his wife Sharon (Beverly
> D'Angelo) in *High Spirits* (1988).

Ease off! You're as persistent as a dog with two dicks.

> Bert Gibson (M. Emmet Walsh) in *White Sands* (1992).

- I don't know quite how to begin.

- Then let me start. I know, by just looking at you, you are the perfect man for my stud farm.

- Stud farm!?

- If it makes it any easier for you I am willing to take on multiple partners.

- Multiple partners!? No offense, ma'am, but wouldn't I find that a tad uncomfortable?

- Well, what if it was with somebody you really trusted, like Mr. Drysdale?

- I don't think this is the sort of thing Mr. Drysdale would want to be involved in.

- Well, you should have seen his face when I showed him the pictures of what I have in mind. He was very excited.

- I don't doubt that.

- Would you like to see the pictures? They're very detailed.

- Not just yet. Don't you think we're moving awful fast?

- Oh, not as far as I'm concerned, Mr. Clampett. I've got my license and I'm ready to breed.

If you put the two of them together in a tank with a shark, the shark would have an identity crisis.

Ella (Geraldine Chaplin) speaking about actresses Marina Rudd (Elizabeth Taylor) and Lola Brewster (Kim Novak) in *The Mirror Crack'd* (1980).

Jim Carrey, *Ace Ventura: Pet Detective*

- Excuse me, ma'am, I could use a glass of iced tea.

Uncle Jed (Jim Varney) thinks he's meeting his future wife, Miss Arlington (Leann Hunley), who, in fact, seeks investors for a horse breeding farm in *The Beverly Hillbillies* (1993).

Come to me, jungle friends.

Ace Ventura (Jim Carrey) greeting his pets when entering his apartment in *Ace Ventura: Pet Detective* (1994).

This man is smart as a gorilla and strong as a fox.

Pete Putrid (Stuart Pankin) to FBI agent Jo Dee Fostar (Billy Zane) in *Silence of the Hams* (1994).

Non·PC

I was in the black studies program. By now I could have been black.

Fielding Mellish (Woody Allen) expressing regret at not having finished college in *Bananas* (1971).

Yes, my little yellow friend.

Inspector Clouseau (Peter Sellers) to his servant Cato (Burt Kwouk). At other times he calls him: "You raving Oriental idiot." *The Return of the Pink Panther* (1982).

Cato is in the hospital. They nearly blew his little yellow skin off.

> Inspector Jacques Clouseau (Peter Sellers) to Dreyfus (Herbert Lom) after a bomb explosion in *The Return of the Pink Panther* (1982).

Is this a black thing?

> Axel Foley (Eddie Murphy) to Chief Lutz (Allen Garfield) in *Beverly Hills Cop II* (1987).

The Irish are the blacks of Europe; Dubliners are the blacks of Ireland, and on our side, we're the blacks of Dublin. So say it: I'm black and I'm proud!"

> Manager (Robert Arkins) in *The Commitments* (1991).

No Absence of Malice

I hate you! Every little bit of you!

> Chief Inspector Dreyfus (Herbert Lom) to Jacques Clouseau (Peter Sellers) in *A Shot in the Dark* (1964).

I hate people I don't like.

> Nicolai Sestrin (Andreas Voutsinas) in *The Twelve Chairs* (1970).

Come on now! You kick out the gooks, the next thing you know, you have to kick out the chinks, the spicks, the spooks, the kikes and all that's going to be left in here is a couple of brain-dead rednecks.

> Adrian Cronauer (Robin Williams) gets ironic with two rednecks in an off-limits bar in *Good Morning, Vietnam* (1987).

You are evil and you must be destroyed.

Ouiser Boudreaux (Shirley MacLaine) in *Steel Magnolias*
(1989).

I hate you more. If hate were people, I'd be China.

Phil Berquist (Daniel Stern) to his wife in *City Slickers*
(1991).

Things That Go Bump in the Night

Inga-Werewolf!

Freddy-Werewolf?

Igor-There!

Freddy-What?

Igor-There wolf. There castle.

Freddy-Why are you talking that way?

Inga (Teri Garr), at the howling of a wolf,
Freddy/Frederick Frankenstein (Gene Wilder) and Igor
(Marty Feldman) in *Young Frankenstein* (1974).

I'm going out for a bite to drink.

Count Vladimir Dracula (George Hamilton) in *Love at
First Bite* (1979).

I do not drink... vine... or smoke shit.

Count Vladimir Dracula (George Hamilton) puts it
differently to Cindy Sondheim/Nina (Susan St. James) in
Love at First Bite (1979) when she offers him champagne
and a joint.

Children of the night... SHUT UP!!!

The Count (George Hamilton) in *Love at First Bite* (1979) is fed up with howling wolves after over seven hundred years of solitude and spoofs the original line, "Listen to them! Children of the night. What music they make," delivered by Count Dracula (Bela Lugosi) listening to the howling wolves in *Dracula* (1931) and Gary Oldman in *Bram Stoker's Dracula* (1993). (2) Also rephrased by Vampiress Odette (Geena Davis) and journalist Gil Turner (Ed Begley, Jr.) in *Transylvania 6-5000* (1985): "Listen, there are the children of the night." "What are they doing out in the daytime?" "They make beautiful music, don't they?" "They sound like wolves to me." (3) In *Ed Wood* (1994) Martin Laudau, as Bela Lugosi, agrees to meet again with Johnny Depp but at another time: "Perhaps we could meet again, Mr. Lugosi?" "Certainly, but now the children of the night are calling."

Good Morning, Vietnam

- Eddy, we're not just anybody, son.

- That's right, Eddy. Your father is a little of everybody and your grandfather's got some of the best blood in Europe flowing through them veins.

> Herman Munster (Fred Gwynne) and Grandpa (Al Lewis) in *The Munsters' Revenge* (1981).

Excuse me, my dear, could I interest you in a little bite?

> Grandpa (Al Lewis) offering lunch (his or hers?) to a young lady in *The Munsters' Revenge* (1981).

- Gozer the Gozerian! Good evening! As the duly designated representative of the city, county and state of New

Ed Wood

York, I order you to cease any and all supernatural activity and to return forthwith to your place of origin or to the nearest convenient parallel dimension. (...)

- Are you a God?

- No.

- Then die!

Dr. Raymond Stantz (Dan Aykroyd) and Gozer (Slavitza Jovan) in *Ghostbusters* (1984).

DR. JEKYLL & MR. HYDE. It must be a duplex.

Fantasy (voice of Whoopi Goldberg) reading the name plate at the entrance of the haunted house in *The Pagemaster* (1994).

Evildoers are easier and they taste better.

Vampire Lestat (Tom Cruise) educating Louis (Brad Pitt) on blood types in *Interview with the Vampire* (1994).

Psycho-Killers, Qu'est-ce que c'est?

It's a weird moon. Moon kills, you know. It feeds off the earth. On a night like this, one of us could get up in the middle of the night, grab an axe and cut someone's head off.

Tripper's (Bill Murray) campfire story in *Meatballs* (1979).

What kind of man gives cigarettes to trees?

Survivalist Donald
Quinelle (Robin
Williams) to assassin
Jack Locke (Jerry
Reed) in *The
Survivors* (1983).

You mean you put down your rock and I put down my sword and we try to kill each other like civilized people?

Westley/Roberts the
Pirate (Cary Elwes) to
Fezzik (André the Giant) in *The Princess Bride* (1987).

Ghostbusters

I think the message to psychos, fanatics, murderers, nutcases, all over the world is: Don't mess with suburbanites because, frankly, we're not going to take it anymore.

Art Weingartner (Rick Ducommun) in *The Burbs* (1989).

- Max! How horrible!

- Well, he deserved it, 99. He was nothing but a KAOS killer.

- Sometimes I wonder if we're any better, Max.

- What are you talking about, 99!? We have to kill, and maim, and destroy. We stand for everything that's good, fine, and decent in the world.

Agent 99 (Barbara Feldon) and her husband, Agent 86,
Maxwell Smart (Don Adams) when KAOS fiend Dementi
(Harold Gould) is struck by artificial lightning in *Get
Smart, Again!* (1989).

It's the so-called normal guys who always let you down. Psychos never scare me. At least they're committed.

> Selina Kyle/Cat Woman (Michelle Pfeiffer) to Bruce Wayne/Batman (Michael Keaton) in *Batman Returns* (1992).

Thank you, Topper. I can kill again. You've given me a reason to live.

> Harbinger (Miguel Ferrer) to Topper Harley (Charlie Sheen) in *Hot Shots! Part Deux* (1993).

Parts Is Parts

Always remember, nature gives us many of our features, but lets us pick our teeth.

> Patricia Harrington (Marion Davies) reading a self-help guide in *The Patsy* (1928).

Oh, I love sitting on your lap. I could sit here all day if you didn't stand up.

> Professor Quincy Adams Wagstaff (Groucho Marx) to Cora (Thelma Todd) in *Horse Feathers* (1932).

- Surely you don't mind my holding your hand?

  - It ain't heavy. I can hold it myself.

> Captain Cumming (Cary Grant) and Lady Lou (Mae West) in *She Done Him Wrong* (1933).

- St. Louis. You were born there?

  - Yes.

  - What part?

  - Why, all of me.

Ace Lamont (John Miljan) and Ruby Carter (Mae West) in *Belle of the Nineties* (1934). Stan Laurel and Oliver Hardy had a similar joke the previous year in *Sons of the Desert* (1933): *Lady-* "Charley tells me you're from Los Angeles. What part?" "Ollie-All of me."

I'll work my brain to the bone for you.

Lawyer Egbert Fitzgerald (Edward Everett Horton) hired to handle Mimi's (Ginger Rogers) divorce in *The Gay Divorcee* (1934).

Your left eye says yes and your right eye says no. Fifi, you're cockeyed.

Prince Danilo (Maurice Chevalier) to Sonia (Jeanette MacDonald) in *The Merry Widow* (1934).

- I must have your golden hair, fascinating eyes, alluring smile, your lovely arms, your form divine...

- Wait a minute, wait a minute. Is this a proposal or are you taking inventory?

Ace Lamont (John Miljan) and Ruby Carter (Mae West) in *Belle of the Nineties* (1934).

On your toes, you heels.

Moe to Larry and Curly in *Calling All Curs* (1939).

- I kinda lost my head.

- You didn't lose your head. It's there but you can't see it.

Prisoner Alan Douglas (William Janney) by Stanley MacLaurel (Stan Laurel) in *Bonnie Scotland* (1935).

After three weeks of this, a leg is nothing to me but something to stand on.

Abner (Guy Kibbee), the producer, watching the female dancers in *42nd Street* (1933).

- You know, if it weren't for two things you'd be a terrific dancer.

  - What's that?

  - Your feet.

> Gracie (Gracie Allen) and George (George Burns) in *A Damsel in Distress* (1937).

Are you eating a tomato, or is that your nose?

> Charlie McCarthy (voice of Edgar Bergen) to Larson E. Whipsnade (W.C. Fields) in *You Can't Cheat an Honest Man* (1939).

What symmetrical digits.

> Cuthbert J. Twillie (W.C. Fields) holding the hand of Flower Belle Lee (Mae West) in *My Little Chickadee* (1940).

- Where did I see your face before?

  - Right where it is now.

> S. Quentin Quale (Groucho Marx) and Joe Panello (Chico Marx) in *Go West* (1940).

'Your eyes, your remarkable eyes.' If he ever looks into my eyes again he'll really see a storm over the pampas.

> Jilted Glenda Crawford (Betty Grable) about Argentinian Ricardo Quintana (Don Ameche) in *Down Argentine Way* (1940).

There's something awfully big about you.... Your nose.

> The waitress, Tiny (Jody Gilbert), to Bill (W.C. Fields) in *Never Give a Sucker an Even Break* (1941).

There's a face I always like to shake hands with.

> Armstrong Custer (Errol Flynn) to Ned Sharp (Arthur
> Kennedy) in *They Died with Their Boots On* (1941).

- You ask her for her lips, then you ask her for her heart, then her hand.

   - What am I doing? Piece work?

> Doc (Bud Abbott) coaching Wishy (Lou Costello) in the
> fine art of seduction in *Rio Rita* (1942).

They give my goosepimples goosepimples.

> Mervin Milgrim (Lou Costello) in *Who Done It?* (1942).
> Joe Mantegna, as Joe Ruffalo, has a similar line when
> Alice, Mia Farrow, takes a drug that makes her
> disappear in *Alice* (1990): "I've got goosepimples on my
> goosepimples."

I've been on the pavement so long my socks have bunions.

> George M. Cohan (James Cagney) in *Yankee Doodle
> Dandy* (1942).

- When I make up my mind...

   - I know! When you make up your mind, you lose your head.

> Jonathan Brewster (Raymond Massey), a homicidal
> maniac, and Dr. Einstein (Peter Lorre), his friend, sidekick
> and plastic surgeon in *Arsenic and Old Lace* (1944).

- I need help.

   - Like I need four thumbs.

> Adrienne Fromsett (Audrey Totter) and Philip Marlowe
> (Robert Montgomery) in *Lady in the Lake* (1946).

- Take your rightful place, Mr. Wooley. Mr. Egan, you sit on Mr. Wooley's left hand and Matt, you sit on his right hand.

  - What do I eat with? My feet?

> The Widow Hawkins (Marjorie Main) sitting Chester Wooley (Lou Costello) at the head of the table in *The Wistfull Widow of Wagon Gap* (1947).

When it bleeds, the Red Sea.

> Cyrano (Jose Ferrer) speaking of his nose in *Cyrano de Bergerac* (1950).

I'd hate to have your nerve in a tooth.

> Holly (Betty Hutton) to Angel (Gloria Grahame) in *The Greatest Show on Earth* (1952).

I'm not the kneecap type.

> Polly's (Jean Peters) answer to George Loomis (Joseph Cotten) when he complains about Rose's (Marilyn Monroe) low-cut dresses in *Niagara* (1953).

- Harry, we should beware of these men. They're desperate characters.

  - What makes you say that?

  - Not one of them looked at my legs.

> Gwendolyn Chelm (Jennifer Jones) to her husband Harry (Edward Underdown) in *Beat the Devil* (1954).

He's got an empty stomach and it's gone to his head.

> Joe (Tony Curtis) speaking of his friend Jerry (Jack Lemmon) in *Some Like It Hot* (1959).

Now you've done it! (...) You tore off one of my chests.

> Daphne (Jack Lemmon) to Josephine (Tony Curtis) in
> *Some Like It Hot* (1959).

- They're only pulling your leg.
  - Well, it almost came off.

> Irma (Shirley MacLaine) and Policeman Paton (Jack
> Lemmon) coming out of the "panier-à-salade" in *Irma La
> Douce* (1963).

- That color looks wonderful with your eyes.
  - Just my right eye; I hate what it does to the left one

> Nick Arnstein (Omar Sharif) to Fanny Brice (Barbra
> Streisand) in *Funny Girl* (1968).

Don't point that finger at me unless you intend to use it.

> Oscar Ungar (Walter Matthau) to Felix Madison (Jack
> Lemmon) in *The Odd Ccouple* (1968).

I swear, Your Grace, by my wife's little black mustache...

> Sancho Panza (James Coco) to Don Quixote (Peter
> O'Toole) in *Man of La Mancha* (1972).

- Your skin, it is so beautiful.
  - Yes, I know. It covers my whole body.

> The Violinist and Sonja (Diane Keaton) in *Life and Death*
> (1975).

It's amazing that brain can generate enough power to keep those legs moving.

> Lex Luthor (Gene Hackman) speaking of Otis (Ned
> Beatty) in *Superman* (1978).

- I almost forgot what you look like. Day by day I erased your face from my mind, little by little, till all I had left was your right ear and three front teeth on the bottom.

- I still carry your picture in a locket. Naturally I had to cut off your head in case Paul found it.

> Lou Peckingpaugh (Peter Falk) and Marlene Duchard (Louise Fletcher) reunited (as in *Casablanca*) in *The Cheap Detective* (1978).

- You know, your eyes lit up the moment you saw me again.

- That battery's been dead a long time.

> Nick Gardenia (Chevy Chase) and his ex-wife Glenda Park (Goldie Hawn) in *Seems Like Old Times* (1980).

Coronary! My heart wouldn't dare attack me.

> Dan Snow (Walter Matthau) who had a coronary, not a heart attack, in *First Monday in October* (1981).

They're not real tits at all, just retreads.

> Sissy (Cher) in *Come Back to the 5 & Dime Jimmy Dean, Jimmy Dean* (1982).

- Is this some kind of bust?

- Yes, it's very impressive, but we'd just like to ask you some questions.

> Mimi Du Jour (K.T. Sullivan), a sexy dancer, and Lt. Frank Drebin (Leslie Nielsen) in *More! Police Squad!—Revenge and Remorse* (1982).

My eyes had a heart attack!

> Charles Lumley III (Henry Winkler) watching Belinda (Shelley Long) prepare breakfast in a sweatshirt and bobbies in *Night Shift* (1982).

Brains! I've never seen so many brains out of their skulls before!

Michael Hfuhruhurr (Steve Martin) in the pickled-brain room of Alfred Necessiter's (David Warner) apartment in *The Man With Two Brains* (1983).

Isn't it awfully nice to have a penis.

Isn't it practical to have it on.

It's swell to have a stiffy.

It's divine to own a dick. (...)

Hooray for the one-eyed trouser snake.

Sung in *Monty Python The Meaning of Life* (1983).

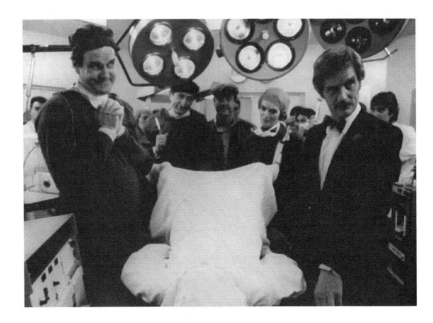

Monty Python's The Meaning of Life

If brains were dynamite you couldn't blow your nose.

Debbie (Mackenzie Phillips) in *American Graffiti* (1973).

If I give my heart to you, I'll have none and you'll have two.

Sung by 'Crocodile' Dundee (Paul Hogan) in *Crocodile Dundee* (1986).

- I know the secret to happiness.

- Oh yeah! What's that?

- A girl with freckles on her tits.

Eddie Jillette (Richard Gere) and his partner Joey in *No Mercy* (1986).

Reverend, you've got balls as big as church bells.

Porn king Jerry Caesar (Dabney Coleman) to the Reverend Whirley (Christopher Plummer) in *Dragnet* (1987).

Alright, twenty 'Something-Better'. Start with:

Obvious: Excuse me! Is that your nose or did a bus park on your face?

Meteorological: Everybody take cover, she's going to blow!

Fashionable: You know, you could de-emphasize your nose if you wore something larger... like Wyoming.

Personal: Well! here we are. Just the three of us.

Punctual: All right, Dillman, your nose was on time, but you were fifteen minutes late.

Envious: Ohhh! I wish I were you. Gosh! To be able to smell your own ear.

Naughty: Pardon me, sir, some of the ladies have asked if you wouldn't mind putting that thing away.

Philosophical: You know it's not the size of a nose that matters, it's what's in it.

Humorous: Laugh and the world laughs with you; sneeze and it's goodbye Seattle.

Commercial: Hi! I'm Carl Shad and I can paint that nose for $39.95.

Polite: Would you mind not bobbing your head, the orchestra keeps changing tempo.

(*Sings*)...: He's got the whole world in his nose.

Sympathetic: Ah!!! What happened? Did your parents lose a bet with God?

Complimentary: You must love the little birdies to give them this to perch on.

Scientific: Say! Does that thing influence the tides?

Obscure: I'd hate to see the grindstone.

Inquiry: When you stop and smell the flowers, are they afraid?

French: Say! The pigs have refused to find any more truffles until you leave.

Pornographic: Finally! A man who can satisfy two women at once.

Religious: The Lord giveth, and he just kept on giving it, didn't He?

Disgusting: Say! Who mows your nose hair?

Terminoid: Keep that guy away from my cocaine.

Aromatic: It must be wonderful to wake up in the morning and smell the coffee-in Brazil.

Appreciative: Oh! How original! Most people just have their teeth capped.

Dirty: Your name wouldn't happen to be dick, would it?

Charlie 'C.D.' Bales (Steve Martin) in *Roxanne* (1987).

Steve Martin in *Roxanne*

You know what, Anderson, you're starting to get so far up my nose I'm beginning to feel your boots on my chin.

Mayor Tilman (R. Lee Ermey) to FBI agent Rupert Anderson (Gene Hackman) in *Mississippi Burning* (1988).

- What do you think?
  - Looks like a penis, only smaller.

Lou Ann McGuinn's (Bernadette Peters) answer to a flasher in *Pink Cadillac* (1989).

Does Pinocchio have wooden balls?

Pedro Carmichael (Peter Falk) in *Tune In Tomorrow* (1990).

That's the spirit, Thing, lend a hand.

> Gomez (Raul Julia) to Thing (a hand without a body) in
> *The Addams Family* (1991).

- Come give me a hand!
- I already have.

> Captain James Hook's (Dustin Hoffman) reply to Peter
> Banning/Peter Pan (Robin Williams) refers to the fact that
> he lost a hand in the original story partly due to Peter. In
> *Hook* (1991).

Look at her. She's doing the shoulder thing.

> Bill Reimers (Emilio Estevez) speaking of sobbing Gina
> Garrett (Rosie O'Donnell) in *Another Stakeout* (1993).

It looks like the upper hand is on the other foot.

> President Tug Benson (Lloyd Bridges) coming to the rescue
> of Topper Harley (Charlie Sheen) in *Hot Shots! Part Deux*
> (1993).

I do love you. I tried to forget you but no matter what I do, your face is always on the tip of my tongue.

> Topper Harley (Charlie Sheen) reunited with Ramada
> (Valeria Golino) in *Hot Shots! Part Deux* (1993).

She insults me, too. My God! If you don't have tits like Dolly Parton no one wants you.

> Cross-dresser Chris (Liev Schreiber) in *Mixed Nuts*
> (1994).

Bill, if you get any sadder you're gonna trip over your lip.

> Marie (Isabella Hofmann) to Bill Rago (Danny DeVito) in
> *Renaissance Man* (1994).

Oh my nose!

> Marcia Brady (Christine Taylor) in *The Brady Bunch Movie* (1995).

Over My Dead Body

- Is he living?

- No, he fell through a trapdoor and broke his neck.

- Was he building a house?

- No, they were hanging him.

> Oliver Hardy asking Stan Laurel about his uncle, hoping he's the rich millionaire recently deceased in *Laurel and Hardy Murder Case* (1930).

Let's drop a rock on him and then we'll make him dead when he's alive.

> Stannie (Stan Laurel) proposing to drop a rock in the well where Silas Barnaby is hiding in *March of the Wooden Soldiers* (Original title: *Babes in Toyland*) (1934).

Moe-Wait a minute! Ain't there another way we can die?

Executioner-You may either have your head cut off or be burned at the stake.

Larry-Cut my head off.

Curly-Not me. I'd rather be burned at the stake.

Larry-Why?

Curly-A hot steak is better than a cold chop.

> In *Restless Knights* (1935).

Either he's dead or my watch is stopped.

> Dr. Hugo Hackenbush (Groucho Marx) taking Stuffy's
> (Harpo Marx) pulse in *A Day at the Races* (1937).

- That's a mean way to die.

- You know any good ways?

> Nick Charles (William Powell) in *Another Thin Man*
> (1939).

That sucker jumped three feet in the air and came down stiff as a board.

> George Hally (Humphrey Bogart) sharpshooting German
> soldiers in *The Roaring Twenties* (1939).

- We're falling two thousand feet!

- That's all right, dear. Don't start worrying until we get down to one-thousand-nine-hundred-and-ninety-nine. It's the last foot that's dangerous.

> The niece (Gloria Jean) and her uncle Bill (W.C. Fields)
> jumping over the cliff in a basket in *Never Give a Sucker
> an Even Break* (1941).

You are going to commit suicide if it's the last thing you do.

> Swami Talpur (Boris Karloff) trying to get Freddy Phillips
> (Lou Costello) to commit suicide while under hypnosis in
> *Abbott and Costello Meet the Killer Boris Karloff* (1949).

- Would you do me a favor, Harry?

- What?

- Drop dead!

> Billie Dawn (Judy Holliday) and Harry Brock (Broderick
> Crawford) in *Born Yesterday* (1950). This dialogue is
> usually remembered simply as:" Do me a favor, drop
> dead!"

I should hang you twice, I think.

The captain of the Louisa (a German gunboat) (Peter Bull) to Charlie Allnut (Humphrey Bogart) in *The African Queen* (1951).

Is this your first crucifixion?

Demetrius (Victor Mature), a slave, to Barabbas in *The Robe* (1953). This phrase inspired the Harvard Lampoon's Awards to create the Victor Mature Award. See also: *Earthquake* (1974).

Harold and Maude

- Well, we lost the procession. (...) What cemetery is it?

- Maybe there's an address on the casket?

Lawyer Harold Fine (Peter Sellers) and hippie Nancy (Leigh Taylor-Young) looking for the right cemeteray in a dayglow-painted hearse in *I Love You, Alice B. Toklas!* (1968).

- Tell me Harold, what do you do for fun? What activity gives you a different sense of enjoyment from the others? What gives you that special satisfaction?

- I go to funerals.

Harold's (Bud Cort) answer to the psychiatrist in *Harold and Maude* (1972).

- What does it feel like to be dead for two-hundred years?

- It's like spending a week-end in Beverly Hills.

Luna Schlosser (Diane Keaton) and Miles Monroe (Woody Allen) in the year 2173 after 200 years of cryogenetic sleep in *Sleeper* (1973).

There are worse things in life than death. I mean if you've ever spent an evening with an insurance salesman you know what I mean.

> Boris Grushenko (Woody Allen) in *Love and Death* (1975).

No pulse, no heartbeat. If condition not change, this man is dead.

> Sidney Wang (Peter Sellers) in *Murder by Death* (1976).

- The essence of suicide is despair.

  - The essence of suicide is you don't collect insurance.

> Doctor Hudson Kane (Stacy Keach) and Captain Cutshaw (Scott Wilson), his patient in *The Ninth Configuration* (1979).

Max-Is this Siegel? How is he?

22-I think he's dying. I'll call an ambulance.

Max-Mr. Siegel, did you see who did it?

Siegel-It was... a man... It was a man who, ugh...

22-Too late.

Max-Better call the morgue.

Siegel-Just a second.

Max-Ambulance.

Siegel-It was a big man, a tall man. I'd say a 42 long.

Max-Did you notice anything else about him?

Siegel-He had a patch over one eyeeee...

Max-Morgue.

Siegel-What's your hurry?

Max-Ambulance.

Siegel-He also had one leg and one arm.

Max-One leg and one arm! Why didn't you tell me that before?

Siegel-You didn't ask me if he was hard to fit? AHHhhh...

Max-Morgue.

Siegel-Just a few minutes.

Max-Ambulance. When you called me you said you had information about the nude bomber.

Siegel-I think... (*Clunk.*)

22-Who should I call?

Max-(*To Siegel*) Morgue?

Siegel-Mmmm...? Ambulance.

> Agent Maxwell Smart (Don Adams), Agent 22 (Andrea Howard) and the mortally (?) wounded fashion designer Jonathan Levinson Siegel (Bill Dana) in *The Nude Bomb* (1980).

He was laying right there, dead as yesterday.

> Aurora (Yvonne Wilder) in *Seems Like Old Times* (1980).

Have you ever talked to a corpse? It's boring!

> Whines a dead (Griffin Dunne) to (David Naughton) in *An American Werewolf in London* (1981).

Dying is easy. Comedy is hard.

> Alan Swan (Peter O'Toole) quoting Edmund King in *My Favorite Year* (1982).

Can't you let me die in peace once in a while?

> Baron Munchausen (John Neville) to Sally Salt (Sarah Polley) in the belly of the whale in *The Adventures of Baron Munchausen* (1989).

And hair color so natural only your undertaker knows for sure.

> The Joker/Jack Napier (Jack Nicholson) in *Batman*
> (1989).

- Max! How horrible!

- Well, he deserved it, 99. He was nothing but a KAOS killer.

- Sometimes I wonder if we're any better, Max.

- What are you talking about, 99!? We have to kill, and maim, and destroy. We stand for everything that's good, fine, and decent in the world.

> Agent 99 (Barbara Feldon) and her husband, Agent 86,
> Maxwell Smart (Don Adams), when KAOS fiend Dementi
> (Harold Gould) is struck by artificial lightning in *Get*
> *Smart, Again!* (1989).

You can't ask me to kill a person! I'm a scientist. We only do continents, countries, occasionally a convention. But a person? Never!

> Conrad (Bernie Kopell) in *Get Smart, Again!* (1989).

- No grief for Lips?

- I'm wearing black underwear.

> Dick Tracy (Warren Beatty) and Breathless Mahoney
> (Madonna) after the death of Lips in *Dick Tracy* (1990).

- Hi, Curly. Kill anybody today?

- Day ain't over yet.

> Mitch Robbins (Billy Crystal) and trail boss Curly (Jack
> Palance) in *City Slickers* (1991).

- She's dead, sir. They took her to the morgue.

- The morgue! She'll be furious.

> Ernest Menville (Bruce Willis) upon learning that his
> immortal wife, Madeline Ashton (Meryl Streep), has been
> transported to the morgue in *Death Becomes Her* (1992).

You kill a few people, they call you a murderer. You kill a million and you're a conqueror. Go figure.

> Erik Qualen (John Lithgow) in *Cliffhanger* (1993).

- Sometimes I have suicidal thoughts. I feel like I want to jump off buildings or slit my wrists or put a bullet through my head.

- Well, have you considered drowning? They say it's like God giving you a big wet hug... forever. STOP CALLING HERE!!!

> Pat (Julia Sweeney) hosting a radio talk show called Love
> Chat in *It's Pat—The Movie* (1994).

You couldn't sneak up on a corpse.

> Bret Maverick (Mel Gibson) to Zane Cooper/Coop
> (James Garner) in *Maverick* (1994).

- Just think of it. Someday we'll be buried here, side by side, six feet under, in matching coffins, our lifeless bodies rotting together for all eternity.

- Cara mia!

Morticia (Anjelica Huston) and Gomez (Raul Julia) in *The Addams Family* (1991).

Title Index

The **Title Index** is an alphabetical list of the movies from which quotes were obtained. The **Cast** and **Character Name Indexes** immediately follow this index.

Cast Index

The **Cast Index** lists the actors attributed to the quotes listed in the book in a straight alphabetical format by last name (names are presented in a first name, last name format, but are alphabetized by last name). The **Character Name, Director, Writer, Keyword,** and **Decade Indexes** immediately follow this index.

Bud Abbott, 53, 99, 103, 104, 109, 110, 113, 118, 120, 121, 145, 166, 211, 246, 294, 328, 361, 362, 375

Don Adams, 86, 129, 137, 183, 186, 208, 209, 216, 217, 218, 248, 263, 325, 341, 343, 355, 371, 387, 388

Stanley Adams, 299

David Adnopoz, 129

Danny Aiello, 12, 176

Eddie Albert, 84

Alan Alda, 6, 54, 100, 315

Fred Allen, 141, 299

Gracie Allen, 45, 89, 140, 141, 165, 177, 194, 242, 243, 243, 251, 252, 374

Karen Allen, 291

Woody Allen, 2, 3, 4, 5, 6, 8, 21, 27, 33, 39, 40, 49, 105, 107, 131, 159, 160, 162, 163, 167, 169, 238, 282, 283, 283, 293, 294, 295, 300, 307, 308, 325, 330, 353, 366, 385, 386

Kirstie Alley, 163

Maria Conchita Alonso, 310

Don Ameche, 374

Eddie 'Rochester' Anderson, 64, 146, 285

André the Giant, 371

Ursula Andress, 339

Dana Andrews, 65

Julie Andrews, 8

Susan Angelo, 185

Eugene J. Anthony, 40

Christina Applegate, 123

Tom Arbold, 98

Eve Arden, 46, 78, 144

Robert Arden, 258

Alan Arkin, 134

Richard Arlen, 95

Curtis Armstrong, 76

Desi Arnaz, 22, 178

Edward Arnold, 191

Tom Arnold, 62

Jean Arthur, 22, 339, 348

Maureen Arthur, 53, 58

Armand Assante, 12, 69, 73, 87, 124, 133, 138, 185, 199, 200, 319

Fred Astaire, 30, 33, 47, 64, 75, 98, 156, 177, 181, 193, 194, 218,

242, 243, 250, 314, 338

Mary Astor, 87

Richard Attenborough, 259

Rene Auberjonois, 329

Lenore Aubert, 113

Mischa Auer, 45

Dan Aykroyd, 97, 106, 116, 187, 190, 203, 220, 232, 308, 310, 318, 370

Lauren Bacall, 237, 256

Barbara Bach, 201

Brian Backer, 34, 231

Irving Bacon, 159

Diedrich Bader, 124

Ross Elliot Bagley, 97, 248

Scott Baio, 111

Scott Bakula, 94

Alec Baldwin, 158

Daniel Baldwin, 63

Lucille Ball, 37, 46, 62, 79, 134, 157, 174, 187, 211, 226, 271, 290, 315, 339

Martin Balsam, 338

Anne Bancroft, 176, 262, 355

George Barbier, 236

Thomas Barbout, 301

Ellen Barkin, 73

Binnie Barnes, 299

Ethel Barrymore, 79, 351

John Barrymore, 56, 153, 235

Lionel Barrymore, 150

Kim Basinger, 50, 123, 167, 185

Barbara Bates, 351

Anne Baxter, 178, 216, 304

Ned Beatty, 377

Warren Beatty, 40, 155, 177, 232, 240, 262, 388

Louise Beavers, 153

Bonnie Bedelia, 55

Noah Beery, Sr., 19

Wallace Beery, 113, 322

Ed Begley, Jr., 231, 369

Leon Belasco, 169

Harry Bellafonte, 272

Ralph Bellamy, 360

James Belushi, 152, 287

John Belushi, 34, 156, 169, 231, 247, 273, 308, 318

Robert Benchley, 298, 299

William Bendix, 186, 350

Annette Bening, 82, 148, 154, 177, 240

Jack Benny, 56, 57, 172, 181

Tom Berenger, 6, 86, 199

Marisa Berenson, 40

Ingrid Bergman, 160, 363

Halle Berry, 21, 125, 200

Willie Best, 337

Brian Beuben, 177

Jack Beutel, 216

Turhan Bey, 125

Earl Billings, 276

Thora Birch, 357

Jacqueline Bisset, 100

Honor Blackman, 169

Sidney Blackmer, 48

Vivien Blaine, 364

Brian Blessed, 355

Joan Blondell, 77, 143

Eric Blore, 98

Humphrey Bogart, 83, 160, 226, 228, 237, 253, 256, 290, 303, 384, 385

Joseph Bologna, 16

Ward Bond, 72, 188, 268

Beulah Bondi, 59

Veda Ann Borg, 351

Roger Bowen, 320

Character Name Index

The **Character Name Index** lists character names attributed to quotes listed in the book in a straight alphabetical order presented in a first name, last name format, but alphabetized by last name. Characters with surname attributes only may not be listed. The **Director** and **Writer Indexes** immediately follow this index.

Director Index

The **Director Index** lists only the films of each director from which the quotes were taken. This is not a comprehensive list of all directors, nor any director's complete list of film credits. Names are presented in a first name, last name format, and alphabetized by last name. The **Cast** and **Character Names Indexes** immediately precede this index; the **Writer Index** immediately follows.

George Abbott
Too Many Girls '40

Jim Abrahams
Airplane! '80
Big Business '88
Hot Shots! '91
Hot Shots! Part Deux '93
Police Squad '82
Ruthless People '86

Alan Alda
The Four Seasons '81
Sweet Liberty '86

Woody Allen
Alice '90
Annie Hall '77
Bananas '71
Broadway Danny Rose '84
Everything You Always Wanted to Know About Sex But Were Afraid to Ask '72
Hannah and Her Sisters '86
Love and Death '75
Manhattan '79
A Midsummer Night's Sex Comedy '82
Sleeper '73
Take the Money and Run '69
What's Up, Tiger Lily? '66

Robert Altman
Come Back to the 5 & Dime Jimmy Dean, Jimmy Dean '82
M*A*S*H '70

Jon Amiel
Tune In Tomorrow '90

Franco Amurri
Flashback '90
Monkey Trouble '94

Michael Anderson, Sr.
Around the World in 80 Days '56

Ken Annakin
Those Magnificent Men in Their Flying Machines '65

Emile Ardolino
Three Men and a Little Lady '90

Hal Ashby
Harold and Maude '72

Anthony Asquith
The Importance of Being Earnest '52
Pygmalion '38

John H. Auer
Wheel of Fortune (AKA: A Man Betrayed) '41

Hy Averback
I Love You, Alice B. Toklas! '68

Dan Aykroyd
Nothing but Trouble '91

Lloyd Bacon
Footlight Parade '33
42nd Street '33
Miss Grant Takes Richmond '49

John Badham
Another Stakeout '93
Blue Thunder '83
Saturday Night Fever '77
Stakeout '87

Roy Ward Baker
Don't Bother to Knock '52

Montague Banks
Great Guns '41

Steven Barron
Coneheads '93

Hall Bartlett
Jonathan Livingston Seagull, 183

Charles T. Barton
Abbott and Costello Meet Captain Kidd '52

Abbott and Costello Meet Frankenstein '48
Abbott and Costello Meet the Killer, Boris Karloff '49
Abbott and Costello Meet the Mummy '55
Buck Privates Come Home '47
Mexican Hayride '48
The Noose Hangs High '48
The Time of Their Lives '46
The Wistful Widow of Wagon Gap '47

Warren Beatty
Dick Tracy '90

William Beaudine
Blues Busters '50

Gorman Bechard
Assault of the Killer Bimbos '87

Richard Benjamin
City Heat '84
Mermaids '90
Milk Money '94
My Favorite Year '82
My Stepmother Is an Alien '88

Robert Benton
Nadine '87

Adam Bernstein
It's Pat—The Movie '94

Armyan Bernstein
Cross My Heart '87

Kathryn Bigelow
Point Break '91

Tony Bill
Untamed Heart '93

Mike Binder
Blankman '94

Claude Binyon
Here Come the Girls '53

William Peter Blatty
The Ninth Configuration '79

John Blystone
Block-Heads '38
Swiss Miss '38

Paul Bogart
Cancel My Reservation '72
Neil Simon's Broadway Bound '92

Peter Bogdanovich
Paper Moon '73

Richard Boleslawski
The Garden of Allah '36

Phillip Borsos
The Grey Fox '82

Frank Borzage
Little Man, What
Now? '34
Strange Cargo '40

Marco Brambilla
Demolition Man '93

Martin Brest
Midnight Run '88

James Bridges
Bright Lights, Big City
'88

Albert Brooks
Lost in America '85

James L. Brooks
Broadcast News '87
Terms of Endearment
'83

Mel Brooks
Blazing Saddles '74
High Anxiety '77
History of the World:
Part 1 '81
The Producers '67
Spaceballs '87
The Twelve Chairs '70
Young Frankenstein
'74

Richard Brooks
Bite the Bullet '75
Cat on a Hot Tin Roof
'58

Otto Brower
Fighting Caravans '31

Clarence Brown
Ah, Wilderness '35

Tod Browning
Dracula '31

Harold Bucquet
Without Love '45

David Burton
Fighting Caravans '31

Tim Burton
Batman '89
Batman Returns '92
Beetlejuice '88
Ed Wood '94

David Butler
Calamity Jane '53
Caught in the Draft
'41
The Princess and the
Pirate '44
The Road to Morocco
'42

Edward Buzzell
At the Circus '39
Go West '40
Song of the Thin Man
'47

Michael Cacoyannis
Zorba the Greek '64

James Cameron
The Terminator 2:
Judgement Day '90
True Lies '94

Martin Campbell
Cast a Deadly Spell
'91

Frank Capra
Arsenic and Old Lace
'44
It Happened One
Night '34
It's a Wonderful Life
'46
A Lady for a Day '33
Meet John Doe '41
Mr. Smith Goes to
Washington '39
State of the Union '48

Topper Carew
Talkin' Dirty After
Dark '91

Michael Caton-Jones
Doc Hollywood '91

Michael Cimino
Year of the Dragon
'85

Bob Clark
Loose Cannons '90

Matt Clark
Da '88

Eddie Cline
My Little Chickadee
'40
Never Give a Sucker
an Even Break '41
The Bank Dick '40

Fred Coe
A Thousand Clowns
'65

Joel Coen
Raising Arizona '87

Chris Columbus
Home Alone '90
Home Alone 2: Lost in
New York '92

Jack Conway
The Girl from Missouri
'34
Honky Tonk '41
Libeled Lady '36
Red-Headed Woman
'32

Francis Ford Coppola
Apocalypse Now '79
Bram Stoker's Dracula
'93
One from the Heart
'82
Peggy Sue Got
Married '86

Roger Corman
The Raven '63

Michael Crichton
Physical Evidence '89

John Cromwell
Since You Went Away
'44

George Cukor
Adam's Rib '49
Born Yesterday '50
Dinner at Eight '33

It Should Happen to
You '54
Let's Make Love '60
Love Among the Ruins
'75
My Fair Lady '64
The Philadelphia Story
'40
Two-Faced Woman
'41
The Women '39

Irving Cummings
Double Dynamite '51
Down Argentine Way
'40
Louisiana Purchase
'41

Michael Curtiz
The Adventures of
Robin Hood '38
Cabin in the Cotton
'32
Casablanca '42
Life with Father '47
Trouble Along the
Way '53
Yankee Doodle Dandy
'42

Morton DaCosta
Auntie Mame '58

Joe Dante
The 'Burbs '89

Martin Davidson
The Lords of Flatbush
'74

Andrew Davis
Code of Silence '85

Walter De Leon
The Ghost Breakers
'40

Roy Del Ruth
Blonde Crazy '31
Topper Returns '41

Rudy DeLuca
Transylvania 6-5000
'85

Cecil B. DeMille
The Greatest Show on
Earth '52
Madam Satan '30
The Plainsman '36
Samson and Delilah
'49
The Ten
Commandments '56
Unconquered '47
Union Pacific '39

Jonathan Demme
The Silence of the
Lambs '91

Howard Deutch
Getting Even with Dad
'94

Danny DeVito
The Mogul '91

Ernest R. Dickerson
Juice '92

Edward Dmytryk
Cornered '45
Million Dollar Legs
'32

Roger Donaldson
Cadillac Man '90
White Sands '92

Stanley Donen
Charade '63
The Grass Is Greener
'60
Royal Wedding '51
Singing in the Rain
'52
Two for the Road
'67

Clive Donner
The Nude Bomb '80
What's New Pussycat?
'65

Richard Donner
Lethal Weapon
'87
Lethal Weapon 2 '89
Maverick '94
Scrooged '88
Superman '78

King Donovan
Promises! Promises!
'63

Gordon Douglas
Robin and the Seven
Hoods '64

Stan Dragoti
Love at First Bite '79
Necessary Roughness
'91

Dennis Dugan
Brain Donors '92

Bill Duke
The Cemetery Club
'92

Allan Dwar
The Three Musketeers
'39

Clint Eastwood
The Eiger Sanction '75
The Outlaw Josey
Wales '76

Thom Eberhardt
Gross Anatomy '89
Without a Clue '88

Blake Edwards
Breakfast at Tiffany's
'61
The Great Race '65
The Pink Panther
Strikes Again '76
The Return of the Pink
Panther '82
Revenge of the Pink
Panther '78
A Shot in the Dark '64
S.O.B. '81
Sunset '88
That's Life! '86

Stephen Elliott
The Adventures of
Priscilla, Queen of
the Desert '94

Nora Ephron
Mixed Nuts '94
This Is My Life '92

Peter Faiman
Crocodile Dundee '86

Ferdinanad Fairfax
Nate and Hayes '83

James Fargo
The Enforcer '76

Felix Feist
George White's
Scandal '45

Bill Fishman
Car 54, Where Are
You? '94
Tapeheads '88

Richard Fleischer
20,000 Leagues
Under the Sea '54

Victor Fleming
Bombshell '33
Gone with the Wind
'39
Reckless '35
Red Dust '32
Test Pilot '38
The Virginian '29
The Wizard of Oz '39

Robert Florey
Cocoanuts '29

John Flynn
Nails '92
Out for Justice '91

Bryan Forbes
The Wrong Box '66

John Ford
Fort Apache '48
My Darling
Clementine '46
The Quiet Man '52
The Searchers '56
Stagecoach '39

Robert Forster
Hollywood Harry '85

Bob Fosse
Cabaret '72

Norman Foster
Mr. Moto's Last
Warning '39

Wallace Fox
The Corpse Vanishes
'47

Melvin Frank
The Court Jester '56

John Frankenheimer
Dead-Bang '89

Harry Fraser
'Neath the Arizona
Skies '34

Stephen Frears
The Grifters '90
Hero '92

William Friedkin
The Night They Raided
Minsky's '68

Sidney J. Furle
Ladybugs '92

Tay Garnett
China Seas '35
A Connecticut Yankee
in King Arthur's
Court '49
Joy of Living '38

Lewis Gilbert
Moonraker '79
Shirley Valentine '89
The Spy Who Loved
Me '77

Terry Gilliam
The Adventures of
Baron Munchausen
'89
The Fisher King '91
Monty Python and the
Holy Grail '75

Paul Michael Glaser
The Running Man '87

Jim Goddard
Reilly: The Ace of
Spies '84

Peter Godfrey
Christmas in
Connecticut '45

Mark Goldblatt
Dead Heat '88

Michael Gordon
Boys' Night Out '62
Cyrano de Bergerac
'50
Pillow Talk '59

Steve Gordon
Arthur '81

Lisa Gottlieb
Across the Moon '94

Edmund Goulding
Dark Victory '39
Grand Hotel '32

Alfred E. Green
Copacabana '47

Ezio Greggio
The Silence of the
Hams '94

Nick Grinde
Million Dollar Legs '32

Christoper Guest
Attack of the 50 Ft.
Woman '93

Val Guest
Casino Royale '67

Taylor Hackford
Against All Odds '84

Mark Haggard
The First Nudie
Musical '75

Piers Haggard
The Fiendish Plot of Dr.
Fu Manchu '80

Randa Haines
Wrestling Ernest
Hemingway '93

Alexander Hall
Goin' to Town '35

Guy Hamilton
Goldfinger '64
The Man with the
Golden Gun '74
The Mirror Crack'd
'80

Curtis Hanson
The Bedroom Window
'86

Renny Harlin
The Adventures of
Ford Fairlane '90

Rowdy Harrington
Road House '89

Anthony Harvey
The Lion in Winter '68

Henry Hathaway
The Dark Corner '46
Go West, Young Man
'36
Niagara '53
The Real Glory '39
True Grit '69

Howard Hawks
Ball of Fire '41
Barbary Coast '35
The Big Sleep '46
Bringing Up Baby '38
Gentlemen Prefer
Blondes '53
His Girl Friday '40
I Was a Male War
Bride '49
Monkey Business '52
Rio Bravo '59
To Have and Have Not
'44
Twentieth Century '34

Ben Hecht
Angels Over
Broadway '40

Amy Heckerling
Fast Times at
Ridgemont High '82
Johnny Dangerously
'84
National Lampoon's
European Vacation
'85

Victor Heerman
Animal Crackers '30

Stuart Heisler
The Glass Key '42

Stephen Herek
Bill & Ted's Excellent
Adventure '89

Douglas Hickox
Brannigan '75

Colin Higgins
Foul Play '78

George Roy Hill
Butch Cassidy and the
Sundance Kid '69
The World According
to Garp '82

Walter Hill
Crossroads '86
48 HRS. '83

Arthur Hiller
The Americanization
of Emily '64
The In-Laws '79
Man of La Mancha
'72
Outrageous Fortune
'87

Alfred Hitchcock
Notorious '46
Rear Window '54
Secret Agent '36
To Catch a Thief '55

Michael Hoffman
Soapdish '91

Tom Holland
Fright Night '47

Dennis Hopper
Chasers '94
Easy Rider '69

James W. Horne
Bonnie Scotland '35
The Bohemian Girl '36
Way Out West '37

Leslie Howard
Pygmalion '38

Ron Howard
Far and Away '92
Night Shift '82
Parenthood '89

Howard Hughes
The Outlaw '43

John Hughes
The Breakfast Club '85
Ferris Bueller's Day
Off '86

Ken Hughes
Casino Royale '67
Sextette '78

Maurice Hunt
The Paleface '48

John Huston
The Asphalt Jungle
'50
The African Queen
'51
Beat the Devil '54
Casino Royale '67
The Maltese Falcon
'41
The Misfits '61
The Treasure of the
Sierra Madre '48

Brian G. Hutton
High Road to China
'83
Kelly's Heroes '70

Peter Hyams
Narrow Margin '90

John Irvin
Raw Deal '86

David S. Jackson
Detonator '93

Mick Jackson
L.A. Story '91

Jim Jarmusch
Night on Earth '91

Norman Jewison
Other People's Money
'91

Phil Joanou
Final Analysis '92

Alan Johnson
To Be or Not to Be '83

Lamont Johnson
Spacehunter '83

Joe Johnston
The Pagemaster '94

Terry Jones
Monty Python and the
Holy Grail '75
Monty Python's The
Meaning of Life '83

Glenn Jordan
The Buddy System '84
Only When I Laugh
'81

Neil Jordan
High Spirits '88
Interview with the
Vampire '94

Lawrence Kasdan
The Big Chill '83
Body Heat '81
I Love You To Death
'90

Elia Kazan
A Streetcar Named
Desire '51

William Keighley
The Man Who Came
to Dinner '42
Torrid Zone '40

Gene Kelly
The Cheyenne Social
Club '70
Hello, Dolly! '69
Singing in the Rain
'52

Erle C. Kenton
Pardon My Sarong
'42

Who Done It? '42

Irving Kershner
The Empire Strikes
Back '80

Alek Keshishian
With Honors '94

Louis King
Bulldog Drummond
Comes Back '37

Randal Kleiser
Grease '78

Andrei Koncalovsky
Homer & Eddie '90

Henry Koster
Harvey '50
The Inspector General
'49
The Rage of Paris '38
The Robe '53

Stanley Kramer
Inherit the Wind '60

Stanley Kubrick
Dr. Strangelove, or:
How I Learned to
Stop Worrying and
Love the Bomb '64

Ken Kwapis
Vibes '88

Gregory La Cava
My Man Godfrey '36
Stage Door '37

Charles Lamont
Comin' Round the
Mountain '51
Hit the Ice '43

John Landis
An American
Werewolf in London
'81
The Blues Brothers '80
National Lampoon's
Animal House '78
Trading Places '83

Sidney Lanfield
The Lemon Drop Kid
'51
My Favorite Blonde
'42
Sorrowful Jones '49
You'll Never Get Rich
'41

Fritz Lang
The Return of Frank
James '40

Walter Lang
But Not For Me '59
Meet the Baron '33
Tin Pan Alley '40

Paul Leder
Molly & Gina '94

Rowland V. Lee
Captain Kidd '45

Michael Lehmann
Heathers '89
Hudson Hawk '91

Robert Z. Leonard
Dancing Lady '33
Duchess of Idaho '50
Ziegfeld Girl '41

Mervyn LeRoy
Mary, Mary '63

Richard Lester
A Funny Thing
Happened on the
Way to the Forum
'66

Brian Levant
The Flintstones '94

Barry Levinson
Bugsy '91
Diner '82
Good Morning,
Vietnam '87
Jimmy Hollywood '94
The Natural '84
Rain Man '88
Tin Men '87

Eugene Levy
Once Upon a Crime '91

Cullin Lewis
The Desert Trail '35

Jerry Lewis
The Ladies' Man '61
The Nutty Professor '63
Which Way to the Front? '70

Luis Llosa
The Specialist '94

Bob Logan
Repossessed '90

Joshua Logan
Bus Stop '56

Arthur Lubin
Buck Privates '41
In the Navy '41
Ride 'Em Cowboy '42

Ernst Lubitsch
Bluebeard's Eighth Wife '38
The Merry Widow '34
Ninotchka '39
The Shop Around the Corner '40
To Be or Not to Be '42

George Lucas
American Graffiti '73
Star Wars '77

Sidney Lumet
A Stranger Among Us '93
Q & A '90
The Verdict '82

David Lynch
Wild at Heart '90

Jonathan Lynn
Clue '86
Nuns on the Run '90

Louis Malle
Crackers '84

Joseph L. Mankiewicz
All About Eve '50
Guys and Dolls '55
The Ghost and Mrs. Muir '47
There Was a Crooked Man '70

Tom Mankiewicz
Dragnet '87

Delbert Mann
Separate Tables '58
That Touch of Mink '62

Edward L. Marin
Johnny Angel '45

Richard Marquand
Return of the Jedi '83

Garry Marshall
Boy! Did I Get a Wrong Number! '66
Destry Rides Again '39
Fancy Pants '50
The Mating Game '59
Monsieur Beaucaire '46
Off Limits '53
Overboard '87
The Perils of Pauline '47
Pretty Woman '90
Valley of the Sun '42
You Can't Cheat an Honest Man '39

Penny Marshall
Renaissance Man '94

Elaine May
Ishtar '87

Archie Mayo
Night After Night '32
A Night in Casablanca '46
The Petrified Forest '36

Paul Mazursky
Bob and Carol and Ted and Alice '69

Down and Out in Beverly Hills '86
The Pickle '93

Leo McCarey
The Awful Truth '37
Belle of the Nineties '34
Duck Soup '33
Going My Way '44
Ruggles of Red Gap '35
Six of a Kind '34

Michael James McDonald
The Crazy Sitter '94

Joseph McGrath
The Bliss of Mrs. Bloom '68
Casino Royale '67
The Magic Christian '69

Norman Z. McLeod
Casanova's Big Night '54
Horse Feathers '32
It's a Gift '34
Monkey Business '31
The Paleface '48
Road to Rio '47
Topper '37

John McTiernan
Last Action Hero '93

Peter Medak
The Ruling Class '72

Gus Meins
March of the Wooden Soldiers (AKA: Babes in Toyland) '34

Alan Metter
Back to School '86

Nicholas Meyer
Volunteers '85

Lewis Milestone
The Front Page '74
The General Died at Dawn '36

David Miller
Love Happy '49

George Miller
The Witches of Eastwick '87

Rob Minkoff
The Lion King '94

Vincente Minnelli
An American in Paris '51
The Bad and the Beautiful '52
Kismet '55

Robert Montgomery
Lady in the Lake '46

Robert Moore
Chapter Two '79
The Cheap Detective '78
Murder by Death '76

Paul Morrissey
Andy Warhol's Frankenstein '74

Russell Mulcahy
Ricochet '91

Eddie Murphy
Harlem Nights '89

Geoff Murphy
Freejack '92

Ronald Neame
First Monday in October '81
The Horse's Mouth '58

Gary Nelson
Get Smart, Again! '89

Ralph Nelson
Soldier in the Rain '63

Mike Nichols
Carnal Knowledge '71
Postcards from the Edge '90
Who's Afraid of Virginia Woolf? '66
Wolf '94

Jack Nicholson
Goin' South '78

Elliot Nugent
The Cat and the Canary '39
My Favorite Brunette '47
Never Say Die '39

Ron Nyswaner
The Prince of Pennsylvania '88

Clifford Odets
None But the Lonely Heart '44

Kenny Ortega
Hocus Pocus '93

Frank Oz
Dirty Rotten Scoundrels '88
Housesitter '92

G.W. Pabst
The Threepenny Opera '31

Alan J. Pakula
The Parallax View '74

Norman Panama
The Court Jester '56
How to Commit Marriage '69
The Road to Hong Kong '62

Jerry Paris
The Grasshopper '70

Robert Parish
Casino Royale '67

Alan Parker
Angel Heart '87
Bugsy Malone '76
Mississipi Burning '88

James D. Parriott
Heart Condition '90

Gabriel Pascal
Major Barbara '41

Richard Pearce
Leap of Faith '93
No Mercy '86

Arthur Penn
Bonnie & Clyde '67

Bill Persky
Serial '80

Donald Petrie
Grumpy Old Men '93
Richie Rich '94

Joseph Pevney
Female on the Beach
'55

Sidney Poiter
Uptown Saturday
Night '74

Roman Polanski
Pirates '86

Sydney Pollack
The Electric Horseman
'79
Three Days of the
Condor '75
Tootsie '82

H.C. Potter
Mr. Blandings Builds
His Dream House
'48
Mr. Lucky '43

Michael Powell
49th Parallel (AKA:
The Invaders) '67

Otto Preminger
Laura '44
River of No Return '54

Jonathon Prince
Camp Nowhere '94

Albert Pyun
Brain Smasher... A
Love Story '93

Richard Quine
How to Steal a Million
'66

Sex and the Single
Girl '64

Gene Quintano
National Lampoon's
Loaded Weapon I
'93

Bob Rafelson
Man Trouble '92
The Postman Always
Rings Twice '81

Harold Ramis
Caddyshack '80
Club Paradise '86

Frederic Raphael
Women & Men.
Stories of Seduction
'90

Nicholas Ray
Rebel Without a
Cause '55

Carl Reiner
All of Me '84
Dead Men Don't Wear
Plaid '82
Fatal Instinct '93
The Jerk '79
The Man With Two
Brains '83
Summer School '87

Rob Reiner
A Few Good Men '93
North '94
Princess Bride '87
This Is Spinal Tap '84
When Harry Met Sally
'89

Irving Reis
The Bachelor and the
Bobby-Soxer '47
The Big Street '42

Karel Reisz
Everybody Wins '90

Ivan Reitman
Ghostbusters '84
Ghostbusters II '89
Meatballs '79
Stripes '81

Burt Reynolds
The End '78

Dick Richards
Farewell, My Lovely
'75

Tony Richardson
Blue Sky '94
Tom Jones '63
Women & Men:
Stories of Seduction
'90

Charles Riesner
The Big Store '41

Michael Ritchie
The Bad News Bear
'76
Cops and Robbersons
'94
Fletch '86
The Scout '94
The Survivors '83

Martin Ritt
The Front '76

Hal Roach
The Devil's Brother
(AKA: Fra Diavolo)
'33

Stephen Roberts
The Ex-Mrs. Bradford
'36

Phil Alden Robinson
Field of Dreams '90

**Charles "Buddy"
Rogers**
The Bohemian Girl '36
March of the Wooden
Soldiers (AKA:
Babes in Toyland)
'34

Charles R. Rogers
The Devil's Brother
(AKA: Fra Diavolo)
'33

Herbert Ross
California Suite '78
The Goodbye Girl '77

Play It Again, Sam '72
Protocol '84
The Seven-Per-Cent
Solution '76
Steel Magnolias '89
The Sunshine Boys '75

Joe Roth
Revenge of the Nerds
II: Nerds in Paradise
'87

Wesley Ruggles
I'm No Angel '33
No Man of Her Own
'32

Richard Rush
The Stunt Man '80

Ken Russell
Salome's Last Dance
'88
Women & Men:
Stories of Seduction
'90

Mark Rydell
The Reivers '69

Gene Saks
The Odd Couple '68

Jay Sandrich
Seems Like Old Times
'80

Mark Sandrich
Carefree '38
Follow the Fleet '36
The Gay Divorcee '34
Top Hat '35

Victor Saville
Kim '50

Franklin J. Schaffner
The Best Man '64

Fred Schepisi
Roxanne '87
The Russia House '90

Victor Schertzinger
Birth of the Blues '41
The Road to
Singapore '40

The Road to Zanzibar
'41

Joel Schumacher
The Client '94
St. Elmo's Fire '85

Martin Scorsese
The Color of Money
'86
Taxi Driver '76

Allan Scott
Carefree '38

Tony Scott
Beverly Hills Cop II '87

Edward Sedgwick
Speak Easily '32

Peter Segal
The Naked Gun 33
1/3: The Final Insult
'94

Susan Seidelman
Desperately Seeking
Susan '85
Making Mr. Right '87

William A. Seiter
A Lady Takes a
Chance '43
Little Giant '46
The Moon's Our Home
'36
Roberta '35
Room Service '38
Sons of the Desert '33
You Were Never
Lovelier '42

David Seltzer
Punchline '88
Shining Through '92

Yahoo Serious
Young Einstein '88

Tom Shadyac
Ace Ventura: Pet
Detective '94

Ken Shapiro
Modern Problems '81

Melville Shavelson
Houseboat '58
Yours, Mine and Ours
'68

Tim Shelan
Seven Days' Leave '42

Ron Shelton
Bull Durham '88

Lowell Sherman
Morning Glory '33
She Done Him Wrong
'33

Donald Siegel
Dirty Harry '63
The Shootist '76

James Signorelli
Easy Money '83

Sylvan Simon
Rio Rita '42

Kevin Smith
Clerks '94

Mel Smith
Radioland Murders
'94

Gene Soks
Mame '74

Barry Sonnenfeld
The Addams Family
'91
Addams Family Values
'93

Penelope Spheeris
The Beverly Hillbillies
'93
The Little Rascals '94
Wayne's World '92

Steven Spielberg
Always '89
Hook '91
Indiana Jones and the
Last Crusade '89
Indiana Jones and the
Temple of Doom '84
1941 '79

Raiders of the Lost Ark
'81

Andrew Stevens
The Skateboard Kid II
'94

George Stevens
Annie Oakley '35
A Damsel in Distress
'37
Giant '56

Ben Stiller
Reality Bites '94

Ben Stoloff
The Affairs of Annabel
'38

Oliver Stone
JFK '91

Mel Stuart
Willy Wonka and the
Chocolate Factory
'71

John Sturges
McQ '74

Preston Sturges
Hail the Conquering
Hero '44
The Lady Eve '41
The Miracle of
Morgan's Creek '44
The Sin of Harold
Diddlebock '47
Unfaithfully Yours '48

Stephen Surjik
Wayne's World 2 '93

Edward Sutherland
Every Day's a Holiday
'37
The Flying Deuces '39
International House
'33
Mississipi '35
One Night in the
Tropics '40

Allan Swan
Look Who's Laughing
'41

David Swift
How to Succeed in
Business Without
Really Trying '67

Senkichi Taniguhi
What's Up, Tiger Lily?
'66

Quentin Tarantino
Reservoir Dogs '92

Frank Tashlin
Artists and Models '55
The Geisha Boy '58
Say One For Me '59
Son of Paleface '52

Lewis Teague
The Jewel of the Nile
'85

Betty Thomas
The Brady Bunch
Movie '95

Richard Thorpe
Double Wedding '37
The Thin Man Goes
Home '44

James Toback
The Pick-Up Artist '87

Jacques Tourneur
Out of the Past '47

Robert Townes
Personal Best '82
Tequila Sunrise '88

Frank Tuttle
Roman Scandals '33

Ron Underwood
City Slickers '91
Speechless '94

**Woodbridge S. Van
Dyke**
After the Thin Man '36
Another Thin Man '39
Manhattan
Melodrama '34
Marie Antoinette '38
Naughty Marietta '35
Love on the Run '36

The Thin Man '34

Buddy Van Horn
Any Which Way You
Can '81
The Dead Pool '88
Pink Caddilac '89

Paul Verhoeven
Total Recall '90

Stephen Verona
The Lords of Flatbush
'74

Charles Vidor
Gilda '46

King Vidor
The Patsy '28

Josef von Sternberg
Macao '52

Hal Walker
At War with the Army
'50
Road to Utopia '45

Richard Wallace
It's in the Bag '45

Raoul Walsh
The Big Trail '31
Dark Command '40
Klondike Annie '36
The Roaring Twenties
'39
The Tall Men '55
They Died with Their
Boots On '41

Charles Walters
Please Don't Eat the
Daisies '60

**Keenen Ivory
Wayans**
A Low Down Dirty
Shame '94

Jack Webb
Pete Kelly's Blues '55

Paul Weiland
City Slickers II: The
Legend of Curly's
Gold '94

Don Weis
Critic's Choice '63
The Munsters' Revenge
'81

Orson Welles
Confidential Report
(AKA: Mr. Arkadin)
'35

William A. Wellman
Beau Geste '39
Lady of Burlesque '43
Nothing Sacred '37
The Public Enemy '31
A Star Is Born '37

Wim Wenders
Paris, Texas '84

Billy Wilder
Buddy Buddy '81
The Front Page '31
The Fortune Cookie
'66
Irma La Douce '63
Kiss Me, Stupid '64
The Major and the
Minor '42
The Private Life of
Sherlock Holmes '70
Some Like It Hot '59
Sunset Boulevard '50

Gene Wilder
The Adventure of
Sherlock Holmes'
Smarter Brother '75

Hugh Wilson
Rustlers' Rhapsody '85

Simon Wincer
Harley Davidson and
the Marlboro Man
'91

Henry Winkler
Cop and a Half '93

Robert Wise
The Sound of Music
'65

William Witney
Roll on Texas Moon '46

David S. Wood
King Ralph '91

Sam Wood
A Day at the Races
'37
Hold Your Man '33
Kitty Foyle '40
A Night at the Opera
'35

William Wyler
Funny Girl '68
How to Murder Your
Wife '65
Jezebel '38

Jean Yarbrough
In Society '44
Lost in Alaska '52

Bud Yorkin
Arthur 2: On the
Rocks '88
Start the Revolution
Without Me '70

Harold Young
The Scarlet Pimpernel
'35

Roger Young
Lassiter '84

Robert Zemeckis
Death Becomes Her
'92
Forrest Gump '94
Who Framed Roger
Rabbit? '88

Howard Zieff
House Calls '78
Unfaithfully Yours '83

Fred Zinneman
High Noon '52
Oklahoma! '55

David Zucker
Aiplane!

The Naked Gun 2
1/2: The Smell of
Fear '91

The Naked Gun: From
the Files of Police
Squad! '88

Police Squad '82

Ruthless People '86

Jerry Zucker
Airplane! '80

Police Squad '82

Ruthless People '86

Writer Index

■ □ □ □ □ □ □ □ □ □ □ ■

The **Writer Index** lists only the films of each writer from which the quotes were taken. This is not a comprehensive list of all writers, nor is it any writer's complete list of film credits. Names are presented in a first name-last name format, and alphabetized by last name. The **Director** and **Character Names Indexes** immediately precede this index; the **Keyword Index** immediately follows.

Jim Abrahams
Airplane! '80
Hot Shots! Part Deux
'93
Hot Shots! '91
Police Squad '82
The Naked Gun: From
the Files of Police
Squad! '88

Rodney Ackland
49th Parallel (U.S. title:
The Invaders) '67

Felix Adler
Blockheads '38
Swiss Miss '38
Way Out West '37

James Agee
The African Queen '51

Alan Alda
The Four Seasons '81
Sweet Liberty '86

Will Aldis
Back to School '86

Scott Alexander
Ed Wood '94

Curt Allen
Hollywood Harry '85

Fred Allen
It's in the Bag '45

Janis Allen
Meatballs '79

Jay Presson Allen
Cabaret '72

Woody Allen
A Midsummer Night's
Sex Comedy '82
Alice '90
Annie Hall '77
Bananas '71
Broadway Danny Rose
'84
Everything You Always
Wanted to Know
About Sex But Were
Afraid to Ask '72
Hannah and Her
Sisters '86
Love and Death '75
Manhattan '79
Play It Again, Sam '72
Sleeper '73
Take the Money and
Run '69
What's Up, Tiger Lily?
'66
What's New Pussycat?
'65

Rod Amateau
Sunset '88

Ken Annakin
Those Magnificient
Men in Their Flying
Machines '65

Robert Ardrey
A Lady Takes a
Chance '43

David Arnott
The Adventures of
Ford Fairlane '90
Last Action Hero '93

Anthony Asquith
The Importance of
Being Earnest '52
Pygmalion '38

Patti Astor
Assault of the Killer
Bimbos '87

Robert J. Avrech
A Stranger Among Us
'93

George Axelrod
Breakfast at Tiffany's
'61
Bus Stop '56
How to Murder Your
Wife '65

Dan Aykroyd
The Blues Brothers '80
Coneheads '93
Dragnet '87
Ghostbusters '84
Ghostbusters II '89
Nothing but Trouble
'91

Peter Aykroyd
Nothing but Trouble
'91

Richard Bach
Jonathan Livingston
Seagull

Graham Baker
Joy of Living '38

Herbert Baker
Artists and Models '55

Sextette '78

Bela Balasz
The Threepenny
Opera '31

Leora Barish
Desperately Seeking
Susan '85

Peter Barnes
The Ruling Class '72

James Lee Barrett
The Cheyenne Social
Club '70

Michael Barrie
The Mogul '91

Hall Bartlett
Jonathan Livingston
Seagull

Ronald Bass
Rain Man '88

Joe Batteer
Chasers '94

S.H. Behrman
The Scarlet Pimpernel
'35
Two-Faced Woman
'41

Edmund Beloin
A Connecticut Yankee
in King Arthur's
Court '49

My Favorite Brunette
'47

Jerry Belson
Always '89
The End '78
The Grasshopper '70

Barbara Benedek
The Big Chill '83

Charles Bennett
Secret Agent '36
Unconquered '47

Mac Benoff
Love Happy '49

Robert Benton
Bonnie & Clyde '67
Nadine '87
Superman '78
There Was a Crooked
Man '70

Roger Berger
Final Analysis '92

Andrew Bergman
Blazing Saddles '74
Fletch '86
The In-Laws '79
Soapdish '91
The Scout '94

Armyan Bernstein
Cross My Heart '87
One from the Heart
'82

Jack Bernstein
Ace Ventura: Pet
Detective '94

Walter Bernstein
The Front '76

Claude Binyon
Mississipi '35

Shane Black
Last Action Hero '93
Lethal Weapon '87

Terry Black
Dead Heat '88

Dennis Blair
Easy Money '83

William Peter Blatty
The Ninth
Configuration '79
A Shot in the Dark '64

Len Blum
Meatballs '79
Spacehunter '83
Stripes '81

Jeffrey Boam
Indiana Jones and the
Last Crusade '89
Lethal Weapon 2 '89

True Boardman
Pardon My Sarong
'42
Ride 'Em Cowboy '42

Sydney Boehm
The Tall Men '55

Alan Boretz
Copacabana '47

William Bowers
Seven Days' Leave '42

William Boyd
Tune In Tomorrow '90

Marie Boyle
The Big Trail '31

Gerard Brach
Pirates '86

Charles Brackett
Ball of Fire '41
Bluebeard's Eighth
Wife '38
The Major and the
Minor '42
Niagara '53
Sunset Boulevard '50

Leigh Brackett
The Big Sleep '46
The Empire Strikes
Back '80
Rio Bravo '59

Irving Brecher
At the Circus '39
Go West '40

Andy Breckman
Arthur 2: On the
Rocks '88

Richard Breen
Mary, Mary '63
Niagara '53
Pete Kelly's Blues '55

Lou Breslow
Great Guns '41

Marshall Brickman
Annie Hall '77
Manhattan '79
Sleeper '73

John Bright
Blonde Crazy '31
The Public Enemy '31
She Done Him Wrong
'33

Oscar Brodney
Harvey '50
Mexican Hayride '48

Albert Brooks
Lost in America '85
The Scout '94

James L. Brooks
Broadcast News '87
Terms of Endearment
'83

Mel Brooks
Blazing Saddles '74

High Anxiety '77
History of the World:
Part 1 '81
The Producers '67
Spaceballs '87
The Twelve Chairs '70
Young Frankenstein
'74

Richard Brooks
Bite the Bullet '75

Gerard Brown
Juice '92

Robert Bruckner
Jezebel '38
Yankee Doodle Dandy
'42

Sidney Buchman
Mr. Smith Goes to
Washington '39

Alfred Bunn
The Bohemian Girl '36

Curtis Burch
Ladybugs '92

Abe Burrows
How to Succeed in
Business Without
Really Trying '67

Val Burton
The Time of Their Lives
'46

Frank Butler
Bonnie Scotland '35
Going My Way '44
My Favorite Blonde
'42
Never Say Die '39
The Perils of Pauline
'47
The Road to Morocco
'42
The Road to
Singapore '40
The Road to Zanzibar
'41

Harry Butler
Caught in the Draft
'41

Michael Butler
Brannigan '75
Code of Silence '85

Frank Buxton
What's Up, Tiger Lily?
'66

Floyd Byars
Making Mr. Right '87

Michael Cacoyannis
Zorba the Greek '64

Betty Camden
Auntie Mame '58
Singing in the Rain
'52

James Cameron
The Terminator 2:
Judgement Day '90
True Lies '94

Leon Capetanos
Down and Out in
Beverly Hill '86

Truman Capote
Beat the Devil '54

James Cappe
The Adventures of
Ford Fairlane '90

Jim Carabatsos
No Mercy '86

Topper Carew
Talkin' Dirty After
Dark '91

Jim Carrey
Ace Ventura: Pet
Detective '94

L.M. Kit Carson
Paris, Texas '84

Robert Carson
Beau Geste '39

Dee Caruso
Which Way to the
Front? '70

David Casci
The Pagemaster '94

Jim Cash
Dick Tracy '90

Nick Castle
Hook '91

Frank Cavett
Going My Way '44

Janus Cercone
Leap of Faith '93

Prescott Chaplin
Never Give a Sucker
an Even Break '41

Graham Chapman
Monty Python and the
Holy Grail '75
Monty Python's The
Meaning of Life '83

Paddy Chayefsky
The Americanization
of Emily '64

Helen Childress
Reality Bites '94

Jerome Chodorov
Louisiana Purchase '41

Patrick Civillo
Homer & Eddie '90

Ron Clark
Revenge of the Pink
Panther '78

John Cleese
Monty Python and the
Holy Grail '75
Monty Python's The
Meaning of Life '83

Ethan Coen
Raising Arizona '87

Lawrence J. Cohen
Start the Revolution
Without Me '70

Harry Colomby
Johnny Dangerously
'84

Adele Commandini
Christmas in
Connecticut '45

Richard Connel
Rio Rita '42

Myles Connolly
State of the Union '48

Steve Conrad
Wrestling Ernest
Hemingway '93

Ernie Contreras
The Pagemaster '94

Dorothy Cooper
Duchess of Idaho '50

Alec Coppel
The Bliss of Mrs.
Bloom '68

Francis Ford Coppola
One from the Heart '82

John Cornell
Crocodile Dundee '86

James Costigan
Love Among the Ruins
'75

Harry Crane
Song of the Thin Man
'47

Michael Cristofer
The Witches of
Eastwick '87

Cameron Crowe
Fast Times at
Ridgemont High '82

Billy Crystal
City Slickers II: The
Legend of Curly's
Gold '94

Jack Cunningham
Mississippi '35

Valerie Curtin
Unfaithfully Yours '83

Michael Curtiz
Casablanca '42

Neil Cuthbert
Hocus Pocus '93

Roald Dahl
Willy Wonka and the
Chocolate Factory
'71

Ian Dalrymple
Pygmalion '38

Bill Dana
The Nude Bomb '80

Rodney Dangerfield
Easy Money '83

Delmer Daves
The Petrified Forest
'36
You Were Never
Lovelier '42

Martin Davidson
The Lords of Flatbush
'74

Jerry Davis
Duchess of Idaho '50

Luther Davis
Kismet '55

Ron Davis
Coneheads '93

Isabel Dawn
The Moon's Our Home
'36
Wheel of Fortune
(AKA: A Man
Betrayed) '41

**Anatole de
Grunwald**
Major Barabara '41

Steven E. de Souza
The Flintstones '94
48 HRS. '83
Hudson Hawk '91

Ricochet '91
The Running Man '87

Gery De Vore
Raw Deal '86

Boyce DeGaw
The Moon's Our Home
'39

Paul Dehn
Godlfinger '64

Walter DeLeon
Birth of the Blues '41
The Cat and the
Canary '39
The Ghost Breakers '40
International House
'33
Little Giant '46
Ruggles of Red Gap
'35
Six of a Kind '34
The Time of Their Lives
'46
Union Pacific '39

Vina Delmar
The Awful Truth '37

Rudy DeLuca
Transylvania 6-5000
'85

Helen Deutsch
Kim '50

I.A.L. Diamond
Buddy Buddy '81
The Fortune Cookie
'66
The Front Page '74
Irma La Douce '63
Kiss Me, Stupid '64
The Private Life of
Sherlock Holmes
'70

Ernest R. Dickerson
Juice '92

Howard Dimsdale
Abbott and Costello
Meet Captain Kidd
'52

Leslie Dixon
Outrageous Fortune
'87
Overboard '87

Rudy Dochtermann
The Fiendish Plot of Dr.
Fu Manchu '80

Bob Dolman
Far and Away '92

**Mary Agnes
Donoghue**
The Buddy System
'84

Martin Donovan
Death Becomes Her
'92

Joseph Dougherty
Attack of the 50 Ft.
Woman '93
Cast a Deadly Spell
'91

Gordon Douglas
Topper Returns '41

Nathan E. Douglas
Inherit the Wind
'60

Brian Doyle-Murray
Club Paradise '86

William A. Drake
Grand Hotel '32
The Three Musketeers
'39

Jay Dratler
The Dark Corner '46
It's in the Bag '45
Laura '44

Hal Dresner
The Eiger Sanction '75

Philip Dunne
The Ghost and Mrs.
Muir '47
The Robe '53

Phil Dusenberry
The Natural '84

Patrick Edgeworth
Raw Deal '86

Dave Edison
Cast a Deadly Spell
'91

Blake Edwards
City Heat '84
The Return of the Pink
Panther '82
A Shot in the Dark '64
S.O.B. '81
Soldier in the Rain '63
That's Life! '86

Michael Elias
The Jerk '79
Serial '80

Stephen Elliott
The Adventures of
Priscilla, Queen of
the Desert '94

Robert Ellis
Tin Pan Alley '40

Jim Emerson
It's Pat—The Movie
'94

John Emerson
The Girl from Missouri
'34

Samuel G. Engel
My Darling
Clementine '46

Richard English
Million Dollar Legs '32

Delia Ephron
Mixed Nuts '94
This Is My Life '92

Nora Ephron
This Is My Life '92
When Harry Met Sally
'89

Jack Epps, Jr.
Dick Tracy '90

Julius J. Epstein
Arsenic and Old Lace '44
The Man Who Came to Dinner '42

Philip C. Epstein
Arsenic and Old Lace '44
The Man Who Came to Dinner '42

John Eskow
Pink Cadillac '89

Howard Estabrook
The Virginian '29

Rich Eustis
Serial '80

John Farrow
Around the World in 80 Days '56

William Faulkner
The Big Sleep '46
To Have and Have Not '44

Jules Feiffer
Carnal Knowledge '71

Earl Felton
20,000 Leagues Under the Sea '54

Frank Fenton
River of No Return '54

Larry Ferguson
Beverly Hills Cop II '87

Michael Fessier
You Were Never Lovelier '42
You'll Never Get Rich '41

Herbert Fields
Mississippi '35

Joseph Fields
Louisiana Purchase '41
A Night in Casablanca '46

Sid Fields
In Society '44

W.C. Fields
The Bank Dick '40
It's a Gift '34
My Little Chickadee

Hal Fimberg
The Big Store '41
In Society '44

Harry Julian Fink
Dirty Harry '71

Rita M. Fink
Dirty Harry '71

Abem Finkel
Jezebel '38

Fred F. Finklehoffe
At War with the Army '50

Carrie Fisher
Postcards from the Edge '90

Jim Fisher
The Beverly Hillbillies '93

Steve Fisher
Johnny Angel '45
Lady in the Lake '46
Song of the Thin Man '47

Jeffrey Fiskin
Crackers '84

F. Scott Fitzgerald
Marie Antoinette '38

John Flynn
Nails '92

Carl Foreman
Cyrano de Bergerac '50
High Noon '52

Garrett Fort
Dracula '31

Jan Fortune
Dark Command '40

Lewis R. Foster
It's in the Bag '45
Million Dollar Legs '32

Robert Foster
Dead-Bang '89

Fredric M. Frank
The Greatest Show on Earth '52
The Ten Commandments '56
Unconquered '47

Harriet Frank, Jr.
The Reivers '69

Melvin Frank
A Funny Thing Happened on the Way to the Forum '66
Monsieur Beaucaire '46

Jeff Franklin
Summer School '87

John Frant
Hit the Ice '43

Devery Freeman
Miss Grant Takes Richmond '49

Everett Freeman
The Princess and the Pirate '44
You Can't Cheat an Honest Man '39

Ken Friedman
Cadillac Man '90

David Fuler
Necessary Roughness '91

Jules Furthman
The Big Sleep '46
Bombshell '33
China Seas '35
The Outlaw '43
Rio Bravo '59

To Have and Have Not '44

John Fusco
Crossroads '86

Bob Gale
1941 '79

George Gallo
Midnight Run '88

Paul Gangelin
Roll on Texas Moon '46

Lowell Ganz
City Slickers '91
City Slickers II: The Legend of Curly's Gold '94
Night Shift '82
Parenthood '89

Herb Gardner
A Thousand Clowns '65

Robert Garland
The Electric Horseman '79

Mick Garnis
Hocus Pocus '93

Oliver H.P. Garrett
Manhattan Melodrama '34

Harvey Gates
The Corpse Vanishes '47

John Gay
Separate Tables '58

Larry Gelbart
Tootsie '82
The Wrong Box '66

Peter George
Dr. Strangelove, or: How I Learned to Stop Worrying and Love the Bomb '64

Chris Gerolmo
Mississipi Burning '88

Robert Getchell
The Client '94

David Giler
The Parallax View '74

Terry Gilliam
The Adventures of Baron Munchausen '89
Monty Python and the Holy Grail '75
Monty Python's The Meaning of Life '83

Dan Gilroy
Chasers '94
Freejack '92

George Gipe
The Man With Two Brains '83

Kubec Glasmon
Blonde Crazy '31
The Public Enemy '31

Mitch Glazer
Scrooged '88

Gayle Glecker
The Lords of Flatbush '74

Jim Goddard
Reilly: The Ace of Spies '84

Ray Golden
The Big Store '41

Gary Goldman
Total Recall '90

James Goldman
The Lion in Winter '68

William Goldman
Butch Cassidy and the Sundance Kid '69
Maverick '94
The Princess Bride '87

Clifford Goldsmith
Life with Father '47

David Zelag Goodman
Farewell, My Lovely '75

Frances Goodrich
After the Thin Man '36
Ah, Wilderness '35
Another Thin Man '39
It's a Wonderful Life '46
Naughty Marietta '35
The Thin Man '34

Leon Gordon
Kim '50

Ruth Gordon
Adam's Rib '49
It Should Happen to You '54

Steve Gordon
Arthur '81

Carl Gottlieb
The Jerk '79

Ed Graczyck
Come Back to the 5 & Dime Jimmy Dean, Jimmy Dean '82

Ronny Graham
Spaceballs '87
To Be or Not to Be '83

Bert Granet
The Affairs of Annabel '38

John Grant
Abbott and Costello Meet Captain Kidd '52
Abbott and Costello Meet Frankenstein '48
Abbott and Costello Meet the Killer, Boris Karloff '49
Abbott and Costello Meet the Mummy '55
Buck Privates '41
Buck Privates Come Home '47

Comin' Round the Mountain '51
In Society '44
In the Navy '41
The Noose Hangs High '48
Pardon My Sarong '42
Ride 'Em Cowboy '42
Rio Rita '42
The Time of Their Lives '46
The Wistful Widow of Wagon Gap '47
Who Done It? '42

Mauri Grashin
Roll on Texas Moon '46

Mike Gray
Code of Silence '85

Charles Grayson
One Night in the Tropics '40

Brian Grazer
Housesitter '92

Adolph Green
Auntie Mame '58
Singing in the Rain '52

Howard J. Green
Morning Glory '33

Paul Green
Cabin in the Cotton '32

Ezio Greggio
The Silence of the Hams '94

Milton Gropper
No Man of Her Own '32

Larry Gross
48 HRS. '83

Frank Gruber
Johnny Angel '45

Paul Guay
The Little Rascals '94

Christopher Guest
This Is Spinal Tap '84

Alec Guiness
The Horse's Mouth '58

Fred Guiol
Giant '56

James Gunn
Lady of Burlesque '43

Dan Guntzelman
Revenge of the Nerds II: Nerds in Paradise '87

Albert Hackett
After the Thin Man '36
Ah, Wilderness '35
Another Thin Man '39
It's a Wonderful Life '46
Naughty Marietta '35
The Thin Man '34

George Hadjinassios
Shirley Valentine '89

Scott Hale
The Shootist '76

Sam Hamm
Batman '89

Curtis Hanson
The Bedroom Window '86

Robert Harling
Soapdish '91
Steel Magnolias '89

Howard Harris
Copacabana '47
The Noose Hangs High '48

Timothy Harris
Trading Places '83

Jim V. Hart
Bram Stoker's Dracula '93

Don Hartman
Life with Father '47

My Favorite Blonde '42
Never Say Die '39
The Princess and the Pirate '44
The Road to Morocco '42
The Road to Singapore '40
The Road to Zanzibar '41

Edmund Hartman
Fancy Pants '50
In Society '44
The Lemon Drop Kid '51
The Paleface '48

Eric Hatch
Topper '37

Lionel Hauser
Dark Command '40

John Michael Hayes
But Not For Me '59
Rear Window '54
To Catch a Thief '55

Lawrence Hazard
Strange Cargo '40

Ben Hecht
Angels Over Broadway '40
Barbary Coast '35
Monkey Business '52
Nothing Sacred '37
Notorious '46
Twentieth Century '34

Joseph Heller
Sex and the Single Girl '64

Sam Hellman
The Return of Frank James '40
The Three Musketeers '39

Buck Henry
Protocol '84

David Lee Henry
Out for Justice '91

F. Hugh Herbert
Dark Command '40

Rowdy Herrington
Road House '89

Stephen Hibbert
It's Pat—The Movie '94

Colin Higgins
Foul Play '78
Harold and Maude '72

Robert Hill
Female on the Beach '55

Samuel Hoffenstein
Laura '44

Paul Hogan
Crocodile Dundee '86

Tom Holland
Fright Night '47

Don Holley
National Lampoon's Loaded Weapon I '93

Geoffrey Homes
Out of the Past '47

Milton Homes
Mr. Lucky '43

Arthur T. Horman
Buck Privates '41
In the Navy '41

Lionel Houser
Christmas in Connecticut '45

Sidney Howard
Gone with the Wind '39

Eric Hughes
Against All Odds '84

John Hughes
The Breakfast Club '85

Ferris Bueller's Day
Off '86
Home Alone '90
Home Alone 2: Lost in
New York '92
Nate and Hayes '83
National Lampoon's
European Vacation
'85

John Hunter
The Grey Fox '82

Gladys Hurlbut
Love on the Run '36

John Huston
The African Queen '51
Beat the Devil '54
Jezebel '38
The Maltese Falcon '41
The Treasure of the
Sierra Madre '48

Willard Huyck
American Graffiti '73
Indiana Jones and the
Temple of Doom '84
Radioland Murders '94

Peter Hyams
Narrow Margin '90

Eric Idle
Monty Python and the
Holy Grail '75
Monty Python's The
Meaning of Life '83
National Lampoon's
European Vacation
'85

W. Peter Iliff
Point Break '91

David Isaacs
Volunteers '85

Vladimir Jabotinsky
Samson and Delilah
'49

David S. Jackson
Detonator '93

Felix Jackson
Destry Rides Again
'39
Rage of Paris '38

Don Jakoby
Blue Thunder '83

Rian James
42nd Street '33

Elsie Janis
Madam Satan '30

Jim Jarmusch
Night on Earth '91

Jim Jennewein
The Flintstones '94
Getting Even with Dad
'94
Richie Rich '94

Jack Jevne
Topper '37

Monica Johnson
The Scout '94

Lawrence E. Johnson
Speak Easily '32

**Mark Steven
Johnson**
Grumpy Old Men '93

Monica Johnson
Lost in America '85

Grover Jones
Dark Command '40
The Virginian '29

Terry Jones
Monty Python and the
Holy Grail '75
Monty Python's The
Meaning of Life '83

Neil Jordan
High Spirits '88

Edmund Joseph
Who Done It? '42

Adrien Joyce
Man Trouble '92

Bert Kalmar
Duck Soup '33
A Night at the Opera
'35
Horse Feathers '32

Steven Kampmann
Back to School '86

Garson Kanin
Adam's Rib '49
It Should Happen to
You '54

Michael Kanin
How to Commit
Marriage '69

Hal Kanter
Artists and Models '55
Here Come the Girls
'53
Let's Make Love '60
Off Limits '53

Larry Karaszewski
Ed Wood '94

Lawrence Kasdan
The Big Chill '83
Body Heat '81
The Empire Strikes
Back '80
Return of the Jedi '83

Gloria Katz
American Graffiti '73
Indiana Jones and the
Temple of Doom '84
Radioland Murders
'94

Edward Kaufman
The Gay Divorcee '34

George S. Kaufman
Cocoanuts '29
A Night at the Opera
'35

Philip Kaufman
The Outlaw Josey
Wales '76
Raiders of the Lost Ark
'81

Robert Kaufman
Love at First Bite '79

Larry Kenner
Jewel of the Nile '85

George Kennett
Boy! Did I Get a
Wrong Number! '66

Doug Kenney
Caddyshack '80

Charles Kenyon
The Petrified Forest '36

Curtis Kenyon
Seven Days' Leave '42

James V. Kern
Look Who's Laughing
'41

Roland Kibbee
A Night in
Casablanca '46

Tom Kilpatrick
Wheel of Fortune
(AKA: A Man
Betrayed) '41

Bruce Kimmel
The First Nudie
Musical '75

Robert King
Speechless '94

David Kirschner
The Pagemaster '94

Robert Klane
National Lampoon's
European Vacation
'85
Unfaithfully Yours '83

Wally Klein
They Died with Their
Boots On '41

Arthur Kober
Meet the Baron '33

David Koepp
Death Becomes Her '92

Larry Konner
The Beverly Hillbillies
'93

Harry Kornitz
The Thin Man Goes
Home '44

John Kostmayer
I Love You To Death
'90

Jim Kouf
Another Stakeout '93
Stakeout '87

Norman Krasna
Let's Make Love '60

Stu Krieger
Monkey Trouble '94

Sid Kuller
The Big Store '41

Harry Kumitz
How to Steal a Million
'66
The Inspector General
'49

Andrew Kurtzman
Camp Nowhere '94

Gregory La Cava
My Man Godfrey '36

**Richard
LaGravenese**
The Fisher King '91

Harold Lamb
The Plainsman '36
Samson and Delilah
'49

Bill Lancaster
The Bad News Bear '76

John Landis
An American
Werewolf in London
'81
Clue '86

Harry Langdon
The Flying Deuces '39

Noel Langley
The Wizard of Oz '39

Leo Lania
The Threepenny
Opera '31

Dale Lanner
Ruthless People '86

Ring Lardner, Jr.
M*A*S*H '70

Jesse L. Lasky, Jr.
Samson and Delilah
'49
The Ten
Commandments '56
Unconquered '47
Union Pacific '39

Jonathan Latimer
The Glass Key '42
Topper Returns '41

S.K. Lauren
A Damsel in Distress
'37

John Law
Casino Royale '67

Dale Lawner
Dirty Rotten
Scoundrels '88

Bert Lawrence
Blues Busters '50

Jerome Lawrence
First Monday in
October '81

Vincent Lawrence
Night After Night '32
Test Pilot '38

J.F. Lawton
Blankman '94
Pretty Woman '90

Norman Lear
The Night They Raided
Minsky's '68

Robert Leco
Abbott and Costello
Meet Frankenstein
'48

Reuben Leder
Molly & Gina '94

Charles Lederer
Gentlemen Prefer
Blondes '53
His Girl Friday '40
I Was a Male War
Bride '49
Kismet '55
Monkey Business '52

Robert E. Lee
First Monday in
October '81

Robert Lees
Buck Privates Come
Home '47
Comin' Round the
Mountain '51
Hit the Ice '43
The Wistful Widow of
Wagon Gap '47

Michael Leeson
The Survivors '83

Ernest Lehman
Hello, Dolly! '69
The Sound of Music
'65
Who's Afraid of
Virginia Woolf? '66

Gladys Lehman
Rio Rita '42

Jerry Leichtling
Blue Sky '91
Peggy Sue Got
Married '86

Peter M. Lenkov
Demolition Man '93

Isobel Lennart
Funny Girl '68
Please Don't Eat the
Daisies '60

Hugh Leonard
Da '88

Alan Jay Lerner
An American in Paris
'51
My Fair Lady '64
Royal Wedding '51

Sonya Levien
Oklahoma! '55
Ziegfeld Girl '41

Kevin Levine
Volunteers '85

Barry Levinson
Diner '82
Jimmy Hollywood '94
Tin Men '87
Unfaithfully Yours '83

Leonard L. Levinson
Look Who's Laughing
'41

Albert E. Lewin
Boy! Did I Get a
Wrong Number! '66

Cecil Lewis
Pygmalion '38

Jerry Lewis
The Ladies' Man '61
The Nutty Professor '63

W.P. Lipscomb
The Garden of Allah
'36
Pygmalion '38

Robert Locash
The Naked Gun 33
1/3: The Final Insult
'94

Bob Logan
Repossessed '90

Helen Logan
Tin Pan Alley '40

Anita Loos
The Girl from Missouri
'34
Hold Your Man '33

Red-Headed Woman
'32
The Women '39

David Loughery
Flashback '90

Edward T. Lowe
Bulldog Drummond
Comes Back '37

George Lucas
American Graffiti '73
Raiders of the Lost Ark
'81
Return of the Jedi '83
Star Wars '77

William Ludwig
Oklahoma! '55

Sidney Lumet
Q & A '90

David Lynch
Wild at Heart '90

Barre Lyndon
The Greatest Show on
Earth '52

Jonathan Lynn
Nuns on the Run '90

Charles MacArthur
Barbary Coast
Twentieth Century '34

Richard Macaulay
The Roaring Twenties
'39
Torrid Zone '40

Philip MacDonald
Mr. Moto's Last
Warning '39

Richard Mack
You Can't Cheat an
Honest Man '39

Aeneas MacKenzie
The Ten
Commandments '56
They Died with Their
Boots On '41

Jeanie Macpherson
The Devil's Brother
(AKA: Fra Diavolo)
'33
Madam Satan '30
The Plainsman '36

Ben Maddow
The Asphalt Jungle '50

John Lee Mahin
Bombshell '33
Naughty Marietta '35

Richard Mailbaum
Goldfinger '64
The Spy Who Loved
Me '77

David Mamet
The Postman Always
Rings Twice '81
The Verdict '82

Babaloo Mandel
City Slickers '91
City Slickers II: The
Legend of Curly's
Gold '94
Night Shift '82
Parenthood '89
Vibes '88

John Lee Manin
Love on the Run '36

**Herman J.
Mankiewicz**
Dinner at Eight '33

**Joseph L.
Mankiewicz**
All About Eve '50
Guys and Dolls '55
Manhattan
Melodrama '34

Tom Mankiewicz
Dragnet '87
The Man with the
Golden Gun '74

Wolf Mankowitz
Casino Royale '67

Albert Mannheimer
Born Yesterday '50

Bruce Manning
The Rage of Paris '38

Lawrence B. Marcus
The Stunt Man '80

Frances Marion
Dinner at Eight '33

George Marion, Jr.
The Gay Divorcee '34
You Can't Cheat an
Honest Man '39

Mitch Markowitz
Good Morning,
Vietnam '87

Charles R. Marlon
Blues Busters '50

Steve Marshal
Revenge of the Nerds
II: Nerds in Paradise
'87

Garry Marshall
Grasshopper '70

Penny Marshall
Renaissance Man '94

D.M. Marshman, Jr.
Sunset Boulevard '50

Frances Martin
One Night in the
Tropics '40
International House
'33
Mississippi '35

Steve Martin
Dead Men Don't Wear
Plaid '82
The Jerk '79
L.A. Story '91
The Man With Two
Brains '83
Roxanne '87

**Troy Kennedy
Martin**
Kelly's Heroes '70

Arthur Marx
Cancel My
Reservation '72

**William
Mastrosimone**
With Honors '94

Chris Matheson
Bill & Ted's Excellent
Adventure '89

Richard Matheson
Loose Cannons '90
The Raven '63

John Mattson
Milk Money '94

Elaine May
Ishtar '87

Edwin Justus Mayer
To Be or Not to Be '42

Steve Mazur
The Little Rascals '94

Paul Mazursky
Bob and Carol and
Ted and Alice '69
Down and Out in
Beverly Hills '86
I Love You, Alice B.
Toklas! '68
The Pickle '93

Leo McCarey
Going My Way '44

Horace McCoy
Valley of the Sun '42

Michael McDowell
Beetlejuice '88

**James Kevin
McGuinness**
China Seas '35

Don McGuire
Tootsie '82

**William Anthony
McGuire**
Little Man, What
Now? '34

Roman Scandals '33

Jay McInerney
Bright Lights, Big City
'88

Norman Z. McLeod
Casanova's Big Night
'54

Irene Mecchi
The Lion King '94

Thomas Meehan
Spaceballs '87

Charles Melson
Swiss Miss '38

Ivan Menchell
The Cemetery Club
'92

Nicholas Meyer
The Seven-Per-Cent
Solution '76

Nancy Meyers
Once Upon a Crime
'91
Protocol '84

Ted V. Mikels
Assault of the Killer
Bimbos '87

John Milius
Apocalypse Now '79

Arthur Miller
Everybody Wins '90
The Misfits '61

Harvey Miller
Protocol '84

Seton I. Miller
The Adventures of
Robin Hood '38

Winston Miller
My Darling
Clementine '46

Sam Mintz
Roberta '35

Ivan Moffa
Giant '56

Jefferson Moffit
Bonnie Scotland '35

Jim Moloney
The Fiendish Plot of Dr.
Fu Manchu '80

Nate Monaster
That Touch of Mink '62

Eddie Moran
Topper '37

Paul Morrissey
Andy Warhol's
Frankenstein '74

Jim Mulholland
The Mogul '91

Jane Murfin
Roberta '35

Eddie Murphy
Harlem Nights '89

Greg Murphy
Without a Clue '88

Warren B. Murphy
The Eiger Sanction '75

M.M. Musselman
The Three Musketeers
'39

Henry Myers
Destry Rides Again
'39

Mike Myers
Wayne's World '92
Wayne's World 2 '93

Rick Natkin
Necessary Roughness
'91

William Neff
I Was a Male War
Bride '49

Gary Nelson
Get Smart, Again! '89

David Newman
Bonnie & Clyde '67
Superman '78
There Was a Crooked
Man '70

Dudley Nichols
Bringing Up Baby '38
Stagecoach '39

Tommy Noonan
Promises! Promises!
'63

Denis Norden
The Bliss of Mrs.
Bloom '68

**William W. Norton,
Sr.**
Brannigan '75

Frank S. Nugent
Fort Apache '48
The Quiet Man '52
The Searchers '56
The Tall Men '55

Ron Nyswaner
Gross Anatomy '89
The Prince of
Pennsylvania '88

Dan O'Bannon
Blue Thunder '83
Total Recall '90

Robert O'Brien
Fancy Pants '50
The Lemon Drop Kid
'51
Say One For Me '59

David Odell
Nate and Hayes '83

Clifford Odets
The General Died at
Dawn '36
None But the Lonely
Heart '44

Michael O'Donoghue
Scrooged '88

James O'Hanlon
Calamity Jane '53

The Plainsman '36

Fred Rinaldo
Abbott and Costello
Meet Frankenstein
'48
Buck Privates Come
Home '47
Comin' Round the
Mountain '51
Hit the Ice '43
The Wistful Widow of
Wagon Gap '47

Clements Ripley
Jezebel '38

Robert Riskin
A Lady for a Day '33
It Happened One
Night '34
Meet John Doe '41
The Thin Man Goes
Home '44

Allen Rivkin
Dancing Lady '33
Meet the Baron '33

Marguerite Roberto
Honky Tonk '41

Jonathan Roberts
The Lion King '94

June Roberts
Mermaids '90

Marguerite Roberts
True Grit '69
Ziegfeld Girl '41

Stanley Roberts
Who Done It? '42

William Roberts
The Mating Game '59

Sam Robins
The Corpse Vanishes
'47

Casey Robinson
Dark Victory '39

Phil Alden Robinson
All of Me '84

Field of Dreams '90

Charles Rogers
Block-Heads '38
Swiss Miss '38
The Flying Deuces '39
Way Out West '37

**Howard Emmett
Rogers**
Hold Your Man '33
Libeled Lady '36

**Sandra Weintraub
Roland**
High Road to China
'83

Lawrence Roman
McQ '74

Jack Rose
Houseboat '58
My Favorite Brunette
'47
The Paleface '48
The Road to Rio '47
Sorrowful Jones '49
Trouble Along the
Way '53

Mark Rosenthal
The Beverly Hillbillies
'93
The Jewel of the Nile
'85

Arthur Ross
The Great Race '65

Robert Rossen
The Roaring Twenties
'39

Eric Roth
Forrest Gump '94

Marc Rubel
Big Business '88

Stanley Rubin
Macao '52

Harry Ruby
Duck Soup '33
Horse Feathers '32

Paul Ruchnick
Addams Family Values
'93

Richard Rush
The Stunt Man '80

Harry Ruskin
Six of a Kind '34

Ken Russell
Salome's Last Dance
'88

Willy Russell
Shirley Valentine '89

Morrie Ryskind
Animal Crackers '30
Cocoanuts '29
My Man Godfrey '36
A Night at the Opera
'35
Room Service '38
Stage Door '37

Lesser Samuels
Strange Cargo '40

Barry Sandler
The Mirror Crack'd
'80

John Sanford
Honky Tonk '41

Alvin Sargent
Other People's Money
'91
Paper Moon '73

Arlene Sarner
Blue Sky '91
Peggy Sue Got
Married '86

Michael Sayers
Casino Royale '67

Joel Sayre
Annie Oakley '35

Richard Schayer
Kim '50

Andrew Scheinman
North '94

Alfred Schiller
The Flying Deuces '39

Murray Schisgal
Tootsie '82

Charles Schnee
The Bad and the
Beautiful '52

Gerald Schnitzer
The Corpse Vanishes
'47

**Bernard C.
Schoenfeld**
The Dark Corner '46
Macao '52

Paul Schrader
Taxi Driver '76

Arnold Schulman
The Night They Raided
Minsky's '68

Joel Schumacher
St. Elmo's Fire '85

David R. Schwartz
Robin and the Seven
Hoods '64
Sex and the Single
Girl '64

Kathryn Scola
One Night in the
Tropics '40

Adrian Scott
Mr. Lucky '43

Allan Scott
Carefree '38
Follow the Fleet '36
Joy of Living '38
Roberta '35
Top Hat '35

Peter S. Seaman
Doc Hollywood '91
Who Framed Roger
Rabbit '88

George Seaton
A Day at the Races '37

Manuel Seff
Footlight Parade '33
Love on the Run '36

Arthur Sellers
Modern Problems '81

David Seltzer
Punchline '88
Shining Through '92

David O. Selznick
Since You Went Away
'44
A Star Is Born '37

Lorenzo Semple, Jr.
The Parallax View '74

Yahoo Serious
Young Einstein '88

Alexandra Seros
The Specialist '94

James Seymour
Footlight Parade '33
42nd Street '33

Ken Shapiro
Modern Problems '81

Stanley Shapiro
Dirty Rotton
Scoundrels '88
Pillow Talk '59
That Touch of Mink '62

Steve Sharon
The Dead Pool '88

Melville Shavelson
Sorrowful Jones '49
Double Dynamite '51
Houseboat '58
The Princess and the
Pirate '44
Trouble Along the
Way '53
Yours, Mine and Ours
'68

**George Bernard
Shaw**
Pygmalion '38
Major Barbara '41

Arthur Sheekman
Duck Soup '33
Monkey Business '31
Roman Scandals '33

Sidney Sheldon
The Bachelor and the
    Bobby-Soxer '47

Ron Shelton
Bull Durham '88

Sam Shepard
Paris, Texas '84

Jack Sher
Critic's Choice '63
Off Limits '53

Standford Sherman
Any Which Way You
    Can '81

Tom Sherohman
Modern Problems '81

Robert Sherwood
The Scarlet Pimpernel
    '35

Harold Shumater
Freejack '92
Ride 'Em Cowboy '42
Ronald Shusett

Charles Shyer
Goin' South '78
House Calls '78
Once Upon a Crime
    '91
Protocol '84

Tom Sierchio
Untamed Heart '93

Stirling Silliphant
The Enforcer '76

**Richard Alan
Simmons**
Female on the Beach
    '55

Neil Simon
California Suite '78
Chapter Two '79

The Cheap Detective
    '78
The Goodbye Girl '77
Murder by Death '76
Neil Simon's
    Broadway Bound
    '92
The Odd Couple '68
Only When I Laugh
    '81
Seems Like Old Times
    '80
The Sunshine Boys '75

Warren Skaaren
Batman '89
Beetlejuice '88
Beverly Hills Cop II '87

Zachary Sklar
JFK '91

Ebbe Roe Smith
Car 54, Where Are
    You? '94

Harold Jacob Smith
Inherit the Wind '60

Kevin Smith
Clerks '94

Paul Gerard Smith
Topper Returns '41

Kathrn Sola
Night After Night '32

Edward Solomon
Bill & Ted's Excellent
    Adventure '89

Bernie Somers
Cops and Robbersons
    '94

Rodolfo Sonego
Once Upon a Crime
    '91

Aaron Sorkin
A Few Good Men '93

Terry Southern
Dr. Strangelove, or:
    How I Learned to

Stop Worrying and
    Love the Bomb '64
Easy Rider '69
The Magic Christian
    '69

Ralph Spence
The Flying Deuces '39
Seven Days' Leave '42
Speak Easily '32

Penelope Spheeris
The Little Rascals '94

Leonard Spigelgass
The Big Street '42
I Was a Male War
    Bride '49

Roger Spottiswoode
48 HRS. '83

Jim Staahl
The Beverly Hillbillies
    '93

Rama Laurie Stagner
Blue Sky '91

Sylvester Stallone
The Lords of Flatbush
    '74

Lynn Starling
The Cat and the
    Canary '39

Ben Starr
How to Commit
    Marriage '69

Mark Stein
Housesitter '92

Norman Steinberg
Blazing Saddles '74
Johnny Dangerously
    '84
My Favorite Year '82

Leonard Stern
Lost in Alaska '52
The Nude Bomb '80

Stewart Stern
Rebel Without a
    Cause '55

**Donald Ogden
Stewart**
Dinner at Eight '33
Kitty Foyle '40
The Philadelphia Story
    '40
Without Love '45

Oliver Stone
JFK '91

Tom Stoppard
The Russia House '90

Peter Stowe
Charade '63

Larry Strawther
Without a Clue '88

Wesley Strick
Final Analysis '92
Wolf '94

Preston Sturges
Hail the Conquering
    Hero '44
The Lady Eve '41
The Miracle of
    Morgan's Creek '44
Never Say Die '39
The Sin of Harold
    Diddlebock '47
Unfaithfully Yours '48

Burt Styler
Boy! Did I Get a
    Wrong Number! '66

C. Gardner Sullivan
Union Pacific '39

Arne Sultan
The Nude Bomb '80

**Miles Hood
Swarthout**
The Shootist '76

Julia Sweeney
I'ts Pat—The Movie
    '94

Jo Swerling
Double Wedding '37
It's a Wonderful Life
    '46

The Real Glory '39

David Swift
How to Succeed in
    Business Without
    Really Trying '67

Ted Tally
The Silence of the
    Lambs '91

Daniel Taradash
Don't Bother to Knock
    '52

Quentin Tarantino
Reservoir Dogs '92

Frank Tashlin
Artists and Models '55
The Geisha Boy '58
The Lemon Drop Kid
    '51
Love Happy '49
Miss Grant Takes
    Richmond '49
The Paleface '48
Son of Paleface '52

David Taylor
Lassiter '84

Dwight Taylor
Follow the Fleet '36
The Thin Man Goes
    Home '44
Top Hat '35

Steve Tesich
The World According
    to Garp '82

Harvey Thew
The Public Enemy '31
She Done Him Wrong
    '33

Carline Thompson
The Addams Family
    '91

Keene Thompson
Fighting Caravans '31
The Virginian '29

Writer Index

Larry Thompson
The Addams Family
'91

James Toback
Bugsy '91
The Pick-Up Artist '87

Peter Torokvei
Back to School '86

Gene Towne
Joy of Living '38

Robert Towne
The Natural '84
Personal Best '82
Tequila Sunrise '88

Dalton Trumbo
Kitty Foyle '40

Glenn Tryon
Roberta '35

Larry Tucker
Bob and Carol and
Ted and Alice '69

Harry Tugend
Birth of the Blues '41

Karl Tunberg
Down Argentine Way
'40

Bonnie Turner
The Brady Bunch
Movie '95
Coneheads '93
Wayne's World '92
Wayne's World 2 '93

Terry Turner
The Brady Bunch
Movie '95
Coneheads '93
Wayne's World '92
Wayne's World 2 '93

Burl Tuttle
'Neath the Arizona
Skies '34

John Twist
Annie Oakley '35
Too Many Girls '40

Gladys Unger
Madam Satan '30

Laslo Vadnay
Copacabana '47

Ladislaus Vajda
The Threepenny
Opera '31

Anthony Veiller
The Ex-Mrs. Bradford
'36
Stage Door '37
State of the Union '48

Stephen Verona
The Lords of Flatbush
'74

Gore Vidal
The Best Man '64

Salka Viertel
Two-Faced Woman '41

Eliot Wald
Camp Nowhere '94

Jerry Wald
The Roaring Twenties
'39
Torrid Zone '40

Edwards Waldman
The Pink Panther
Strikes Again '76

Frank Waldman
The Pink Panther
Strikes Again '76
The Return of the Pink
Panther '82
Revenge of the Pink
Panther '78

Ira Wallach
Boys' Night Out '62

Darrell Ware
Down Argentine Way
'40

Dale Wasserman
Man of La Mancha '72

Daniel Waters
The Adventures of
Ford Fairlane '90
Batman Returns '92
Demolition Man '93
Heathers '89
Hudson Hawk '91

Maurine Watkins
Libeled Lady '36
No Man of Her Own
'32

Damon Wayans
Blankman '94

**Keenen Ivory
Wayans**
A Low Down Dirty
Shame '94

Hugh Wedlock
George White's
Scandal '45

Herschel Weingrod
My Stepmother Is an
Alien '88
Trading Places '83

Robert L. Welch
Son of Paleface '52

William Welch
Promises! Promises!
'63

Orson Welles
Confidential Report
(AKA: Mr. Arkadin)
'35

William A. Wellman
A Star Is Born '37

William K. Wells
Meet the Baron '33

Richard Wesley
Uptown Saturday
Night '74

Mae West
Belle of the Nineties
'34
Every Day's a Holiday
'37

Go West, Young Man
'36
Goin' to Town '35
I'm No Angel '33
Klondike Annie '36
My Little Chickadee
'40
Night After Night '32
She Done Him Wrong
'33

Donald E. Westlake
The Grifters '90

John T. Weville
Never Give a Sucker
an Even Break '41

Norman Wexler
Saturday Night Fever
'77

Rod Whitaker
The Eiger Sanction '75

Billy Wilder
Ball of Fire '41
Bluebeard's Eighth
Wife '38
The Fortune Cookie
'66
Kiss Me, Stupid '64
The Major and the
Minor '42
Ninotchka '39
Some Like It Hot '59

Gene Wilder
The Adventure of
Sherlock Holmes'
Smarter Brother '75
Young Frankenstein
'74

Hugh Williams
The Grass Is Greener
'60

Margaret Williams
The Grass Is Greener
'60

Tennessee Williams
A Streetcar Named
Desire '51

Hugh Wilson
Rustlers' Rhapsody '85

Arthur Wimperis
The Scarlet Pimpernel
'35

P.J. Wolfson
Dancing Lady '33
The Perils of Pauline
'47
Reckless '35

Christopher Wood
Moonraker '79
The Spy Who Loved
Me '77

David S. Wood
King Ralph '91

Bronte Woodard
Grease '78

P.G. Woodhouse
A Damsel in Distress
'37

Waldemar Young
The Plainsman '36

Kazuo Yamada
What's Up, Tiger Lily?
'66

Paul Yawitz
The Affairs of Annabel
'38

Dorothy Yost
The Gay Divorcee '34

Waldemar Young
Test Pilot '38

Robert Zemeckis
1941 '79

Paul Zindel
Mame '74

David Zucker
Airplane! '80
Police Squad '82
The Naked Gun: From
the Files of Police
Squad! '88

The Naked Gun 33
 1/3: The Final Insult
 '94
The Naked Gun 2
 1/2: The Smell of
 Fear '91

Jerry Zucker
Airplane! '80
Police Squad '82
The Naked Gun: From
 the Files of Police
 Squad! '88

Alan Zweibel
North '94

Keyword Index

All references in the **Keyword Index** are to page numbers within the text. Character names are sorted under the first name, while all other names are sorted by last name. The **Decades Index** immediately follows this index.

Keyword Index

Decade Index

The **Decades Index** lists each decade with the corresponding movies in order of release year.

Gone with the Wind
'39
Mr. Moto's Last
Warning '39
Mr. Smith Goes to
Washington '39
Never Say Die '39
Ninotchka '39
Oily to Bed, Oily to
Rise '39
The Real Glory '39
The Roaring Twenties
'39
Saved by the Belle '39
Stagecoach '39
The Three Musketeers
'39
Three Sappy People
'39
Union Pacific '39
We Want Our
Mummy '39
The Wizard of Oz '39
The Women '39
Yes, We Have No
Bonanza '39
You Can't Cheat an
Honest Man '39

1940's
Angels Over
Broadway '40
The Bank Dick '40
Cookoo Cavaliers '40
Dark Command '40
Down Argentine Way
'40
From Nurse to Worse
'40
The Ghost Breakers
'40
Go West '40
His Girl Friday '40
Kitty Foyle '40
My Little Chickadee
'40
No Census, No
Feeling '40
Nutty but Nice '40
One Night in the
Tropics '40
The Philadelphia Story
'40
The Return of Frank
James '40
The Road to
Singapore '40

The Shop Around the
Corner '40
Strange Cargo '40
Tin Pan Alley '40
Too Many Girls '40
Torrid Zone '40
You Nazty Spy! '40

All the World's a
Stooge '41
An Ache in Every
Stake '41
Ball of Fire '41
The Big Store '41
Birth of the Blues '41
Buck Private '41
Caught in the Draft
'41
49th Parallel (AKA:
The Invaders) '41
Great Guns '41
Honky Tonk '41
I'll Never Heil Again
'41
In the Navy '41
In the Sweet Pie and
Pie '41
The Lady Eve '41
Look Who's Laughing
'41
Louisiana Purchase
'41
Major Barbara '41
The Maltese Falcon
'41
Meet John Doe '41
Never Give a Sucker
an Even Break '41
374, 384
The Road to Zanzibar
'41
So Long, Mr. Chumps
'41
Some More of Samoa
'41
They Died with Their
Boots On '41
Topper Returns '41
Two-Faced Woman
'41
Wheel of Fortune
(AKA: A Man
Betrayed) '41
You'll Never Get Rich
'41

Ziegfeld Girl '41

The Big Street '42
Casablanca '42
Even as I.O.U. '42
The Glass Key '42
Loco Boy Makes Good
'42
The Major and the
Minor '42
The Man Who Came
to Dinner '42
Matri-Phony '42
My Favorite Blonde
'42
Pardon My Sarong
'42
Ride 'Em Cowboy '42
Rio Rita '42
The Road to Morocco
'42
Seven Days' Leave '42
Three Smart Saps '42
To Be or Not to Be '42
Valley of the Sun '42
What's the Matador?
'42
Who Done It? '42
Yankee Doodle Dandy
'42
You Were Never
Lovelier '42

Dizzy Detectives '43
Dizzy Pilots '43
Hit the Ice '43
I Can Hardly Wait '43
Lady of Burlesque '43
A Lady Takes a
Chance '43
Mr. Lucky '43
The Outlaw '43
Spook Louder '43
They Stooge to Conga
'43
Three Little Twirps '43

Arsenic and Old Lace
'44
Busy Buddies '44
Catherine Was Great
'44
Crash Goes the Hash
'44
Going My Way '44

Hail the Conquering
Hero '44
Idle Roomers '44
In Society '44
Laura '44
The Miracle of
Morgan's Creek '44
No Dough, Boys '44
None but the Lonely
Heart '44
The Princess and the
Pirate '44
Since You Went Away
'44
The Thin Man Goes
Home '44
To Have and Have Not
'44
The Yoke's On Me '44

Booby Dupes '45
Captain Kidd '45
Christmas in
Connecticut '45
Cornered '45
George White's
Scandal '45
Here Come the Co-Eds
'45
Idiots Deluxe '45
If a Body Meets a
Body '45
It's in the Bag '45
Johnny Angel '45
Micro-Phonies '45
The Road to Utopia
'45
Without Love '45

Beer Barrel Polecats
'46
The Big Sleep '46
A Bird in the Head '46
The Dark Corner '46
Gilda '46
It's a Wonderful Life
'46
Lady in the Lake '46
Little Giant '46
Monsieur Beaucaire
'46
My Darling
Clementine '46
A Night in
Casablanca '46
Notorious '46

The Postman Always
Rings Twice '46
Roll on Texas Moon
'46
Three Loan Wolves
'46
The Time of Their Lives
'46
Uncivil War Birds '46

All Gummed Up '47
The Bachelor and the
Bobby-Soxer '47
Buck Privates Come
Home '47
Copacabana '47
The Corpse Vanishes
'47
Fright Night '47
The Ghost and Mrs.
Muir '47
Half-Wit's Holiday '47
Life with Father '47
My Favorite Brunette
'47
Out of the Past '47
The Perils of Pauline
'47
The Road to Rio '47
The Sin of Harold
Diddlebock '47
Sing a Song of Six
Pants '47
Song of the Thin Man
'47
The Wistful Widow of
Wagon Gap '47
Unconquered '47

Abbott and Costello
Meet Frankenstein
'48
Crime on their Hands
'48
Fort Apache '48
The Hot Scots '48
Mexican Hayride '48
Mr. Blandings Builds
His Dream House
'48
The Noose Hangs
High '48
The Paleface '48
Shivering Sherlocks
'48
Silver Rider '48

Decade Index

Which Way to the
Front? '70

Bananas '71
Carnal Knowledge '71
Dirty Harry '71
Willy Wonka and the
Chocolate Factory
'71

Cabaret '72
Cancel My
Reservation '72
Everything You Always
Wanted to Know
About Sex *But
Were Afraid to Ask
'72
Harold and Maude
'72
Man of La Mancha
'72
Play It Again, Sam '72
The Ruling Class '72

American Graffiti '73
Paper Moon '73
Sleeper '73

Andy Warhol's
Frankenstein '74
Blazing Saddles '74
The Front Page '74
The Lords of Flatbush
'74
Mame '74
The Man with the
Golden Gun '74
McQ '74
The Parallax View '74
Uptown Saturday
Night '74
Young Frankenstein
'74

The Adventure of
Sherlock Holmes'
Smarter Brother '75
Bite the Bullet '75
Brannigan '75
The Eiger Sanction '75
Farewell, My Lovely
'75

The First Nudie
Musical '75
Life and Death '75
Love Among the Ruins
'75
Love and Death '75
Monty Python and the
Holy Grail '75
The Sunshine Boys '75
Three Days of the
Condor '75

The Bad News Bear
'76
Bugsy Malone '76
The Enforcer '76
The Front '76
Murder by Death '76
386
The Outlaw Josey
Wales '76
The Pink Panther
Strikes Again '76
The Seven-Per-Cent
Solution '76
The Shootist '76
Taxi Driver '76

Annie Hall '77
The Goodbye Girl '77
High Anxiety '77
Saturday Night Fever
'77
The Spy Who Loved
Me '77
Star Wars '77

California Suite '78
The Cheap Detective
'78
The End '78
Foul Play '78
Goin' South '78
Grease '78
House Calls '78
National Lampoon's
Animal House '78
Revenge of the Pink
Panther '78
Sextette '78
Superman '78

Apocalypse Now '79
Chapter Two '79

The Electric Horseman
'79
The In-Laws '79
The Jerk '79
Love at First Bite '79
Manhattan '79
Meatballs '79
Moonraker '79
1941 '79
The Ninth
Configuration '79

1980's
Airplane! '80
The Blues Brothers '80
Caddyshack '80
The Empire Strikes
Back '80
The Fiendish Plot of Dr.
Fu Manchu '80
Holy Moses! '80
The Nude Bomb '80
Seems Like Old Times
'80
Serial '80
The Mirror Crack'd
'80
The Stunt Man '80

An American
Werewolf in London
'81
Any Which Way You
Can '81
Arthur '81
Body Heat '81
Buddy Buddy '81
First Monday in
October '81
The Four Seasons '81
History of the World:
Part 1 '81
Modern Problems '81
The Munsters' Revenge
'81
Only When I Laugh
'81
The Postman Always
Rings Twice '81
Raiders of the Lost Ark
'81
S.O.B. '81
Stripes '81
Come Back to the 5 &
Dime Jimmy Dean,
Jimmy Dean '82

Dead Men Don't Wear
Plaid '82
Diner '82
Fast Times at
Ridgemont High '82
The Grey Fox '82
A Midsummer Night's
Sex Comedy '82
More! Police Squad
'82
My Favorite Year '82
Night Shift '82
One from the Heart
'82
Personal Best '82
Police Squad '82
The Return of the Pink
Panther '82
Tootsie '82
The Verdict '82
The World According
to Garp '82

The Big Chill '83
Blue Thunder '83
Easy Money '83
48 HRS. '83
High Road to China
'83
The Man With Two
Brains '83
Monty Python's The
Meaning of Life '83
Nate and Hayes '83
Return of the Jedi '83
Spacehunter '83
The Survivors '83
Terms of Endearment
'83
To Be or Not to Be '83
Trading Places '83
Unfaithfully Yours '83

Against All Odds '84
All of Me '84
Broadway Danny Rose
'84
The Buddy System '84
City Heat '84
Crackers '84
Ghostbusters '84
Indiana Jones and the
Temple of Doom '84
Johnny Dangerously
'84
Lassiter '84

The Natural '84
Paris, Texas '84
Protocol '84
Reilly: The Ace of
Spies '84
This Is Spinal Tap '84

The Breakfast Club '85
Code of Silence '85
Desperately Seeking
Susan '85
Hollywood Harry '85
The Jewel of the Nile
'85
Lost in America '85
Moonlighting '85
National Lampoon's
European Vacation
'85
Rustlers' Rhapsody '85
St. Elmo's Fire '85
Transylvania 6-5000
'85
Volunteers '85
Year of the Dragon
'85

Back to School '86
The Bedroom Window
'86
Club Paradise '86
Clue '86
The Color of Money
'86
Crocodile Dundee '86
Crossroads '86
Down and Out in
Beverly Hills '86
Ferris Bueller's Day
Off '86
Fletch '86
Hannah and Her
Sisters '86
Mae West '86
No Mercy '86
Peggy Sue Got
Married '86
Pirates '86
Raw Deal '86
Ruthless People '86
Sweet Liberty '86
That's Life! '86

Angel Heart '87

Assault of the Killer
  Bimbos '87
Beverly Hills Cop II '87
Broadcast News '87
Cross My Heart '87
Dragnet '87
Good Morning,
  Vietnam '87
Ishtar '87
Lethal Weapon '87
Making Mr. Right '87
Nadine '87
Outrageous Fortune
  '87
Overboard '87
The Pick-Up Artist '87
Princess Bride '87
Raising Arizona '87
Revenge of the Nerds
  II: Nerds in Paradise
  '87
Roxanne '87
The Running Man '87
Spaceballs '87
Stakeout '87
Summer School '87
Tin Men '87
The Witches of
  Eastwick '87
Will Rogers: Look
  Back in Laughter '87

Arthur 2: On the
  Rocks '88
Beetlejuice '88
Big Business '88
Bright Lights, Big City
  '88
Bull Durham '88
Da '88
Dead Heat '88
The Dead Pool '88
Dirty Rotten
  Scoundrels '88
High Spirits '88
Midnight Run '88
Mississipi Burning '88
My Stepmother Is an
  Alien '88
The Naked Gun: From
  the Files of Police
  Squad! '88
The Prince of
  Pennsylvania '88
Punchline '88
Rain Man '88

Salome's Last Dance
  '88
Scrooged '88
Sunset '88
Tapeheads '88
Tequila Sunrise '88
Vibes '88
Who Framed Roger
  Rabbit? '88
Without a Clue '88
Young Einstein '88

The Adventures of
  Baron Munchausen
  '89
Always '89
Batman '89
Bill & Ted's Excellent
  Adventure '89
The 'Burbs '89
Dead-Bang '89
Get Smart, Again! '89
Ghostbusters II '89
Gross Anatomy '89
Harlem Nights '89
Heathers '89
Indiana Jones and the
  Last Crusade '89
Lethal Weapon 2 '89
Parenthood '89
Physical Evidence '89
Pink Cadillac '89
Road House '89
Shirley Valentine '89
Steel Magnolias '89
When Harry Met Sally
  '89

1990's
The Adventures of
  Ford Fairlane '90
Alice '90
Cadillac Man '90
Dick Tracy '90
Everybody Wins '90
Field of Dreams '90
Flashback '90
The Grifters '90
Heart Condition '90
Home Alone '90
Homer & Eddie '90
I Love You To Death
  '90
Loose Cannons '90
Mermaids '90
Narrow Margin '90
Nuns on the Run '90

Postcards from the
  Edge '90
Pretty Woman '90
Q & A '90
Repossessed '90
The Russia House '90
The Terminator 2-
  Jugement Day '90
Three Men and a Little
  Lady '90
Total Recall '90
Tune In Tomorrow '90
Wild at Heart '90
Women & Men.
  Stories of Seduction
  '90
The Addams Family
  '91
Bugsy '91
Cast a Deadly Spell
  '91
City Slickers '91
Doc Hollywood '91
The Fisher King '91
Harley Davidson and
  the Marlboro Man
  '91
Hook '91
Hot Shots! '91
Hudson Hawk '91
JFK '91
King Ralph '91
L.A. Story '91
The Mogul '91
The Naked Gun 2
  1/2: The Smell of
  Fear '91
Necessary Roughness
  '91
Night on Earth '91
Nothing but Trouble
  '91
Once Upon a Crime
  '91
Other People's Money
  '91
Out for Justice '91
Point Break '91
Ricochet '91
The Silence of the
  Lambs '91
Soapdish '91
Talkin' Dirty After
  Dark '91

Batman Returns '92
Brain Donors '92

The Cemetary Club
  '92
Death Becomes Her
  '92
Far and Away '92
Final Analysis '92
Freejack '92
Hero '92
Home Alone 2: Lost in
  New York '92
Housesitter '92
Juice '92
Ladybugs '92
Man Trouble '92
Nails '92
Neil Simon's
  Broadway Bound
  '92
Reservoir Dogs '92
Shining Through '92
This is My Life '92
Wayne's World '92
White Sands '92

Addams Family Values
  '93
Another Stakeout '93
Attack of the 50 Ft.
  Woman '93
The Beverly Hillbillies
  '93
Brain Smasher... A
  Love Story '93
Bram Stoker's Dracula
  '93
Coneheads '93
Cop and a Half '93
Demolition Man '93
Detonator '93
Fatal Instinct '93
A Few Good Men '93
Grumpy Old Men '93
Hocus Pocus '93
Hot Shots! Part Deux
  '93
Last Action Hero '93
Leap of Faith '93
National Lampoon's
  Loaded Weapon I
  '93
The Pickle '93
A Stranger Among Us
  '93
Total Instinct '93
Untamed Heart '93
Wayne's World 2 '93

Wrestling Ernest
  Hemingway '93

Ace Ventura: Pet
  Detective '94
Across the Moon '94
The Adventures of
  Priscilla, Queen of
  the Desert '94
Blankman '94
Blue Sky '94
Camp Nowhere '94
Car 54, Where Are
  You? '94
Chasers '94
City Slickers II: The
  Legend of Curly's
  Gold '94
Clerks '94
The Client '94
Cops and Robbersons
  '94
The Crazy Sitter
  '94
Ed Wood '94
The Flintstones '94
Forrest Gump '94
Getting Even with Dad
  '94
Interview with the
  Vampire '94
It's Pat—The Movie
  '94
Jimmy Hollywood
  '94
The Lion King '94
The Little Rascals '94
A Low Down Dirty
  Shame '94
Maverick '94
Milk Money '94
Mixed Nuts '94
Molly & Gina '94
Monkey Trouble '94
The Naked Gun 33
  1/3: The Final Insult
  '94
North '94
The Pagemaster '94
Radioland Murders
  '94
Reality Bites '94
Renaissance Man '94
Richie Rich '94
The Scout '94
The Silence of the
  Hams '94

The Skateboard Kid II
 '94
The Specialist '94
Speechless '94
True Lies '94
Victim of Desire '94
With Honors '94
Wolf '94

The Brady Bunch
 Movie '95